The S Corporation Desk Book

Michael Schlesinger, J.D.

PRENTICE HALL
Englewood Cliffs, New Jersey 07632

Prentice-Hall International (UK) Limited, *London*
Prentice-Hall of Australia Pty. Limited, *Sydney*
Prentice-Hall Canada, Inc., *Toronto*
Prentice-Hall Hispanoamericana, S.A., *Mexico*
Prentice-Hall of India Private Limited, *New Delhi*
Prentice-Hall of Japan, Inc., *Tokyo*
Simon & Schuster Asia Pte. Ltd., *Singapore*
Editora Prentice-Hall do Brasil, Ltda., *Rio de Janeiro*

© 1988 *by*
PRENTICE-HALL, Inc.
Englewood Cliffs, NJ

10 9 8 7 6 5 4 3 2 1

Printed in the United States of America

Library of Congress Cataloging-in-Publication Data

Schlesinger, Michael
    The S corporation desk book / Michael Schlesinger.
      p.   cm.
    Includes index.
    ISBN 0-13-785635-0
    1. Subchapter S corporations—Taxation.   I. Title.
KF6491.S34 1988
343.7305'267—dc19
[347.3035267]   88-4116
                                        CIP

ISBN 0-13-785635-0

PRENTICE HALL
BUSINESS & PROFESSIONAL DIVISION
A division of Simon & Schuster
Englewood Cliffs, New Jersey 07632

This book is dedicated to my wife Lauren and my sons, Philip and Charles, whose patience and understanding made this book a reality.

About the Author

MICHAEL SCHLESINGER, B.A., J.D., LL.M (Taxation), is a member of the New York Bar. Mr. Schlesinger is a partner in the firm of Schlesinger & Sussman of New York, New York, and Clifton, New Jersey, and has been admitted to practice before the New York State Bar, the Federal District Courts for the Southern and Eastern Districts of New York, the U.S. Court of Appeals for the 2nd and 7th Circuits, the U.S. Tax Court, the U.S. Court of Claims, and the Internal Revenue Service. Mr. Schlesinger is a member of the New York State Bar Association and the Tax Section of the New York Bar. He is also a member of the New York County Lawyer's Association and a member of the Faculty Bank, New York State Society of Certified Public Accountants.

Mr. Schlesinger is also the author of two tax columns, one that appears in *The Practical Accountant* and is entitled "Tax Planning Idea of the Month" and one that appears periodically in *Variety*. Additionally, he is the author of numerous tax articles in national publications. He is also a former contributing editor to *Business Taxes Interpreted*.

Mr. Schlesinger has been a lecturer to the National Society of Public Accountants, the American Institute of Certified Public Accountants, the Practicing Law Institute, the Empire State Association of Public Accountants, the National Association of Enrolled Agents, the Florida Society of Enrolled Agents, the New York State and New Jersey Societies of Certified Public Accountants, the National Conference of Certified Public Accountant Practitioners, the New Jersey Association of Public Accountants, the Independent Accountants of Illinois, the American Institute of Banking, the New York County Lawyers Association, and the Federal Tax Forum.

Contents

About the Author   iv

What This Book Will Do for You   xxii

A Word from the Author   xxvi

Acknowledgments   xxviii

Chapter 1

TAX CONSIDERATIONS INVOLVED IN ELECTING S CORPORATION STATUS • 1

1.1   A General Overview of the Taxation of S Corporation Income • 3

1.2   How S Corporations Can Generate Substantial Tax Savings
      Through Income Splitting Among Family Members • 4

      A. Gift of S Corporation Stock – 4
      B. Two Methods for Maintaining Control of the S Corporation
         When Splitting Income Among Family Members – 5
      C. When Income Splitting Should Not Occur – 5
      D. The Consequences of Section 1366(e)'s Reallocation Rules – 6
      E. The Effect That the Tax Reform Act of 1986 (the TRA) Has on
         Tax Planning – 7
         1. Tax Rates – 7
         2. The Alternative Minimum Tax – 7

1.3   Pertinent Income Tax Reasons for Establishing S Corporations • 8

      A. Immediate Deduction for Losses – 8
      B. No Add-On Minimum Tax – 9
      C. No Personal Holding Company Tax – 9
      D. No Recharacterization of Pass-Through Items – 9

1.4   Calendar or Fiscal Year for Reporting Income • 9

      A. General Discussion – 9
      B. The Mechanics – 10
         1. New S Corporations – 10
         2. Existing S Corporations – 10
         3. The Fiscal Year Based on Business Purposes – 11
         4. Tiered Structures—S Corporation Which Is a Member of a
            Partnership – 12

5. S Corporation Makes the S Election Status for Fiscal Year, Not the Shareholders – 12
6. Section 7519's Interest-Free Deposit – 12
7. Refund of Required Payment – 16
8. Tax Planning Under Sections 444 and 7519 – 16

1.5 Cash or Accrual Basis for Reporting Income: How to Make the Choice • 17

A. General Discussion – 17
B. Existing C Corporations Converting to S Corporations—Change of Accounting Method Barred – 18
C. S Corporation Can Use a Different Accounting Method Than Predecessor Partnership – 18

Endnotes for Chapter 1 – 18

Chapter 2

THE ELEMENTS OF THE S CORPORATION ELECTION • 21

2.1 Statutory Requirements to Be an S Corporation • 23
2.2 Limits on Numbers of Shareholders • 23

A. How to Count Shareholders – 23
1. Time for Counting Shareholders – 23
B. Constructive Ownership Rules Do Not Apply – 24
C. Stock Held by a Nominee – 24
D. Treatment of Stock Held by a Custodian Under the Uniform Gifts to Minors Act (UGMA) – 24
E. How Stock Held by Joint Tenants and Tenants in Common Is Treated – 25
F. How Stock Held by a Husband and Wife Is Treated – 25
1. Community Property States – 25
2. Death of a Spouse – 26

2.3 Types of Entities and Individuals That Can Be Shareholders • 26

A. General Discussion – 26
B. Tax Planning Potentials and Pitfalls for Each Type of Shareholder – 26
1. Estates – 26
2. Grantor, Section 678 Trust, Testamentary, Qualified S Corporation Trusts, and Voting Trusts – 27
a. Voting Trusts, 27
b. Grantor Trusts, 27
c. Testamentary Trusts, 28
d. Section 678 Trusts, 28
e. Qualified S Corporation Trusts, 28

C. The Five Statutory Requirements – 29
D. The Election to Be Treated as a Qualified S Corporation Trust – 29
E. The Bankrupt Shareholder – 30

2.4   Who Cannot Be an S Corporation Shareholder? • 30

A. Nonresident Aliens – 30
B. Nonqualifying Trusts – 30
C. Partnerships – 31
D. Corporations – 31

2.5   S Corporation Cannot Be a Member of an Affiliated Group • 31

A. Two Situations Where an S Corporation Can Have a Subsidiary – 32
    1. Inactive Subsidiaries – 32
    2. Transitory Subsidiaries – 33
        a. Section 338 Transaction, 33

2.6   S Corporation Can Be a Member of a Controlled Group • 34

A. Tax Rates of C Corporations Are Unchanged if S and C Corporations Are Members of a Controlled Group – 34

2.7   Only Domestic Corporations Can Be S Corporations • 35

2.8   Five Types of Corporations That Cannot Be S Corporations • 35

2.9   S Corporation Can Only Have One Class of Stock • 36

A. S Corporation Can Have Voting and Nonvoting Stock – 36
    1. Tax and Business Planning Possibilities with Voting and Nonvoting Common Stock – 36
        a. Shifting Income Among Family Members, 36
        b. Raising Business Capital, 37
        c. Attracting Key Personnel, 37
B. Debt as a Second Class of Stock – 38
    1. Why S Corporate Shareholders Prefer Lending Money to S Corporations Rather than Acquiring More Stock – 38
    2. Section 1361(c) (5)'s Safe Harbor for Debt – 39

Endnotes for Chapter 2 – 39

Chapter 3

TIMING AND MANNER OF AN S CORPORATION ELECTION • 43

3.1   New Corporations—Filing • 45

A. Consents – 45
    1. Manner in Making Consents – 45

2. When and Where to Elect—New Corporation and C
Corporations Electing S Corporate Status – 46
3. Time for Meeting Requirements – 47
4. There Can Be No Termination or Revocation Within the
Prior Four Years – 47

3.2   The Form 2553 and Existing S Corporations • 48

3.3   Who Signs Form 2553? • 48

A. Stock Held by a Nominee – 48
B. Minors—Stock Held by a Custodian Under the Uniform Gift to
Minors Act – 48
C. Joint Tenants – 49
D. Spouses – 49
E. Community Property – 49
F. Estates – 49
G. Voting Trusts – 49
H. Grantor Trusts – 50
 I. Testamentary Trusts – 50
J. Section 678 Trusts – 50
K. Qualified S Corporation Trusts – 50
L. The Bankrupt Shareholder – 50
M. Gift of S Corporate Stock – 50
N. Conditional Sale of Stock – 50
O. Incompetent Individual – 5022

3.4   Burden of Proof Regarding Filing Form 2553 • 51

3.5   What Corporate Officer Signs the Form 2553? • 52

3.6   The Tax Considerations with Respect to C Corporations Converting
to S Corporations • 52

A. Repayment of Loans to Retirement Plans – 52
B. Accounting Method – 52
C. Investment Credit – 52
D. Permitted Tax Year – 53
E. Tax on Passive Investment Income and Loss of Income – 53
F. Loss of Fringe Benefits – 53
G. Tax on Capital Gains – 54
H. No Carryforward or Carryback of C Losses, Investment Tax
Credits, Foreign Tax Credit, and So On – 54
 I. Conversion from C Corporation to S Status—LIFO
Recapture – 54

Endnotes for Chapter 3 – 55

Chapter 4

SUBCHAPTER S INCOME AND EXPENSES • 57

4.1   Income Taxed at One Level—An Overview • 59

    A. Separately Stated Items – 60
    B. Nonseparately Stated Items—Gross Income – 61

4.2   Accounting Method and Tax Year for Reporting Income • 61

4.3   Elections Regarding Gross Income • 61

4.4   Capital Gains and Losses • 62

    A. The Effect of the Tax Reform Act of 1986 – 62
    B. General Discussion – 62

4.5   Section 1231 Transactions • 63

    A. The Effect Caused by the Tax Reform Act of 1986 – 63
    B. General Discussion – 63

4.6   Dealer Transactions • 63

    A. The Effect Caused by the Tax Reform Act of 1986 – 63
    B. General Discussion – 64

4.7   Section 1239 Conversion of Capital Gains to Ordinary Income • 65

    A. The Effect Caused by the Tax Reform Act of 1986 – 65
    B. General Discussion – 65

4.8   Property Distributions to Shareholders • 62

    A. Exceptions to Section 1363(d) – 66
    B. Section 1374's Tax on Distribution and in Liquidation of an S
       Corporation – 67

4.9   Earning and Profits • 67

    A. When an S Corporation Will Have Earnings and Profits – 67
    B. Earnings and Profits Can Penalize an S Corporation Under
       Sections 1375 and 1362(d)(3) – 67
    C. Methods to Eliminate Earnings and Profits – 68
    D. The Tax Consequences of Reductions in Earnings and
       Profits – 68

        1. Dividends – 68
        2. Investment Credit Recapture – 68
        3. Subchapter C Transactions – 68

4.10   Discharge of Indebtedness Income—Section 108(d)(7) • 68

    A. Sections 108(d)(7)(A) and (B) – 68

B. Contribution of Debt to an S Corporation—Section
    108(d)(7)(C) – 69

Endnotes for Chapter 4 – 69

Chapter 5

CORPORATE DEDUCTIONS • 71

5.1   Introduction • 73

5.2   Investment Interest • 73

5.3   Charitable Contributions • 74

5.4   Taxes • 74

    A. Foreign Taxes – 74
    B. State Income Taxes – 75

5.5   Trade or Business Expenses—Section 162 • 75

5.6   Fringe Benefits—Sections 79, 101, 105, 106, 119 • 76

    A. Partnership Rules Apply to S Corporation Fringe Benefits—
    Section 1372 – 76

        1. Definition of 2% or More Shareholders – 76
    B. Fringe Benefits for S Corporations in Existence as
    of 9/28/82 – 77

5.7   Retirement Plans—Section 401 et Seq. • 77

    A. Introduction – 77
    B. Comparison of S Corporate Plans with Other Self-Employed
    Plans – 77
    C. Unreasonable Contributions – 78
    D. Planning Possibilities with S Corporate Retirement Plans – 78

5.8   Amortization of Organizational Expenses—Section 248 • 79

5.9   Section 179 Expensing of Recovery Property • 79

5.10   Section 465 At Risk Limitation • 81

5.11   Hobby Losses—Section 183 • 81

5.12   Losses and Expenses Owed to Shareholders—Section 267 • 82

    A. Section 267(a)(1)—Losses – 82

        1. Disallowances of Losses – 82
        2. Definition of Related Person – 82
        3. Effect of Disallowed Loss on Basis and Later
        Transactions – 83
    B. Section 267(a)(2)'s Suspension of Expenses and Interest – 84

5.13 Vacation Homes, Personal Residences, and the Like—Section 280A • 84

5.14 Corporate Interest—Section 163(h)(1) • 86

5.15 Legal Expenses, Accounting Fees, and So On • 86

5.16 Reasonable Compensation • 86

     A. The Dichotomy Between Salary and Distributions in Respect to Stock Under Section 1368 – 86
     B. Self-employment Tax Under Section 1401 and Distributions with Respect to Stock Under Section 1368 – 88
     C. Reasonable Compensation – 88

Endnotes for Chapter 5 – 89

Chapter 6

S CORPORATION INCOME TAXES • 91

6.1 Three Situations Where the S Corporation Is Liable for Income Tax • 93

6.2 Tax on Capital Gains for C Corporations Electing S Status • 93

     A. Background – 93
     B. Section 1374's Tax – 93
     C. Methods to Overcome Old Section 1374 Tax – 94

          1. Fail One or More of Old Section 1374(a)'s Three Prescribed Requirements – 95

               a. The Effect of Ltr. Rul. 8651019 in Counting the 3-Year Period, 95

          2. How the S Corporation Incurs Long- and Short-Term Capital Gains to Permissible Limits – 95
          3. Use Installment Sale Reporting Under Section 453 to Report the Capital Gain – 96

     D. Two Statutory Exceptions to Old Section 1374(a)'s Tax on Capital Gains – 97
     E. Liquidate Under Section 337 to Avoid Old Section 1374(a)'s Tax – 98
     F. Computation of Old Section 1374's Tax – 99

          1. Income Tax Under Section 1374(b) – 99
          2. Old Section 1374(c)(3) Limits on Tax Calculated Under Old Section 1374(b) – 100
          3. Correlation Between Tax on Passive Investment Income Under Section 1375 and Tax on Capital Gains Under Old Section 1374 – 101

     G. The Minimum Tax – 102

1. When an S Corporation Is Liable for Minimum Tax – 102
2. Computing the Minimum Tax Under Pre-TRA Rules – 102
H. The Effect That the Corporate Income Tax Paid Under Old Section 1374(b) and Section 56 Has on Shareholders—Section 1366(f)(2) – 103

6.3   Tax from Recomputing a Prior-Year Investment Credit • 104

6.4   Tax on Excess Passive Investment Income • 105

A. Consequences of Passive Investment Rules on S Corporations – 105
B. When Tax Liability Will be Imposed on Passive Investment Income – 105
1. The Effect That the Tax Reform Act of 1986 Has on Passive Investment Income – 106
C. Definition of Pertinent Terms Under Section 1375 and 1362 – 107
1. Passive Investment Income – 107
2. Rents – 107
a. Real Property, 107
b. Personal Property, 109
c. Who Provides Services?, 109
3. Royalties – 109
4. Interest – 110
5. Dividends – 110
6. Annuities – 111
7. Sales or Exchanges of Stock or Securities – 111
D. Gross Receipts – 113
E. Net Passive Income – 115
F. Excess Net Passive Income – 115
G. Taxable Income – 115
H. Tax Computed Under Section 1375 – 116
1. Credits Against Section 1375 Tax – 117
2. Coordination with New Sections 1374 and 1375(c)(2) – 117
I. Waiver of Section 1375 Tax—Section 1375(d) – 117
J. Reduction in Pass-through for Section 1375 Tax—Section 1368(f)(3) – 118
K. Section 1368(e)(3)'s Method to Reduce S Corporation's Earnings and Profits – 118

6.5   When an S Corporation Is Never Liable for Tax for Excessive Passive Investment Income Under Section 1375 and Subject to Termination Under Section 1367(d)(3) • 118

A. S Corporations Started After the Effective Date of the Subchapter S Revision Act of 1982 That Never Were C Corporations – 118

B. S Corporation Has No Rents, Royalties, Interest, Dividends, Annuities, and Sale or Exchange of Stock or Securities – 119

C. C Corporation That Converts to S Status and Has No Earnings and Profits or Eliminates Them Before Electing S Status – 119

D. S Corporation Has No Taxable Income or Net Passive Investment Income – 119

6.6   State Corporate Taxes • 119

6.7   Section 1374—Tax Imposed on Certain Built-in Gains • 120

A. C Corporations that Elected S Corporation Status Before 12/31/86 – 120

B. Corporations Electing S Status After 12/31/86 – 120

1. Corporations Electing S Status from Inception – 120
2. C Corporations Electing S Status After 12/31/86 (the "10-Year Taint" Rules) – 120
3. Counting the 10-Year Period – 122

Endnotes for Chapter 6 – 123

Chapter 7

BASIS AND LOSSES: PASSIVE LOSS RULES • 127

7.1   When a Shareholder Takes Items of Income, Loss, and So On, into Account • 129

A. Taxable Year of Inclusion – 129

1. When Stock Ownership Remains Unchanged – 129
2. Change of Stock Ownership During the Year – 130

B. Specific Situations for Reporting S Corporate Incomes, Losses, and So On – 131

1. Death of a Shareholder – 131
2. Closing of the Books of the S Corporation—Section 1362(e)(3) – 131
3. Change of More than 50% Interest in the S Corporation—Section 1362(e)(6)(D) – 131

C. Termination of S Shareholder Status – 131
D. Elections That Affect the Computation of Income, Expense, and So On – 132
E. Year in Which Items Are Included – 132

7.2   Basis • 132

A. The Importance of Basis—The Road Map – 132
B. How to Compute Stock Basis – 132

1. Cost Basis – 132
2. Increases in Basis—Section 1367(a)(1) – 133

3. Decreases in Basis—Sections 1367(a)(2)(A) – (E) – 133
4. Investment Tax Credit Adjustment – 133
5. Other Items Affecting Basis – 134
   a. Items Must Be Reported—Section 1367(b)(1) and Section 6241–6245 Requirements, 134
   b. Basis Cannot Be Reduced Below Zero, 134
   c. Shareholders Cannot Use Unsecured Demand Promissory Notes to Create Basis, 134
   d. Section 1244 Stock, 134
   e. Worthless Stock, 134
   f. Section 465—"At-Risk" Rules, 134
6. Examples of Application of the Basis Rules – 135
C. Debt Basis – 136
D. What Constitutes Debt – 136
   1. Guarantee of Shareholders – 136
   2. Worthlessness of Debt – 136
   3. The Mechanics of Debt as It Applies to Basis – 137
      a. How Is Debt Value Determined for Section 1367(b)(2)(A), 137
      b. Restoration of Basis in Debt—Section 1367(b)(2)(B), 137
      c. Examples Illustrating the Debt Rules Set Forth in Chapters 7.2 C and D, 137
E. Payment of Shareholder's Debt, or How to Convert Ordinary Income into Capital Gains – 138

7.3   Timing of Basis Determination • 139

A. The Mechanics of the Basis Computations – 140

7.4   The Section 1366(d) Rules • 141

A. Section 1366(d)(1)—Losses Cannot Exceed Basis in Stock and Debt – 141
B. Section 1366(d)(2)—Carryover Losses – 142
C. Section 1366(d)(3)—Carryover of Disallowed Losses in Posttermination Years – 142
   1. Posttermination Transition Period—Section 1371(e) – 142

7.5   Identity of Pass-through Losses • 143

7.6   Sections 165(g) and 166(d)'s Rules—Section 1367(b)(3) • 145

7.7   How to Create Basis So That Current Losses Can Be Deductible • 145

7.8   Preparer Penalties and Basis • 145

7.9   Passive Income and Losses • 145

A. Introduction – 145
   1. Taxpayers Subject to the Rules – 146
   2. Exceptions to the Passive Loss Rules – 146

3. Examples of How the Passive Loss Rules Generally
   Work – 146
4. Definition of Passive Activities – 147

   a. Material Participation, 147
   b. Material Participation by Entities, 149
B. Operation of the Passive Loss Rules – 150
C. Portfolio Income and Expenses – 150

   1. Self-charged Interest – 151
D. Rental Activities – 152
E. Distinguishing Among Activities – 155
F. Tax Credits – 153
G. Taxable Dispositions – 153
H. Conversion of Activities – 154
I. Death of a Taxpayer – 154
J. Gifts of Passive Loss Property – 155
K. Nonrecognition Exchanges Under Section 351, 721, or
   1031 – 155
L. Phase-in Rules – 155
M. Investment Income Expense – 156
N. Disposition of Interest in Partnerships and S
   Corporations – 156

Endnotes for Chapter 7 – 157

Chapter 8

DISTRIBUTIONS AND THE ACCUMULATED ADJUSTMENT ACCOUNT • 161

8.1   Introduction • 163

8.2   Distributions Within S Corporations Without Earnings and
      Profits—Section 1368(b) • 163

      A. Distributions from S Corporations in Excess of Stock Basis,
         Long-Term or Short-Term Capital Gains – 165
      B. Fiscal Year S Corporations – 166
      C. Section 1368 Distribution Rules and Debt – 166

8.3   Distribution in S Corporations with Earnings and Profits • 168

      A. Means to Eliminate Earnings and Profits – 168
      B. The Accumulated Adjustments Account (AAA)—Section
         1368(e)(1) – 169

         1. Treatment of Tax-Exempt Income and Expense – 170
         2. AAA May Be Reduced Below Zero – 170
         3. AAA Transferable and not Affected by Stock Transfers – 170
         4. Redemptions Under Section 302(a) and 303(a)—Section
            1368(e)(1)(B) – 170

5. Investment Tax Credit Recapture – 171
6. An Example of the AAA Computation – 171
C. The Order Applying Distributions If the S Corporation Has Earnings and Profits—Section 1368(c) – 172
1. Classification of the Gain, Distribution Rules, Fiscal Year S Corporation, Priority Rules, and So On – 172
2. An Example of the Distribution Rules – 172
D. AAA Can Be Less than Zero – 174
E. AAA Is Transferable – 174
F. AAA Is Included in Distributions Pro Rata – 175
G. Operation of Section 1368(e)(3) Election – 175
1. Reasons Why a Shareholder Would Want to Make a Section 1368(e)(3) Election – 176

8.4   Distributions in S Corporations with PTI • 176

8.5   Property Distributions—Section 1363(d) • 179

A. The Effect of Complete Liquidations and Reorganizations on Property Distributions Under Sections 1363(d) and (e) – 179
B. The Characterization of the Gain Realized, Shareholders Basis, and the Effect That the Property Distribution Will Have on The S Corporation Under Sections 1374 and 1375 – 179
C. Tax Planning Under Section 1363(d) – 180
D. AAA and Earnings and Profits – 181

8.6   Posttermination Distributions • 181

A. Dividend Election Under Section 1371(e)(2) – 182

Endnotes for Chapter 8 – 182

Chapter 9

INCOME AND ESTATE TAX PLANNING FOR S CORPORATIONS, AUDIT PROCEDURES, AND STATUTE OF LIMITATIONS PROBLEMS • 183

9.1   Tax Planning for S Corporations • 18530

9.2   Providing Funds for the Elderly • 185

9.3   Providing Funds for Children—The Effect That the "Kiddie Tax" Has on Income Tax Planning with S Corporations • 185

9.4   Providing Funds for Other Relatives • 186

9.5   Retirement Plan and Fringe Benefits • 186

A. Employee Stock Ownership Trusts Cannot Be Holders of S Corporate Stock – 187
B. Retirement Plans Are Subject to Creditor Attack – 187

9.6   Social Security Benefits and S Corporations • 187

9.7   Distribution of Earnings Generally Not Subject to Self-employment
       Tax • 187

9.8   Shareholders' Agreement • 188

9.9   S Corporation Can Be a Shareholder in a C Corporation • 188

       A. Reasons Why an S Corporation Wants to Be a Shareholder in a
          C Corporation – 188

9.10   S Corporation Can Be a Partner in a Partnership • 189

       A. Reasons Why an S Corporation Wants to Be a Partner – 189
          1. Section 704 – 189
          2. Partnership Basis Rules – 189

9.11   Estate and Gift Tax Planning • 190

       A. Estate Tax – 190
          1. Estate Tax Planning – 190
             a. The Shareholders' Agreement, 191
             b. Private Annuities, 191
             c. The *Cain* Redemption, 192
       B. Gift Tax – 19219

9.12   Sale of the S Corporate Business • 193

       A. Introduction – 193
       B. Sale of Assests – 193
          1. The Effect That C Corporate Assets Will Have on the Sale—
             Section 1374 – 193
          2. Tax Consequences of Sale of S Corporate Assets – 194
             a. Investment Tax Credit Recapture, 194
             b. What to Do with Unwanted Assets Not Needed by the
                Purchaser of the Corporate Business, 194
       C. Sale of Stock – 194
       D. Reorganizations—Mergers, Recapitalizations, and So On – 194

9.13   Section 1244 Election • 195

9.14   Investment Tax Credit Recapture • 195

9.15   Below-Market Loans—Section 7872 • 197

       A. Loans from Shareholders to S Corporations – 197
       B. Loans from the S Corporation to the S Shareholder – 197

9.16   Other Areas of Tax Planning • 197

9.17   Statute of Limitations • 198

       A. Statute of Limitations at Corporate Level—Section 6037 – 198
          1. Filing Tax Court Petition – 198

    B. Statute of Limitations—Shareholder Level – 199
    C. Unified Determinations – 19904

9.18   Audit of S Corporations • 199

    A. Unified Determinations – 199

9.19   Shareholder Debt—Pros and Cons • 200

9.20   The Danger of Having the S Corporation Owning Tax-Exempt
        Bonds and Stock and Securities • 200

    A. Tax-Exempt Bonds – 200
    B. Stock and Securities – 201

Endnotes for Chapter 9 – 201

Chapter 10

REVOCATION AND TERMINATION OF S STATUS; TAX CONSEQUENCES ON SALE OF S CORPORATE STOCK; REDEMPTIONS, PARTIAL LIQUIDATIONS, LIQUIDATIONS, AND REORGANIZATIONS UNDER SECTION 368(a) • 203

10.1   Termination and Revocation of S Status—Statutory Grounds • 205

10.2   Voluntary Revocation of S Status—Section 1362(d)(1) • 205

    A. Reasons for Revoking S Status – 206
    B. Effective Date of Revocation—Sections 1362(d)(1)(C)
       and (D) – 206
       1. Section 1362(d)(1)(C) – 206
       2. Section 1362(d)(1)(D) – 207
    C. Revocation of Intentional Termination Under Section
       1362(d)(1)(D) or Section 1362(d)(1)(C)(ii) – 208

10.3   Failure to Remain as an S Corporation—Section 1362(d)(2) • 208

    A. Notification of Termination – 209

10.4   S Corporation Having Subchapter C Earnings and Profits and
       Deriving More than 25% of Its Gross Receipts from Passive
       Investment Income for Three Consecutive Years—Section
       1362(d)(3) • 209

    A. Definition of Subchapter C Earnings and Profits – 210
    B. Elimination of Subchapter C Earnings and Profits—Section
       1368(e)(3) – 210

10.5   Waiver of Termination—Section 1362(f) • 211

10.6   Election After Termination—Section 1362(g) • 212

10.7   The Tax Effects of Termination • 213

  A. The S Termination Year – 213

    1. When Tax Returns Are Due for S and C Short Years—
        Section 1362(e)(6)(B) – 214
    2. Overlap Between Sections 1362(e)(3) and 1377(a)(2), the
        Mechanics of the Section 1362(e)(3) Election – 215
    3. Distribution of Money by the Corporation with Respect to Its
        Stock During a Posttermination Period – 215

  B. The Tax Consequences to the C Corporation in the C Short
      Year and Thereafter – 216

    1. Tax Consequences Shared by Both Types of C
        Corporations – 216

      a. Borrowing from the Retirement Plan, 216
      b. Members of a Controlled Group, 216
      c. Investment Tax Credit Recapture, 216
      d. Estimated Taxes, 216

    2. S Corporations That Have C Corporate Attributes – 217

  C. Closing the Book Under Section 1362(e)(6)(D) – 217

10.8   Tax Effects of S Shareholders Selling Stock Interests • 217

  A. Computation of Seller's Gain and Loss – 217
  B. Character of Seller's Gain or Loss – 218
  C. The Tax Consequences of the Sale – 218

    1. Risks in Sale of Stock – 219
    2. Investment Tax Credit Recapture – 219
    3. Depreciation Recapture—Sections 1245, 1250, et Seq. – 220
    4. No Step-up in Basis of Assets Unless Section 338 Is
        Elected – 220

  D. Reasons Why a Seller of S Corporate Stock Wants a Section
      1377(a)(2) Election to Close the Books and Steps to Be Taken
      to Obtain the Closure – 221

    1. The Steps to Be Taken to Make the Section 1377(a)(2)
        Election – 222

  E. Reasons Why a Stock Sale Is Desired – 222

    1. Situations Involving Assets Subject to Section 452C – 223
    2. The Assets on S Corporate Books Have a Shorter
        Depreciation Life than If the Purchaser Bought the Assets
        Outright – 224

  F. Selling More than a 50% Interest—Closing of the Books Under
      Section 1362(e)(6)(D) – 224
  G. How S Shareholders Report Income, Loss, and So On, If There
      Has Been a Change of S Corporate Stock Ownership During the
      Year Less than 50% and the Books of the S Corporation Are
      Not Closed Pursuant to Section 1377(a)(2) – 224

10.9   Redemption of an S Shareholder's Interest in the Corporation,
         Partial Liquidations • 225

         A. Redemptions – 225
         B. Partial Liquidations – 226

10.10   Liquidations of S Corporation Under Sections 337, 338, 333, and
         332 • 226

         A. Section 337 Liquidations – 226
            1. The Ameliorative Relief Prescribed in Section 633 of the
               TRA – 227
         B. Section 338 Liquidations – 228
         C. Section 333 Liquidations – 228
         D. Section 332 Liquidations – 229

10.11   Reorganizations • 229

         A. Introduction – 229
         B. Statutory Merger and Consolidations—Section
            368(a)(1)(A) – 230
            1. Reelection of S Status After the Merger – 230
            2. Investment Tax Credit Recapture – 231
            3. Postmerger Distributions – 231
         C. Sections 368(a)(1)(B) and (C) Reorganizations – 231
         D. Section 368(a)(1)(D) Reorganizations – 232
            1. Business Purpose – 232
            2. Reelection of S Status for the Spun-off Corporation – 232
         E. Recapitalizations—Section 368(a)(1)(E) – 233
         F. F Reorganizations—Section 368(a)(1)(F) – 233
         G. Hybrid Mergers—Sections 368(a)(2)(D) and (E) – 233

Endnotes for Chapter 10 – 234

Appendices   **235**

FORM	CHAPTER
1. Form 2553 · 238	3.1
2. Consent to Election to Be Treated As an S Corporation · 240	3.1A
3. Transmittal Letter for Form 2553 · 241	3.4
4. State Taxation of S Corporations	5.4B; 5.16; 6.6
5. Section 1368(e)(3) Election to Distribute Earnings and Profits Before Accumulated Adjustments Account · 246	6.4K; 8.3G

 6. Filled-in Return—Distributions Where   8.2
    S Corporation Has No Earnings and
    Profits · 254

 7. Filled-in Return—Distributions Where   8.3
    S Corporation Has No Earnings and
    Profits · 254

 8. Filled-in Return—Distributions Where   8.6
    S Corporation Has No Earnings and
    Profits · 265

 9. Filled-in Return—Distributions Where   8.9
    S Corporation Has Earnings and
    Profits · 283

10. Filled-in Return—Distributions Where   8.10
    S Corporation Has Earnings and
    Profits · 291

11. Shareholders' Agreement   9.8; 10.3
    Provisions · 300

12. Form 8082   9.18

13. Notice of Revocation of Subchapter S   10.2
    Election Under Section 1362(a) · 304

14. Consent to Election to Have Items   10.7A; 10.7A2
    Assigned Under Normal Accounting
    Rules—Section 1362(e)(3)(B) · 305

15. Election to Close Books Upon   10.8D1
    Termination of Interest by S
    Corporation Shareholder—Section
    1377(a)(2) · 306

16. Shareholder Consent—Section   10.8D1
    1377(a)(2) · 307

17. Sample Returns · 314

Tables   **321**

     I. Table Setting Forth in General Terms the Method of
        Computing S Corporation Income and Expenses ● 323
    II. Table of Internal Revenue Code Sections ● 325
   III. Table of Tax Reform Act of 1986 Sections ● 337
    IV. Table of Treasury Regulations ● 338
     V. Table of Cases ● 340
    VI. Table of Revenue Rulings ● 342
   VII. Department of Labor Opinions, Revenue Procedures,
        Announcements, Technical Memoranda ● 343
  VIII. Table of Private Letter Rulings ● 344

Index   **345**

What This Book Will Do for You

S corporations have always been shrouded in complexity and fraught with tax planning dilemmas. With the passing of the Tax Reform Act of 1986 (TRA), and the Omnibus Budget Reconciliation Act (OBRA), and the promulgation of the Temporary Passive Loss Regulation, the issues arising in tax preparation and planning for S corporations and their shareholders have become still more complicated.

While the TRA did not actually change many provisions of the law in regard to S corporations, the impact it had on the area has been tremendous and forces taxpayers to reexamine their perspective. Because of the loss of Section 337 liquidations for C corporations and the punitive alternative minimum tax, many business owners have made the switch from C corporation to S corporation status. S corporations now prove to be a less expensive method of accumulating capital—the top individual tax rate is 33% compared to the top corporate rate of 34%. However, the passive loss rules, the harsh tax treatment of Section 1374 when C corporations elect S status, and the complex basis rules in regard to distributions make the S corporation a perilous tax trap for the unwary. Now, more than ever, to make competent tax planning decisions with your clients, you need to be armed with current and authoritative information on the hundreds of tax planning issues that arise in regard to S corporations.

The S Corporation Desk Book was written specifically to give you this kind of guidance in one handy volume. Rather than covering every single case, ruling, or procedure on a particular point, I've attempted, instead, to give you the main case or point in each area of S corporation taxation—just enough so that you can quickly grasp the situation at hand without wading through pages of text. Also, because there are so many gray areas in S corporation taxation, I've given you not only the facts but also an interpretation of how a particular ruling or section of the law impacts on certain tax planning scenarios. The information is organized into 10 chapters; what follows is a brief summary of what these chapters cover and a sampling of the kinds of solutions and answers you'll find within.

Chapters 1, 2, and 3 outline the pros and cons of electing S corporation status post–TRA and the statutory requirements for making the election as well as the timing and manner necessary. You'll discover

- How to choose between cash and accrual basis for reporting income and between a calendar or fiscal year.

- Methods for maintaining control of the S corporation when income is split among family members.
- Tips and tactics for filing Form 2553 (if a single mistake is made on this crucial form, all benefits sought by using an S election could be lost).
- How to prevent unwarranted tax consequences from arising when converting from C corporation to S corporation status.

Chapters 4 and 5 discuss how you can determine S corporate income and expense as well as define which items are passed through to shareholders as separately stated items and which are not. Chapters 7 and 8 then discuss how these items of income, expense, and so on that have been reported on shareholders' individual returns, are distributed to shareholders. You'll find out

- How to "pigeon hole" various items of income, expense, and loss on Form 1120S.
- How the Internal Revenue Service will now recharacterize S corporation capital gains into ordinary income and techniques for eliminating earnings and profits to avoid severe tax penalties.
- How to create a blueprint for building up basis so that if losses occur, shareholders can readily deduct them on their returns.
- When passive income will be created for shareholders under the passive loss rules.
- The full implications of the Section 469 limit on passive activity losses, along with dozens of tax planning options for determining when the losses and credits can be claimed by the taxpayer.
- How to set up an accumulated adjustment account (AAA) for distribution of S corporate earnings and profits.
- How to create capital gains through the operation of S corporations.

Chapter 6 shows you how to treat the three types of taxes that can arise at the shareholder level. In addition, Chapter 6 covers state corporate income taxes and tells you

- How to avoid old Section 1374's tax on S corporation capital gains.
- How to determine the amount of tax liability imposed on an S corporation's passive investment income post–TRA 1986.
- When an S corporation will never be liable for tax at the corporate level.

Chapter 9 gives you up-to-the-minute income and estate tax planning guidelines for S corporations as well as audit and statute of limitations procedures. You'll discover

- Numerous ways to use S corporations in income and estate tax planning scenarios despite congressional restrictions.

- The pros and cons of S corporations becoming shareholders of C corporations (plus hidden advantages for the S corporation that becomes a partner in a partnership).

- Planning devices for reducing estate tax—from the *Cain* redemption to private annuities.

- How to eliminate the harsh effects of investment tax credit recaptures.

Chapter 10 is a broad-ranging chapter that covers revocation and termination of S status, the tax consequences of the sale of S corporate stock, redemptions, partial liquidations, and reorganizations under Section 368(a). You'll find out

- Exactly which types of inadvertent terminations are covered under Section 1362, what the consequences of these terminations are and ways to minimize them.

- Possible tax traps for those who rush to sell their S corporate stock now that corporate liquidations are no longer in vogue.

- How to take advantage of relief prescribed in Section 633 of TRA 1986 for easing the damaging effects of changes made to Section 337 liquidations.

- How S corporations and shareholders can benefit from tax-free reorganization under Section 368 (plus a full discussion of eight different types of reorganization).

Because the coverage within *The S Corporation Desk Book* is so broad, I've included several features that help you find the information you need quickly and better understand it once you find it. As you'll see, the table of contents is written in outline form, with each segment of the book enumerated both for ease of location within the text and for use in the multitude of cross-references throughout. With this outline and the index, you'll have two means of gaining instant access to topics within the area of S corporation taxation and procedures. You'll also find these helpful features throughout the book:

Tax pointers   Serve to point out pitfalls and opportunities as well as relevant cases and revenue rulings.

Examples   Make each point come alive with hypothetical situations involving corporations, shareholders, and numbers. Several of the examples serve as *work-*

	sheets for computations, such as determining basis and setting up an accumulated adjustment account.
Sample forms, agreements, and returns	Are included in the Appendix and are referred to often within each chapter. Among the helpful forms you'll find are Form 2553, a sample transmittal letter for Form 2553, filled-in returns for five different complex tax planning scenarios involving distributions and income, a sample shareholders' agreement provision, a revocation of S election, and much more.
Tables	Of cases, statutes, treasury regulations and rulings, and procedures make it easy for you to solve specific problems quickly.

It is my hope that all these elements will remove the mystery surrounding S corporations and enable you to face the challenge of S corporation taxation with confidence and competence.

A Word from the Author

This book provides, in a single volume, a complete guide and reference tool for the tax practitioner, to solve the many problems arising in regard to S corporate taxation. While this book does not cover every single case, ruling, or procedure on a particular point, the reader is provided with the main case or point in a particular area, so that this situation can be understood quickly. Further, the appendices contain filled-in tax returns illustrating tax treatment for the examples in the text. To assist the reader, tax planning situations are presented throughout the book. In addition, there is one specific chapter portion directed toward tax planning situations so that the reader, once he or she understands the tax ramifications of a particular situation, can adopt various tax planning approaches to address specific problems.

This book also contains many sections specifically addressing the problems raised by the Tax Reform Act of 1986 (TRA), the Omnibus Budget Reconciliation Act (OBRA), and the Temporary Regulations dealing with Passive Loss Rules. While the TRA did not change very many provisions of the law in regard to S corporations, the impact that it had on the area has been tremendous and must be addressed.

The S Corporation Desk Book is organized into 10 chapters. The paragraphs that follow set forth a brief summary of what is included in each. It should be noted that in writing this book, I have attempted to make the table of contents read like an index, so that the reader will have two easy means to solve a problem: the table of contents and the index. In addition, I have provided a table of cases, statutes, treasury regulations, rulings, and procedures so that the reader will have an easy-to-use way to solve a specific problem. The appendices are also coded to specific chapter provisions, so that the reader, once he or she locates the form to be used, can go directly to the specific chapter reference to review the law and requirements in regard to the form.

Chapter 1, Tax Considerations Involved in Electing C Corporation Status, provides a general overview of the taxation of S corporate income, whether a calendar or fiscal year should be adopted for reported income, as well as cash or accrual basis. In addition, Chapter 1 discusses some tax planning situations.

Chapter 2, The Elements of the S Corporation Election, details the specific requirements that are imposed in the Code to become an S corporation. Chapter 3, Timing and Manner of an S Corporation Election, complements Chapter 2 by providing further details about the S corporate election. Chapter 3 also offers tax planning suggestions in regard to C corporations converting to S status.

Chapters 4, 5, 7, and 8 detail how S corporate income, expenses, and the like are reported on the corporate and shareholders' tax returns. Chapter 4, S Income and Expenses, details mainly how income items are reported on the S corporate tax return. Chapter 5 discusses the treatment of corporate deductions such as legal expenses and accounting fees, reasonable compensation, fringe benefits, and more. Chapter 7 discusses basis and the procedure for taking losses. In addition, Chapter 7 covers the passive loss rules set forth in the Tax Reform Act of 1986 and the Temporary Passive Loss Regulations as they pertain to S corporations. Chapter 8 outlines the procedures regarding distributions and the accumulated adjustment account.

Chapter 6 covers the three types of taxes that can arise at the shareholder level, namely, tax from recomputing a prior year's investment credit, tax on excess passive investment income, and the tax imposed by Section 1374. In addition, Chapter 6 considers state corporate income taxes and instances when an S corporation will never be liable for tax at the corporate level.

Chapter 9, Income and Estate Tax Planning for S Corporations, Audit Procedures, and Statute of Limitations Problems, covers many areas. The variety of tax planning situations included cover some discussion of the planning possibilities under the Tax Reform Act of 1986. Chapter 9 also discusses the pros and cons of shareholder debt, the audit of S corporations, statute of limitations problems, and below-market loans.

Chapter 10 is also a broad-ranging chapter. In it, there is coverage of revocation and termination of S status, the tax consequences on the sale of S corporate stock, redemptions, partial liquidations, liquidations, and reorganizations under Section 368(a).

Because the Tax Reform Act of 1986 has basically reduced the effectiveness of Section 337 liquidations, the reader will find discussion throughout the text on how to sell the corporate business.

In regard to the appendices, aside from offering the reader samples of filled-in tax returns, there are sample forms to be used by S corporations in connection with their operations.

This book is intended to remove some of the mystery surrounding S corporations and their complexities. Because of its thoroughness, multitudinous examples, and tax pointers, *The S Corporation Desk Book* should provide the reader with a unique resource tool. It is also a major addition to any tax library.

Michael Schlesinger

Acknowledgments

This book took a number of years to write mainly due to the complexity of the topic. Complicating the writing of this book was Congress, which kept changing the law, forcing me to rewrite some chapters. As is true with any book of this consequence, it could not have been written without the help of many people: the individuals who typed and helped me proof the various versions of the manuscript of this book, Arlene Pizarro, Peter Rubie, Debra Clancy, Christine Rubing, and Alexandra Nicolescu; Jeffrey Katz, Esq., and Bruce Di Cicco, Esq., Paul Silby, CPA, who read the early chapters; the National Conference of Certified Public Accountant Practitioners (Westchester-Rockland Chapter) who checked my filled-in tax returns; Barrie Rosen, Esq., who checked my footnotes and citations and shepardized them; and most of all my wife Lauren and children, Philip and Charles, who did without a husband and father for periods of time so this book could be written. Also deserving a special note is my editor, Bette Schwartzberg, who had the patience and understanding to wait for this book, and the librarians and staff at the American Institute of Certified Public Accountants in New York City, who assisted me when I was researching and writing this book.

1

Tax Considerations Involved in Electing S Corporation Status

1.1 A GENERAL OVERVIEW OF THE TAXATION OF S CORPORATION INCOME

In an effort to overcome the rigidity in operating a business in either the corporate or partnership form, and to combine some of the desirable traits of both, Congress, in 1958, created a hybrid called an S corporation (formerly known as a Subchapter S corporation, which Congress changed to S corporation in the Subchapter S Revision Act of 1982).

The best generalization, albeit a broad one, due to the hybrid concept of an S corporation, is that it generally combines some of the aspects of partnership taxation, but provides shareholders with limited liability for state law purposes with respect to creditors, bankruptcy, and the like.

It is important to note, however, that although the S corporation's taxation in many ways resembles a partnership, there are many situations where partnership tax law does not apply (e.g., an S corporation cannot allocate income as a partnership can under Section 704(b)). Consequently, due to the complex rules governing it, an S corporation can become a trap for the unwary, if care is not exercised.

With respect to S corporation ordinary income and loss, it is basically not taxed at the corporate level; rather, it is passed through to the shareholders as in a partnership.[1] Likewise, this is true for foreign income and loss, tax-exempt interest, charitable contributions, and passive income.[2]

Consequently, this is one of the reasons why individuals elect S corporation status to operate their corporations—they seek not to be plagued by the tax technicalities of "regular Form 1120 corporations," hereinafter referred to as "C corporations" (tax on accumulated surplus, disguised dividends, personal holding company taxation, etc.).

The text that follows contains a detailed discussion about the advantages and disadvantages of S corporation taxation. Additionally, tax planning ideas are set forth to take advantage of the quirks in the law as well as offer methods to avoid the pitfalls.

1.2 HOW S CORPORATIONS CAN GENERATE SUBSTANTIAL TAX SAVINGS THROUGH INCOME SPLITTING AMONG FAMILY MEMBERS

A. Gift of S Corporation Stock

By gifting stock among family members on creation of the S corporation, substantial tax savings can result. An example will clarify:

EXAMPLE 1-1

F, who is in the 50% federal income tax bracket, is the father of two minor children over the age of 14, who have no taxable income. He plans to establish an S corporation and estimates that it will earn $125,000 each year.

F plans to withdraw $45,000 in salary each year. If F owns all the S corporation stock, he will achieve no tax savings since all the corporation's income (salary, taxable income, etc.,) will be taxed to F in his tax bracket.

If, however, F gave each of his two minor children over the age of 14 a 20% interest in the corporation, keeping 60% control for himself, there would be tax savings since $32,000 of corporate income after salary would go to these two minor children, directly ($125,000 less $45,000 = $80,000; $80,000 × 20% × 2 = $32,000).

TAX POINTERS

1. With respect to gift tax, F would probably pay no gift tax if he gifted stock to his children upon formation of the corporation, unless the corporate capitalization of the S corporation was greater than the annual exclusion of $10,000 for each beneficiary.

   If F decided to gift the stock to his children in Example 1-1 at a date later than inception, since he did not feel the corporation would be profitable until a date in the future thereby keeping all the losses for himself, F would have a problem, since he must calculate a value for the stock for gift tax purposes.

2. There is also a problem with respect to gifts of stock to minor children, if the gift is made under the Uniform Gifts to Minors Act (UGMA), in that a donor cannot be a custodian. If the donor acts as the custodian and dies before the minor reaches majority, the donor will have the gift included in his or her estate.[3]

Consequently, F, in Example 1-1, when he gives away stock under the UGMA, must make sure that an individual other than himself, such as his wife, siblings, or parents, acts as the custodian.

3. The Service under Section 1366(e) has the ability to reallocate income in S corporations where family members are shareholders (see discussion at Chapter 1.2.D).

4. Care must be exercised in making the S election. For example, in *T. J. Henry Associates,*[4] a father transferred stock from himself to himself as custodian for his four minor children, and as custodian he did not consent to the S corporation election. The Tax Court sustained the termination of the S corporation election.[5]

B. Two Methods for Maintaining Control of the S Corporation When Splitting Income Among Family Members

One major difficulty with splitting income among family members is for the donor to maintain control of the S corporation.

One method of control is the adoption of a shareholders' agreement, which contains various restrictive provisions on transfer and operation of the corporation (e.g., a provision that a selling or deceased shareholder must first offer the stock that is being disposed of to the surviving shareholder(s) and/or the corporation before offering it to others). (See Chapter 9.8 for a discussion of shareholders' agreements.) The other is establishing voting and nonvoting stock issuing the nonvoting stock to the family members with the parents keeping the voting stock. (See Chapter 2.9.A.1 for a discussion of this topic.)

C. When Income Splitting Should Not Occur

If F in Example 1-1 projected losses instead of income during the early years of operation of the S corporation, then there is no tax benefit for him to make his children shareholders. An example will clarify:

EXAMPLE 1-2

Assume the same facts as in Example 1-1, except that F, who is in the 50% federal income tax bracket, believes the corporation will lose $100,000 each year for several years after F takes out his salary of $45,000.

Assuming that F keeps all the S corporation stock, and that F has sufficient basis in his stock to take losses (see discussions of basis in Chapters 7 and 8) incurred by his S corporation, F will be able to lower, during the first year of operation, his personal taxable income by $55,000 each year ($45,000 salary, $100,000 loss).

If F made his two minor children over the age of 14 20% shareholders each, and they had no taxable income, they would obtain no benefit from their $40,000 (40 × $100,000) of losses, thereby not reaping any basic tax savings for F, since his portion of the loss would be reduced from $100,000 to $60,000.

D.   The Consequences of Section 1366(e)'s Reallocation Rules

Section 1366(e) specifically engrafts the family partnership rules of 704(e)(3) to S corporations. Consequently, if an individual who is a member of a family (e.g., F) renders services for the corporation or furnishes capital to the S corporation without receiving reasonable compensation, the Service can make an adjustment by Section 1366(e) in the income taxes of all concerned, to reflect the true value of such services or capital.

For purposes of definition, the rules define the family of the individual to include a spouse, ancestors (e.g., father and mother), lineal descendants (e.g., children and grandchildren), and any trusts for the primary benefit of such persons.[6]

TAX POINTER

It is to be noted that the family partnership rules are an amorphous concept, and thus continual review should be made of the area to prevent falling into the grasp of such rules. An example will illustrate the impact of the Section 1366(e) reallocation rules.

EXAMPLE 1-3

Assume in Example 1-1 that F, instead of transferring only a 40% interest in his S corporation to his children, transferred 100% to them. Furthermore, he drew no salary, in an effort to shift all the income to his children. The Service, under these circumstances, would probably allocate a reasonable salary to F. It is also possible that even if F took a salary, the Service could raise the salary issue, claiming that the salary was unreasonably low.

TAX POINTERS

1. The Service is not always successful in reallocating income among family members. In *Trucks, Inc.* v. *U.S.*,[7] the Court refused to reallocate income from a family S corporation to a family member when such member worked less than 10 hours each year for the corporation. In *Edwin D. Davis*,[8] an or-

thopedic surgeon formed two corporations in connection with his practice, one to carry out physical therapy treatment and the other to perform an X-ray function. Davis made gifts of 90% of the stock to his children keeping 10% of it for himself. Both corporations elected S status. Each corporation owned equipment, employed other persons, and paid no salary to Davis (he worked less than 20 hours per year for the corporations). The Court refused to allocate income on his referral of work to these two corporations since he did not receive referral fees when he referred work to unrelated radiologists and physical therapists in the past.

2. Section 1366(e) reallocation rules by definition allow the Service to reallocate income to non-S shareholders as well as to shareholders. Thus, inadequate rent, salary, and the like paid to an individual could cause reallocation under Section 1366(e).

E. The Effect That the Tax Reform Act of 1986 (the TRA) Has on Tax Planning

With any tax planning ventures, the TRA must be consulted as well to determine if benefits will be obtained. For instance, the passive loss rules set forth in Section 469 (discussed at Chapter 7.9) must be consulted to determine if the tax planning will yield desirable results. Thus, in Example 1-1, if the children are not materially participating in the business, it must be asked if they are the best recipients of the passive income, or is there another person (e.g., a brother of F) who could use the passive income to offset losses. Likewise, Section 1 has to be consulted if the tax planning involved minors under the age 14 as to whether or not it pays to have minors receive income. If the minors are under 14, they are taxed at the parent's highest tax rate pursuant to Section 1. Thus it may not pay to have minors under the age of 14 as S corporate shareholders.

1. Tax Rates

In 1987 and thereafter, Sections 1 and 11 basically prescribe that the top tax rate for C corporations will be higher than that for individuals. For instance, the top corporate tax rate is 34% in 1988 while the top individual rate is 33%.

2. The Alternative Minimum Tax

Congress in the TRA expanded and revised the alternative minimum tax for taxable years beginning after 1986 to cause more corporations to be subject to income tax. To accomplish this objective, Congress created some new categories for alternative minimum taxation, with perhaps the most perplexing being the tax on adjusted net book income (Section 56(f)(1) et seq.). Basically, Section 56(f)(1) prescribes that the alternative minimum taxable income of any C corporation is increased by one-half the amount by which its "adjusted net book income" exceeds its alternative minimum taxable income. The effect is that if a C corporation had only tax-exempt income from tax-exempt bonds other than specified private activity bonds,[9] it would pay a tax on this income, assuming it exceeded the exemption amount of $40,000.[10] The corporation will also lose the effect of Section 243's 70%-80% dividend received credit since 100% of the dividends would be subject to tax. Consider the following example, simplified for illustrative purposes.

EXAMPLE 1-4

D, Inc., is a C corporation and for 1988 has the following income: net income from sales, $48,000; dividends, $10,000; and tax-exempt bond income other than from specified private activity bonds, $200,000. Its taxable income will be $50,000: $48,000 + [$10,000 − ($10,000 × 80% dividends received credit)]; however, its alternative minimum taxable income is $64,000: ([$48,000 + $10,000 + $200,000] − [$50,000]) × 50% − $40,000 exemption. This example assumes that the corporation owns more than 20% of the stock of the corporation *delivering* the dividend.

1.3   PERTINENT INCOME TAX REASONS FOR ESTABLISHING S CORPORATIONS

Here is set forth a brief summary of the income tax reasons, besides income splitting and the one level of taxation discussed previously, as to why corporations elect S status.

A.   Immediate Deduction for Losses

If heavy start-up losses are expected or where an operating C corporation anticipates a period of heavy losses, an S election should be considered since S corporate losses are deductible in the year incurred to the extent of a shareholder's basis in S corporation stock and loans to the corporation.

TAX POINTERS

1. If the shareholder does not have sufficient basis in stock and loans, these unusable losses may be carried forward indefinitely and taken when the shareholder's basis is restored. (See Chapter 7 for a discussion about this point.)

2. Losses from an S corporation can be used to offset the shareholder's income from other sources without reallocation under Section 269.[11] Also, if the loss from an S corporation is passive, Section 469 enacted under the Tax Reform Act of 1986 prescribes that it can only be used to offset passive income. (See discussion at Chapter 7.9.)

B. No Add-On Minimum Tax

S corporations basically do not pay the minimum tax on preference items imposed by Section 55 et seq., as do C corporations. Instead, the S corporate shareholders include in their minimum tax calculation the pass-through of preference items to determine if they are liable for any minimum tax. With respect to a C corporation that becomes an S, Section 1374 imposes a tax on certain "built-in gains."

C. No Personal Holding Company Tax

An S corporation, unless it has C earnings and profits, can engage in 100% passive investment activities without adverse tax consequences or additional tax liability. In contrast, a C corporation can have a tax imposed on it by Section 541 et seq. for its passive investment activities, depending upon the number of its shareholders and the dollar amount of its passive income. (See Chapters 6.4 and 6.5 for a further discussion.)

D. No Recharacterization of Pass-Through Items

By Section 1366(a)(1)(A), S corporations pass through certain items of income, expense, and the like to the shareholder without recharacterization. Consequently, S corporation charitable contributions are not subject to the 10% limitation imposed on C corporations by Section 170(b)(2). However, S corporations cannot take advantage of two charitable contribution techniques: contributions of inventory (Section 170(e)(3)(A)) and scientific equipment (Section 170(e)(4)(D)) available to C corporations. (See Chapter 5.3 for a discussion about this topic.)

1.4 CALENDAR OR FISCAL YEAR FOR REPORTING INCOME

A. General Discussion

An S corporation, pursuant to Section 444 can use a fiscal year to report its income where there is a new or existing corporation. The price to be paid to obtain this fiscal year is that Section 444(c)(1) prescribes that the S corporation must make an interest-free deposit with the Service roughly equal to the tax being deferred for the shareholder with the Corporation adjusting the deposit each year to reflect the S corporation's income (i.e., if the S corporation's income goes up the deposit has to go up—if the income decreases a refund has to be made.[12]

B.   The Mechanics

1.   New S Corporations

Section 444(a) prescribes that a new S corporation can elect a fiscal year that has a deferral period of three months or less. In regard to what fiscal period the corporation can choose, Congress has mandated that the fiscal year must end on 9/30, 10/31, or 11/30.[13]

2.   Existing S Corporations

For existing S corporations desiring fiscal year status there are a number of rules. Section 444(b)(3) prescribes that in a literal reading of the statute, that if an S corporation used a fiscal year starting in 1986, the corporation can elect to keep that fiscal year (the three month rule for new S corporations set forth in Section 444(b)(1) is not applicable). An example will illustrate:

EXAMPLE 1-5

When XYZ Inc., elected S status in 1980, it chose a 2/28 fiscal year ending. XYZ, Inc., can elect under Section 444 to keep the 2/28 fiscal year or a calendar year under Section 1378 for reporting purposes.

In regard to an S corporation that already has a taxable year, and wishes to change the year to a fiscal year, the corporation can change to fiscal year under Section 444(b)(ii); however, the corporation can only choose a fiscal year that results in a deferral period not longer than the shorter of three months or the deferral period of the year that is being changed. Thus, if an S corporation has a fiscal year of 7/31, it can elect a fiscal year of 9/30, 10/31, or 11/30—if the corporation has a fiscal year ending 10/31, it can only elect an 11/30 fiscal year or keep its existing 10/31 year.

As to a C corporation that elected S status during the period 9/18/86 to 1/1/88 and pursuant to Section 1378 reported its income under a calendar year basis, the Omnibus Budget Reconciliation Act of 1987 (OBRA) Section 10206(d)(4) prescribes that the corporation generally may choose a fiscal year which produces a deferral period not longer than the shorter of three months or the deferral period of the C corporation. So, if a C corporation that had a fiscal year ending 6/30/87 elected S status in 1987, it could choose a fiscal year of 9/30, 10/31, 11/30, or 6/30 pursuant to the special provision of OBRA.

3.   The Fiscal Year Based on Business Purpose

An S corporation under Section 1378(b) can elect a fiscal year based on business purpose. Congress has prescribed that the S corporation may use a fiscal year if it meets one of three tests:

a.   *Revenue Procedure 74-33*

This procedure allows the tax year to conform to the S corporation's normal business year. If an S corporation received permission to use a fiscal year under Revenue Procedure 74–33, then it can continue to use the fiscal year without obtaining IRS approval.[14]

b.   *Revenue Procedure 83-25*

This procedure allows an S corporation to adopt a taxable year conforming to a fiscal year where (1) 25% or more of an S corporation's gross receipts for the 12-month period are recognized in the last two months of such period and (2) this 25% test has been met for three consecutive 12-month periods.[15]

c.   *Business Reason*

Congress, in the Tax Reform Act of 1986, prescribed that the Treasury Department is authorized to prescribe other tests permitting an S corporation to adopt fiscal year reporting. However, the Tax Reform Act of 1986 Conference Committee has prescribed that the following reasons will not suffice to adopt a fiscal year:

1. The fact that a particular business involved the use of price lists, model years, and the like that change on an annual basis
2. The use of a particular year for administrative purposes, for example, for promotion of staff and retirement of shareholder
3. The use of a particular year for regulatory or financial accounting purposes
4. The hiring patterns of a particular business

As of this writing, it is not clear if the S corporation which uses a fiscal year based on business purpose has to make an election and make a deposit under Section (444(c)(i) discussed in Chapter 1.4.B.6.

4. Tiered Structures—S Corporation Which Is a Member of a Partnership

As discussed at Chapter 2.4.C, an S corporation can be a partner in a partnership. However, Section 444(d)(3) prescribes that if an S corporation is part of a tiered structure (i.e., the S corporation is a partner in the partnership), the S corporation cannot make an election under Section 444 for a fiscal year unless it is part of a structure composed of one or more partnerships or S corporations all having the same taxable year. Thus, as the Conference Committee Report to OBRA stated, if:

> a June partnership that has traditionally used a taxable year ending June 30 is owned by calendar year individuals and an S corporation that has also traditionally used a taxable year ending June 30[;] [t]he partnership and S corporation may make elections under this provision to continue to use their taxable years ending June 30 providing the election is made by both entities.

TAX POINTER

Section 444(d)(3) could prove troublesome to an S corporation which is a minority partner in a partnership, since it will be unable, due to its minority status, to cause the partnership to change to a fiscal year desired.

5. S Corporation Makes the S Election Status for Fiscal Year, Not the Shareholders

Section 444(d)(1) prescribes that the corporation makes the election for fiscal year status, not the shareholders. Thus, majority rule shall prevail and the minority shareholder will have no veto power over this election.

6. Section 7519's Interest-Free Deposit

Section 444(c)(1) prescribes that if an S corporation made an election for a fiscal year under Section 444, it must make a "required payment" as prescribed by Section 7519 (in reality, this required payment is an interest-free deposit to the government). Section 7519 requires that for every year that the fiscal year election is in effect, a required payment is required to be made pursuant to Section 7519(f)(2) on April of the calendar year following the calendar year in which the election year begins, or at such later date as may be prescribed by the Treasury Department.

In terms of the operation of Section 7519, it is complex. Detailed below are the definitional provisions under Section 7519 and examples as to how Section 7519 operates.

Required Payment

Section 7519(b) prescribes that a required payment for an election year is equal to the excess of: 1) the product of the applicable percentage (as defined below) of the adjusted highest Section 1 tax rate multiplied by the S corporation's net base-year income over; 2) the amount of the required payment for the preceding election year. For purposes of definition, the adjusted highest Section 1 tax rate is prescribed by Section 7519(b) as 36% for election years beginning in 1987. For all other election years, the adjusted highest Section 1 rate is the rate of tax imposed by Section 1 as of the end of the year preceding the election year plus 1 percentage point. Section 7519(c) provides that if the previous year's required payment is greater than the current year's payment then the corporation is entitled to receive a refund of the difference, although Section 7519(f)(4) prescribes that the Government will not pay any interest on this refund.

Applicable Percentage

Section 7519(d)(4) defines applicable percentage as follows:

If the applicable election year of the partnership or S corporation begins during:	The applicable percentage is:
1987	25
1988	50
1989	75
1990 or thereafter	100

Base Year Income

Section 7519(d)(1) prescribes that the base year is the tax year preceding the election year. An S corporation's net base income is equal to the sum of the deferred ratio multiplied by the corporation's net income for the base year plus the excess (if any) of: 1) the deferred ratio multiplied by the aggregate amount of applicable payments made by the entity during the base year, over; 2) The aggregate amount of the applicable amount of the applicable payments made during the deferred period of the base year.

Deferred Ratio

Section 7519(e)(1) defines deferred ratio as the ratio that the number of months in the deferred period of the base year bears to the number of months in the S corporation's tax year.

Net Income

Section 7519(d)(2)(B) defines net income as the amount (not less than zero) determined by taking into account the aggregate amount of the S corporation's items (other than credits) described in Section 1366(a). If an S corporation was a C corporation for the base year its taxable income for that year is treated as its net income for that year.

Applicable Payments

Section 7519(d)(3) prescribes that applicable payments are amounts paid or incurred by an S corporation that are includable in a shareholder's gross income other than gains from the sale or exchange of property between the owner and the S corporation and dividends paid.

$500 Threshhold Payment

Section 7519(a)(2) prescribes that an S corporation does not have to make a required payment if the total of required payments for the current year and all preceding election years does not exceed $500. An amount not required to be paid is not considered part of the required payment for the preceding election year for the purpose of determining the amount of the required payment for the current election year. An example will illustrate:

EXAMPLE 1-6

In its first election year, an S corporation's required payment would be $350; in its second election year, the S corporation's required payment would be an additional $350. In its first election year the S corporation does not have to make a required payment; however, in its second election year it will make a required payment of $700.

Two situations could arise which would require Section 7519 rules to come into effect—where there are applicable payments made to shareholders and where there are not. The examples set forth below illustrate the applicability of Section 7519.

EXAMPLE 1-7

Without Applicable Payment To Shareholders

ABC, Inc., is a 6/30 fiscal year S corporation having $132,000 of net income for the fiscal year ending 6/30/87 and $140,000 for the fiscal year ending 6/30/88.

	Fiscal Year Ended	
	6/30/87	6/30/88
Base Year Net Income	132,000	140,000
Deferred Ratio	6/12	6/12
Deferred base-year net income	66,000	70,000
Rate for Required Payment	36%	29%
	23,760	20,300
Applicable Percentage	25%	50%
	5,940	10,150
Net Required Payment, 1988	5,940	
TOTAL Required Payment on 4/15/89		10,150
LESS: 1988 Payment		5,940
TOTAL DUE		4,210

EXAMPLE 1-8

With Applicable Payment to Shareholders

XYZ, Inc., is an 8/31 fiscal year S corporation. In 1987, the base year net income after deducting the applicable payment is $450,000. The applicable payment is $120,000, consisting of $30,000 rent payments paid to XYZ's sole shareholder, A, in four equal quarterly installments at the beginning of each calendar year quarter.

Base Year Net Income	450,000
Deferred Ratio	4/12
Deferred base-year net income (4/12 × 450M)	150,000
Total applicable payments	120,000
Deferred Ratio	4/12
Applicable payment ratio amount (4/12 × 120M)	40,000
Less: Actual applicable payments during base-year deferred period:	
Quarterly Rent	30,000
Applicable payment component	10,000
Required Payment Calculation	
Deferred base-year net income	150,000
Applicable payment component	10,000
	160,000
Rate for Required Payment	36%
	57,600
Applicable Percentage	25%
1988 Required Payment	14,400

To ensure proper reporting, Section 7519(f)(4) prescribes penalties. Further, as discussed in this Section, Section 7519(f)(3) provides that no interest is due or allowable on any refund due the S corporation in a year in which it has a negative required payment. However, if a required payment is not made timely, it is treated as a tax for purposes of determining interest. Additionally, Section 7519(g) prescribes that the Treasury is to prescribe regulations necessary to carry out Section 7519 including a means for annualizing an S corporation's income and applicable payments if the base year is a tax year of less than 12 months.

7. Refund of Required Payment

Section 7519(c) prescribes that if the required payment for a year is less than its required payment for the prior year, the S corporation shall be entitled to a refund of such excess. Thus, if an S corporation can make its net income decrease in the current year it can obtain a refund of the reduction from the prior year of the required payment. However, Sections 7519(f)(3) states that no interest shall be paid by the Service on any refunds to be made. Accordingly, an S corporation can obtain a refund under Section 7519 if it causes its net income to decrease from the prior year by, inter alia, declaring salaries to shareholder-employees.

Not discussed in Section 7519, however, is what occurs if an S corporation decides to return to calendar year status, or it liquidates, it terminates its S status or it is acquired in a merger. As of this writing, there is no indication how the government will treat these situations. Presumably, the tax payer will receive a refund of any required payments.

8. Tax Planning Under Sections 444 and 7519

As the above discussion indicates, electing fiscal year status for an S corporation is a very complicated procedure. Besides that, the S corporation, if it is making money, must make a tax payment with the Internal Revenue Service which gathers no interest nor gives the shareholders of the fiscal year S corporation any tax benefit. Presumably, if an S corporation fails to make a proper tax payment under any of the Code provisions, this required payment is probably subject to attachment by the Service for payment of the erroneously paid taxes by the S corporation.

Another problem that could arise with a fiscal year S corporation is when stock changes hands between shareholders. For example, suppose a shareholder sells stock in a fiscal year S corporation to another shareholder. In terms of valuing the stock for sale purposes, the sale price must also reflect the selling shareholder's portion of the required payment(s). Likewise, if a gift is made of S corporation stock, the amount of the required payment that would be allocated to the shares being given has to be added to the value for gift tax purposes.

1.5 CASH OR ACCRUAL BASIS FOR REPORTING INCOME: HOW TO MAKE THE CHOICE

A. General Discussion

An S corporation, like any other corporation, can elect either the accrual method or cash-basis method to report income and expense, providing it is not a tax shelter. (If the corporation is a tax shelter, TRA Section 801 prescribes that the corporation must use the accrual method to report its income. As to the definitions of a tax shelter, it is complex, but see generally Sections 6661(b)(2)(C)(ii) and 1256(e)(3)(B) and other definitional areas). The S corporation is not bound by the accounting method of its shareholders. However, if the S corporation elects the accrual basis to report income and expense, the S corporation, pursuant to Section 267(a)(2), is basically put on the cash-basis method for purposes of deducting business expenses and interest owed to certain related-party cash-basis taxpayers.[16]

As to who these certain related parties are, Section 267(e) defines them to be:

- Any shareholder who owns stock in the corporation.
- Any person as defined in Section 267(b) or 707(b)(1) related to a shareholder.[17]

The consequences of Section 267(a)(2)'s proscription is that the S corporation will receive the deduction for the expense items when the amount is "includible" in the recipient's income.

TAX POINTER

Section 267 provides, with respect to this matching of corporation deduction and related-party income, that there is no time limit when these accrued items must be paid, as was the case under law prior to the Subchapter S Revision Act of 1982.

Examples will clarify and illustrate the deductibility of expenses and interest.

EXAMPLE 1-6

Alpha Corporation, an S corporation, is owned by two unrelated individuals, A and B, who report their income on cash basis. B owns 1 share, and A owns 99 of Alpha Corporation. Alpha Corporation adopts the accrual method to report its income and the calendar year basis for reporting income. Alpha Corporation, on January 1, 19XX, signs a lease with A.

As of 12/31/XX, Alpha Corporation has accrued $6,000 of rent owed to A. Because A has not received the $6,000 rent by 12/31/XX, Alpha Corporation cannot deduct the $6,000 of rent on its Form 1120S for 19XX.

EXAMPLE 1-7

Assume the same facts as in Example 1-6, except that, on January 1 of the next year (19XY), Alpha Corporation delivers a $6,000 check to A who deposits the check and reports it as income. Alpha Corporation will be able to deduct $6,000 rent in 19XY on its Form 1120S.

EXAMPLE 1-8

Assume the same facts as in Example 1-7, except that Alpha Corporation delivers a $6,000 rent check to A on 12/31/XX and A deposits the check that day. Alpha Corporation will obtain a deduction for $6,000 rent expense in 19XX.

B. Existing C Corporations Converting to S Corporations— Change of Accounting Method Barred

At least two court cases have held that an S corporation may not adopt a method of accounting different from the method it used as a C corporation, without obtaining the Service's consent.[18]

C. S Corporation Can Use a Different Accounting Method than Predecessor Partnership

An S corporation can elect a different accounting method than a predecessor partnership.[19]

ENDNOTES FOR CHAPTER 1

1. Section 1366(B).
2. Id. For a more detailed explanation of the tax treatment of S corporate ordinary income, deductions, capital gains, and the like, see Chapters 4 and 5.
3. See *Lober* v. *U.S.,* 346 U.S. 335 (1945); Rev. Rul. 57-366, IRB 1957-32, 20.
4. 80 T.C. 47.
5. For a further discussion about termination and the tax effects of same, see Chapter 10.

6. Section 704(e)(3).

7. 588 F. Supp. 638 (Neb. 1984), aff'd on other issue, 52 AFTR 2d 5209 (8th Cir 1985).

8. 64 T.C. 1034 (1975).

9. Section 57(a)(5)(C)(i).

10. Section 55(d)(2).

11. Rev. Rul. 76-363, 1976-2 C.B. 90; *Modern Home Fire & Casualty Insurance Co.* 54 T.C. 839 (1970), acq. 1970-2 C.B. XX (1970).

12. Section 7519(c).

13. Section 444(b)(4).

14. 1974-2 C.B. 489 (cited with approval in the Conference Committee Report to the Tax Reform Act of 1986 at II-319).

15. 1983-1 C.B. 698 (cited with approval in the Conference Committee Report to the Tax Reform Act of 1986 at II-319).

16. S. Rep. No. 640, 97th Cong., 2d Sess. 24, reprinted in 1982-2 C.B. 718, 729 states: "The bill places a Subchapter S corporation on the cash method of accounting for purposes of deducting business expenses and interest owed to a related party cash basis taxpayer. . . ." See also H.R. Rep. No. 826, 97th Cong., 2d Sess. 23, reprinted in 1982-2 C.B. 730, 740.

17. Note, also, if a shareholder owns more than 50% of profits interest in a partnership, the partnership and the S corporation are related for this purpose (Section 707(b)(1)(A)). Additionally, the restriction on the deduction by the S corporation in a partnership year only applies if the corporation and shareholder to whom the expense or interest is being paid are related on the last day of the corporation's year in which the amount would normally be deductible.

18. *Weiss* v. *Comm.*, 395 F. 2d 500 (10th Cir. 1968), aff'g Para. 67,124 P-H Memo, TCM 1967-125, *William H. Leonhart*, Para. 68, 097 P-H Memo TCM 1968-98.

19. Because by definition Section 381(a) does not apply to the incorporation of a partnership, Section 381(c)(4), which is set forth below, cannot apply:

> The acquiring corporation shall use the method of accounting used by the distributor or transferor corporation on the date of distribution or transfer unless different methods were used by several distributor or transferor corporations or by a distributor or transferor corporation and the acquiring corporation. If different methods were used, the acquiring corporation shall use the method or combination of methods of computing taxable income adopted pursuant to regulations prescribed by the Secretary.

2

The Elements of the S Corporation Election

2.1 STATUTORY REQUIREMENTS TO BE AN S CORPORATION

Because an S corporation is a creature of statute, Congress has prescribed certain basic requirements that must be met by a corporation to achieve S corporation status. Section 1361(b) prescribes that an S corporation must (1) be a domestic corporation, (2) have only 35 shareholders, (3) not be a member of an affiliated group, (4) have only one class of stock, and (5) have only eligible shareholders (e.g., individuals, decedents' estates, certain prescribed trusts, no nonresident aliens).

TAX POINTER

Because the limitation of the number of shareholders, estate planning becomes difficult, especially if a shareholder has a large family and wishes to bestow stock upon members of said family. Further, in contrast to a C corporation and a partnership, an S corporation is not a good vehicle to raise investment capital, due to the limited number of shareholders permitted.

2.2 LIMITS ON NUMBERS OF SHAREHOLDERS

A. How to Count Shareholders

1. Time for Counting Shareholders

Rev. Rul. 78-390[1] prescribes that an S corporation may not have more than 35 shareholders at any particular time during the year. Thus, an S corporation will not be disqualified if cumulatively it has a total of more than 35 shareholders during a taxable year due to transfers, but will lose its status if at any time in the taxable year it has more than 35 shareholders.

TAX POINTER

Beware of the consequences of attempts to subvert Section 1361(b)'s mandate. If the Service detects an attempt to subvert the 35 shareholder numerical requirement of Section 1361(b), it will be struck down. For instance, in Rev. Rul. 77-220,[2] issued when S corporations were limited to only 10 shareholders, 30 individuals formed three corporations, each with 10 shareholders, with each corporation capitalized in the same amount. Each corporation elected S corporation status, and then the three S corporations formed a partnership to operate a small business. The Service deemed the three corporations as one and struck down the elections.

B. Constructive Ownership Rules Do Not Apply

In Section 318, a parent is deemed to own the stock of children, grandchildren, parents, and spouse. Section 1361(b) does not apply such rules for counting shareholders (with the exception of a spouse), so that these people are counted separately (e.g., if a father and his 2 children are shareholders of an S corporation, there are 3 shareholders, not one, for purposes of arriving at the 35 shareholder numerical limit of Section 1361(b).

With respect to a husband and wife, as discussed shortly, they are counted as one shareholder for purposes of determining Section 1361(b)'s 35 shareholder limit.[3]

C. Stock Held by a Nominee

If stock is held by a nominee, the beneficial owner will be treated as a shareholder for purposes of the 35 shareholder numerical limit of Section 1361(b). Likewise, stock held by an agent is deemed to be stock owned by the principal.[4] An example will illustrate:

EXAMPLE 2-1

ADF, Inc., an S corporation, issued 15 stock certificates, 13 to individuals, 1 to A, who was the agent for B, and 1 to D, who is holding the stock as a nominee for Q, R, and S, 3 individuals. ADF, Inc., has 17 shareholders, although only 15 certificates were issued: the 13 individuals, B and Q, R and S.

TAX POINTER

See Chapter 3.3.A as to who must make the S corporate election on Form 2553 when stock is held by a nominee.

D. Treatment of Stock Held by a Custodian Under the Uniform Gifts to Minors Act (UGMA)

When stock is held by a custodian under the UGMA, the minor is deemed the owner, not the custodian.[5] Thus, if one person acts as a custodian for four different minors, there are four shareholders (see discussion at Chapter 1.2A, Tax Pointer 2, as to the estate tax consequences of custodianship situations under UGMA).

TAX POINTER

See Chapter 3.3.B as to who must make the S corporate election on Form 2553.

E. How Stock Held by Joint Tenants and Tenants in Common Is Treated

If two or more unmarried persons own S corporation stock as joint tenants, tenants in common, and so on, each person counts as a shareholder[6] (as to married individuals, see discussion below).

TAX POINTER

See Chapter 3.3.C as to who must make the S corporate election on Form 2553.

F. How Stock Held by a Husband and Wife Is Treated

Section 1361(c)(1) states that if stock is held jointly by a husband and wife, either as joint tenants or as tenants in common, the husband and wife are treated as one shareholder, although both spouses must personally consent to the S corporation election.[7] If a husband and wife each own stock separately, as well as jointly, they are still treated as one shareholder.[8]

TAX POINTER

See Chapter 3.3.D as to who must make the S corporate election on Form 2553.

1. Community Property States

In a community property state, the husband and wife are treated as one shareholder if they each own stock, regardless of whether or not they each own stock as common property.

TAX POINTER

See Chapter 3.3.E as to who must make the S corporate election on Form 2553.

2. Death of a Spouse

If a spouse dies, stock owned by the surviving spouse and the estate of the deceased spouse will be treated as one shareholder. Likewise, if both spouses die, the two estates will be treated as one shareholder.

2.3 TYPES OF ENTITIES AND INDIVIDUALS THAT CAN BE SHAREHOLDERS

A. General Discussion

Section 1361(b)(1) imposes limitations on who can be a shareholder of an S corporation. For instance, corporations, employee stock ownership trusts (ESOPs), partnerships, nonresident aliens, and certain types of trusts cannot be shareholders, while estates, resident aliens, and certain types of trusts can. Consequently, tax planning possibilities become limited. For instance, because an ESOP cannot be an S corporate shareholder, a valuable means of stimulating employee performance is lost.

B. Tax Planning Potentials and Pitfalls for Each Type of Shareholder

1. Estates

Section 1361(b)(1)(B) prescribes that an estate can own stock in an S corporation. Note, however, if the administration of a decedent's estate is unduly prolonged, the Service may deem the estate to be a trust, which will cause the S corporation to lose its status.[9]

Consequently, if a shareholder dies, providing in the will that a testamentary trust is to be established, which by its terms will invalidate the S corporation election, the executor or personal representative of the estate cannot unreasonably delay the administration of the estate before establishing the trust in an attempt to keep the S corporation alive.

TAX POINTERS

1. If an estate is kept open to hold stock during the period that estate taxes are paid on a deferred basis, under Section 6166A, this will not cause the S corporation to be terminated.[10] (For a further discussion of estate planning with S corporations, see Chapter 9.11.)

2. See Chapter 3.3.F as to who must make the S corporate election on Form 2553.

2.   Grantor, Section 678 Trust, Testamentary, Qualified S Corporation Trusts, and Voting Trusts

Section 1361(b)(1)(B) permits only five types of trusts to own stock in an S corporation. The five trusts are (1) voting trusts, (2) grantor trusts, (3) Section 678 trusts, (4) testamentary trusts (under limited circumstances), and (5) Qualified S Corporation Trusts. Consequently, income and estate tax planning is severely limited, since by definition, trusts that do not fit the definition (e.g., nongrantor inter vivos trusts where all the trust income is not required to be distributed each year) cannot be shareholders. Below is set forth a brief discussion of these allowable trusts.

a.   *Voting Trusts*

Section 1361(c)(2)(A)(iv) basically does not define what requirements a trust must meet to qualify as a "voting trust," except to state that each trust beneficiary must be an eligible shareholder of an S corporation.

Proposed Reg. Section 1.1371-1(d)(3), which was proposed under the former law, sets forth a number of requirements, among them the following: (1) that the trust be in writing, (2) that it give the right to vote stock to one or more trustees, (3) that all distributions are for the benefit of the beneficial owners, (4) that title and possession of the S corporation stock vest in the beneficiaries at the end of the trust, and (5) that under its terms, or by state law, the trust terminate on or before a specific time period or event.

TAX POINTER

See Chapter 3.3.G as to who must make the S corporate election on Form 2553.

b.   *Grantor Trusts*

Section 1361(c)(2)(A)(i) generally allows a grantor trust (a trust that is treated entirely as owned by the grantor under Sections 671–677) to be a shareholder of an S corporation, providing the grantor is an individual and not a nonresident alien. A common example of a "grantor trust" is the revocable inter vivos trust, which is often used as an estate planning device to minimize state probate of assets.

Section 1361(c)(2)(A)(ii) prescribes that after the death of the grantor, the trust may continue as a shareholder for up to either 60 days or 2 years after the grantor's death (the 2-year period applies if the grantor's gross estate includes the entire corpus of the trust).

TAX POINTER

See Chapter 3.3.H as to who must make the S corporate election on Form 2553.

c. Testamentary Trusts

Sections 1361(b)(1)(B) and 1361(c)(2)(A)(iii) prescribe that a trust that receives S corporation stock under a will can remain as a shareholder for up to 60 days. As discussed at Chapter 9.11, these restrictions on testamentary trusts severely limit estate planning, thereby forcing a testamentary trustee to either sell the stock quickly or make a distribution to the beneficiaries of the stock, assuming they are all eligible shareholders.

TAX POINTERS

1. There is one advantage to transferring stock to a testamentary trust, however, in that frequently, a sale can be made from a trust without court approval, whereas a sale by an estate could require it.

2. See Chapter 3.3.I as to who must make the S corporate election on Form 2553.

d. Section 678 Trusts

Section 1361(c)(2)(A)(i), in conjunction with Section 678, allows a trust owned by the person other than a grantor to be an S corporation shareholder. The person treated as the owner must be an individual and not a nonresident alien. At the death of the deemed owner, Section 1361(c)(2)(A)(ii) states that the trust may continue as a shareholder for either 60 days or 2 years after the deemed owner's gross estate includes the entire corpus of the trust).

TAX POINTER

See Chapter 3.3.J as to who must make the S corporate election on Form 2553.

e. Qualified S Corporation Trusts

In 1981, Congress established the concept of a Qualified S Corporation Trust to own stock in an S corporation. Since then, the definition has been revised in 1982 and 1984. Basically, a Qualified S Corporation Trust is a "simple trust."[11] Examples of trust that can qualify as S Corporation Trust are QTIP marital deduction trusts, Section 2503(b) trusts for minor children, trusts that pay income for life to a beneficiary,[12] trusts that will terminate when a beneficiary attains a certain age, and so on. (Other examples of Qualified S Corporation Trusts are found in Ltr. Ruls. 8514018 and 8435153.[13])

C. The Five Statutory Requirements

To have a trust qualify as a Qualified S Corporation Trust, it has to comply with Section 1361(d). The requirements are briefly set forth below, and it is to be noted that the requirements are strict:

1. All the assets of the trust must be distributed during the life of the current income beneficiary if the trust ends during the life of the current income beneficiary.

2. The trust must distribute or be required to distribute all its income currently to the sole income beneficiary.

3. The income interest of the current income beneficiary must terminate on the earlier of (a) the death of the beneficiary or (b) the termination of the trust.

4. The terms of the trust must require that any corpus distributed during the life of the current income beneficiary be distributed only to that beneficiary.

5. There can only be one income beneficiary during the life of the current beneficiary.

TAX POINTERS

1. Although there is a restriction as set forth regarding one income beneficiary, Section 1361(d)'s definition does not preclude a trust from having multiple income beneficiaries after the death of the current income beneficiary.

2. A Qualified S Corporation Trust is not limited to owning stock only in an S corporation—it can own other property in other situations (e.g., stock in a C corporation).

D. The Election to Be Treated as a Qualified S Corporation Trust

Besides the foregoing, Section 1361(d)(1) prescribes that the Qualified S Corporation Trust will not qualify as an S corporate shareholder unless the beneficiary irrevocably elects to have the trust qualify for the special tax treatment. The Service, in Temp. Reg. Section 18.1361-1, has prescribed the manner in which the beneficiary must elect. Care must be exercised with respect to the election, since Section 1361(d)(2)(D) prescribes that the beneficiary must make the election within 2 months and 16 days after the trust acquires the S corporation stock. If the election is premature or late, it could cause the S corporation to lose its status as such, because there is not a qualified shareholder.

TAX POINTERS

1. Care should be taken with respect to whom is selected to be the trustee of the Qualified S Corporation Trust. For example, if a minor child is a beneficiary and the child's parent is the trustee, and if any of the trust income is used for the minor child's support, the trust may lose its qualification, because all the S corporate income is not passing through to the beneficiary, and thus the corporation's S corporate status will be destroyed.

2. Since Section 1361(d) allows state law and the trust instrument to define what is trust income and corpus, there is room for tax planning, because depending on where the parties want to be, certain items could be classified as corpus rather than income and thereby save income taxes.

3. See Chapter 3.3.K as to who must make the S corporate election on Form 2553.

E.   The Bankrupt Shareholder

In 1980, when Congress passed Section 1361(c)(3), it ended a long-running feud between the Service and the courts by providing that a shareholder who has filed under any provision of the bankruptcy code can be an S corporation shareholder.

TAX POINTER

See Chapter 3.3.L as to who must make the S corporate election on Form 2553.

2.4   WHO CANNOT BE AN S CORPORATION SHAREHOLDER?

A.   Nonresident Aliens

Section 1361(b)(1)(C) prescribes that nonresident aliens cannot be shareholders.

B.   Nonqualifying Trusts

As discussed previously, a number of trusts cannot qualify for S corporation purposes. Note also that Section 1361(c)(2)(A) prescribes that a foreign trust cannot be a shareholder.

C. Partnerships

Section 1361(b)(1)(B) prescribes that a partnership cannot be an S corporation shareholder.[14] However, a partnership can apparently act as a nominee or trustee of an allowable trust and not destroy the S corporation election.[15] Note, the Service will also strike down attempts to subvert this prohibition on partners owning stock in an S corporation. (See Rev. Rul. 77-220, discussed at Tax Pointer in Chapter 2.2.A.1.)

TAX POINTER

Note that while a partnership cannot be an S corporate shareholder, the S corporation can be a partner in a partnership. (See discussion at Chapter 9.10.)

D. Corporations

Section 1361(b)(1)(B) prescribes that a corporation, whether foreign or domestic, cannot own stock in an S corporation. However, a corporation can apparently hold title to the stock as a nominee or trustee of an allowable trust.[16]

TAX POINTER

Note that while a corporation cannot be a shareholder in an S corporation, an S corporation can basically own stock in a C corporation providing it is not a member of an affiliated group. (See discussion at Chapter 9.9 and as set forth below.)

2.5 S CORPORATION CANNOT BE A MEMBER OF AN AFFILIATED GROUP

Section 1361(b)(2)(A) states that for an S corporation to keep its status, it cannot be a member of an affiliated group.[17] Further, Section 1362(b)(2)(B)(i) states that the S corporation can never be a member of an affiliated group at any time during its taxable year. The following example will clarify:

EXAMPLE 2-2

A, Inc., a calendar year corporation, owned 100% of two subsidiaries that were actively engaged in manufacturing. Until 19XX, it filed consolidated returns with its subsidiaries. In January 19XY, A, Inc., sold off its two subsidiaries and wants to elect S status. Because A, Inc., is a member of an affiliated group for part of its taxable year, it can only elect S status for the years after 19XY.

An affiliated group would exist if an S corporation owns directly at least 80% of the voting power of all stock and at least 80% of each class of nonvoting stock of a subsidiary.[18] There is no requirement that consolidated returns be filed for the affiliated group for this prohibition to exist.[19] If the S corporation owns 79% of a subsidiary's stock, then there is no affiliated group.[20] Further, it is to be noted that the rules of attribution have no applicability. Thus, an S corporation could own 79% of a subsidiary's stock and an S corporation shareholder could own the rest, with there still being no affiliated group.[21]

TAX POINTER

By the logic of Sections 1504 and 1361, an S corporation could have complete ownership and not lose its election by having the S corporation own 50% of the stock of each of the subsidiaries and then have the subsidiaries own 50% of each other's stock.

A.   Two Situations Where an S Corporation Can Have a Subsidiary

Even if the S corporation owns too much of the subsidiary's stock, this will still not cause the S corporation parent to lose its S corporate status in two situations:

1.   Inactive Subsidiaries

Section 1361(c)(6) permits an S corporation to own 100% of a subsidiary, providing that the subsidiary

1. Has not begun business at any time on or after the date of its incorporation.
2. Has no taxable income during the taxable year of the parent corporation.

The requirements for Section 1361(c)(6)'s exemption, however, are quite strict. The regulations prescribe that acquiring operating assets may constitute the beginning of business destroying the S corporation election,[22] and it has been held that the election is lost when a subsidiary borrows money, incurs expenses, and plans its business(es).[23]

TAX POINTERS

1. Because of Section 1361(c)(6)'s strictures, this exception to the general rule of "no affiliated groups" has little utility. Its

only recognized use is to allow a subsidiary to reserve or hold a corporate name[24]—a very limited use.

2. If an 80% or more subsidiary of the S corporation has taxable gross income, this will automatically cause the S corporation to lose its election.[25]

2.   Transitory Subsidiaries

A transitory subsidiary occurs when an S corporation acquires a subsidiary but only for a very limited period of time and purpose. For instance, in Rev. Rul. 73-496,[26] an S corporation purchased the stock of another corporation, liquidating it 29 days later. The Service sustained the S election, since the momentary control was part of a liquidation process.

TAX POINTER

Ltr. Rul. 7812051 held that ownership of a subsidiary for over 100 days caused termination of S corporate status even though the need to maintain the subsidiary was due in part to a requirement of federal agency approval.

a.   *Section 338 Transaction*

Although S corporations could have used Section 334(b)(2) to acquire assets of a corporation through purchase of the stock of the corporation, Section 338, the successor to Section 334(b)(2), precludes an S corporation from buying the stock of the corporation to liquidate it and obtain a step up in value of its assets. The consequences to an S corporation, if it attempts to use Section 338 to acquire assets of a subsidiary, is loss of its election.[27] Thus, S corporations are precluded from a valuable negotiating device to conduct business. An example will clarify:

EXAMPLE 2-3

MN, Inc., is an S corporation. A, who owns AB, Inc., a C corporation, is approached by MN, Inc., to sell MN, Inc., the stock of AB, Inc. MN, Inc., pointed out to A that Section 338 precludes an S corporation from buying the stock of a corporation and then liquidating it to get a step up in basis for the corporation's assets. A, for tax reasons unique to A (i.e., the double tax under Section 337), advises that it cannot sell the assets to MN, Inc., under Section 337; therefore, the deal cannot be consummated.

TAX POINTER

For further discussion about Section 338, see Chapter 10.10.B.

2.6 S CORPORATION CAN BE A MEMBER OF
A CONTROLLED GROUP

Although Section 1361(b)(2)(A) precludes an S corporation from being a member of an affiliated group, there is nothing in the law to prevent it from being a member of a controlled group (i.e., brother-sister corporations as defined by Section 1563(a) connected through common ownership by individuals, estates, or trusts). This could arise in various situations, for example, when the same shareholders owns a C and an S Corporation or two or more S corporations (e.g., brother-sister corporations). The consequences of an S corporation being a member of a controlled group is that certain tax situations become affected, for example, membership in retirement plans,[28] targeted jobs credit,[29] and research credit.[30] An example will illustrate:

EXAMPLE 2-4

X, a taxpayer, owns all the stock in ABC, Inc., an S corporation, and XYZ, Inc., a C corporation. X establishes a profit sharing plan in XYZ, Inc., where there are many employees but very little profits, and a pension plan in ABC, Inc., where X is the sole employee. By Section 410 et seq., because ABC, Inc., and XYZ, Inc., are members of a controlled group, the employees of ABC, Inc., and XYZ, Inc., have to be combined to see if the top-heavy rules of Section 401 et seq., have not been abridged, if the proper amount of contributions are being made, and so on. (For a discussion of retirement plans, see Chapter 5.7.)

A. Tax Rates of C Corporations Are Unchanged if S and C Corporations Are Members of a Controlled Group

The S corporation, by being a member of a controlled group, does not affect the tax rates of C corporation(s) that are member(s) of the controlled group, accumulated earnings credit of the corporation(s), and so on.[31] An example will clarify:

EXAMPLE 2-5

A forms ABC, Inc., a C corporation, to engage in a venture. It is profitable, and A is contemplating another venture. In 19X3, A forms IMN, Inc., to engage in this new enterprise, which elects S corporation status on formation. Both IMN, Inc., and ABC, Inc., earn $100,000 each in 19X3. ABC, Inc.'s corporate income tax for 19X3 will be computed by using the tax rates under Section 11 without allocation as would be required for brother-sister C corporations under Section 1561 et seq., and A, as sole shareholder of IMN, Inc., will report $100,000 of income on A's Form 1040.

TAX POINTER

Although Section 1561 et seq. will not affect any of the graduated tax rates when a C and an S corporation are members of a controlled group, Section 482 can apply to reallocate income.[32]

2.7　ONLY DOMESTIC CORPORATIONS CAN BE S CORPORATIONS

Section 1361(b)(1) prescribes that only "domestic corporations" can be S corporations. However, the term "domestic"[33] for S corporation purposes is not defined in the Code. Rather, Treas. Reg. Section 1.1371-1(b) (adopted under former Code Section 1371) prescribes that for a corporation to be an S corporation, it must be "created or organized in the United States or under the law of the United States or of any State or Territory." Accordingly, by definition, corporations organized in a foreign country cannot be S corporations, even though the corporation may have assets and do business in the United States.

TAX POINTER

While Section 1361(b)(1) may limit where an S corporation must be formed, there is no limitation on the location where an S corporation must do business. Consequently, an S corporation could have 100% income from foreign countries and still qualify for S status.

2.8　FIVE TYPES OF CORPORATIONS THAT CANNOT BE S CORPORATIONS

Section 1361(b)(2) states that, notwithstanding the fact that all the other requirements of S corporate status have been satisfied (e.g., the corporation only has 35 individual shareholders, the shareholders are not nonresident aliens), the corporation to elect S corporate status must not be engaged in five ineligible activities:

1. An affiliated group (discussed in Chapter 2.5)
2. A financial institution that is a bank as defined in Section 585(a)(2) or to which Section 593 applies
3. An insurance company subject to tax under Subchapter L of the Code

4. A corporation where an election under Section 936 applies (i.e., a corporation electing the Puerto Rico and possession tax credit)

5. A DISC or former DISC

2.9 S CORPORATION CAN ONLY HAVE ONE CLASS OF STOCK

For a corporation to qualify as an S corporation, Section 1361(b)(1)(D) provides that it can only have one class of stock. As discussed in Chapter 10.11.E, this one class of stock requirement severely limits estate and income tax planning possibilities since S corporations are prohibited from adopting recapitalizations, creating preferred stock, and so on. However, there are some planning possibilities, as discussed below.

A. S Corporation Can Have Voting and Nonvoting Stock

While Section 1361(b)(1)(D) prohibits more than one class of stock, Section 1361(c)(4) permits an S corporation to have voting and nonvoting common stock, providing that such shares have the same economic rights in the stock to dividends and liquidation proceeds. This consequence of this statutory exception to Section 1361(b)(1)(D)'s rule is greater flexibility with respect to tax and business planning.

1. Tax and Business Planning Possibilities with Voting and Nonvoting Common Stock

a. *Shifting Income Among Family Members*

As discussed in Chapter 1.2.A, one tax planning device is to shift income by having various family members (i.e., children over the age of 14) own stock in the S corporation together with the parents. To prevent loss of control over corporate affairs, the S corporation can issue nonvoting common stock to the children over the age of 14 and voting common stock to the parents. An example will illustrate:

EXAMPLE 2-6

A and B, husband and wife, who have three minor children, C, D, and E, plan to start AB, Inc., an S corporation. To keep control over the corporation, A and B will have AB, Inc., issue all voting common stock to themselves and nonvoting common stock to their three children, C, D, and E.

TAX POINTER

Care must be taken not to run afoul of the reallocation rules of Section 1366(e). (See discussion in Chapter 1.2.D.)

b. Raising Business Capital

While an S corporation due the strictures of Section 1361(b)(1)(D) cannot issue preferred stock, it can issue something that resembles it, namely, nonvoting common stock. An example will clarify:

EXAMPLE 2-7

Beta owns all the voting comon stock in Alpha, Inc., as S corporation. Alpha, Inc., needs to raise additional capital, so it issues nonvoting common to B. B is willing to make the investment giving all the control to Alpha, Inc., to Beta because by definition both sets of stock have the same economic rights to dividends and liquidation proceeds.

TAX POINTER

Recent private letter rulings have indicated that corporations can have a great deal of flexibility in raising business capital (see, e.g., Ltr. Rul. 8247017, agreement giving minority shareholders the option of having their stock redeemed under certain conditions did not create a second class of stock).

c. Attracting Key Personnel

Frequently, key personnel who are running a business want equity participation in the business to compensate them for their efforts. While an S corporation as a matter of law cannot establish an ESOP (see discussion at Chapter 2.3.A), it can establish nonvoting common stock to furnish the employees with an equity interest in the corporation. Or, alternatively, and in combination with issuing nonvoting stock to the key personnel, the S corporation can issue voting stock but restrict its rights by a shareholders' agreement. In Rev. Rul. 85-161,[34] a shareholder-employee could only transfer his stock after obtaining the consent of all the holders of the S corporation voting stock, and, if the consent could not be obtained, then the shareholder must sell the stock to the other shareholder or the S corporation at book value. These provisions also apply in the event of the death or disability of the shareholder-employee.

TAX POINTERS

1. In determining whether there is more than one class of stock, Reg. Section 1.1371-1(g) (adopted under former Code Section

1371) prescribes that only issued and outstanding stock is considered. The fact that the articles of incorporation provide for other classes of stock that have not been issued will not disqualify the S corporate election.

2. Care must be taken in issuing stock since state law may create a difference in shareholder rights to receive dividends or liquidation proceeds. (See, e.g., Rev. Rul. 71-522,[35] where two classes of stock were found, and thus no S election, because one set of subscribers to stock paid cash for the stock and the others intangible property.)

3. If nonvoting stock and/or voting stock is issued to key personnel to furnish them with equity participation, the key personnel could be taxed for the value of the stock furnished and/or a gift tax situation could occur, depending upon how the key personnel is furnished the stock.

B.   Debt as a Second Class of Stock

Under Section 1361(b)(1), which defines the elements for S corporation formation, there is no restriction about S corporations incurring debt. However, there is a potential problem if debt is not issued pro rata to stock ownership in that it could be classified as a second class of stock and thus destroy the S corporation election. Fortunately, due to case law, the Service's position in this area[36] and Section's 1361(c) S's safe harbor debt rules (Chapter 2.9.B.2), there is slight chance that debt could create a second class of debt.[37]

In regard to what type of situations are not treated as a second class of stock, the following should be noted:

> *Sam Novell*[38]—certain disproportionate advances were deemed "loans and not advances of equity capital."
>
> *August F. Nielsen Co.*[39]—debt was not in proportion to stock ownership, but the debt did not affect the stockholder's corporate control and thus not classified as stock.
>
> *James L. Stinnett, Jr.*[40]—noninterest-bearing notes did not carry with them the right to vote, participate in earnings growth or decision making, and so on; thus the debt is not classified as a second class of stock.

1.   Why S Corporate Shareholders Prefer Lending Money to S Corporations Rather than Acquiring More Stock

Under state law, creditors on dissolution of a corporation are paid before shareholders. Therefore, to protect themselves when they advance money to the corporation, shareholders attempt to do so by means of debt rather than acquire more stock, subject to the rules regarding second class of stock.

2. Section 1361(c)(5)'s Safe Harbor for Debt

In 1982, Congress, sympathetic to the reclassification problem of debt as a second class of stock, created a safe harbor for debt in Section 1361(c)(5). With respect to S shareholder loans, Section 1361(c)(5)(A) prescribes that "straight debt" will not be considered a second class of stock if the shareholder loans

1. Are in writing.
2. Have an unconditional promise to pay in money a sum certain on a specified date or on demand.
3. Have an interest rate and interest payment dates that are not contingent on the S corporation's profits, discretion, or similar factors.
4. Are not convertible directly or indirectly into S corporate stock.
5. Are owed to a creditor that would be a permitted S shareholder.

Accordingly, if S corporations observe the rules of Section 1361(c)(5) with respect to incurring debt to S corporate shareholders, no problems should arise with respect to loss of S corporate status.

TAX POINTERS

1. The interest rate should be able to be computed by outside factors such as the prime rate.[41]
2. If the debt falls outside of the safe harbor test set forth in Section 1361(c)(5) (i.e., it is not in writing), it still will not be classified as a second class of stock if the debt is incurred proportional to stock ownership.[42]
3. See Chapter 9.19 for the tax planning possibilities with S corporate debt.

ENDNOTES FOR CHAPTER 2

1. 1978-2 C.B. 220 (10 shareholder limit under prior law not violated when corporation had cumulative total of 15 shareholders during taxable year, but no more than 10 shareholders at any one time).
2. 1977-1 C.B. 263.
3. Section 1361(c)(1).
4. Reg. Section 1.1371-1(d)(1) (adopted under former Code Section 1371: "nominee,

agent, guardian, or custodian" generally not considered an S corporation share-holder).

5. Rev. Rul. 66-226, 1966-2 C.B. 356.

6. Reg. Section 1.1371-1(d)(1) (adopted under former Code Section 1371).

7. Temp. Reg. Section 18.1362-2(b)(2) and Reg. Section 1.1372-(3)(a) (adopted under former Code Section 1372).

8. Reg. Section 1.1371-1(d)(2)(i) (adopted under former Section 1371).

9. See, e.g., *Old Virginia Brick Co., Inc.*, 44 T.C. 724 (1965), aff'd 367 F. 2d 276 (4th Cir. 1966) (estate that began in 1941 that consented to S corporation status in 1959 and lost S corporation election by Reg. Section 1.641(b)–(3)(a) since estate "terminated" and was succeeded by a "testamentary trust").

10. Rev. Rul. 76-23, 1976-1 C.B. 264. But see Ltr. Rul. 7951131 (Service refused to rule, claiming a fact question, that estate could be kept open during pendency of federal estate tax audit without becoming a trust).

11. Section 651(a) defines a simple trust as one that provides that "all of its income is required to be distributed currently" and that does not make any distributions in a given year other than its current income.

12. Ltr. Rul. 8336069 (testamentary trust that paid income to a widow for her life a Qualified S Corporation Trust).

13. For an example of a Qualified S Corporate Trust that did not qualify, see Ltr. Rul. 8434091 (a trust that could pay income and corpus to either a woman or her son found not to be Qualified S Corporate Trust).

14. See also *Frederick J. Kling*, 41 T.C.M. 1133 (1981) (partnership owned all the stock of S corporation; partners denied deduction of corporate losses as distributive share).

15. Reg. Section 1.1371-1(d)(1) (adopted under former Code Section 1371); see also *Ray Guzowski*, Para. 67, 145 P-H Memo T.C. (1967).

16. Reg. Section 1.1371-1(d)(1) (adopted under former Code Section 1371).

17. Two examples of where an S corporation lost its election are *Barnes Motor & Parts Co. v. U.S.*, 309 F. Supp. 298 (C.E.D., N.C. 1970) (S corporation owned more than 80% of stock of two corporations), and *Olive E. Qualley*, Para. 76, 208 P-H Memo T.C. (1976) (S corporation purchased stock of two subsidiaries and attempted to use their losses).

18. Section 1504(a).

19. Reg. Section 1.1371-1(c)(1) (adopted under former Code Section 1371; *Olive E. Qualley*, Para. 76, 208 P-H Memo T.C. (1976).

20. See, e.g., Ltr. Rul. 8219071 (2/12/82) (parent corporation becomes eligible to be S corporation by reducing ownership in subsidiary's stock below 80%).

21. Examples of this stock ownership situation are Ltr. Rul. 8451049 (corporation eligible for S status if it transferred 21% of its DISC subsidiary's stock to its

shareholders), and Ltr. Rul. 8421025 (corporation eligible for S status if the beneficiary of its shareholder, a trust, bought 21% of the stock of its DISC subsidiary).

22. Reg. Section 1.1371-1(c)(2)(ii) (adopted under former Code Section 1371).

23. Ltr. Rul. 8215007 (12/23/81).

24. Section 1361(c)(6)(B).

25. Id.

26. 1973-2 C.B. 312.

27. Sections 338(a), 1371(a)(2).

28. Section 410.

29. Section 52(a).

30. Section 30(f).

31. Section 1561(a).

32. See, e.g., *William H. Bell III*, Para. 82, 660 P-H Memo T.C. (1982) (income paid to S corporation by related corporation should be adjusted downward by Section 482), but see *Bank of Winnfield & Trust Co. v. U.S.*, 540 F. Supp. 219 (W.D., La. 1982) (no allocation of insurance premiums from an S corporation to a bank controlled by the stockholders of S corporation).

33. Note, the term "domestic" is defined generally by Section 7701(a)(4) to mean "when applied to a corporation created or organized in the United States or under the law of the United States or any State."

34. 1985-41 IRB 22.

35. 1971-2 C.B. 316.

36. The Service announced in TIR1248 (7/27/73) that it would change Reg. Section 1.1371-1(g) (adopted under former Code Section 1371), which gave rise to the cases listed at footnotes 38–40. Further, the Service announced that it would not litigate the issue of a second class of stock in cases factually similar to the four major cases in the area, including the *Stinnett* case discussed at endnote 40.

37. See discussion in *Stinnett* (endnote 40) and Estate of *William M. Allison*, 57 T.C. 174 (1971).

38. 54 T.C. 221 (1970).

39. Para. 68, 011 P-H Memo T.C. (1968).

40. 54 T.C. 221 (1970).

41. See H.R. Rep. No. 826, 97th Cong. 2d Sess. 8, and S. Rep. No. 640, 97th Cong. 2d Sess. 8.

42. See, e.g. *W. C. Gammon*, 46 T.C. 1 (1966) (debt issued in proportion to stock ownership is not second class of stock).

3

Timing and Manner of an S Corporation Election

3.1 NEW CORPORATIONS—FILING

Although a corporation may satisfy all the requirements of the statute to be an S corporation, it does not become one automatically—the corporation must file a Form 2553 (Appendix 1) to elect this status.

TAX POINTER

Care should be used in filing Form 2553. The Service does not rule on the validity of the S election when received. Thus, if a mistake is made in filing the form,[1] or if the election is not made timely,[2] all the benefits sought by using an S election could be lost. Note, further, the shareholders bear the burden of proof if there is any factual question relating to the validity of the election.[3] (See discussion infra at Chapter 3.4 regarding burden of proof.)

To make the S corporation election on Form 2553, several factors have to occur.

A. Consents

Section 1362(a)(2) requires that all shareholders on the day an election is made must consent to the election. If the election is filed after the first day of a corporation's taxable year, Section 1362(b)(2)(B)(ii) requires the consent of any person who held stock during the taxable year and before the election. If a shareholder does not consent, the election will not take effect until the next taxable year. An example will illustrate:

EXAMPLE 3-1

ABC, Inc., is a C corporation whose stock is owned entirely by A. ABC, Inc., reports on the calender year, and on 2/01/X3, X buys all A's stock, with the intention of having ABC, Inc., become an S corporation as of 1/1/X3. If X does not obtain A's consent on the Form 2553, the election will not be effective until 1/01/X4.

1. Manner in Making Consents

The shareholders make the consent by signing where indicated on the form. Once a shareholder has consented to a valid election, the shareholder cannot later withdraw the consent.[4] Also, a corporation cannot file its election until it is incorporated.[5] To overcome last-minute situations, it is possible for shareholders to sign a consent form (Appendix 2) and then attach the consent form to the actual Form 2553. By using this approach, the corporation is saved the task of sending the Form 2553 all over the country to obtain necessary signatures.

TAX POINTERS

1. Care must be used in filling out the Form 2553 since failing to state the number of shares owned by each shareholder can cause the S corporate election to be invalid.[6]

2. A corporate secretary cannot sign the Form 2553 as an officer of the S corporation since the secretary is not listed as an officer who can sign the Form 1120S under Temp Reg. Section 18.1362-1(a). The only persons who can sign the Form 2553 are the S corporation president, vice president, treasurer, assistant treasurer, chief accounting officer, or any other officer duly authorized to act.[7]

2.   When and Where to Elect–New Corporations and C Corporations Electing S Corporate Status

Section 1362(b)(1)(B) provides that a corporation may elect S corporation status on or before the fifteenth day of the third month of its taxable year (under the law prior to 1983, the corporation had 75 days to make this election). An example will illustrate:

EXAMPLE 3-2

ABC, Inc., is a calendar year corporation. On 1/01/X3, the shareholders of ABC, Inc., decide they want to elect S corporation status. They have until 3/15/X3 to file the election. (Under the law prior to 1983, the shareholders would have had until 3/16/X3 to file the election.)

With respect to corporations formed other than on January 1, Section 1362(b)(4) provides that the election is to be made within 2 months and 15 days after the start of the taxable year, regardless of when that taxable year ends. An example will illustrate:

EXAMPLE 3-3

A, B, and C form ABC, Inc., on 12/1/87 and desire S corporate status. The shareholders must file the Form 2553 on or before 2/15/88 for the taxable year 12/1–12/31/87.

3. Time for Meeting Requirements

Section 1362(B)(2)(B)(i) prescribes that a corporation, if it wants to elect S corporation status, must satisfy all S corporation requirements on every day during the taxable year before the election is made. If the corporation cannot meet this requirement, then the election will be effective for the following taxable year. An example will illustrate:

EXAMPLE 3-4

ABC, Inc., is a calendar year corporation. ABC, Inc., has two shareholders: AXY, a partnership, and Q, an individual. On 1/10/X3, Q buys out AXY's stock interest and then elects S status. ABC, Inc., cannot be an S corporation for 19X3 because it failed to meet all the requirements of S status on every day of the taxable year (i.e., it had an improper shareholder for 10 days). Consequently, ABC, Inc., will have S status starting 1/01/X4.

4. There Can Be No Termination or Revocation Within the Prior Four Years

Section 1362(g) provides that if a corporation's S status has been terminated after 1982, then the corporation and any successor corporation shall not be eligible to make an election to acquire S status until the fifth year after the termination of the election unless the Service consents to an earlier election.

As to grounds that the Service has permitted reelection, they usually revolve around the fact that there was a substantial change of ownership of the corporation (i.e., more than 50% after the year of termination).[8] In the absence of a substantial change of ownership, an S corporation can reelect S status if it can show that (1) termination was reasonably beyond the control of the corporation and its substantial shareholders and (2) the substantial shareholder did not participate in the plan to terminate the election.[9] With respect to situations allowing reelection and denial of the request, the Service has issued a large number of private letter rulings on this point, and the reader is respectfully directed to consult them to determine if a particular fact matter fits the reader's situation. (For a more detailed discussion of this area, see Chapter 10.6.)

TAX POINTER

A request to reelect S status does not affect the time to timely file an S election. Thus, a corporation may consider filing a timely election while its request for reelection is pending. An example where this occurred is in Ltr. Rul. 8203017.

3.2 THE FORM 2553 AND EXISTING S CORPORATIONS

If a corporation has already elected S status and a new shareholder joins the corporation, Section 1362(d) prescribes that the election continues without any actions to be undertaken by the S shareholders. If any shareholder does not want the S corporation, however, the shareholder can take one of two steps:

1. File the consent to revocation, providing the shareholder can round up more than 50% of the shares of stock of the corporation (Chapter 10.2), or
2. Do a terminating event (e.g., transfer stock to a nonpermitted shareholder, e.g., a partnership). (See Chapter 10.3.) However, the corporation's shareholder agreement might prevent this.

Thus, the new shareholder of the S corporation should do a careful investigation before becoming a shareholder in an existing S corporation if the new shareholder does not want S status in the future. The new shareholder could find himself in a very difficult situation with no legal way of extracation.

3.3 WHO SIGNS FORM 2553?

Chapters 2.2 and 2.3 discussed who could be a shareholder. Below is detailed who signs the shareholder's consent portion of the Form 2553 with respect to the various individuals, trusts, and so on that can be S corporate shareholders.

A. Stock Held by a Nominee

The beneficial owner must sign the Form 2553.

B. Minors—Stock Held by a Custodian Under the Uniform Gift to Minors Act

Temp. Reg. Section 18.1362-2(b)(2) states that the Form 2553 must be signed by the minor or the minor's legal representative. If the minor has no legal representative, then the minor's natural or adoptive parent can sign the consent form. Rev. Rul. 66-116[10] prescribes that a custodian under the Uniform Gifts to Minors Act does not have the capacity to sign the consent for a minor. Rev. Rul. 68-227[11] provides that if the custodian happens to be the minor's legal representative or parent, and if no legal representative has been appointed, the custodian may then consent in the capacity as legal representative or parent.

TAX POINTER

Note the term "minor" is not defined by the Code or regulations with respect to S corporate situations. Presumably, the state law, where the S corporation is formed, will define the term "minor."[12]

C. Joint Tenants

Temp. Reg. Section 18.1362-2(b)(2) provides that each tenant in common, joint tenant, and so on is treated as a separate shareholder who must consent to the S corporate election.

D. Spouses

Even though Section 1361(c)(1) provides that a husband and wife are treated as 1 shareholder for purposes of the 35 shareholder limit, Reg. Section 1.1371-1(d)(2), adopted under former Code Section 1371, provides that they both must sign the consent form.[13]

E. Community Property

Temp. Reg. Section 18.1362-2(b)(2) provides that if stock is community property, each person having a community property interest is treated as a shareholder and must sign the consent.

F. Estates

Temp. Reg. Section 18.1362-2(b)(2) provides that an executor or an administrator of an estate will sign the consent on behalf of the estate. In the event that there are multiple executors or administrators, Temp. Reg. Section 18.1362-(2)(b)(2) implies that only one executor or administrator may have to consent.

G. Voting Trusts

For taxable years starting after 1982, Section 1361(c)(2)(B)(iv) provides that each beneficiary of the trust is a shareholder. Accordingly, each beneficiary should sign the consent form, and it would be advisable to have the trustee of the trust sign the consent as well.

H.   Grantor Trusts

Under a grantor trust, the grantor is treated as a shareholder and therefore must sign the consent. (If there are multiple grantors, then each must sign the consent.)

I.   Testamentary Trusts

Because Section 1361(c)(2)(B)(iii) treats the estate as a shareholder rather than the trust, the executor of the estate makes the consent, not the trustee.

J.   Section 678 Trusts

Temp. Reg. Section 18.1362-2(b)(2) asserts that each deemed owner of the trust should consent to the election.

K.   Qualified S Corporation Trusts

The income beneficiary who is the deemed owner of the stock should sign. Because the law is not clear on this point, most likely the trustee should sign as well.

L.   The Bankrupt Shareholder

If the individual shareholder is in bankruptcy under Title 11, the bankruptcy estate consents to the election presumably[14] by the administrator of the estate signing the Form 2553.

M.   Gift of S Corporate Stock

If the gift of stock is incomplete, the donor should sign the consent.[15] If the gift is complete, then the donee will sign as the stockholder.

N.   Conditional Sale of Stock

If the conditional sale of stock occurs, the buyer can only sign the form when the buyer becomes the beneficial owner of the stock.[16]

O.   Incompetent Individual

If a conservatorship has been established for an incompetent person, the conservator is the individual who signs the form.

3.4 BURDEN OF PROOF REGARDING FILING FORM 2553

As stated previously, the S shareholders bear the burden of proof with respect to establishing that a valid Form 2553 was filed timely and that all the elements with respect to the election (i.e., proving the dates that the corporation first began business, acquired assets, or had shareholders, as the case may be) were met. Accordingly, certain steps should be taken to prove that filing of Form 2553 was timely and that the facts reported therein are correct; namely,

1. File the Form 2553 by means of certified mail, return receipt requested, and ask that the Service stamp and return an enclosed copy of the letter when received. (See Appendix 3 for a sample letter.)

2. If the S corporation is a new one, have the attorney and accountant for the corporation at the time the corporation is formed coordinate so that the corporate records and balance sheet reflect the same dates for having assets and shareholders and doing business.

3. Use the current Form 2553 in effect to file the election. While Temp. Reg. Section 18.1362-1(a) does not require one version of a Form 2553 over another, care should be taken to use the most current form to ensure that all information the Service seeks has been provided so that a proper election can be made. (See Appendix 1.)

TAX POINTERS

1. The Service has no statutory power to waive an untimely election.

2. Taxpayers who have not used certified mail to file the Form 2553 have prevailed to show timely filing.[17]

3. The timely mailing rule of Section 7502 applies, so if the Form 2553 is postmarked on the last day of the election period, the election will be good although the Service may receive the Form 2553 several days later.

4. The filing of a Form 1120S for many years does not stop the Service from raising the issue of an initial improper election.[18]

5. An S corporation can issue a different number of shares from that detailed on the Form 2553 and not lose its election.[19]

6. While Section 1362(f) allows the Service to waive any S qualifications with respect to certain inadvertent terminations (see Chapter 10.5 for a discussion of this topic), there is no provision that allows the Service to treat an improper election as valid.

3.5   WHAT CORPORATE OFFICER SIGNS THE FORM 2553?

Temp. Reg. Section 18.1362-1(a) provides that the Form 2553 can be signed by any person who is authorized to sign the Form 1120S. Section 6062 states that the individuals who can sign the Form 1120S are the president, vice president, treasurer, assistant treasurer, chief accounting officer, or any officer duly authorized so to act. It is to be noted that the corporate secretary is not one of the listed signatories.

3.6   THE TAX CONSIDERATIONS WITH RESPECT TO C CORPORATIONS CONVERTING TO S CORPORATIONS

Before a C corporation becomes an S corporation, certain points should be considered to prevent unwarranted tax consequences from arising. Some of the factors to consider are the following:

A.   Repayment of Loans to Retirement Plans

As illustrated in Chapter 5.7.B, more than 5% of S corporate shareholders cannot borrow money from their retirement plans because it is a prohibited transaction under Section 4975. Accordingly, prior to electing S status, 5% or more of shareholder participants in the C corporation retirement plan should repay their loans to prevent penalties from being imposed under Section 4975.[20]

B.   Accounting Method

As discussed in Chapter 1.5.B, it appears that an S corporation cannot adopt a method of accounting different from the method used as a C corporation without obtaining the Service's prior consent.

C.   Investment Credit

Section 1371(d)(1) prescribes that an S corporate election will not trigger the recapture of any investment tax credit, assuming that the C corporation assets are still subject to investment tax credit (see Chapter 6.3). Instead, the S corporation, pursuant to Section 1372(d)(2), is liable for any recapture of investment tax credit claimed during a prior non–S corporation year, if the S corporation disposes of the asset prior to the expiration of its useful life.

D. Permitted Tax Year

Chapter 1.4 discussed the fact that an S corporation can only have a fiscal year under limited circumstances with an interest-free deposit being made to the Service. Consequently, when a fiscal year C corporation converts to S, it should give serious consideration to reporting its income using calendar year status to avoid the complications of the interest-free deposit required by Sections 444 and 7519. An example will illustrate:

EXAMPLE 3-5

AB, Inc., is a fiscal year C corporation engaged in manufacturing with its fiscal year ending 7/31/XX. It has three shareholders—Murray, Arlene, and Al, all individuals. On 8/1/XX it adopts S status. Rather than make the "required payment" as prescribed by Sections 444 and 7519, AB, Inc., adopts calendar year status pursuant to Section 1378. Consequently, AB, Inc., will file two tax returns for 19XX—Form 1120 for the fiscal period ending 7/31/XX and a Form 1120S for the period 8/1–12/31/XX.

E. Tax on Passive Investment Income and Loss of Income

In Chapter 10.4 the point was illustrated that if the C corporation on conversion to an S corporation has one dollar or more of earnings and profits, then earnings and profits could cause the S corporation to lose its status pursuant to Section 1362(d)(3), if for three consecutive years, the S corporation has gross receipts in excess of 25% from passive investment income in each of the years. Further, as discussed in Chapter 6.4, the S corporation will, if it flunks the passive investment income test in a year when it has earnings and profits, pay an income tax on the lower of the excess net passive income or its taxable income.

Consequently, to avoid this problem, the C corporation may consider before electing S status, to eliminate all earnings and profits by declaring a dividend or opting as discussed in Chapter 6.4.K to have a special distribution made under Section 1368(e)(3).

F. Loss of Fringe Benefits

As was pointed out in Chapter 5.6, Section 1363(b)(2) denies certain fringe benefits tax free to 2% or more shareholders of S corporations if the S corporation was formed or elected S status after 9/28/82. Examples of fringe benefits that are affected are medical care, group term life insurance, and the exclusion from income of meals and lodging furnished for the convenience of the employer. Consequently, prior to converting from C to S status, the shareholders of the C corporation should determine the impact that the loss of tax-free fringe benefits will have on their tax picture so that there will not be any adverse tax consequences caused by the election.

G.   Tax on Capital Gains

Chapter 6.7 discussed new Section 1374(a), which imposes a tax on "built-in gains" subject to certain restrictions that the S corporation inherits when a C corporation elects S status after 12/31/86. Section 1374 was amended by the Tax Reform Act of 1986 (the TRA) to prevent a C corporation from taking an end-run around Sections 337 and 338, which were likewise amended by the Tax Reform Act of 1986. New Section 1374's tax applies to sales of these inherited assets or distributions to shareholders for a period of 10 years after the C corporation elects S status. Consequently, if a C corporation has assets that have built-in appreciation, it should give very serious thought about liquidating under Section 337 before 12/31/88 rather than converting to S status because of the prohibitive tax imposed under Section 1374. (See Chapter 6.7.)

H.   No Carryforward or Carryback of C Losses, Investment Tax Credits, Foreign Tax Credit, and So On

Section 1371(b)(1) provides that no carryforwards and no carrybacks arising from transactions while the S corporation was in C status can be carried to a taxable year for which it is an S corporation. Examples would be net operating loss (NOL) carryforwards under Section 172, investment tax credit carryforwards under Sections 38, 39, and so on. Although NOLs that arise when the S corporation was a C cannot be carried forward to S years, Section 1371(b)(3) provides that for purposes of determining the number of years the NOL can be carried forward, the years that the corporation is an S are counted. This counting procedure prescribed by Section 1371(b)(3) becomes of importance to a C corporation that converts to an S that has an NOL—the NOL could be lost forever if the S never terminates its election or terminates it beyond the period of carryforward set forth in Section 172.

I.   Conversion from C Corporation to S Status—LIFO Recapture

Congress, in the Tax Reform Act of 1987, has added Section 1363(f) to prescribe that when a C corporation that maintains its inventories under LIFO and converts to S status it must recapture the excess of the inventory's value using a FIFO cost flow assumption over its LIFO value as of the close of its last tax year as a C corporation (hereinafter the "LIFO recapture amount").

The tax that will be generated by the inclusion in income of the LIFO recapture amount is payable in four equal installments, with the first installment to be paid on or before the due date of the corporate tax return (without regard to extensions) for the corporation's last year as a C corporation. The three remaining installments are due on the due date of the corporation's tax returns for the three succeeding tax years (without regard to extensions). No interest is payable on these installments if they are paid by the respective due dates.

In terms of defining the LIFO recapture amount, Section 1363(d)(3) prescribes that it is the excess of the inventory's value using FIFO over its LIFO value at the close of the corporation's last year as a C corporation. (Note: If the corporation uses the retail method for valuing inventories under LIFO, that method will be used to make FIFO valuation.) An example will illustrate the effect of the changes:

EXAMPLE 3-6

ABC, Inc., which uses LIFO converts from C to S on 1/1/8X. At the time of conversion, the corporation had the following transaction with its inventory:

Opening Inventory 1,000 units at $5	$ 5,000
Purchases: 2,000 units at $7	14,000
Sales: 2,000 units at $8	16,000
Ending Inventory 1,000 units at $5	5,000

The FIFO ending inventory would be $7,000 ($7 × 1,000 units). The LIFO recapture amount is $2,000 ($7,000 − 5,000).

The effective date of the amendment to Section 1363 applies to corporations that elect S status after 12/17/87 unless; 1) On or before 12/17/87 a Board of Directors resolution to elect S status has been filed (by the electing corporation or by a former parent of the electing corporation if the former parent has been merged into the electing corporation); and 2) The S election is made before 1989.

ENDNOTES FOR CHAPTER 3

1. See, e.g., *T. H. Campbell & Bros., Inc.,* Para. 75, 149 P-H Memo T.C. (1975) (stamping Form 2553 "ACCEPTED" did not stop Service from arguing successfully that Form 2553 was not filed timely); *Ray Mora,* Para. 72, 123 P-H Memo T.C. (1972) (corporation's filing of Form 1120S for five years without objection by Service did not prevent Service from asserting deficiencies for sixth year on grounds no Form 2553 had been filed); and *Rowland* v. *U.S.,* 315 F. Supp. 596 (W.D., Ark. 1970) (defense of laches could not be used against Service regarding striking

down S election). But, see *McClelland Farm Equip. Co. v. U.S.,* 601 F. 2d 365 (8th Cir. 1979) (Form 2553 received by Service too early, deemed filed timely to allow S corporation status).

2. Ltr. Rul. 8442053 (Service has no authority to "retroactively validate" a late election).

3. See, e.g., *Wesley A. Ober,* Para. 80, 513 P-H Memo T.C. (1980) (no valid election filed, Service could not find Form 2553 allegedly filed by the corporation; taxpayers offered no direct evidence of mailing other than the normal course of business in their lawyer's office).

4. Temp. Reg. Section 18.1362-2(a).

5. Ltr. Rul. 8530100.

6. *Brutsche* v. *Comm.,* 585 F. 2d 436 (10th Cir. 1978).

7. Section 6062.

8. Reg. Section 1.1372-5(a) (adopted under former Code Section 1372) prescribes that if there was a change in ownership of more than 50% after the year of termination, it will tend to establish that consent should be granted.

9. Id.

10. 1966-1 C.B. 198, amplified by 68-227, 1968-1 C.B. 381.

11. 1968-1 C.B. 381.

12. See, e.g., Rev. Rul. 71-287, 1971-2 C.B. 317 (the terms "minor" and "majority" were determined by the California Uniform Gifts to Minor Act).

13. Accord, *Homer W. Forrester,* 49 T.C. 499 (1968).

14. While Temp. Reg. Section 18.1362-2(b)(2) does not have a specific reference to bankruptcy, it does discuss estates in general. Presumably, this language applies to bankruptcy situations.

15. See, e.g., *Finley G. Auld,* Para. 78, 508 P-H Memo T.C. (1978) (stock was still deemed to be held by father, since beneficial ownership of stock was not transferred to son; son's letter to the Service advised that he had not consented to S corporate election treated as a nullity).

16. See, e.g., *Pacific Coast Music Jobbers, Inc.,* 55 T.C. 866, 878 (1971), aff'd 457 F. 2d 1165 (5th Cir. 1972).

17. See, e.g., *Mitchell Offset Plate Serv., Inc.,* 53 T.C. 235 (1969), acq. 1970-1, C.B. XVI (1970).

18. See, e.g., *Ray Mora,* Para. 72, 123 P-H Memo T.C. (1972) (Service challenged filing Form 2553 even though corporation filed Form 2553 for five years; Court stated Service not estopped to challenge Form 2553 even if Service audited all five years of prior returns and "accepted" all returns).

19. Rev. Rul. 74-150, 1974-1 C.B. 241 (facts contained in Form 2553 that are not relevant to the corporation's qualification or as an S corporation will not invalidate an otherwise valid election).

20. DOL Opinion No. 84-44a.

4

Subchapter S Income and Expenses

4.1 INCOME TAXED AT ONE LEVEL—AN OVERVIEW

A prime reason for establishing an S corporation is that the Code generally provides for one level of taxation at the shareholder level.[1] However, if you have attempted to prepare a Form 1120S, you can become quite confused, since while basically S corporate income, expense, loss, and so on are reported at the shareholder level, you have to know how to "pigeon hole" various items. Any resemblance that the Form 1120S with its separately stated items reflected on Schedules K and Form K-1, the Schedule M, and so on has to a financial statement is purely happenstance. For instance, charitable contributions are treated as an expense item by C corporations on the Form 1120 to arrive at taxable income, but with S corporations, the shareholders report the contribution on their Form 1040 as an itemized deduction. The text below discusses the law in general as to reporting the various items of income, expense, gain, loss, and so on. (As to how to prepare a Form 1120S, see the Appendix, which sets forth typical factual situations and filled-in forms.)

TAX POINTER

It is important to understand the concept of S corporate income and loss for purposes of making adjustments to basis and the accumulated adjustment account.

With respect to a broad generalization of the way income, loss, and so on are reported on Form 1120S, there are, as discussed in more detail below, two types of income and loss: "separately stated items" that are passed through directly to shareholders on Schedule(s) K (and K-1) and items that are aggregated in the front of the Form 1120S, lines 1–20, with the total of line 21 passed through to shareholders on the Schedule(s) K (and K-1), line 1. The total of the separately stated items and the net income or loss of the S corporation (i.e., the total of the Schedules K, and K-1, items) is then applied to the shareholder's basis in his, her, or its stock and debt in the S corporation. If loss exceeds the shareholder's basis, the shareholders can only take loss to the extent of the shareholder's basis in debt and stock. With respect to distribution, these are made from the accumulated adjustments account.

Chapter 4 discusses S corporate income items, Chapter 5 discusses S corporate expenses, Chapter 6 discusses taxes what the S corporation pays on its income, Chapter 7 discusses basis, and Chapter 8 discusses accumulated adjustments account.

A.   Separately Stated Items

The reason that some items are passed through to S shareholders as separate items and others are aggregated and reported as net income and loss is found in Section 1366(a)(1). The basic rule of pass-through under Section 1366(a)(1) is that an item of income, expense, and so on remains separate if its separate treatment can affect the tax liability of any shareholder, with the remainder of the items combined to form either ordinary income or ordinary loss. Unfortunately, the Code does not specify all the items that require separate treatment. Additionally, as the Code changes, so will these items of income, expense, and so on. To complicate matters further, the Tax Reform Act of 1986 (TRA) has repealed the capital gains deduction; however, Congress has left intact the statutory structure to compute short- and long-term capital gains and losses, Section 1231 treatment, and so on. In fact, the TRA Conference Committee stated that "the current statutory structure for capital gains is retained in the Code to facilitate reinstatement of a capital gains rate differential if there is a future tax rate increase."[2] It should be further noted that in regard to individual capital gains, (1) Sections 1(g) and 1(j) specifically provide that the tax rate on long-term capital gains cannot exceed 33%, and (2) capital losses are netted against capital gains; however, the $3,000 limit for deducting capital losses in excess of capital gains is retained.

In summary, even though the long-term capital gains deduction is repealed, it will still be necessary to distinguish between ordinary income and losses and capital gains and losses to compute the capital loss limitation.[3]

Thus, as of this writing presumably the following items will probably be among those that commonly pass through separately to S shareholders to be reported and lumped with the shareholder's income, expense, capital gains and losses, and so on:

Income Items

Net short-term capital gain and loss

Net long-term capital gain and loss

Net gain and loss from involuntary conversions due to casualty or theft

Net Section 1231 gain or loss

Foreign income and loss

Tax-exempt income

Passive income

Portfolio income

<u>Deductions</u>

Charitable contributions

Section 179 expense deductions

Certain foreign taxes

Investment interest expenses

Oil and gas productions for purposes of depletion

B. Nonseparately Stated Items—Gross Income

The Code does not define the gross income of an S corporation; however, Section 1363(b) states that taxable income of an S corporation "shall be computed in the same manner as in the case of an individual." Thus, for the most part, as the foregoing text illustrates, the S corporation computes its gross income and deductions as would an individual.[4] (See Table I following the appendices, which generally sets forth a flow chart as to how to compute S corporation income and expense.) Accordingly, an S corporation has income under the reallocation of income rules prescribed by Section 482,[5] transfer of installment debt under Section 453(d),[6] assignment of income principles,[7] cancellation of debt rules,[8] and so on. Likewise, an S corporation is not taxed on items that are excluded from gross income under Sections 101–133 (e.g., tax-exempt interest).[9]

TAX POINTERS

1. For various reasons, tax-exempt bonds should not be held by S corporations. (See discussion infra at Chapter 8.3.B.1.)

2. S corporation gross income is reported on Form 1120S, page 1, line 1(a).

4.2 ACCOUNTING METHOD AND TAX YEAR FOR REPORTING INCOME

See Chapters 1.4 and 1.5 for discussion of these topics.

4.3 ELECTIONS REGARDING GROSS INCOME

With respect to elections regarding gross income such as the Section 1033 election to avoid the recognition of gain on an involuntary conversion, Section 1363(c)(1) prescribes that most of the elections are made at the corporate level by the S corporation rather than by the shareholders. Examples of elections made by the S corporation are the deduction for intangible drilling costs, avoiding installment reporting, and research and development costs. As to the elections not made at the corporate level, Section 1363(c)(2) prescribes that the shareholders must make the elections. For instance, the shareholders must make the election regarding the tax treatment with respect to investment interest, foreign tax credit, and mining and exploration expenditures.

4.4 CAPITAL GAINS AND LOSSES

A. The Effect of the Tax Reform Act of 1986

As was stated in Chapter 4.1.A, the TRA has eliminated the capital gains deduction, thereby basically treating capital gains and losses the same as ordinary income and losses. However, Congress has kept the distinction between capital gains and losses and ordinary income and loss. Accordingly, because distinctions are made between ordinary and capital items, discussion is made below in an effort to pigeon hole items.

B. General Discussion

Generally, with respect to capital gains and losses, the S corporation like an individual reports its gains and losses from capital transactions on Schedule D. If capital losses exceed capital gains in any year, these losses are passed through to the shareholders without reduction. As to holding period, the same rules that apply to individuals to determine long-term and short-term gain and loss apply to S corporations.

TAX POINTER

In certain limited circumstances, S corporations can pay a tax on net capital gains. (For instances when this might occur, see discussion in Chapters 6.2 and 6.7.)

The *Arrowsmith*[10] and *Corn Products*[11] doctrines do apply to S corporations to recharacterize capital gains and loss transactions.[12] (It is beyond the scope of this book to discuss or define the *Arrowsmith* and the *Corn Products* doctrines; however, discussion of these topics can be found in any general textual discussion about capital gains, including *P-H Federal Taxes*; see discussion at Para 32, 177, Vol. 7, *P-H Federal Taxes*, 1987.

TAX POINTER

Capital gain and losses are reported on Form 1120S Schedules
D, K, and K-1, lines 4d and e.

4.5 SECTION 1231 TRANSACTIONS

A. The Effect Caused by the Tax Reform Act of 1986

Before reading this discussion, refer to Chapter 4.1.A to understand why
there is a separate discussion for Section 1231.

B. General Discussion

Generally, Section 1366 prescribes that the S corporation's Section 1231
gain and loss on property are passed through separately to be aggregated
with the shareholder's other Section 1231 gains and losses. With respect to
the recharacterization of Section 1231 gains to ordinary income as prescribed
by Section 1231(c), it is reported on the S corporation Form 4797 and is
aggregated with the other ordinary income items on Form 1120S, page 1. An
example will illustrate:

EXAMPLE 4-1

ABC, Inc., an S corporation, in 19XX sold equipment at a loss producing
a $2,000 net Section 1231 loss. The next year 19XI, ABC, Inc., sold land
it held for two years for a $5,000 gain. ABC, Inc., in 19XI will report
Section 1231 $3,000 gain on the Form 1120S, Schedules K and K-1, and
$2,000 as ordinary income on Form 1120S, page 1, line 4.

TAX POINTER

Section 1231 gain and losses are reported on Form 4797 with
the net results being reported on Form 1120S, page 1, line 4,
or Schedule K and K-1, line 5, depending on the computations
done on the Form 4797.

4.6 DEALER TRANSACTIONS

A. The Effect Caused by the Tax Reform Act of 1986

Before reading this discussion, the reader is referred to Chapter 4.1.A
to understand why there is a separate discussion for dealer transactions.

B. General Discussion

In determining whether an S corporation has realized a capital gain or loss rather than ordinary income and loss, the Service normally will not look at the activities of the shareholders; rather it looks at the corporation's activities. However, Reg. Sec. 1.1375-1(d), which was adopted under former Code Section 1375, provides that if the S corporation "is availed of by any shareholder or group of shareholders owning a substantial portion of the stock of such corporation for the purpose of selling property which in the hands of such shareholder or shareholders would not" be a capital asset, then profit on the sale will be ordinary income to the corporation, even if the property was a capital asset in its hands. Further, in determining the character of the asset in the hands of the stockholder, the activities of other S corporations in which the individual is a stockholder will be taken into account.

In other words, this means that, if an S corporation holds a property interest as a capital asset and has a substantial stockholder who is a dealer in such property, the corporation's capital gain on the sale of the property could be converted into ordinary income. An example will illustrate:

EXAMPLE 4-2

A, who owns 55% of ABC, Inc., an S corporation, is a dealer in real estate. The other stock of ABC, Inc., is owned by A's children. ABC, Inc., has as its only asset a piece of real estate that it is selling for a gain of $100,000. The $100,000 gain on the sale may be classified as an ordinary income transaction rather than a capital gain, because of A's controlling interest and dealer status.

TAX POINTERS

1. As to how much control the dealer must have to taint the character of the corporate gain, it is not clear. However, a recent Technical Memorandum shed some light on the Service's position with respect to when dealer status will be found.

   In Tech. Mem. 8537007, an S corporation owned mineral property with the following shareholders: a father owned 55% of the stock and was assumed to be a dealer in mining properties and his children owned the rest. A Section 1231 gain resulted from a corporate transaction that was treated as a capital gain and was not recharacterized as ordinary income under Reg. Sec. 1.1375-1(d). No recharacterization was made because the corporation offered the property for sale only after failing to raise funds for the mineral property's development.

2. The Service has not always been successful in converting capital gain to ordinary income. For instance, in *George* v.

Buono,[13] the Court did not believe that the corporation's three largest shareholders were dealers, and land was treated as a capital asset even though it was purchased for resale, and the corporation received subdivision approval prior to sale as a single parcel. Other cases where the Service lost its recharacterization argument are *Carmelo* v. *Ofria*[14] (S corporation qualified for capital gain on sale of unpatented invention) and *Est. of Walter K. Dean*[15] (land held for development and sale to customers in the ordinary course of business treated as held for investment when sold producing capital gains).

4.7   SECTION 1239 CONVERSION OF CAPITAL GAINS TO ORDINARY INCOME

A.   The Effect Caused by the Tax Reform Act of 1986

Before reading this discussion, the reader is referred to Chapter 4.1.A to understand why there is a separate discussion for Section 1239.

B.   General Discussion

Section 1239 recharacterizes as ordinary income gain realized in the sale or exchange of capital or Section 1231 assets between certain "related persons." Section 1239's rule applies only if the property transferred will be in the hands of the transferee property subject to depreciation. As to related persons, Sections 1239(b) and (d) define them to be, as they pertain to S corporations:

1. A person and an S corporation when such person owns directly or indirectly 50% or more of the value of the outstanding stock (1239(b)(1)

2. An employer- and employee-controlled welfare benefit fund or such fund controlled by a party related to the employees per the rules of Section 1239 (Section 1239(d))

With respect to Section 1239(b)(1)'s 50% ownership test, Section 318's attribution rules basically apply to determine stock ownership with certain modifications. An example of the application of the rules of Section 1239 as they apply to S corporations is set forth below:

EXAMPLE 4-3

An individual owns 49% of the stock (by value) of Corporation X, an S corporation, and a trust for A's children owns the remaining 51% of the stock. A's children are deemed to own the stock owned for their benefit by the trust in proportion to their actuarial interests in the trust (Section

318(a)(2)(B)). A, in turn, constructively owns the stock so deemed to be owned by his children (Section 318(a)(1)(A)(ii)). Thus, A is treated as owning all the stock of Corporation X, and any gain A recognizes from the sale of depreciable property to Corporation X is treated under Section 1239 as ordinary income.

4.8 PROPERTY DISTRIBUTIONS TO SHAREHOLDERS

Section 1363(d) mandates that generally, when an S corporation distributes appreciated property (other than an obligation of the corporation) the distribution is treated as if the property had been sold to the shareholder at fair market value. This gain, in turn, will pass through to shareholders by Section 1366, and its character will likewise pass. Thus, if the S corporation distributes appreciated Section 1231 property to a shareholder, the shareholders will, in turn, recognize Section 1231 gain at the shareholder level. The shareholder's basis in the property is the fair market value. An example will clarify:

EXAMPLE 4-4

AB, Inc., an S corporation owned entirely by T, distributes in 19XX, in a non–Section 1374 transaction,[16] capital stock of a N.Y. Stock Exchange Company to T. AB, Inc.'s basis is $10,000, and on the date of the transfer, the stock's value was $17,000. AB, Inc., purchased the stock several years ago. T's basis in the stock is $17,000, and T realizes as the sole shareholder of AB, Inc., a $7,000 long-term gain.

Further, it is to be noted that the distribution of appreciated property could trigger tax under Sections 1374 and 1375. (See discussion at Chapters 6.2–6.5 and 10.4.)

A. Exceptions to Section 1363(d)

Section 1363(e) provides that Section 1363(d)'s recognition rule regarding gain does not apply to reorganization(s) and division(s) involving the S corporation under Section 354, 355, or 356.

TAX POINTER

Depending on the type of asset, Sections 1239, 1245, and 1250 should apply to the distribution.

B.   Section 1374's Tax on Distribution and in Liquidation of an S Corporation

Under prior law, an exception was made in Section 1363(e) to Section 1363's taxation for complete liquidation of the S corporation when appreciation of property was involved. The TRA changed this, and now Section 1374 applies to tax the gain, subject to TRA Section 633(d). (See Chapters 6.2 and 6.7 for discussion of this point.)

4.9   EARNINGS AND PROFITS[17]

A.   When an S Corporation Will Have Earnings and Profits

Under prior law, an S corporation could have earnings and profits (e.g., from being the beneficiary of a life insurance contract). Under current law, Section 1371(c)(1) states that an S corporation by definition cannot have any earnings and profits from its operations. The only way an S corporation could have earnings and profits would be as follows:

1. Be a C corporation with earnings and profits and convert to S status

2. Be an S corporation formed prior to 1983 and have earnings and profits from the years prior to 1983

3. Acquire the earnings and profits of a C corporation in a merger, or similar arrangement pursuant to Sections 368, 381(c)(2), and 1371(c)(2)

4. Be a corporation that is the product of a tax-free division under Section 355

B.   Earnings and Profits Can Penalize an S Corporation Under Sections 1375 and 1362(d)(3)

As discussed in Chapters 6.4 and 10.4, the S corporation could be severely penalized by having one dollar or more of earnings and profits. Under Section 1375, the S corporation would pay an income tax at the higher rate of tax specified in Section 11(b) on its excess passive investment income. Further, under Section 1362(d)(3) (Chapter 10.4), the $1 or more of earnings and profit could cause this corporation to lose its S election if it had too much passive income for three consecutive years.

C.   Methods to Eliminate Earnings and Profits

One obvious way to eliminate earnings and profits is to declare a dividend. However, due to the complexities of S corporate taxation, an S corporation, unless all the shareholders receiving distributions elect otherwise under Section 1368(e)(3), has to go through detailed steps to make the dividend distribution. (See discussion at Chapter 8.3 et seq. for the rules regarding distributions as they apply to earnings and profits.) (For a discussion of the mechanics of Section 1368(e)(3), see Chapter 6.4.K.)

D.   The Tax Consequences of Reductions in Earnings and Profits

1.   Dividends

As discussed generally in Chapter 8.3, dividends reduce earnings and profits.

2.   Investment Credit Recapture

As discussed in Chapter 6.3, an S corporation could be liable for investment credit recapture. Any payment of tax for the investment credit recapture reduces earnings and profits by the amount of the tax.

3.   Subchapter C Transactions

Section 1371(c)(2) prescribes that earnings and profits are adjusted for Subchapter C transactions. Thus, C earnings and profits have to be adjusted for redemptions, liquidations, reorganizations, divisions, and so on (See discussion generally at Chapter 8.3 et seq.)

4.10   DISCHARGE OF INDEBTEDNESS INCOME— SECTION 108(d)(7)

A.   Sections 108(d)(7)(A) and (B)

Prior to the Tax Reform Act of 1986, generally if debt of an insolvent debtor or of a debtor in bankruptcy is discharged, the debtor was allowed to exclude the debt discharge from income, but had to reduce tax attributes starting with net operating losses (NOLs) for the taxable year the debt is discharged. In regard to S corporations, they basically do not have NOLs because all the corporation's losses and deductions are passed through to its shareholders.

B. Contribution of Debt to an S Corporation—Section 108(d)(7)(C)

When a shareholder contributes debt to an S corporation as a contribution to capital, corporate income does not result to the extent that the basis of the old debt had previously been reduced by the pass-through of losses from the corporation. An example will illustrate:

EXAMPLE 4-5

At the beginning of 19X1, A, Inc., a calendar year S corporation, which has one shareholder, B, has on its balance sheet, corporate stock, $200, and loan from B, $100. At the end of 19X1, A, Inc., has a loss of $250, which pursuant to Chapter 7, reduces B's stock basis to zero and the debt to $50. In 19X2, B contributes the note to A, Inc. The consequence is that both B and A, Inc., have no income from the cancellation of the indebtedness; A, Inc's assets are not changed, and B's stock basis is raised to $50.

ENDNOTES FOR CHAPTER 4

1. Sections 1363(a), 1363(b).
2. Conference Committee Report II, H.R. Conf. Rep. No. 841, 99th Cong., 2d Sess. (1986) at 106 (hereinafter Conf. Rep. or Conference Report).
3. Conf. Rep. p. II-106. It is to be noted that neither the TRA or the Senate and Conference Committee Reports to the TRA contain any directives to the Internal Revenue Service to eliminate or simplify the forms on which capital gains and losses or Section 1231 calculations are made.
4. An S corporation would not be taxed as an individual when it deals with its own stock. In this instance Section 1032 would apply to exempt an S corporation from taxation when it issues stock in exchange for property. See, also, Ltr. Rul. 8417042 (1/24/84). (S corporation recognized no gain under Section 1032 when it issued its stock in a merger.) Further, in some instances, the nonrecognition of income rules apply in certain instances, namely, Section 354 (exchanges of stock as security in a reorganization) or Section 311(a)(1) (distributions of a corporation's own stock or rights to acquire its stock).
5. See, e.g., *Robert A. Hennessey,* Para. 77, 122 P-H Memo T.C. (1977) (interest income allocated to S corporations under Section 482 because of interest-free loan to related corporations). But see, *Bank of Winnfield & Trust Co.* v. *U.S.,* 540 F. Supp. 219 (W.D., La. 1982) (court refused to sustain Section 482 allocation).
6. *Dessauer* v. *Comm.,* 449 F. 2d 562 (8th Cir. 1971).
7. *Stedwell Johnston,* Para. 76, 142 P-H Memo T.C. (1976).
8. *Ralph L. Brutsche,* 65 T.C. 1034 (1976), rev'd on other grounds, 585 F. 2d 436 (10th Cir. 1978).

9. See, e.g., *M. Lucile Harrison,* 59 T.C. 578 (1973), Acq. 1973-2 C.B. 2 (1973) (Section 101 applied to exempt from taxation insurance proceeds received by S corporation).

10. *Arrowsmith* v. *Comm.,* 344 U.S. 6 (1952).

11. *Corn Prods. Ref. Co.* v. *Comm.,* 350 U.S. 46 (1955).

12. An example where the *Arrowsmith* doctrine was applied is *David Bresler,* 65 T.C. 182 (1975), acq. 1976-2 C.B. 1 (1976) (most of payment received by S corporation in antitrust suit settlement characterized as ordinary income because prior loss in the sale of corporation's business reflected as ordinary loss). In *Estate of John F. Shea,* 57 T.C. 15 (1971), acq. 1973-2 C.B. 3 (1973), the Service asserted the *Corn Products* doctrine, but the court rejected its application because of the facts involved.

13. 74 T.C. 187 (1980), acq. 1981-2 C.B. 1 (1981).

14. 77 T.C. 524 (1981), non acq. 1983-1 C.B. 1 (1983).

15. Para. 75, 137 P-H Memo T.C. (1975).

16. For a definition and discussion about Section 1374, see Chapters 6.4 and 6.7.

17. For a definition of earnings and profit, see generally Sections 312 and 316.

5

Corporate Deductions

5.1 INTRODUCTION

As discussed in Chapter 4 and Table I following the appendices, an S corporation computes its deductions in the same manner as an individual, subject to certain exceptions, with certain deductions passing through as separate items and others being aggregated. The discussion below will discuss deduction situations that normally arise with respect to the majority of S corporations.

5.2 INVESTMENT INTEREST

Section 163(d)(1) imposes a limit on the amount of interest expense that a person can deduct with respect to debt incurred to purchase or carry investments. Basically, the amount of allowable interest expense is equal to the amount of net investment income[1] subject to a phase-in rule.[2] It is beyond the scope of this book to offer any detailed discussion of this topic. Examples of items that would be classified as investment income per Section 163(d) would be amounts treated as portfolio income under the passive loss rules (see Chapter 7.9.B), gain from the disposition of investment property (Section 163(d)(5)(A)), and income from a trade or business when the taxpayer does not materially participate, providing that the activity is not a "passive activity" under the passive loss rules (Section 163(d)(5)(A)(ii)).[3] With respect to S corporations, Section 1366(a)(1)(A) requires that the corporation's investment interest expense and investment income and expense pass through to the shareholders as separate items. The consequence of this pass-through is that if the shareholder's share of investment interest of the S corporation together with his or her personal share of investment interest exceeds the Section 163(d)(1) limitations just set forth, the shareholder may not deduct the investment interest in excess of such limitations. The consequence of Section 163(d)(1)'s limitations is illustrated in the following example.

EXAMPLE 5-1

Taxpayer is a shareholder in an S corporation engaged in the automobile business, which is very profitable distributing most of its income to the shareholders. Taxpayer has large investment interest deductions that were incurred borrowing money to engage in various investment activities other than real estate. If the income taxable to taxpayer could be construed as dividend income (i.e., investment income) rather than as automobile business income, taxpayer due to Section 163(d)'s definition could deduct more investment interest. However, Section 163(d) now prevents this. (For treatment under prior law see Tax Pointer 1.)

TAX POINTERS

1. Under prior law, *William H. Crook*[4] allowed the S corporate income in Example 5-1 to be classified as dividend income, and this allowed a shareholder to deduct more investment interest. Tax Reform Act of 1984, Section 1066, allowed an S shareholder for 1983 and 1984 to elect to have the *Crook* reclassification of income occur if the S corporation has an S election in effect for 1982–84.

2. See discussion at Chapter 7.9.M as to the effect that investment interest has in the area of passive income and loss.

5.3   CHARITABLE CONTRIBUTIONS

An S corporation does not claim charitable deductions; rather, these deductions are passed through as separate items to the shareholders (subject to Section 1366(d)(1)'s basis limit discussed in Chapter 7) reportable on line 7 of Form 1120S, Schedules K and K-1. The shareholder deducts the contributions on his, her, or its tax return subject to the charitable contribution limits prescribed by Section 170.

TAX POINTERS

1. S corporate shareholders may deduct charitable contributions without regard to Section 170(b)(2)'s 10% limit imposed on contributions.

2. S corporations are deprived of two favorable charitable contribution techniques provided to C corporations, namely, contribution of inventory (Section 170(e)(3)(A)) and contributions of scientific equipment (Section 170(e)(4)(D)).

5.4   TAXES

A.   Foreign Taxes

An S corporation does not deduct foreign taxes; rather, these taxes are passed through to the shareholder pursuant to Section 1366(a)(1)(A) and are reported on the Form 1120S, Schedules K and K-1, at line 15.

A shareholder has the choice of either deducting the foreign taxes as an itemized deduction or claiming a foreign tax credit on Form 1116.

B. State Income Taxes

In a number of states, an S corporation may be liable for franchise taxes. The deduction should pass through to the shareholder under Section 1366 and be reported on Form 1120S, Schedule K-1. (See Appendix 4, which details how each state taxes S corporate income.)

TAX POINTER

If an S Corporation is liable for state franchise taxes, care must be exercised as to how corporate income is paid to shareholder-employees (i.e., salaries or distributions with respect to stock pursuant to Section 1368). If a distribution is made under Section 1368, it probably will be construed as a dividend for state corporate tax purposes, while if salary is used to pay out corporate income, there is the risk that the salary could be deemed unreasonable. For a discussion of these points, see Chapter 5.16.

5.5   TRADE OR BUSINESS EXPENSES—SECTION 162

An S corporation can deduct trade or business expenses under Section 162. Sections 1363(b)(2) and 703(a)(2)(E) provide that Section 212 cannot be used by an S corporation for deduction of expenses.

For an S corporation to deduct expenses under Section 162, it needs to be engaged in a trade or business. The expenses are deducted on page 1 of Form 1120S.

TAX POINTERS

1. One of the prime reasons that a shareholder-employee(s) form(s) S corporations is due to the fact that, if the trade or business deduction expenses paid to shareholder-employees are disallowed, there is only one level of taxation (i.e., at the shareholder level) rather than two levels of taxation in the case of a disallowance in a C corporation.

2. There are certain Code sections that allow deduction of expenses, whether or not the S corporation is engaged in a trade or business. These Sections are 163 (interest), 164 (taxes), and 183 (hobby loss expenses, which are deductible up to the amount of income).

5.6   FRINGE BENEFITS—SECTIONS 79, 101, 105, 106, 119

A.   Partnership Rules Apply to S Corporation Fringe Benefits— Section 1372

Under prior law, one key reason for electing S status was the tax-free benefits available to shareholder-employees such as medical reimbursement plans, $50,000 group term life insurance, and so on. However, when it adopted the Subchapter S Revision Act of 1982, Congress decided to eliminate the prior fringe benefit rules and substitute instead the partnership rules. Accordingly, Section 1372(a)(1) and (2) provides that 2% or more S corporate shareholders in corporations electing S status after 9/28/82 cannot have the following fringe benefits tax free:

1. Medical reimbursement plans under Sections 105 and 106
2. $50,000 group term life insurance under Section 79
3. $5,000 death benefit exclusion under Section 101(b)
4. Exclusion from income of meals and lodging furnished for the convenience of the employer under Section 119

TAX POINTERS

1. If the S corporation pays these benefits for the 2% or more shareholder-employees, the S corporation will not be able to deduct them pursuant to Sections 1363(b)(2) and 703(a)(2)(E). Instead, these nondeductible items are passed through to the shareholders basically as additional income. If the benefit is a medical one, the 2% or more shareholder-employee will be allowed the medical expense to the extent he or she can deduct it as an itemized deduction under Section 213.

2. The S corporation can deduct all fringe benefits for all 2% or less shareholders and the rank and file employees subject to ERISA standards.

1.   Definition of 2% or More Shareholders

Section 1372(b) defines a 2% or more shareholder as any person who owns or is considered to own under Section 318's attribution rules "on any day during the taxable year of the S corporation more than two percent of the outstanding stock of such corporation or stock possessing more than two percent of the total combined voting power of all stock of such corporation."

B. Fringe Benefits for S Corporations in Existence as of 9/28/82

If an S corporation was in existence on 9/28/82 and had fringe benefits for 2% or more shareholders on that date, the Subchapter S Revision Act of 1982 did not take them away or make them taxable; rather, it provided in the Subchapter S Revision Act of 1982, Section 6(d), that the rules set forth in Chapter 5.6.A do not apply but only up to taxable years beginning before December 31, 1987. Further, Subchapter S Revision Act of 1982, Section 6(d), provided that the transitional rules set forth above will cease to apply and the rules set forth in Chapter 5.6.A will apply and become effective when the following first occurs:

1. The first day of a taxable year beginning after 12/31/82 in which the S corporation (using the passive income rules in existence prior to the adoption of the Subchapter S Revision Act of 1982) has passive investment income greater than 20% of its gross receipts

2. The first day of a taxable year beginning after 12/31/82 on which the S corporation's election is terminated

3. The first day of a taxable year beginning after 12/31/82 on which more than 50% of the S stock is newly owned

With respect to defining transfer of 50% of the stock or more, the rules are the same as under prior law concerning the transfer with respect to S corporations having fiscal year status.

5.7 RETIREMENT PLANS—SECTION 401 ET SEQ.

A. Introduction

It is beyond the scope of this book to present a detailed discussion about retirement plans. However, a brief discussion is set forth regarding certain pertinent points concerning this area.

B. Comparison of S Corporate Plans with Other Self-employed Plans

While parity, which came into existence in the Tax Equity and Fiscal Responsibility Act of 1982 (TEFRA), did much to eliminate the disparity with respect to retirement plans for various entities, some differences remain. For instance, a 5% or more shareholder-employee-participant can borrow from his or her retirement plan in a C corporation, but Section 4975(c)(1)(B) and

(d) precludes a shareholder-employee-participant who, as an officer or employee, owns directly, or by Section 318, more than 5% of the stock in any day of the taxable year from borrowing from the plan.

TAX POINTER

> It should be noted that due to Section 163(h)(1)'s limitations on the deduction of interest loans from pension plans, this exception that allows participants in C corporate plans to borrow from retirement plans will soon lose utility.

C. Unreasonable Contributions

Reg. Section 1.404(a)-1(b) prescribes that contributions to a qualified retirement plan are deductible to the extent that the contributions together with other compensation are reasonable in amount. The case of *La Mastro*[5] offers an example where disallowance will occur. In *La Mastro,* an S corporation was formed 14 days before the end of the S corporation's taxable year. The sole shareholder-employee took a salary, and the S corporation established a defined benefit plan for the sole shareholder-employee that created a loss for the taxable year. The Tax Court disallowed the contribution to the plan treating the contribution as unreasonable.

D. Planning Possibilities with S Corporate Retirement Plans

As with retirement plans for C corporations, partnerships, and so on, there are planning possibilities for S corporate retirement plans. Because retirement plans have the potentiality for accumulating vast assets, the reader should consider tax planning for the S corporation with retirement plan assets.

One area to explore is prohibited transaction exemptions. For instance, in prohibited transaction exemptions (PTEs) 85-68, a corporation was able to factor its secured accounts receivables with its retirement plan, and in PTE 79-10, a corporation that owned land and a building was able, instead of making only a regular cash contribution, to contribute the land and building, leasing the building back. By doing this, the corporation accomplished the following:

- Any future appreciation arising from the land and building passes to the retirement plan.

- If the building was fully depreciated, the corporation now has a rental deduction that is paid to a related entity.

- There is a negative side and that is that the retirement plan assets are tied somewhat to the employer's financial condition (if the employer cannot pay the rent, the plan will have to evict the employer and obtain a new tenant) (real estate, by definition, is illiquid; if the land and building depreciate in value rather than appreciate, the retirement plan made a bad investment, etc.).

TAX POINTERS

1. In regard to retirement plans it should be noted that while the control group provisions of Section 1561 et seq. do not apply to S corporations so that an individual can be a 100% shareholder in an S and C corporation and not have the Section 11(c) corporate rate adjusted, Prop. Reg. Section 1.414(b)(1)-(a) does affect retirement plans to limit deductions. For a more detailed discussion about controlled corporations, see Chapter 2.6.

2. An S corporation cannot have an employee stock ownership trust (ESOP). (See Chapter 2.3.A.)

5.8 AMORTIZATION OF ORGANIZATIONAL EXPENSES— SECTION 248

Section 1363(b)(3) provides that an S corporation can amortize its organization expenses. Thus, S corporations can amortize over 60 months or more fees for legal service for organizing the corporation, drafting the bylaws, and the like, plus the state filing fees for forming the corporation. Additionally, fees for accounting services relative to the organization can be amortized under Section 248. However, commissions and other expenses incurred in selling and issuing the capital stock of a corporation cannot be deducted by the corporation—they merely reduce the amount of capital raised through the sale of stock.[6]

5.9 SECTION 179 EXPENSING OF RECOVERY PROPERTY

Section 179(d)(8) allows shareholders of an S corporation to expense $10,000 each year of recovery property. The rule is the same as with partnerships. The Section 179(d)(8) dollar limitation applies at both the shareholder and corporate level, effective for qualified property placed in service after 1986.

The S corporation makes the election to expense the asset under Section 179 rules.[7] When the S corporation elects to expense the assets under Section

179, the corporation must reduce the basis of the property by the amount of expensing.[8] Further, if more than $200,000 of qualifying property is placed in service during the taxable year, Section 179(b)(2) prescribes that the expense deduction is reduced dollar for dollar. Thus, the Section 179 expense deduction is unavailable if the S corporation in and/with its shareholders acquires more than $210,000 of property. Further, Section 179(b)(3) prescribes that the expensed amount may not exceed the taxable income from the S corporation's (or the shareholder's) active trade or business, subject to a carryover. Section 179(b)(3)(B) prescribes the carryover that the Section 179 election disallowed because there was insufficient taxable income carried forward to the succeeding tax years. Examples will illustrate:

EXAMPLE 5-2

A, Inc., an S corporation in 1987 purchased $15,000 of recovery property. A, Inc., has one shareholder, R. The S corporation has $25,000 of taxable income from its trade or business. The S corporation elects to expense $10,000 of the assets under Section 179. R will have a $10,000 expense deduction on his or her tax return.

EXAMPLE 5-3

Assume the same facts as in Example 5-2, except that A, Inc., only had $6,000 of income. R would only be able to take a $6,000 Section 179 deduction of her or his tax return.

EXAMPLE 5-4

AB, Inc., an S corporation, is composed of two equal shareholders, A and B. A and B are both married and file joint returns with their spouses. AB, Inc., in 1987 elects to expense under Section 179, $5,000 of the cost of new recovery property it purchased. A and B in addition to being shareholders of AB, Inc., are each engaged as sole proprietors in separate businesses. A, in her proprietorship, acquires a qualifying asset for $7,500, and B acquires a qualifying asset in his proprietorship for $10,000. Accordingly, A on her tax return will report $10,000 of Section 179 expense deductions, $2,500 from AB, Inc., and $7,500 from her proprietorship. Likewise, B will have a $10,000 expense deduction ($2,500 from AB, Inc., and $7,500 from his proprietorship).

TAX POINTER

The Tax Reform Act of 1986 does not prescribe what will occur with any unused expense deductions if the S corporation goes out of business or the S shareholder dies.

5.10   SECTION 465 AT-RISK LIMITATION

Section 465 prescribes that a taxpayer's loss deduction from certain activities cannot exceed the amount the taxpaper has "at risk" in the activity at the end of the taxable year. The taxpayer can deduct in later years the portion of the loss that exceeds the amount at risk, providing that the taxpayer can satisfy Section 465's rules. Examples of activities to which Section 465 applies are film or video tapes, real property, and oil and gas property.

Prior to the Subchapter S Revision Act of 1982 (the SSRA), Section 465's risk limitation rules applied at both the shareholder and corporate level. Now, Section 465(a)(1)(B) has been amended to provide that Section 465 only applies at the shareholder level. Prop. Regs. Section 1.465-10(d) states that a shareholder's amount at risk generally includes both the S corporate shareholder's stock and funds loaned by the shareholder to the corporation. Section 465(a) prescribes that Section 465 applies on an activity-by-activity basis. Accordingly, the loss from one activity cannot be deducted against another because the shareholder is at risk with respect to the other activity. Although the law is not exactly clear as to how the mechanics of Section 465 applies to S corporations, the example below sets forth the probable result of a typical factual situation.

EXAMPLE 5-5

X is the sole shareholder of AB, Inc., an S corporation. X acquires his stock in AB, Inc., for $100 cash. In 19XX, AB, Inc., has the following transactions: loss from geothermal property, $100; ordinary income, $10. Under Section 465, X would be able to deduct the loss of $100 incurred in the geothermal property because of X's $100 cash basis in his stock and report the $10 of ordinary income.

5.11   HOBBY LOSSES—SECTION 183

Section 183 prescribes that if an S corporation is found not to engage in a profit-making activity, it will be permitted only limited deductions with respect to the activity.

TAX POINTER

Hobby loss disallowance is not a problem for an S corporation during the first two years of its life since Section 183(d) prescribes a presumption that an activity will not be considered a hobby loss if the activity has produced a profit in three out of five consecutive years (with horses, the activity must produce a profit two out of seven years). The Service is expanding its cases subject to hobby losses. For instance, in *Albert H. Payne*,[9] an individual taxpayer was denied deductions in connection with a tax consultation service operated by the taxpayer when activity generally decreased and the taxpayer did not try to replace or obtain new clients. Foreseeably, this case would apply to S corporations and involve other situations involving professionals (lawyers, architects, etc.). The reader is referred to other cases under Section 183 for applicability.

5.12   LOSSES AND EXPENSES OWED TO SHAREHOLDER— SECTION 267

Section 267(a)(1) and (f)(2) disallows or suspends the deduction of certain losses, and Section 267(a)(2) suspends the deduction of certain expenses.

A.   Section 267(a)(1)—Losses

1.   Disallowance of Losses

Section 267(a)(1) prescribes that an otherwise deductible loss on a sale or exchange of property is nondeductible if the transaction is between certain related parties as detailed below. It makes no difference that the transaction is bona fide and/or arises in the ordinary course of business.

2.   Definition of Related Person

Section 267(b) basically defines who the related person(s) are as they pertain to S corporations. They would be

1. An individual and a corporation controlled by said individual (Section 267(b)(2)).

2. An S corporation and a C corporation, if the same persons own more than 50% in value of the stock of each corporation (Section 267(b)(12)).

3. Two S corporations, if the same persons own more than 50% in value of each corporation's stock (Section 267(b)(11)).

4. Two corporations that are members of the same controlled group (Section 267(b)(3) and (f)(1)) (see discussion at Chapter 2.6 and the tax pointer at 5.7.D for other instances where the controlled group provisions apply to S corporations).

5. A corporation and a partnership if the same persons own more than 50% in value of the corporation's stock and more than 50% of the partnership's capital or profits interest (Section 267(b)(10)).

With respect to stock ownership, Section 267(c) prescribes certain constructive rules of ownership. For instance, Section 267(c)(1) prescribes that "stock owned, directly or indirectly by or for a corporation, partnership, estate or trust shall be considered as being owned proportionately by or for its shareholders, partners or beneficiaries."

3. Effect of Disallowed Loss on Basis and Later Transactions

Section 267 acts in a dual capacity: it disallows the losses between the related parties, and it reduces the basis of the transferee. When the transferee disposes of the property at a later date, Section 267(d) and Reg. Section 1.267(d)-1 state that the transferee's gain will be recognized only to the extent that it exceeds the loss disallowed earlier on the particular property. Examples of the operation of Section 267(d) are set forth below:

EXAMPLE 5-6

A and B are related parties. A sells property to B that has an adjusted basis of $25,000 for $21,000, generating a loss of $4,000. By Section 267(a)(1) the $4,000 loss is disallowed. B's basis is $21,000, and when B has depreciated the asset to $19,000, B sells it to an unrelated third party for $24,000. B's recognized gain is $1,000 ($5,000 − $4,000).

EXAMPLE 5-7

Assume the same facts as in Example 5-6 except that B sold the property to an unrelated party for $15,000. B's recognized loss is $4,000 ($19,000 − $15,000).

TAX POINTERS

1. Losses can arise indirectly. For example, a loss was disallowed to a taxpayer on the sale of corporate stock to a related party who was the sole bidder at an IRS forced tax sale.[10]

2. Reg. Section 1.267(d)-1(b) prescribes that if several items or classes of items are sold or exchanged where the loss is disallowable, an allocation based on fair market value is to be done.

3. Reg. Section 1.267(d)-1(c)(3) prescribes the holding period for the property acquired in the hands of the transferee.

B.   Section 267(a)(2)'s Suspension of Expenses and Interest

Section 267(a)(2), 267(b), and 267(e) prescribe that payments made by an accrual S corporation to its cash-basis shareholder(s) cannot be accrued and deducted by the corporation in one year and paid in the next. Section 267(a) converts an accrual-basis corporation to a cash-basis one for purposes of deducting interest and expense (such as salary) paid to cash-basis shareholders. Thus, the S corporation will deduct the expense and/or interest in the year the shareholder reports the payment and income. In connection with Section 267(a)(2) the following should be noted:

1. The rule for disallowance applies based on the payee; thus, if the shareholder is on an accrual basis and makes a payment to a cash-basis S corporation, the deductibility by the shareholder of the payment will depend when the S corporation recognizes income.

2. As to who is covered by this rule, Section 267(a)(2) prescribes that the corporation and payor are "related" on the last day of the corporation's year in which the payment would be deductible. Thus, the Section 267(a)(2)'s recharacterization will apply even if the relationship between the parties terminates before the expense or interest are includible in gross income by the recipient (i.e., if a calendar year S corporation in 19X1 accrues an item of expense to an S shareholder, Y, and Y redeems his stock interest in 19X1 with payment being made of the accrued expense by the S corporation to Y in 19X2, the S corporation deducts the expense in 19X2). In regard to who is a "related" shareholder, Section 267(e)(1)(B)(ii) prescribes that it is any shareholder no matter how much of an ownership interest the shareholder has and any person related to the shareholder within the meaning of Sections 267(b) or 707(b)(1). An example applying the rules regarding related parties would be an S corporation and a partnership where the shareholder in the S corporation owns directly or indirectly more than 50% of the capital and/or profit interest in the partnership.[11]

5.13   VACATION HOMES, PERSONAL RESIDENCE, AND THE LIKE— SECTION 280A

In an attempt to limit liability from negligence action, breach of contract suits, and so on, an individual may decide to place his or her vacation home or residence in an S corporation. However, Section 280A prescribes that the deduction for the vacation home and residence is limited. While it is beyond the scope of this book to discuss in detail Section 280A, certain points should be noted:

1. Section 280A(c)(5) prescribes the amount and type of deduction for the personal residence and vacation homes.

2. Section 280A(f)(2) and Prop. Reg. Section 1.280A-1(e)(5) prescribes that with respect to personal use of a vacation home or personal residence owned by an S corporation, it is determined by the total amount of personal use by all the S corporate shareholders, and if two or more S shareholders use the home on the same day, it only counts as one personal use day.

3. Prop. Reg. Section 1.280A-1(e)(1) prescribes which person will be deemed to occupy the vacation home or residence as personal use.

Examples of how Section 280A applies to S corporations are set forth below:

EXAMPLE 5-8

A, B, and C form an S corporation, P, Inc., in which each holds a one-third interest. P, Inc., acquires a dwelling unit that C rents from P, Inc., at fair rental for use as C's principal residence. All items of income, gain, loss, deduction, or credit of P that are related to the unit are allocated one-third to each shareholder. Under these circumstances, the personal use of the unit by C is not treated as personal use by P, Inc. Consequently, the use of the unit by C does not subject A and B to the limitations of Section 280A(c)(5) with respect to their shares of the items related to the unit. C, however, is subject to the limitations of Section 280A(c)(5) with respect to C's share of those items.

EXAMPLE 5-9

X, Inc., an S corporation in which A and B are shareholders, is the owner of a fully equipped recreational vehicle. During the month of July, the vehicle is used by three individuals. A uses the vehicle on a 7-day camping trip. D, who is B's daughter, rents the vehicle from X, Inc., at fair rental for 10 days. E rents the vehicle at fair rental for 12 days under an arrangement whereby B is entitled to use an apartment owned by F, a friend of E, for 9 days. X, Inc., is deemed to have used the dwelling unit for personal purposes on any day on which any of its shareholders would be deemed to have so used the unit. Therefore, X, Inc., is deemed to have used the recreational vehicle for personal purposes on 29 days.

TAX POINTER

Section 280A only applies to individuals, partnerships, trusts, estates, and S corporations; it does not apply to C corporations.

5.14   CORPORATE INTEREST—SECTION 163(h)(1)

The Tax Reform Act of 1986 prescribes that consumer interest is not deductible subject to a phase-in. However, Section 163(h)(1) provides that corporate interest is still deductible. It remains to be seen what will occur in this area. Obviously, shareholders in an S corporation will attempt to run through the S corporation's interest items that would be disallowed personally under Section 163(h)(1). Most likely, the Service will be quick to strike down these obvious subterfuges.

5.15   LEGAL EXPENSES, ACCOUNTING FEES, AND SO ON

Section 67 prescribes a 2% floor on certain miscellaneous itemized deductions. Examples of covered items would be tax preparation fees, legal fees in connection with tax matters, financial planning, and subscriptions to financial publications. Shareholders of S corporations in an attempt to maneuver around Section 67 may attempt to have their S corporation pay these expenses. It remains to be seen how the Service will attack these maneuvers. However, there will most likely be a recharacterization.

5.16   REASONABLE COMPENSATION

A.   The Dichotomy Between Salary and Distributions in Respect to Stock Under Section 1368

In the case of a shareholder-employee, the question often arises as to how to compensate them—salaries or distributions of cash under Section 1368. (For a detailed discussion of Section 1368, see Chapters 7 and 8.)

An example will illustrate:

EXAMPLE 5-10

A, Inc., is an S corporation with no earnings and profits. A, Inc., has one shareholder, X, who is also the only employee of the corporation. In 19X1 it has $100 of taxable income. If A, Inc., distributes the $100 of income to X as a distribution with respect to stock, X will report $100 of income. Likewise, if A, Inc., pays X $100 of salary, A, Inc.'s taxable income will be zero (in fact, it could be a loss situation because of payroll taxes), and X will report $100 of income.

While Example 5-10 illustrates that basically the net effect of corporate payments to a shareholder-employee is the same, whether the payment is made by salary or an actual distribution, the choice of corporate payments could impact on other areas. For instance, salary payments form the basis for corporate contributions to qualified retirement plans, are treated as active income for purposes of Section 469's passive income rules (see discussion at Chapter 7.9), generate employment taxes and social security for retirement purposes, and so on. Cash distributions with respect to stock basically do not generate tax consequences to the shareholder-employee, although if the distribution is in excess of the shareholder-employee's basis in stock (see Chapter 8.2) or the accumulated adjustment account if the S corporation still has earnings and profits (see Chapter 8.3), the distribution would generate taxable income to the shareholder-employee.

Besides these reasons for payments of salaries, there are others, depending on how the S corporation is established. For instance, salaries reduce the effect that an inadvertent termination of S status will have on the shareholder-employee. As discussed in Chapter 10.5, an S corporation can inadvertently terminate if adequate steps are not taken to guard against same (but see Chapter 9.8 for discussion as to how the limit inadvertent terminations). If the corporation pays salaries instead of distributions, the result will be that the corporation will obtain a deduction for salary instead of having a nondeductible dividend, as could be the case of a distribution in the year of termination. (See Chapter 8.6.)

Another reason would be state taxes. In some states (see Appendix 4), S corporations are not recognized for tax purposes. Thus, if the corporate earnings were distributed in the form of a distribution instead of salaries, state law could treat the distribution as a dividend, thereby creating a double tax situation.

TAX POINTER

Care, however, must be exercised, if salaries are going to be used to distribute corporate earnings so that no adverse tax results can occur. For instance, if the S corporation has no earnings and profits, the shareholder-employee has no basis in stock or debt (see Chapter 7.4 for a discussion of basis), and the salary would create a loss for the corporation, the shareholder-employee will have ordinary income under Section 61, but will not be able to deduct the loss because of lack of basis pursuant to Section 1367(a)(2). An example will illustrate this tax pointer.

EXAMPLE 5-11

A, Inc., a calendar year S corporation, has one shareholder, D. D, as of 1/1/X1, has no basis in her stock or debt; thus any loss for A, Inc., will be suspended for D pursuant to Section 1367(a)(2). In 19X1, A, Inc., pays D a salary of $200 and reports a $200 loss. The tax consequences to D are that she will report $200 of salary as ordinary income, but since she has no basis in stock or debt, she will have to defer the $200 loss until she obtains basis.

B. Self-employment Tax Under Section 1401 and Distributions with Respect to Stock Under Section 1368

As discussed in Chapter 5.16.A, instead of taking salary, a shareholder-employee may decide, because the tax effect is basically the same as that illustrated in Example 5-10, to take a distribution of income with respect to stock. The current law seems to indicate that a distribution of income with respect to stock pursuant to Section 1368 is not subject to self-employment tax. For instance, Section 1401, by definition, excludes S corporation distributions from self-employment tax (in comparison, note that partnership distributions are subject to self-employment tax).[12]

Further, Rev. Rul. 59-221,[13] issued under prior law, states that S corporate distributions with respect to stock are not self-employment income.[14] Thus, if a shareholder-employee is not concerned about retirement plan contributions, later social security benefits, and the like, then cash distributions in respect to stock under Section 1368 is the method to be used.

TAX POINTER

Since the cash distribution under Section 1368 is not subject to self-employment tax, by definition, then, the shareholder cannot take an IRA contribution with respect to same.

C. Reasonable Compensation

While it may seem strange that the issue of reasonable compensation would arise in S corporations because of the one level of tax concept, it does arise. As discussed at Chapter 5.7.C, it can arise if the S corporation attempts to take an excessive deduction in retirement plan. It can also arise in S corporations where family members are shareholders. For instance, in *Roob* v. *Comm.*,[15] the stock of an S corporation was owned in equal proportions by the taxpayer, his wife, and his children. The parents were the only shareholders who rendered services to the corporation. The Service's reallocation of income from the children to the father was sustained. Example of where the Service has lost is *Rocco v. Comm.*[16] and *Edwin D. Davis*[17] (discussed at Chapter 1.2.D, Tax Pointer 1). Under prior law the Service was successful in *Gary N. Cromer*[18] in challenging an attempt to take out S corporate income as salary instead of a distribution of income with respect to stock. Applying the rationale of *Cromer* to S corporations today, the Service may attempt to disallow salaries where the attempt is made to reduce taxable income for purposes of the passive income rules of Section 1375, which is discussed in Chapter 6.4. Related to this is the fact that if the Service is successful in challenging salary as unreasonable, this could affect the amount of the deduction to a retirement plan.

It is to be noted that the Service could challenge situations where S corporate shareholder-employees attempt to reduce salaries to bypass the withholding requirement for employment taxes, FICA, and the like. Rev. Rul. 74-44,[19] issued under prior law, holds that an S corporation can be considered liable for FICA and related payroll taxes on dividend distributions if the distribution actually represented disguised salaries to its actively employed shareholders.

ENDNOTES FOR CHAPTER 5

1. Section 163(d)(4)(A) defines "net investment income" generally as the excess of (1) investment income over (2) investment expenses. Investment income is defined in Section 163(d)(4)(B) as gross income from property held for investment, including any net gain attributable to disposition of the property held for investment, but only to the extent that it is not derived from the conduct of a trade or business.

2. Section 163(d)(6).

3. A probable example of a situation that could be covered by this provision would be a working interest in oil or gas property. (See Chapter 7.9, endnote 21, for a definition of a working interest in oil or gas property.)

4. 80 T.C. 27 (1983), aff'd without published opinion, 747 F. 2d 1463 (5th Cir. 1984).

5. 72 T.C. 377 (1979). See also *Bianchi,* 66 T.C. 324 (1976).

6. Reg. Section 1.248-1(b)(3)(i).

7. Section 1363(c)(1), Prop. Treas. Reg. Section 1.179-1(h).

8. Prop. Treas. Reg. Section 1.179-1(f)(2). Note, however, that because a trust or estate shareholder cannot deduct the expense, the S corporation does not reduce the basis for the expense allocated to the trust or estate.

9. Para. 86,093 P-H Memo T.C.

10. *Merritt, Sr.* v. *Comm.*, 22 AFTR 2d 5442 (5th Cir. 1968), aff'g 47 T.C. 519.

11. I.R.S. Publication, 589, "Tax Information on S Corporations" (1986), page 9.

12. Reg. Section 1.1402(a)-1(b).

13. 1959-1 C.B. 225.

14. It also should be noted that Schedule K-1 to Form 1120S contains no line to report self-employment income. In contrast, Form 1065 Schedule K-1 does.

15. 50 T.C. 891 (1968).

16. 57 T.C. 826 (1972).

17. 64 T.C. 1034 (1975).

18. Para. 80, 263 P-H Memo T.C. 1980.

19. 1974-1 C.B. 287.

6

S Corporation Income Taxes

6.1 THREE SITUATIONS WHERE THE S CORPORATION IS LIABLE FOR INCOME TAX

An S corporation can be liable for three income tax situations: (1) a tax under Section 1374 (Chapter 6.7.B.2 deals with C corporation electing S status after 12/31/86, and Chapter 6.2 deals with C corporation electing S status before 1/1/87, even though the election does not go into effect until after 12/31/86[1]), (2) tax arising from recomputing a prior-year investment credit that the S corporation took while it was a C corporation (Section 1371(d)(2)), and (3) tax on passive investment income (Section 1375).

6.2 TAX ON CAPITAL GAINS FOR C CORPORATIONS ELECTING S STATUS

A. Background

Congress recognized a problem shortly after creating S corporations—that they could be used for tax avoidance with capital gains. An example will illustrate the abuse that could have been practiced before the law was changed:

EXAMPLE 6-1

A C corporation in 1963 foresees large capital gains in 1964. Accordingly, it adopts S status in 1964, passing the capital gains and the money equal to the capital gains to the shareholders. In 1965, the corporation terminates its election and continues to conduct business. By adopting the C-S-C approach, the corporation was able to avoid capital gains tax at the C level and passed out the gains to the shareholders.

To overcome the problem, Congress in 1966 adopted Section 1378. When the Subchapter S Revision Act of 1982 was adopted, Section 1378 became Section 1374, and it has been modified since. (See Chapter 6.7.B.2.)

B. Section 1374's Tax

1. Introduction

As indicated in Chapter 6.1, it appears that two versions of Section 1374 apply to S corporations: one for C corporations electing S status after 12/31/86 ("new" Section 1374) and one applying to C corporations electing S status prior to 1/1/87 ("old" Section 1374). Presumably, the old Section 1374 result will be what is detailed in Chapters 6.2.B.2 through 6.2.G.[2] If Section 1374 applies to the transaction, be it old Section 1374 or new Section 1374, the consequence is that the S corporation pays the tax under Section 1374 on the gain with the S corporate shareholder(s) being taxed on the net amount of gain after the tax. To illustrate, assume that an S corporation, X, Inc., which had one shareholder, D, engaged in a transaction in 198X that produced a $100,000 gain and that the transaction was subject to a Section 1374 tax of $25,000 that X, Inc., paid to the Service. D would only report as the gain on the transaction $75,000 ($100,000 − $25,000).

2. Old Section 1374(a)'s Tax

Old Section 1374(a) will impose a tax on S corporate capital gains arising from converting a C corporation into S status if certain conditions set forth below are met in a taxable year for three consecutive years following conversion of the corporation to S status, namely, the corporation's

1. Net capital gain exceeds $25,000 (old Section 1374(a)(1)).
2. Net capital gain exceeds 50% of its taxable income (old Section 1374(a)(1)).
3. Taxable income exceeds $25,000 (old Section 1374(a)(2)).

As can be seen, the definition of long- and short-term capital gain and loss is important. As discussed at Chapter 4.1.A, the Tax Reform Act of 1986 (TRA) kept the current statutory structure as well as the format to define long- and short-term capital gain and loss. Thus, there should be little difficulty to do the computations to apply old Section 1374.

If an S corporation fails to meet any of the foregoing conditions (i.e., it has no taxable income in the taxable year), the S corporation will pay no tax on the capital gains incurred, and the gains will be passed tax free to the shareholders. As can also be seen by the definition, old Section 1374's tax is not a subjective one depending on the taxpayer's motives[3]; rather it is a mechanical test.

TAX POINTER

See discussion at Chapter 6.2.C for ways to overcome old Section 1374's tax.

C. Methods to Overcome Old Section 1374 Tax

With careful planning, old Section 1374 does not have to be a trap. From the statutory framework, certain key maneuvers can be followed to avoid the imposition of the tax.

1. Fail One or More of Old Section 1374(a)'s Three Prescribed Requirements

As discussed in Chapter 6.2.B.2, old Section 1374 has three key steps that must be met. By flunking one or more of the steps, there can be no tax. An example will illustrate:

EXAMPLE 6-2

AB, Inc., is a C corporation. AB, Inc., elected S status on 12/31/86. AB, Inc., projected that in 1987 when it had its first full year of S status, it would have the following tax results—a net capital gain of $30,000 from sale of corporate assets and taxable income of $55,000. Accordingly, it will be liable for old Section 1374's tax, because its net capital gain and taxable income are greater than $25,000 (capital gain $30,000, taxable income $55,000) and the net capital gain is greater than 50% of taxable income (50% of taxable income is $27,500, net capital gain is $30,000). However, if AB, Inc., can reduce (1) the net capital gain below $25,000, (2) make the taxable income below $25,000, or (3) make sure the ratio of capital gains to taxable income is below 50%, it will not have an old Section 1374 tax problem in the first year of its existence.

TAX POINTER

One means of reducing taxable income is to declare salaries to shareholder-employees of the S corporation. (With respect to risks involved in doing this, see Chapter 5.16.C.)

a. The Effect of Ltr. Rul. 8651019 in Counting the 3-Year Period

Ltr. Rul. 8651019 involved a pre-TRA fiscal year C corporation (fiscal year 3/31) that elected S status and adopted a calendar year to report income. During its first full year of operation as an S corporation, the corporation changed its mind and requested fiscal year reporting (9/30) that the Service approved. For purposes of old Section 1374(a)'s tax, the corporation's fiscal year 4/1–12/31 and 1/1–9/30 counted as two taxable years for purposes of the 3-year test of Section 1374.

2. How the S Corporation Incurs Long- and Short-Term Capital Gains to Permissible Limits

Old Section 1374(a)'s tax is geared to net capital gains (net long-term capital gain—long-term capital gain less long-term capital loss—less net short-term capital loss), not "gross" capital gains. Accordingly, if sufficient capital losses (long or short) can be generated in the taxable year in question to offset the capital gains so that old Section 1374(a)'s threshold limits will not be reached, the S corporation's "net capital gains" can be passed through to the shareholders tax free.[4]

TAX POINTER

As is true with any tax strategy, the taxpayer should evaluate the effect of accelerating a capital loss to wipe out an old Section 1374 tax on capital gains.

3. Use Installment Sale Reporting Under Section 453 to Report the Capital Gain

As discussed in Chapter 6.2.B.2, old Section 1374's tax only applies to the first 3 years of an S corporation's existence. If old Section 1374 will apply a tax on the capital gains, the S corporation should sell the asset reporting the capital gains by means of an installment sale under Section 453 using Form 6252 recognizing only $25,000 each year for the first 3 years of old Section 1374's applicability. The reason why $25,000 of capital gains can be recognized is that, as discussed in Chapter 6.2.B.2, old Section 1374 only applies if the S corporation has more than $25,000 in a tax year and old Section 1374's tax only applies to gain, not when it makes a sale. An example will illustrate:

EXAMPLE 6-3

Assume the same facts as in Example 6-2, and that AB, Inc., projects it will have during its first year as an S corporation $30,000 of net capital gain and $55,000 of taxable income. To overcome taxation of the net capital gains under old Section 1374, AB, Inc., when it sells the capital gain property will do so by means of an installment sale that will be calculated to provide no more than $25,000 of capital gains in each year. Thus, in the first year of AB, Inc.'s existence as an S corporation, it will realize $25,000 of capital gains and in the next, $5,000 (total $30,000).

TAX POINTER

Section 453A prescribes that the seller when it engages in certain types of seller financing will realize constructive receipt of income under a formula involving the seller's installment sales for the year and its outstanding borrowings. For a discussion of Section 453A's taxation, see Chapter 10.8.E.

D. Two Statutory Exceptions to Old Section 1374(a)'s Tax on Capital Gains

1. Old Sections 1374(c)(1) and (2)

As detailed in Chapter 6.2.A, old Section 1374(a)'s basic design was to prevent an S corporation from being used for a "one-shot" purpose to pass capital gains for one year and then allow the corporation to return to C status. In accordance with that design, old Section 1374(c)(1) and (2) provided two exceptions: (1) old Section 1374(a) will not tax capital gains during a taxable year if the S corporation was one for its last 3 years (old Section 1374(c)(1)) and (2) if a corporation has been in existence for less than 4 years but an S election has been in place for each year (old Section 1374(c)(2)). Examples of these two exceptions are illustrated below:

EXAMPLE 6-4

XYZ, Inc., was formed as a C corporation in 1976. In 1980, it elected S status, and in 1987, it has $100,000 of net capital gains. Old Section 1374(a) will not apply because of Old Section 1374(c)(1) (i.e., it was an S corporation for more than 3 years). Likewise, new Section 1374 does not apply since XYZ, Inc., was an S corporation before 1/1/87. (See Chapter 6.7.A.)

EXAMPLE 6-5

MN, Inc., was formed in 1985 and elected S status on formation. During 1987, it sells a capital asset it purchased in 1985 for $75,000 of net capital gains. Old Section 1374(a) does not apply to tax the $75,000 gain because of old Section 1374(c)(2) (i.e., it has been an S corporation for its entire existence, and thus it does not have to satisfy the 3-year test). Likewise, new Section 1374 does not apply since MN, Inc., was an S corporation before 1/1/87. (See Chapter 6.7.A)

To prevent circumvention of old Sections 1374(c)(1) and (2) by the S corporation engaging in certain tax-free transactions, Congress added old Section 1374(c)(3). An example of the abuse Congress attempted to prevent is set forth below:

EXAMPLE 6-6

X in 19XX forms AB, Inc., taking back 100% of the stock of the corporation and elects S status for the corporation. X also owns 100% of MN, Inc., which is a C corporation. In 19X1, MN, Inc., has a capital asset that will yield on sale $100,000 of net capital gains. In 19X1, X merges MN, Inc., into AB, Inc., forming ABMN, Inc., in an attempt to fit into the exception set forth in old Section 1374(c)(2) and then sells the capital asset. Old Section 1374(c)(3) prevents the result. Likewise, new Section 1374, subject to TRA Section 633(d), could reach this situation (see discussion at Chapter 6.7.B depending on when the merger took place.

Old Section 1374(c)(3) refuses to allow the exceptions of old Section 1374(c)(1) and (2) to apply to a merger of an S and C corporation if three conditions are met as set forth in Reg. Section 1.1378-2(b)(2), adopted under former Code Section 1378 (the predecessor to old Section 1374):

1. The property must be acquired by an S corporation during the period beginning 36 months before the first day of the S corporation's taxable year and ending on the last day of such year.

2. The basis of the property in the hands of the S corporation must be determined, in whole or in part, by reference to the basis of any property in the hands of another corporation.

3. The other corporation was not an S corporation throughout the period beginning on the later of (a) 36 months before the first day of the S corporation's taxable year or (b) the time such other corporation came into existence, and ending on the date the other corporation transferred the property, the basis of which is used to determine, in whole or in part, the basis of the property in the hands of the S corporation.

An example of the operation of old Section 1374(c)(3) is set forth below:

EXAMPLE 6-7

Assume the same facts as in Example 6-6 except that instead of selling the capital gain property in the same year as the merger, ABMN, Inc., holds the property for four years before selling it. Because ABMN, Inc., held the property for more than 36 months, old Section 1374(c)(3) does not apply to the transaction to impose taxation under old Section 1374(a). Note, new Section 1374 may apply to tax this transaction depending on when the merger took place.

E. Liquidate Under Section 337 to Avoid Old Section 1374(a)'s Tax

Assuming that the S corporation would be subject to old Section 1374(a)'s tax on net capital gain because it cannot avail itself of one of the exceptions or loopholes discussed therein, the corporation can sell the tainted assets, liquidate under Section 337, and beat old Section 1374, providing that the corporation meets the tests of TRA Section 633(d). (See discussion at Chapter

10.10.A.) The reason why old Section 1374 would have no effect on a Section 337 liquidation is that old Section 1374(a) only applies to recognized gains, and Section 337, by definition, is not a recognized gain under old Section 1374.

F. Computation of Old Section 1374's Tax

If an S corporation finds itself in a taxable transaction under old Section 1374(a), it would be liable for two taxes, the income tax computed under Section 1374(b) and the minimum tax pursuant to Section 56 in existence pre–TRA (hereinafter "old" Section 56). However, when the TRA was enacted, the Code provisions providing for minimum tax under Section 56, namely, Sections 58(d) and 57(a)(9)(B) were deleted, so it remains to be determined if the corporation will be subject to old Section 56 minimum tax for taxable years beginning after 12/31/86 if the gains tax under old Section 1374 applies.[5] A discussion is found in Chapter 6.2.G as to how old Section 56 would tax old Section 1374 situations, assuming the tax would have applicability.

1. Income Tax Under Section 1374(b)

Old Section 1374(b) prescribes that the S corporation pay income tax on the lower of

1. The corporate alternative tax on the net capital gain in excess of $25,000 (Old Section 1374(b)(1)).[6]

2. The Section 11 tax on the corporation's entire taxable income (Old Section 1374(b)(2)).

For purposes of computing the corporate tax under old Section 1374(b)(2), old Section 1374(b)(2) prescribed that the taxable income upon which the tax is computed in the same manner as a C corporation except that the S corporation cannot take a deduction for a net operating loss under Section 172, a deduction under Sections 243, 247, 249, and 250 et seq. An example will illustrate the computation of tax under old Section 1374(b).

EXAMPLE 6-8

AB, Inc., an S corporation, in 1987 is subject to tax under old Section 1374(a). It had $100,000 of taxable income and $25,000 of net capital gain by Section 1374(b)(2). The old Section 11 tax rates on $100,000 of taxable income is $25,750.[7] By old Section 1374(b)(1), the alternative minimum tax rate is 28%[8] and the tax is $14,000 (28% × $75,000 − $25,000). Accordingly, because the alternative tax is less than the old Section 11 tax ($25,750), the old Section 1374(b) tax is $14,000 (as to the effect of the old Section 1374(b)'s tax on the shareholders, see discussion at Chapter 6.2.H.) (This example assumes that the pre–TRA Section 11 and alternative capital gain rate would apply to this situation rather than the new Section 11 rates.)

EXAMPLE 6-9

Assume the same facts as in Example 6-8, except that the taxable income is $35,000. The old Section 11 tax is $5,550 (15% × 25,000 plus 18% × 10,000). Because the old Section 11 tax is less than the old alternative minimum tax calculation, the old Section 1374(b) tax is $5,550.

2.   Old Section 1374(c)(3) Limits on Tax Calculated Under Old Section 1374(b)

If the S corporation were liable for tax under old Section 1374(a) because of the substituted basis rules of old Section 1374(c)(3), old Section 1374(c)(3) imposed a limit on the amount of tax that can be imposed by old Section 1374(b), namely, that the tax cannot exceed 28% of the amount of net capital gain attributable to the property with a substituted basis, assuming that the old Section 1201(a) applies.[9] The reason for this limitation was to limit taxation just to property with a substituted basis. Accordingly, other capital gains would not be taxed to the corporation. An example will illustrate:

EXAMPLE 6-10

AB, Inc., was incorporated as a C corporation. In 1986, it was merged into an S corporation, CD, Inc., that had been such for five years. ABCD, Inc.'s taxable income for 1987 was $100,000, and its net capital gain for 1987 was $135,000, composed of $60,000 of transactions from CD, Inc.'s assets and $75,000 of AB, Inc.'s assets. The old Section 1374(b)(1) tax would be $25,750. The old Section 1374(b)(2) tax as modified by old Section 1374(c) would be $14,000: (($75,000 − $25,000) × 28%); the $60,000 of CD, Inc.'s net capital gain does not enter into the calculation since it is not subject to tax by old Section 1374(a) and (c)). (This example assumes that the old Sections 11 and 1201(a) tax are in effect.)

TAX POINTERS

1. It is to be noted that two calculations are performed with respect to S corporations and old Section 1374: one to determine the amount of taxable income to be passed to the shareholder under Section 1363(b) and one to determine the amount of tax under old Section 1374, assuming old Section

1374(a) imposes taxation (i.e., computing tax income using Form 1120 to determine taxable income).

2. As discussed in Chapters 2.6 and 5.7, an S corporation can be a member of a controlled group. Accordingly, if an S corporation is liable for tax under Section 1374(a) and it is a brother-sister corporation with a C corporation, it has to for purposes of old Section 1374(b)(2)'s tax to compute its tax pursuant to Section 1561.[10]

3. A 5% negligence penalty can be imposed against an S corporation if it wrongly states that an S election had been in place for three years when in fact it had not been.[11]

3. Correlation Between Tax on Passive Investment Income Under Section 1375 and Tax on Capital Gains Under Old Section 1374

As discussed in Chapter 6.4, if a C corporation converts to an S but does not dispose of its C earnings and profits timely, this corporation can pay a tax on passive investment income as per Section 1375. It is possible under old Section 1374 and Section 1375 for capital gain to be taxed under both sections. Accordingly, to prevent double taxation of the capital gains under both sections, Section 1375(c)(2) contains a coordination provision that provides that the capital gain is taxed in full as passive investment income under Section 1375.

For purposes of old Section 1374, the gain is then reduced by the "excess net passive income" attributable to the gain from the capital assets. An example will illustrate. (Before consulting this example, the reader may want to consult the example found at Chapter 6.4.H.)

EXAMPLE 6-11

Assume that corporation M, an S corporation, has for its taxable year in 1987 total gross receipts of $200,000; passive investment income of $100,000 (discussed in Chapter 6.4); $60,000 of which is interest income; and expenses directly connected with the production of such interest income in the amount of $10,000. Assume also that at the end of the taxable year corporation M has Subchapter C earnings and profits. (See Chapter 6.4.) Since more than 25% of corporation M's total gross receipts are passive investment income, and since corporation M has Subchapter C earnings and profits at the end of the taxable year, corporation M will be subject to the tax imposed by Section 1375. The amount of excess net passive investment income is $45,000: ($100,000 − $10,000) $90,000 × ($50,000/$100,000). Assume that the other $40,000 of passive investment income is attributable to net capital gain and that there are no expenses directly connected with such gain. Under these facts, $20,000 of the excess net passive income is attributable to the net capital gain: $45,000 × ($40,000/ $90,000). Accordingly, the amount of gain taken into account under old Section 1374(b)(1) and the taxable income of corporation M under old Section 1374(b)(2) shall be reduced by $20,000.

G. The Minimum Tax

1. When an S Corporation Is Liable for Minimum Tax

Old Sections 1363 and 58(d), in effect pre–TRA, provided that if an S corporation paid tax under old Section 1374(b), it was liable for minimum tax under Section 58(d) with respect to the net capital gains.

Whether the minimum tax will be imposed against S corporations for tax years after 12/31/86 remains to be determined. (See discussion at Chapter 6.2.F.) Below is set forth a discussion as to how the minimum tax would apply under pre–TRA rules.

2. Computing the Minimum Tax Under Pre–TRA Rules

Computing the corporate minimum tax was a six-step process under pre–TRA law:[12]

Step 1. Compute the tax that would be imposed on the S corporation's income as if it were a C corporation.

Step 2. Compute the tax as in step 1 except exclude the lesser of

    a. The part of the excess of net long-term capital gain over the short-term capital loss that is more than $25,000 or

    b. The part of the excess of net long-term capital gain over the net short-term capital loss that is due to property with a substituted basis

Step 3. The amount figured in step 2 is subtracted from the amount figured in step 1.

Step 4. Subtract the amount of tax actually imposed on the capital gain from the amount figured in step 3.

Step 5. Divide the result in step 4 by the 46% tax rate that applied to ordinary corporations.[13] The result is the amount of the tax preference.

Step 6. Determine the minimum tax using Form 4626. The tax equaled 15% of the amount by which the amount of tax preference determined in step 5 exceeded the greater of $10,000 or the tax due under old Section 1374(b).[14]

An example taken from I.R.S. Publication 589, "Tax Information on S Corporations" (1985), illustrates the computations:

EXAMPLE 6-12

Blue Corporation, an S corporation, files its return on a calendar year basis. Blue Corporation has taxable income of $125,000 for 19XX that includes net capital gains of $50,000. Blue Corporation is subject to the capital gains tax at the corporate level because the $50,000 net capital gains resulted from the sale of property with a substituted basis acquired within the 48-month period ending December 31, 19XX. The capital gains item of tax preference of Blue Corporation is figured as follows:

Step 1. Ordinary tax on taxable income of the S corporation	$37,250
Step 2. Ordinary tax on taxable income less capital gain on property with a substituted basis ($125,000 − $50,000) or $75,000	15,750
Step 3.	$21,500
Step 4. Capital gains tax actually imposed	14,000
Difference	$ 7,500
Step 5. Amount of tax preference ($7,500 divided by 0.46)	$16,304

The minimum tax is 15% of the tax preferences that exceed the capital gains tax: $16,304 − $14,000 = $2,304 × 15%, or $346. (This example uses the tax rates in effect pre–TRA and assumes old Sections 1374 and 56 apply.)

TAX POINTER

The only credit that could have been used to reduce old Section 1374(b)'s tax was the credit allowed by Section 34 that relates to certain fuels and oils and was computed on Form 4136.

H. The Effect That the Corporate Income Tax Paid Under Old Section 1374(b) and Section 56 Has on Shareholders— Section 1366(f)(2)

Assuming old Sections 1374(b) and 56 apply,[15] pre–TRA Section 1366(f)(2) (hereinafter "old" Section 1366(f)(2)) prescribed that taxes imposed under old Sections 1374(b) and 56 reduce the amount of long-term capital gains that the corporation passes through to the shareholders. Old Section 1366(f)(2)(B) prescribed that if the amount of these taxes exceeded the long-term capital gains, the excess was used to reduce the gain on the sale or exchange of Section 1231 property. (For purposes of this reduction, the term "long-term capital gain" does not include any gain from the sale or exchange of any Section 1231 property.) An example will illustrate the application of old Section 1366(f)(2):

EXAMPLE 6-13

X owns 100% of the stock of FG, Inc., a C corporation that converted to an S on 1/1/19XX. During its first year of its existence, FG Inc., had $225,000 of capital gains and paid taxes on the capital gains under old Section 1374 and Section 56 amounting to $60,000. By old Section 1366(f)(2), X reports in 19XX on his Form 1040, Schedule D, $165,000 of capital gains ($225,000 less $60,000).

As discussed in Chapters 6.4 and 8.3.B.5, if the predecessor C corporation had earnings and profits on conversion to S corporate status, the tax generated by the investment credit recapture and paid by the S corporation will reduce the S corporation's accumulated earnings and profits.

TAX POINTERS

1. If the amount of tax on recomputing the investment tax credit on the Form 4255 is greater than $40, the S corporation will be required to make estimated tax payments.
2. Recomputation of investment tax credit could arise if the S corporation makes a distribution of its predecessor assets to its shareholders.

6.3 TAX FROM RECOMPUTING A PRIOR-YEAR INVESTMENT CREDIT

As discussed in Chapter 3.6.C, when a C corporation elects S corporate status, the election does not trigger the recapture of investment tax credit of any assets upon which the C corporation took the credit. However, Section 1371(d)(2) prescribes that if the S corporation makes an early disposition of its predecessor's assets, it, not the shareholders, will pay the tax on the recapture filing Form 4255.

TAX POINTER

See Chapter 9.14 for more detailed discussion of investment tax credit and Chapter 10.8.C.2 for a discussion about investment credit recapture when a shareholder disposes of S corporation stock.

6.4 TAX ON EXCESS PASSIVE INVESTMENT INCOME

A. Consequences of Passive Investment Rules on S Corporations

While it may seem that this segment of the book may be irrelevant in that today, S corporations, which have been such for all their years of existence and have no C corporation earnings and profits due to mergers, and so on, have no problems if they have 100% passive investment income, there still remains the problem for C corporations that convert to S status in that passive investment income could be their downfall. For instance, if a C corporation composed of 20 individual shareholders actively operates an office building, apartment house, and so on as a landlord, providing cleaning services, trash removal, and so on, it will not be taxed as a personal holding company under Section 543 for its rental income. Yet, let this same corporation convert to an S corporation and have one dollar of earnings and profits from C corporation status, and it will find itself subject to the onerous provisions of Sections 1362(d)(3) and 1375. Further, it is to be noted that too much passive income for too long a period of time could lead to termination of S status. (See Chapter 10.4.)

TAX POINTER

See Chapter 6.4.B.1 for the effect that Section 469 will have on S corporations earning passive income.

B. When Tax Liability Will Be Imposed on Passive Investment Income

As discussed in Chapter 10.4, if a C corporation converts to an S corporation and it has "passive investment income" in excess of 25% of "gross receipts" (for a definition of "gross receipts," see Chapter 6.4.D and "earnings and profits" from the C corporate years in each of 3 years, it will lose its S status under Section 1362(d)(3) on the first day of the taxable year that follows the third year. Notwithstanding this termination, if the C corporation turned S corporation has in any of its taxable years "passive investment income" (see definition on page 106) in excess of 25% of the S corporation's "gross receipts" for that taxable year and "earnings and profits" (see definition on page 106) from C corporate years, it could become liable for a tax on that passive investment income pursuant to Section 1375. However, before Section 1375 can impose tax, four tests have to be satisfied in the tax year in question; namely, the S corporation must have

1. Subchapter C earnings and profits at the close of the taxable year (Section 1375(a)(1)). (See Chapter 10.4.A for a definition of the term "Subchapter C earnings and profits.")

2. Passive investment income that is more than 25% of "gross receipts" (Section 1375(a)(2)). (See Chapter 6.4.C.1 for a definition of the term passive investment income and Chapter 6.4.D for the term "gross receipts."

3. Net passive income (Section 1375(b)(2)). (See Chapter 6.4.E for a definition of the term.)

4. Taxable income for the years (Section 1375(b)1(B)). (See Chapter 6.4.G for the definition of "taxable income.")

Although the reasons have changed slightly for punishing S corporations under Sections 1362(d) and 1375, the basic reason is to penalize the shareholders if the S corporation never distributes the C corporation's earnings and profits. An example of Section 1375's penalty tax is set forth below:

EXAMPLE 6-14

MN, Inc., a C corporation, is formed in 19X0 to engage in the architectural drafting business. In 19X2, it elects S status when it has $10 of earnings and profits. In 19X9, more than six years after it elects S status while it still has $10 of earnings and profits, it has passive investment income in excess of 25% of its gross receipts arising from rents it receives from leasing personal property where it did not render significant services. MN, Inc., must pay an income tax at the highest rate specified in Section 11(b)[16] of 34% pursuant to Section 1375. (See Chapter 6.4.H for an example of the computation of the tax.)

TAX POINTER

By definition, if the S corporation has no "earnings and profits" from a C corporation, no loss of election under Section 1362(d)(3)(1) or Section 1375 tax can arise (see discussion below).

1. The Effect That the Tax Reform Act of 1986 Has on Passive Investment Income

As detailed at Chapter 7.9, the Tax Reform Act of 1986 has prescribed new rules (namely, Section 469) regarding passive income and individuals. Sections 1375 and 1362 just deal with the effect of passive income from rents, royalties, interest, dividends, annuities, and income arising from the sale or exchange of stock or securities at the corporate level, not how it is characterized at the individual level. If a corporation is subject to tax under Section 1375 and termination under Section 1362, a shareholder could also be subject to Section 469's rules regarding the characterization of the income. An example would be a C corporation that converts to S status and is engaged in certain rental situations (e.g., triple net leases), which pursuant to Section 469(c)(2) is a passive activity.

C. Definition of Pertinent Terms Under Sections 1375 and 1362

Initially, it should be noted that basically the terms that apply to termination of the S election for "passive investment income" in excess of 25% of gross receipts under Section 1362(d)(3) apply with equal force to the tax imposed under Section 1375. The terms, some of which are shared in common, are set forth below:

1. Passive Investment Income

For Section 1375's tax and Section 1362(d)(3)'s termination of S corporate status to plague an S corporation, Section 1362(d)(3)(D)(i) prescribes that an S corporation must have six types of "gross receipts" in its income: (1) rents, (2) royalties, (3) interest, (4) dividends, (5) annuities, and (6) sale or exchange of stock as securities only to the extent of net capital gains therefrom.

2. Rents

While Section 1372(d)(3)(D)(i) includes rents in the term "passive investment income," it does not define the term. Consequently, the term is defined by the courts and the Service. With respect to the Service's definition, Reg. Section 1.1372-4(b)(5)(vi), adopted under former Code Section 1372, a predecessor to Sections 1375 and 1362, provides that "rent" means the "amounts received for the use of, or right to use, property (whether real or personal) of the corporation."

a. *Real Property*

In regard to real property, Reg. Section 1.1372-4(b)(5)(vi) provides that the term "rents" means amounts received for the use of, or right to use, property of the corporation. The term "rents"

> does not include payments for the use or occupancy of rooms or other space where significant services are also rendered to the occupant, such as for the use or occupancy of rooms or other quarters in hotels, boarding houses, or apartment houses furnishing hotel services, or in tourist homes, motor courts or motels. Generally, services are considered rendered to the

occupant if they are primarily for his convenience and are other than those usually or customarily rendered in connection with the rental of rooms or other space for occupancy only. The supplying of maid service, for example, constitutes such services; whereas the furnishing of heat and light, the cleaning of public entrances, exits, stairways and lobbies, the collection of trash, etc., are not considered as services rendered to the occupant. Payments for the use or occupancy of entire private residences or living quarters in duplex or multiple housing units, of offices in an office building, etc., are generally "rents" under (the predecessor statute to Sections 1362 and 1375). Payments for the parking of automobiles ordinarily do not constitute rents. Payments for the warehousing of goods or for the use of personal property do not constitute rents if significant services are rendered in connection with such payments.[17]

As can be seen from the above definition, if the S corporation renders significant services to the occupants as well as services other than those customarily rendered by a landlord (i.e., supplying of maid service), the S corporation, even though it might have 100% real estate rental income, will not be subject to Sections 1375 and Section 1362(d)(3). However, as set forth below, the demarcation line as to what is prohibited passive investment income and what is not, is not easy to define.

Consider these examples of passive investment income pertaining to real property.

- Reg. Section 1.1372-4(b)(5)(vi) adopted under former Code Section 1372 prescribes that operating a motel does not produce passive investment income "rents" because of the services involved. However, renting an entire motel to one party under a 1-year lease caused an S corporation to lose its status.[18] Renting vacation bungalows caused an S corporation to lose its election.[19]

- The following situations did not cause loss of S corporate status for the renting activities: renting tennis and handball courts to players; providing them with locker room, parking facilities, lessons, and so on,[20] and charging fees for attendant parking lot.[21]

- Rents received from tenants by S corporation that owned a shopping mall caused loss of election.[22] However, rents received in connection with the operation of a mobile home park did not cause the loss of the S election.[23]

TAX POINTER

The regulations have an all-or-nothing test to determine passive investment income from rental activities. If there are not sufficient services provided in rental situations, then the S election will be lost. In contrast, a C corporation engaged in real estate rentals can be exonerated from personal holding tax per Section 543(b)(3) if it can show basically that 50% or more of its adjusted ordinary gross income and dividends paid for the tax year equal or exceed the amount, if any, by which the corporation's nonrent personal holding company income for the year exceeds 10% of its ordinary gross income.

b. Personal Property

In regard to personal property, basically the only test to determine if the S corporate status is kept is the amount of "significant services" that are rendered by the S corporation. If the services are significant, then the S corporation will not lose its status from the rents. It is not necessary, as is the case with real property, that the service be of a type not customarily rendered. Thus, S corporations have not lost their S status by renting housewares,[24] clothes,[25] golf carts,[26] motion pictures,[27] short- and long-term leases for motor cars,[28] aircraft,[29] warehousing, and so on. As to the types of activity that will sustain S status, they usually revolve around the type of work performed. For example, in the case of leasing airplanes, amounts received by an S corporation from the lease of an aircraft without pilot, fuel, or oil will terminate S status, but amounts received from full-service charter will not cancel the status.[30]

TAX POINTER

Before switching to S status, the C corporation, if it is involved with rental activities concerning personal property, should check the cases and rulings to determine if its rental activities will constitute passive investment income. If it appears that the passive investment income will be generated, then the S corporation should seek means to provide significant services to prevent the imposition of Sections 1362 and 1375.

c. Who Provides Services?

The regulations do not focus upon who must supply the services, either the landlord S corporation or independent contractors hired by the landlord's corporation. Basically, there is no problem as to who renders the services; they just must be significant.[31]

3. Royalties

As is the case with "rents," "royalties" are not defined by statute. Reg. Section 1.1372-4(b)(5)(v), which was adopted under former Code Section 1372, states that "royalties" include amounts received for the privilege of using patents, copyrights, oil, gas, and minerals; however, amounts received for timber, coal, and domestic iron ore under Sections 631(b) and (c) basically are not "royalties." Further, the Service has ruled that payments received by an S corporation for broadcast rights to athletic events will not terminate S corporate status.[32]

4. Interest

Reg. Section 1.1372-4(b)5(viii), which was adopted under former Code Section 1372, states that interest "means any amounts received for the use of money (including tax-exempt interest and amounts treated as interest under Section 483)." However, Section 1362(d)(3)(D)(ii) excludes from consideration interest on an obligation acquired in the ordinary course of the S corporation's trade or business from the sale of inventory type goods.[33] Consequently, C corporations converting to S corporation status with retained earnings and profits should give careful consideration to how much interest will be earned during each taxable year, lest interest earned during the year together with the other five types of income exceed 25% of gross receipts. In this regard, it should be noted that presumably interest under Sections 1273 and 1283 is included to determine the 25% gross receipts test.

TAX POINTERS

1. Since interest from installment sales under Section 453 is included in determining the 25% gross receipts test, care should be taken not to exceed the 25% test by generating too much interest from having too much principal being financed for too long a period of time.

2. The fact that interest is unavoidable has no effect on disallowance. In Ltr. Rul. 7727027, an S corporation lost its status because of interest received from a condemnation award—the S corporation, if it wanted to be compensated from the governmental taking, had to accept the interest on the award.

3. Interest expense may not be used to reduce interest income.[34]

5. Dividends

As discussed in Chapters 2.5 and 9.9, an S corporation can own the stock of a C corporation so long as its ownership does not create an affiliated group. Section 1362(d)(3)(D)(i) prescribes that any dividends received will be passive investment income. Reg. Section 1.1372-4(b)(5)(vii) adopted under former Code Section 1372 states that dividends are composed of three categories:

1. Dividends as defined in Section 316 (i.e., any distribution of property made by a corporation to its shareholders out of its current earnings and profits and those accumulated after 2/18/13 out of earnings and profit.

2. Amounts included in gross income by Section 551 (i.e., income relating to foreign personal holding company income taxed to U.S. shareholders).

3. Consent dividends arising under Section 565 (i.e., those distributions made to avoid the imposition of personal holding company tax under Section 543 or improper accumulation of surplus).

TAX POINTER

Before a C corporation converts to S status, it should review its investment portfolio to determine the effect that dividends will have on passive investment income. The corporation may decide to change its portfolio to acquire low-dividend stocks; however, as discussed in Chapters 6.4.C.7 and 6.7, if the C corporation sells the stocks after converting to S status, the capital gains realized from the sales could generate passive investment income.

6. Annuities

Reg. Section 1.1372-4(b)(5)(ix), adopted under former Code Section 1372, defines the term "annuities" as "the entire amount received as an annuity under an annuity, endowment or life insurance contract, regardless of whether only part of such amount could be includible in gross income under Section 72."

7. Sales or Exchanges of Stock or Securities

Section 1362(d)(3)(D)(i) includes gross receipt from sales or exchanges of stock or securities as passive investment income but only to the extent of gains therefrom. Reg. Section 1.1372-4(B)(5)(x) adopted under former Code Section 1372 as set forth below prescribes a lengthy definition for determining the amount of passive investment income to be included:

1. In accordance with Section 1362(d)(3)(D)(i), only gains from the sale or exchange of stock or securities is included in the definition to determine if an S corporation has more than 25% passive investment.

2. Because only gains are included to determine passive investment income, transactions where basis only is recovered reduce passive investment income. Losses, however, are not included and do not offset gains.

3. Reg. Section 1.1372-4(b)5(x), adopted under former Code Section 1372, does not define "stock as securities." Rather, the regulation incorporates the broad definition of "stock or securities" for personal holding companies under Reg. Section 1.543-1(b)(5)(i) to define the term.

4. The fact that the gains arise from an active business conducted by the S corporation (i.e., a regular dealer in stock or securities) is of no consequence. The gains will be counted to determine the 25% passive investment income test. Section 1362(d)(3)(D)(v) prescribes that option and commodities dealers will not have passive investment income arising from dealing in "Section 1256 contracts."

5. Section 1362(d)(3)(D)(iv) prescribes that liquidating distributions received from a corporation where the S corporation owns more than 50% of each class of stock will not result in any passive investment income.

Examples will illustrate the general application of the above points:

EXAMPLE 6-15

AB, Inc., is a C corporation engaged in a bookkeeping service business that converted to S status five years ago in 1982. At the time of conversion, it had $1.00 of earnings and profits. In 1987, it had the following transactions from selling stock: basis, $10,000; sales price, $50,000; gain, $40,000. AB, Inc.'s gross receipts from its bookkeeping business were $160,000. AB, Inc.'s passive investment income from stock or securities is $40,000, which is less than 25% of its gross receipts. (See Chapter 6.4.D for a definition of the term "gross receipts": ($160,000 + $40,000) × 25% = $50,000.) Thus there is no tax under Section 1375 and complications under Section 1362(d)(3). (Note, no tax could arise under new Section 1374 on the gain since AB, Inc., was an S corporation before 1/1/87. See discussion at Chapter 6.7. No tax would arise under old Section 1374 since AB, Inc., was an S corporation for more than 3 years at the time the capital gains arose. See Chapter 6.2.B.2.

EXAMPLE 6-16

Assume the same facts as in Example 6–15, except that AB, Inc.'s gross receipts from its bookkeeping service was only $80,000. AB, Inc., would have more than 25% of its gross receipts from passive investment income ($80,000 + $40,000) = $120,000; $120,000 × 33.3% = $40,000. A tax computation would result under Section 1375 and 1987 would count as 1 year toward termination status under Section 1362(d)(3).

EXAMPLE 6-17

Assume the same facts as in Example 6-16. In addition, AB, Inc., sold stock having a $300,000 basis for $210,000, realizing a loss of $90,000.

Because a loss was generated on the transaction, the amount realized from the sale of stock, $300,000, is not included, and the loss of $90,000 cannot be used to offset the gain realized in Example 6-16.

D. Gross Receipts

Once the tainted items of passive investment income have been determined for the S corporation, it is necessary to perform a computation to see if these items exceed 25% of gross receipts for purposes of Section 1375's tax and Section 1362(d)(3)'s termination of S status. The term "gross receipts" is not specifically defined in Sections 1375 or 1362(d)(3). However, in Reg. Section 1.1372-4(b)(iv), adopted under former Section 1372, the predecessor to Sections 1375 and 1362(d)(3), a definition is found. A cursory discussion is set forth below of the term "gross receipts."

Reg. Section 1.1372-4(b)(5)(iv)'s definition of gross receipts is complicated with many items being included and excluded. Reg. Section 1.1372-4(b)(iv) prescribes that gross receipts

- means the total amount received or accrued under the method of accounting used by the S corporation in computing its taxable income. The term "gross receipts" is not synonymous with "gross income," and the "total amount of gross receipts" is not reduced by returns and allowances, rent, and deduction.
- will include the total amount received or accrued during the corporation's taxable year from the sale-exchange (including a sale or exchange to which Section 337 applies) of any kind of property from investments and for services rendered by the corporation.
- does not include amounts "received in nontaxable sales or exchanges [other than those to which Section 337 applies] except to the extent that gain is recognized by the corporation," amounts received as a loan, as a repayment of a loan (as a contribution to capital), or on the issuance by the corporation of its own stock.

Thus, tax-free exchanges arising under Sections 354, 361, and 1031 by definition should not be included in "gross receipts." Boot received in the exchange, however, should be included in "gross receipts."

TAX POINTER

Obviously, if an S corporation foresees a potential tax situation under Sections 1375 and 1362(d)(3), it will attempt to raise its gross receipts with nonpassive investment income items so as to flunk the 25% test of these two statutory sections. For example, the S corporation could run sales on inventory items lowering the price to generate volume.

Examples illustrating the operation of the rules regarding "gross receipts" as found in Reg. Section 1.1372-4(b)(5)(iv)(b) are set forth below.

EXAMPLE 6-18

A corporation on the accrual method sells property (other than stock or securities) and receives payment partly in money and partly in the form of a note payable at a future time. The amount of the money and the face amount of the note would be considered gross receipts in the taxable year of the sale and would not be reduced by the adjusted basis of the property, the costs of sale, or any other amount.

EXAMPLE 6-19

A corporation has a long-term contract as defined in Paragraph (a) of Reg. Section 1.451-3 with respect to which it reports income according to the percentage-of-completion method as described in Paragraph (b)(1) of Reg. Section 1.451-3. The portion of the gross contract price, which corresponds to the percentage of the entire contract that has been completed during the taxable year, shall be included in gross receipts for such year.

EXAMPLE 6-20

A corporation, which regularly sells personal property on the installment plan, elects to report its taxable income from the sale of property (other than stock or securities) on the installment method in accordance with Section 453. The installment payments actually received in a given taxable year of the corporation shall be included in gross receipts for such year.

TAX POINTERS

1. By definition, the Service could increase an S corporation's gross receipts by reallocation under Section 482 and/or the assignment-of-income doctrine.

2. When an S corporation is a partner, it includes for purposes of gross receipts, the partnership gross receipts rather than the S corporation's distributive share of partnership income.[35] An example will illustrate:

EXAMPLE 6-21

AB, Inc., an S corporation, is a 50% general partner in XYZ Co., a partnership engaged in a retailing venture. In 1987, XYZ Co. had the following: gross receipts from operations, $400,000; deductions, $350,000; net income, $50,000. Thus, AB, Inc.'s share of XYZ Co.'s income is $25,000; however, for purposes of Sections 1375 and 1362(d)(3), the S corporation includes for purposes of gross receipts $200,000 (50% × $400,000).

E. Net Passive Income

Section 1375(b)(2) defines "net passive income" as the S corporation's passive investment income (see Chapter 6.4.C.1 as to how this is computed) less "deductions allowable . . . which are directly connected with the production of such income" with the exception of the deductions allowable under Sections 241–250 and net operating losses under Section 172. Section 1375 does not define the term "directly connected." Consequently, general tax principles must define this term. An example will illustrate:

EXAMPLE 6-22

AB, Inc., an S corporation that has earnings and profits from a predecessor C corporation, is the owner of an office building that only collects rents, and it renders no significant services to its tenants. The rents for the taxable year 19X5 total $100,000. In addition, AB, Inc., has various maintenance expenses such as cleaning, rubbish removal, fuel, and utilities, expenses that total $90,000. The net passive income is $10,000 ($100,000 − $90,000).

TAX POINTERS

1. As Example 6-22 illustrates, if the S corporation does not have a profit with respect to its passive investment income activities, there can be no tax under Section 1375.

2. See Chapter 6.4.H for an example of how the passive investment tax under Section 1375 is computed.

F. Excess Net Passive Income

As detailed in Chapter 6.4.H, Section 1375's tax is imposed on the lower of "taxable income" or "excess net passive income." Section 1375(b)(1)(A) prescribes that "excess net passive income" means an amount that bears the same ratio to "net passive income" (see Chapter 6.4.E for a definition of the term) for the taxable year as the amount by which passive investment income (see Chapter 6.4.C.1 for the definition of the term) for the taxable year exceeds 25% of the S corporation's "gross receipts" (see Chapter 6.4.D for a definition of the term), for the taxable year bears to the passive investment income for the year. A practical illustration of this definition is found in the worksheet set forth in Chapter 6.4.H.

G. Taxable Income

Section 1375(b)(1)(B) prescribes that, if an S corporation has no taxable income as computed under Section 63(a), it cannot be liable for tax under

Section 1375. If it does have taxable income, but its taxable income is less than its excess net passive income (see Chapter 6.4.F for a definition of excess net passive income), Section 1375's tax will be imposed on the taxable income.

TAX POINTER

The method to compute taxable income for purposes of Section 1375 is the same as it is for purposes of old Section 1374's tax on capital gains, subject to adjustments prescribed by new Section 1374(d)(4). (See Chapter 6.2.H.1, which details the computation.)

H. Tax Computed Under Section 1375

As discussed in Chapter 6.4.B, the S corporation has to satisfy four elements for tax to be imposed under Section 1375: (1) Subchapter C earnings and profits at the end of the taxable year, (2) passive investment income more than 25% of the S corporation's gross receipts, (3) net passive investment income, and (4) taxable income. If these four elements are satisfied, the S corporation is taxed pursuant to Section 1375(a) and (b)(1)(B) on the lower of its taxable income as computed pursuant to new Section 1374(d) or its excess passive net income. The proposed regulations under Section 1375 set forth an elaborate means to determine the tax. A simple means is found by using the worksheet found in the instructions for Form 1120S, which is set forth below, modified to reflect the TRA:

EXAMPLE 6-23

AB, Inc., is a corporation engaged in the renting of buildings without providing significant services. At the end of its first year as an S corporation (12/31/88), it has the following: $10 of Subchapter C earnings and profits from its years as a C corporation, $100,000 of rental income, $20,000 of management fees expense, $5,000 of real estate taxes, $8,000 of utilities, and $17,000 of other operating expenses. AB, Inc., will pay a tax under Section 1375 of $12,750, computed as follows:

(1) Enter gross receipts for the tax year $100,000
(2) Enter passive investment as defined in Section 1362(d)(3)(D)   100,000
(3) Enter 25% of line 1 (if line 2 is greater than 3, continue computation)   25,000
(4) Enter excess passive investment income (subtract line 3 from line 2)   75,000
(5) Enter expenses directly connected with the production of income on line 2 (20,000 + 5,000 + 8,000 + 17,000)   50,000

(6) Enter net passive investment income (subtract line 5 from line 2)	50,000
(7) Divide amount on line 4 by amount on line 2	75%
(8) Enter excess net passive income (multiply line 6 by line 7)	37,500
(9) Enter taxable income [100,000 − (20,000 + 5,000 + 8,000 + 17,000)]	50,000
(10) Tax on excess net passive income—enter 34% of the smaller of line 8 or line 9.	12,750

1. Credits Against Section 1375 Tax

Section 1375(c)(1) prescribes that only Section 34's credit for federal tax on gasoline and special fuels can reduce Section 1375's tax.

2. Coordination with New Sections 1374 and 1375(c)(2)

If an S corporation has gain that would result in tax both under Sections 1374 and 1375, Section 1375(c)(2) prescribes Section 1375's tax is imposed in full and Section 1374's tax is reduced by the portion of the excess net passive investment income for the taxable year that is attributable to the gain.

I. Waiver of Section 1375 Tax—Section 1375(d)

Section 1375(d) and Proposed Reg. Section 1.1375A-1(d)(2) prescribe grounds for the waiver of Section 1375's tax. Basically, the S corporation must show to the satisfaction of the Service that it used good faith and diligence to determine that it did not have Subchapter C earnings and profits, how the S corporation learned of its mistake, and what steps will be taken to distribute the earnings and profits. Proposed Reg. Section 1.1375A-1(d)(2) prescribes that the request for a waiver be made in the form of a ruling request and mandates that the date the waiver is to become effective, all the Subchapter C earnings and profits have to be distributed. A possible example of when Section 1375(d) could come into play is set forth below:

EXAMPLE 6-24

A, Inc., a corporation, converted to S status on 1/1/87. Before converting to S status, A, Inc., distributed all its earnings and profits to its shareholders as a dividend so that on 1/1/87, A, Inc.'s books showed zero for earnings and profits. A, Inc., on electing S status engaged in 100% passive investment income activities. In 1988, the Service commenced an audit on A, Inc., when it was a C corporation. When the audit was concluded in 1989, the Service found that A, Inc., had earnings and profits. Unless the corporation obtains relief under Section 1375(d), it will be liable for tax under Section 1375(a) and possible termination under Section 1362(d)(3)(D).

J. Reduction in Pass-through for Section 1375 Tax— Section 1368(f)(3)

As was the case with Section 1374's tax, the Section 1375 tax pursuant to Section 1366(f)(3) reduces the amount of the pass-through to the shareholders. An example will illustrate:

EXAMPLE 6-25

Assume the same facts as in Example 6–23. The amount of passive investment that is taxed to the shareholders is $87,250 ($100,000 − $12,750).

K. Section 1368(e)(3)'s Method to Reduce S Corporation's Earnings and Profits

Instead of distributing the C corporation earnings and profits before the S election, an S corporation pursuant to Section 1368(e)(3) can earmark, providing all shareholders who receive a distribution in the taxable year elect that the distributions be from C earnings and profits and be considered a dividend to the extent of earning and profits. An example illustrating the operation of the election under Section 1368(e)(3) is found at Chapter 8.3.G; for a sample form to make the election under Section 1368(e)(3), see Appendix 5.

Until all the earnings and profits are distributed by this route, the shareholders will be liable for the tax under Section 1375, and if there remain any earnings and profits after three years from the inception of S status, then Section 1362(d)(3) will terminate the election. To do a Section 1368(e)(3) election, all the shareholders who would receive a distribution must consent.

TAX POINTER

As discussed in Chapter 8.3.G.1, there are tax reasons for distribution of C earnings and profits other than to eliminate a problem under Sections 1375 and 1362(d)(3).

6.5 WHEN AN S CORPORATION IS NEVER LIABLE FOR TAX FOR EXCESSIVE PASSIVE INVESTMENT INCOME UNDER SECTION 1375 AND SUBJECT TO TERMINATION UNDER SECTION 1362(d)(3)

A. S Corporations Started After the Effective Date of the Subchapter S Revision Act of 1982 That Never Were C Corporations

By definition of Sections 1362(d)(3), 1375, and so on, an S corporation can have no earnings and profits after the effective date of the Subchapter S

Revision Act of 1982. Accordingly, if an S corporation has been one during the entire period of its existence, never was involved with a C corporation that has earnings and profits created by merger, was formed as a product of a tax-free division under Sections 312(b) and 355 or otherwise, Sections 1375 and 1362(d)(3) can have no effect on the S corporation during its entire existence.

B. S Corporation Has No Rents, Royalties, Interest, Dividends, Annuities, and Sale or Exchange of Stock or Securities

If an S corporation does not have income from the six types of prescribed income set forth in Section 1362(d)(3)(D)(i) (i.e., rents, royalties, interest, dividends, annuities, and sale or exchange of stock or securities), it can never have difficulty with Section 1375 and termination under Section 1362(d)(3). An example will illustrate:

EXAMPLE 6-26

AB, Inc., was formed 1/1/85 and elected S status on that date. Since inception, it has only engaged in manufacturing activities. Sections 1375 and 1362(d)(3) have no effect on AB, Inc.

C. C Corporation That Converts to S Status and Has No Earnings and Profits or Eliminates Them Before Electing S Status

As discussed generally in Chapter 6.7.B, a C corporation that converts to S status and has no earnings and profits from inception of S corporate status will never be plagued with Sections 1362(d)(3) and 1375. This might arise when the C corporation was operating at a loss. As to the tax consequences of the conversion to S status, when the C corporation has net operating losses, see Chapter 3.6.H.

D. S Corporation Has No Taxable Income or Net Passive Investment Income

As discussed in Chapter 6.4.J, if the S corporation has no net passive investment income or taxable income as these terms are defined, there can be no tax under Section 1375.

6.6 STATE CORPORATE TAXES

Appendix 4 sets forth what states recognize S status and those that do not. For a further discussion of this point, see Chapter 5.4.B.

6.7   SECTION 1374—TAX IMPOSED ON CERTAIN BUILT-IN GAINS

A.   C Corporations That Elected S Corporate Status Before 12/31/86

As discussed in Chapter 6.2, the version of Section 1374 in effect prior to the change made by the TRA applies to corporations electing S status before 12/31/86.

B.   Corporations Electing S Status After 12/31/86

1.   Corporations Electing S Status from Inception

Section 1374(c)(1) states that Section 1374's tax will not apply to corporations that elect S status from inception.

2.   C Corporations Electing S Status After 12/31/86 (the "10-Year Taint" Rules)

To prevent an end-run around Sections 336, 337, and 338, which generally impose a double tax on a corporation when it disposes of appreciated assets, Congress amended Section 1374 to impose basically the same type of Section 337 double tax on C corporations that convert to S status. Congress in Section 1374(a) has prescribed a corporate-level tax generally on any gain that arises before the conversion of a C corporation to S status after 12/31/86. This corporate-level tax will be imposed in any tax year where the gain arises through sale or distribution of corporate assets held by the C corporation on the day S status was elected within 10 years of the day the S election was made.[36] The total amount of gain to be recognized is limited to the corporation's aggregate net "built-in gain"[37] when the C corporation was converted to S status with gains arising on sales or distributions of property being presumed to be "built-in gains" unless the taxpayer can show to the contrary that the appreciation occurred after conversion.[38] An example will illustrate:

EXAMPLE 6-27

A, Inc., is a C corporation. At the time it converted to S status in 1987 it had only one asset, a piece of land having a cost of $200 and a fair market value of $1,000. In 1990, A, Inc., sold the land for $1,000. Section 1374 will apply to the $800 of gain.

Section 1374 does not detail how to compute or calculate the amount of "built-in gain" (presumably, C corporations that elect S status at the time of conversion will have an appraisal made of the corporate assets to determine the exact amount of built-in gain). In regard to built-in gains, the following should be noted:

1. Section 1374(d)(2) prescribes that Section 1374 can only tax assets held on the first day the S election took effect. Thus, presumably, assets acquired after that date will be subject to only one level of taxation, at the shareholder level.

2. Section 1374(c)(2) limits the amount of gain that can be taken into account under Section 1374 to the net amount by which the value of all the corporate assets exceed the adjusted basis on the first day the S election took effect. If the C corporation, on conversion to S status, had assets worth less than book value as well as assets worth more than book value, foreseeably the total of built-in gain will be lower. Applying Section 1374(2) to Example 6-27, foreseeably, if the land were sold for $5,000 instead of $1,000, $4,000 of the gain will be subject to one level of tax at the shareholder level and $800 to tax under Section 1374.

3. Section 1374(b)(1) prescribes that the amount of tax computed on the C corporate gain is made by applying the highest tax rate per Section 11(b) to the lesser of (a) the recognized built-in gains in the S corporation for the tax year, or (b) the amount that would be the taxable income for the corporation for the tax year if it were not an S corporation. Section 1374(b)(3)(B) provides that the corporation will be allowed to continue to take into account all of its C corporate tax attributes such as unexpired net operating loss capital loss carryovers to offset the tax.

TAX POINTERS

1. A simple reading of Section 1374(b)(1) indicates that an S corporation subject to Section 1374 can avoid tax if it sells assets in year(s) in which a loss would be generated.

2. Foreseeably, this loss could be generated by paying salaries and bonuses to shareholder-employees in the year the S corporation recognizes built-in gains. An S corporation can avoid Section 1374's grasp by holding the tainted asset for more than 10 years.

3. Rev. Rul. 86-141[39] prescribes that if a C corporation made the S election in 1986 even though it was not effective until a taxable year beginning in 1987, Section 1374's tax does not apply. Rather, old Section 337 and Section 1374's tax applies. For a discussion of old Section 1374, see Chapter 6.2, and for Section 337, Chapter 10.10.A.

4. The sale of inventory can create a problem under Section 1374. Ann. 86-128[40] prescribes that Section 1374(a) apparently will tax the sale of inventory in the regular course of business. (Note, however, as discussed in Chapter 3.6.I, if the C corporation used LIFO and converted to S status, Section 1361(f) will tax the inventory appreciation lying therein. Presumably, there is no double tax and Section 1363(f) will override Section 1374). Ann. 86-128 will also probably apply to completed contract method of accounting situations and to change of accounting method situations. Also, Ann. 86-128 will apply to S corporations trying to reduce their Section 1374 tax by contributing depreciation property.

a. *Coordination with the 2-Year Liquidation Transition Rule Under Section 337 (TRA Section 633(d))*

As discussed in Chapter 10.10, Congress has imposed a double tax on corporations liquidating under Section 337 beginning 1/1/87. However, Congress in TRA Section 633(d) provides a 2-year transition period for certain corporations that meet prescribed tests to have the old version of Section 337 apply. The tests that the corporation has to meet to have the pre–TRA one level of taxation apply to a Section 337 liquidation are twofold: (1) the corporation's stock must have a value of $5,000,000 or less on the date a liquidation plan is adopted (if the corporation's stock has a value of over $5,000,000 but less than $10,000,000, TRA Section 633(d)'s transition rule still applies, but it is subject to a phase out), and (2) it must satisfy a stock ownership test.

To satisfy the stock ownership test, the corporation on or after 8/1/86 must be owned by ten or fewer "qualified persons" owning more than 50% of the value of the stock.[41] ("Qualified persons" are individuals, estates, and trusts defined in Section 1361(c)(2)(A). (TRA Section 633(d)(6)(B) sets forth special attribution rules that apply to define stock ownership.)

In terms of priority, Revenue Ruling 86-141[42] states that if the S corporation meets the conditions of TRA Section 633(d) (e.g., one whose value does not exceed $10,000,000 and more than 50% of whose stock is held by no more than 10 qualified persons), it can qualify for relief from Section 1374, providing the S election is made before 1/1/89.

3. Counting the 10-Year Period

In regard to the 10-year counting period set forth in Section 1374, it remains to be seen what effect Ltr. Rul. 8651019 will have. As discussed at Chapter 6.2.C.1.a, Ltr. Rul. 8651019 involved a pre–TRA fiscal year C corporation (fiscal year ending 3/31) electing S status that chose to report its income on a calendar year basis and then switched to a fiscal year basis (9/30) during its first full year of operation. The effect for old Section 1374 was that the two fiscal year periods 4/1–12/31 and 1/1–9/30 were counted as 2 years for purposes of old Section 1374's 3-year test.

ENDNOTES FOR CHAPTER 6

1. Conference Committee Report H.R., Conf. Rep. No. 84, 99th Cong. 2d. Sess. (1986), II-203 (hereinafter referred to as Conference Report).

2. It should be noted that prior to the Subchapter S Revision Act of 1982, there used to be a Section 1374 entitled "Corporation Net Operating Loss Allowed to Shareholders." This Section 1374 will be called "former Section 1374," and no discussion will be made in the text unless specifically designated.

3. See, e.g., *Warrensburg Board & Paper Corp.*, 77 T.C. 1107 (1981) (former Code Section 1378 applied to gain from insurance recovery, taxpayer's motivation irrelevant).

4. Section 1222(11) defines a "net capital gain" as an excess of net long-term capital gain for the taxable year over net short-term capital loss for such year.

5. Note, the Conference Report II-203 does not discuss this point.

6. The TRA eliminated Section 1201(a)'s 28% alternative capital gains tax rate (hereinafter, the "old" Section 1201(a) tax) and substituted instead the following: The alternative capital gains tax rule is increased 34% effective for tax years beginning after 1986. However, the alternative gains tax does not apply unless the top regular corporation rate under Section 11 is higher than 34% (determined without regard to the phase-out of the lower graduated rates). Thus, the alternative tax does not apply for tax years beginning on or after July 1, 1987, when the new top 34% regular tax rate becomes fully effective. See also endnote 5, supra.

   As to how Section 1201(a)'s tax rate will apply to Section 1374 situations remains to be seen. However, for purposes of discussion, a 28% rate shall be used.

7. While endnote 1 indicates that law under old Section 1374 is to apply, there is no discussion as to what corporate tax rate is to apply—the new rate under Section 11 or the rate in effect pre–TRA (hereinafter referred to sometimes as "old Section 11 tax" or "old Section 11 rates"). For discussion purposes, the old Section 11 rate shall be used: 15% on taxable income up to $25,000, 18% on taxable income in excess of $25,000 up to $50,000, 30% on taxable income in excess of $50,000 up to $75,000, and 40% on taxable income in excess of $75,000 up to $100,000.

8. See endnote 6, supra.

9. Id.

10. Reg. Section 1.1563-1(b)(2)(ii)(c).

11. *Warrensburg Board & Paper Corp.*, endnote 3.

12. These computation steps were taken from I.R.S. Publication 589, "Tax Information on S Corporations" (1985).

13. This assumes the old Section 11 corporate tax rate remains in effect.

14. This assumes that this pre–TRA tax rate will be the one used.

15. See discussion of endnotes 1, 6, and 7, supra.

16. The top corporate tax rate for C corporations in 1988 and thereafter will be 34%; for 1987, a blended rate applies: for calendar year C corporations the top rate will be 40% while for fiscal year C corporations ending June 30, the top rate will be 46%.

17. Reg. Section 1.1372-4(b)(5)(vi) adopted under former Section 1372.

18. Rev. Rul. 78-307, 1978-2 C.B. 222.

19. *Feingold* v *Comm.*, 49 T.C. 461 (1968).

20. Rev. Rul. 76-48, 1976-1 C.B. 265.

21. Ltr. Rul. 7907059.

22. *McIlhinney* v. *Comm.*, Para. 79, 473 P-H Memo T.C. (1979), aff'd without published opinion, 642 F. 2d 442 (3rd Cir. 1981).

23. Ltr. Rul. 7718007.

24. Rev. Rul. 64-232, 1964-2 C.B. 334.

25. Rev. Rul. 65-83, 1965-1 C.B. 430.

26. Id.

27. Rev. Rul. 75-349, 1975-2 C.B. 349.

28. Rev. Rul. 65-40, 1965-1 C.B. 429 (short-term leasing).

29. Rev. Rul. 81-197, 1981-2 C.B. 166.

30. Id.

31. Ltr. Rul. 8211103.

32. Rev. Rul. 71-407, 1971-2 C.B. 318.

33. An example where interest was excluded is found in Ltr. Rul. 8515056 where a corporation developed and sold lots on an installment basis charging interest on the financing.

34. *Llewellyn* v. *Comm.*, 70 T.C. 370 (1978).

35. Rev. Rul. 71-455, 1971-2 C.B. 310.

36. Sections 1374(a) and 1374(d)(2). Because Section 1374's tax applies for 10 years from conversion, from C status, this is why Section 1374 is referred to as the "10-year-taint rule" in regard to former C corporate assets owned by the S corporation.

37. Sections 1374(a) and 1374(d)(2).

38. Section 1374(d)(2)(A).

39. I.R.B. 1986–49.

40. I.R.B. 22, 1986–51.

41. It should be noted that concurrent Resolution No. 395, Section 74, if adopted would have required that these qualified individuals own the stock in the corporation for 5 years.

42. I.R.B. 1986-49.

7

Basis and Losses: Passive Loss Rules

Chapters 4 and 5 discussed, basically, how to determine S corporate income and expense as well as which items are passed through to shareholders as separately stated items and which are not. Chapters 7 and 8 will now discuss briefly how these items of income, expense, and so on, which have been reported on the shareholder's individual tax returns are distributed to the shareholders. Two concepts will be discussed: basis and accumulated adjustments account.

7.1 WHEN A SHAREHOLDER TAKES ITEMS OF INCOME, LOSS, AND SO ON, INTO ACCOUNT

Section 1377(a)(1) prescribes that for taxable years beginning after 1982, all items of income, loss, credits, and deductions that pass through to the shareholders are to be allocated on a per share, per day basis. Section 1366(a)(1) prescribes that items of income, loss, and so on are reported by the shareholders in the shareholder's taxable year that includes the last day of the S corporation's year. Chapter 4.1 detailed the two categories of income that pass through to the shareholders: separately stated items (e.g., capital gains and losses, Section 1231 gains and losses, charitable contributions; see Chapter 4.1.A) and nonseparately stated items (i.e., Form 1120S, page 1, line 21; see Chapter 4.1.B).

A. Taxable Year of Inclusion

In regard to determining how much income should be reported by an S shareholder, two situations could arise: when a shareholder is an S shareholder for the entire year and when ownership changes.

1. When Stock Ownership Remains Unchanged

If an S shareholder remains as such for the entire year, the method to determine each S shareholder's income, loss, and so on is relatively simple under Section 1377(a)(1). Basically, the items of income, loss, and so on are multiplied by the stock percentage of each shareholder and are reported on the shareholder's Form 1120S, K-1. An example will illustrate:

EXAMPLE 7-1

A, Inc., a calendar year S corporation, is composed of two shareholders, X and Y, sisters, who own 50 shares each. They have both held their stock interest for the entire year of 19X7. In 19X7, A, Inc., has ordinary income of $60,000 (Form 1120S, page 1, line 21). X and Y would each report $30,000 of income for the year 19X7.

2. Change of Stock Ownership During the Year

Initially, it should be noted that a sale of stock will have no effect on the amount of the S corporation's income or loss for the year. In regard to determining how much income, loss, and so on each shareholder reports, it is necessary to do a three-part test as set forth in I.R.S. Publication 589, "Tax Information on S Corporations" (1986) at page 9. The three-part test to determine the amount to be reported per share is as follows:

1. Divide the item by the number of days in the S corporation's tax year (to figure the daily amount of the item).

2. Multiply the daily amount of the item by the percentage of stock owned by the shareholder on that day (to figure the shareholder's daily part of the daily amount of the items).

3. Total the shareholder's daily parts of the daily amount of the item (to figure the shareholder's pro-rata share of the item for the tax year).

The example below will illustrate how the three-part test works, except that a shorthand version has been used:

EXAMPLE 7-2

Assume the same facts as in Example 7-1, except that Y sells 25 of her shares in A, Inc., 90 days before the end of the year to Z. Z is a qualified S shareholder. The shareholders will report the $60,000 of corporate income as follows:

STEP 1

Shareholder	% of Stock	% of Year	% for Year
X	50%	100.0%	50.000%
Y	50	75.3[*]	37.650
	25	24.7[†]	6.175
Z	25	24.7[†]	6.175
			100.000%

[*] 275/365.
[†] 90/365.

STEP 2

Total amount of income:	X (50% × $60,000)	= $30,000
Total amount of income:	Y [(37.65% + 6.175%) × $60,000] =	26,295
Total amount of income:	Z (6.175% × $60,000)	= 3,705
	Total	$60,000

TAX POINTER

> Note, under the pro-rata allocation method, an S shareholder transferring stock at some time during the S corporate year, unless the books are closed for the shareholder pursuant to Sections 1362(e)(3) or (e)(6)(D) (Chapters 10.7.A.2 and 10.7.C), the shareholder will be entitled to deduct a proportionate amount of income, loss, and so on, even though such items might have been incurred at a time when the shareholder did not own stock in the S corporation.

B. Specific Situations for Reporting S Corporate Income, Loss, and So On

1. Death of a Shareholder

When a shareholder dies, Section 1366(a)(1) prescribes that his or her pro rata share of income, loss deductions, and credits up to the date of death are includible on the decedent's final Form 1040. In regard to items of income, loss, and so on after the decedent's death, these items are reported by the decedent's estate or heirs acquiring the decedent's stock. (As to the valuation to the decedent's stock for estate tax purposes, see Chapter 9.11.A.)

2. Closing of the Books of the S Corporation—Section 1362(e)(3)

As discussed at Chapter 10.7.A.2, a selling shareholder pursuant to Section 1362(e)(3) can have the books of the S corporation closed. Accordingly, the reader is directed to Chapter 10.7.A.2 for the specific provisions regarding closing of the books.

3. Change of More than 50% Interest in the S Corporation— Section 1362(e)(6)(D)

Section 1362(e)(6)(D) mandates that the corporate books of the S corporation have to be closed on the date when there is a change in ownership greater than 50% in the S corporation in the event there is termination of S status. (See Chapter 10.7.C for a discussion of the specific provisions regarding this area.)

C. Termination of S Shareholder Status

For the consequences of what happens if the S corporation's status is terminated pursuant to Section 1362(d), see generally Chapters 10.1 through 10.7.

D.   Elections That Affect the Computation of Income, Expense, and So On

Section 1363(c) prescribes that elections that affect the computation of items derived from an S corporation are generally made by the corporation except for the three elections that are made separately by each shareholder. These three shareholders' elections are limitations on "investment indebtedness" interest (for a discussion of the term "investment indebtedness" interest, see Chapter 5.2); Section 617, deduction and recapture of certain mining exploration expenditures; and Section 901, taxes paid to foreign countries and U.S. possessions.

E.   Year in Which Items Are Included

As discussed at Chapter 1.4.A, it is possible that an S corporation could have a taxable year different from its shareholders. The rules of Section 1366(a)(1) set forth in the introductory part of Chapter 7.1 apply to require that the items of income, loss, and so on are picked up in the taxable year by the S shareholder that includes the last day of the S corporation year. Thus, for example, assume that the S corporation was on a permitted fiscal year of October 31, 1987 and the S shareholders were calendar year taxpayers, the S corporate items of income, loss, and so on, for the fiscal year ended 10/31/87 are reported on the S shareholder's tax returns for 1987.

7.2   BASIS

A.   The Importance of Basis—The Road Map

Section 1366(d) prescribes that S corporate losses and deductions that pass through to shareholders are deductible by the shareholders to the extent that the shareholders have basis in stock and loans to the S corporation. Accordingly, it is important to determine how to compute basis so that if losses occur, the S corporate shareholders can deduct them on their tax returns.

B.   How to Compute Stock Basis

1.   Cost Basis

While the Code prescribes various provisions regarding adjustment to basis, there is no express statutory provision defining how to compute stock basis and, for that matter, debt basis. The general code provisions dealing with basis apply, that is, Section 351 to cover capital contributions, date of death value (or the alternate valuation date if it applies) for valuing stock acquired by inheritance, and so on.

2. Increases in Basis—Section 1367(a)(1)

Once cost basis has been determined, Section 1367(a)(1) prescribes certain increases in basis. These are as follows:

1. Separately stated items of income (Section 1367(a)(1)(A)) (capital gains, Section 1231 gains, etc.). (See Chapters 4.1.A, 4.4, and 4.5 for a full discussion of this topic.)
2. Nonseparately stated items of income (Section 1367(a)(1)(B)) (the S corporation ordinary income found on Form 1120S, page 1, line 21). (See Chapter 4.1.B for a full discussion of this topic.)
3. Excess of the deduction for depletion over the basis of the property subject to depletion.

3. Decreases in Basis—Sections 1367(a)(2)(A)–(E)

The decreases to cost basis are as follows:

1. Distributions that are not includible in the shareholder's income (Section 1367(a)(2)(A)). Items in this category would be distribution of items that have already been taxed to the shareholder (e.g., accumulated adjustment account (AAA), previously taxed income (PTI). (See Chapters 8.3 and 8.4 for a discussion of this topic.)
2. Separately stated items of loss and deduction (Section 1367(a)(2)(B)) (e.g., capital losses, Section 1231 losses). (See Chapters 4.1.A, 4.4, and 4.5 for a discussion of this topic.)
3. Nonseparately computed loss (Section 1367(a)(2)(C)) (this is the shareholder's share of "taxable loss" on Form 1120S, page 1, line 21). (See Chapter 4.1.B for a full discussion of this topic.)
4. Corporate expense not deductible in computing taxable income and not properly chargeable to a capital account (Section 1367(a)(2)(D)) (e.g., fines and penalties).
5. The amount of the shareholder's deductions for depletion of oil and gas wells under Section 611 (Section 1367(a)(2)(E)).

4. Investment Tax Credit Adjustment

Under pre–TRA law, taxpayers, if investment credit property was involved, would generally be required to reduce basis of property by 50% of the investment tax credit allowed (unless the taxpayer elected to take a lesser credit). If asset basis had been reduced, and there was investment tax credit recapture due to a disposition of the asset, sale, and so on, Section 48(q)(6) prescribes that the basis of the asset is increased by 50% of the recapture. Therefore, S corporate shareholders must increase their basis in their stock to reflect the change in basis.

5.   Other Items Affecting Basis

a.   *Items Must Be Reported—Section 1367(b)(1) and Section 6241– 6245 Requirements*

Section 1367(b)(1) prescribes basically that for basis of an S corporate shareholder to be adjusted for pass-through items of income, loss, and so on, the items affecting basis are to be reported on the shareholder's tax return. Sections 6241–6245, as discussed at Chapter 9.18, have prescribed certain audit requirements. Accordingly, in regard to basis, treatment of S corporate items must be reported on the shareholder's return consistent with the treatment of the items on the S corporation return. Thus, there will be a symmetry between basis for the S corporate shareholder and the amount of income, loss, and so on that the shareholder reports on his, her, or its tax return.

b.   *Basis Cannot Be Reduced Below Zero*

Section 1367(a)(2) prescribes that basis can never be adjusted below zero. Thus, any losses in excess of basis are carried over and deducted in the year when basis is restored. (See discussion at Chapter 7.2.D.3.b.)

c.   *Shareholders Cannot Use Unsecured Demand Promissory Notes to Create Basis*

Rev. Rul. 81-187[1] prescribes that a shareholder cannot use an unsecured demand promissory note payable to the corporation for the purchase of stock to establish basis. When the note is paid, basis will then be increased by the amount of the payment under the note.

d.   *Section 1244 Stock*

See Chapter 9.13 for a discussion of this topic.

e.   *Worthless Stock*

See Chapter 7.6 for discussion of this topic.

f.   *Section 465—"At-Risk" Rules*

See Chapter 5.10 for a discussion of this topic.

6. Examples of Application of the Basis Rules

Set forth below are examples of the application of the basis rules:

EXAMPLE 7-3

A, Inc., is a calendar year S corporation composed of one shareholder, B. In 19X7, A, Inc., had the following items on its tax return (no distributions were made during the year):

Capital stock	$10,000*
Ordinary income, Form 1120S, page 1, line 21	6,000
Charitable contributions	600
Penalty	200

* This equaled B's cost basis for the stock.

B's basis is computed as follows:

Basis, beginning of the year		$10,000
Increases:		
Ordinary income		6,000
Decreases:		
Penalty	(200)	
Charitable contributions	(600)	800
Basis, end of year		$15,200

EXAMPLE 7-4

Assume the same facts as in Example 7-3, but that C acquired his stock in A, Inc., because of B's death (the estate tax valuation was $15,000). C's basis at the beginning of 19X7 would be $15,000, not $10,000, and C's ending basis would be $20,200. (For a discussion of step-up in basis at death, see Chapter 9.11.A.)

EXAMPLE 7-5

Assume the same facts as in Example 7-3, except that instead of having income of $6,000, it was a loss of $6,000. B's basis for 19X7 would be $3,200 computed as follows:

Basis, beginning of the year		$10,000
Decrease:		
Penalty	(200)	
Charitable contributions	(600)	
Loss	(6,000)	6,800
Basis, end of year		$ 3,200

C. Debt Basis

Besides having basis in stock, an S corporate shareholder pursuant to Section 1367(b)(2)(A) can have basis if the shareholder lends money to the S corporation either by a note or by "open account" (i.e., checks, cash, and so on, where no note is signed by the corporation). Section 1367(b)(2)(A) prescribes that once stock basis of a shareholder is reduced to zero by the items affecting basis as set forth in Section 1367(a)(2)(B)–(E) (see Chapter 7.2.B.3.b–e) any excess items reducing basis are applied to reduce (but not below zero) shareholder's basis in debt. Reg. Section 1.1376-2(b)(3), promulgated under former Section 1376, the predecessor to Section 1367, states that if there is more than one indebtedness, the reduction shall be applied to each such indebtedness in proportion to the basis of the various debts.

D. What Constitutes Debt

Because of the importance of debt, there have been a number of cases, rulings, and so on, defining the term. Initially, case law holds that debt means debt owing by the corporation to the shareholder, not to a third party.

1. Guarantee of Shareholders

Generally, the case law indicates that the guarantee of corporate debt will not increase basis. However, Rev. Rul. 70–50[2] prescribes that when the shareholder makes a payment under the guarantee, basis is increased by the amount of the payment. (But, see *Selfe* v. *U.S.*,[3] which held that a shareholder who guaranteed a corporate debt is entitled to a factual determination as to whether this debt is eligible for basis for S corporate basis purposes.) A variation of the guarantee occurs when a shareholder substitutes his, her, or its note for a guarantee of a corporate debt. Rev. Rul. 75-144[4] holds that a shareholder's substitution of his own note for his corporation's note to a bank, which then released the corporation from its liability, resulted in basis to the shareholder equal to the face of the note. In regard to a situation that will not generate basis, Rev. Rul. 69-125[5] prescribes that debt does not include loans made by a partnership composed of the shareholders.

For a more detailed discussion of the area, the reader is directed to read the case law, rulings, and so on, discussing this area.

2. Worthlessness of Debt

For a discussion of this area, see Chapter 7.6.

3. The Mechanics of Debt as It Applies to Basis

As discussed in the introductory part to Chapter 7.2.C, debt comes into play to absorb S corporate losses after stock basis is reduced to zero.

a. *How Is Debt Value Determined for Section 1367(b)(2)(A)*

For purposes of shareholder's debt, the shareholder's basis for the debt will generally be cost as per Section 1012. However, if the debt is generated in a Section 351 exchange, then the debt, by definition, will be determined by its fair market value. If the S corporation is on the accrual basis (see Chapter 1.5 for a discussion of this point) and is indebted to a shareholder, then by general tax principles, the shareholder has basis in this debt to the extent the shareholder includes the items generating debt into income.

b. *Restoration of Basis in Debt—Section 1367(b)(2)(B)*

Section 1367(b)(2)(B) prescribes that when a shareholder's basis in debt has been reduced below the shareholder's original basis in the debt, then any net increase in debt due to operations from the S corporation (i.e., the rules of Section 1367(a) discussed generally at Chapter 7.2.A–B) are to occur first before any increase in stock basis.

c. *Examples Illustrating the Debt Rules Set Forth in Chapters 7.2.C and D*

EXAMPLE 7-6

A, Inc., is a calendar year S corporation with one shareholder, D, a bachelor. A, Inc., commences operations on 1/1/X7. D's stock basis is $5,000, and he lends the corporation $10,000 by means of a note. At the end of its first year of operations, A, Inc., has a loss of $12,000. A, Inc., makes no distribution to D during the taxable year. Pursuant to Section 1367(b)(2)(A), which requires that stock basis be reduced first, D has a basis of $3,000 in his debt computed as follows:

	19X7	
	Basis in Stock	Basis in Debt
Starting basis	$5,000	$10,000
$12,000 loss for the year	(5,000)	(7,000)
Basis at end of year	$ –0–	$ 3,000

EXAMPLE 7-7

Assume the same facts as in Example 7-6. In 19X8, A, Inc., has a profit of $27,000, and the corporation makes no distribution to D during the year. D's basis in this debt is $10,000, and his basis in stock is $20,000 computed as follows:

	Basis in Stock	Basis in Debt
Starting basis	$ –0–	$ 3,000
$27,000 ordinary income	20,000	7,000
Ending basis	$20,000	$10,000

TAX POINTERS

1. Note, under the law prior to the Subchapter S Revision Act of 1982, reductions to debt basis were not restored.

2. Care must be used in the operation of the basis rules to ensure that shareholders start with sufficient basis, expecially if the shareholders are incorporating a partnership or proprietorship. In *George W. Wiebusch*,[6] a proprietorship was incorporated that had liabilities in excess of basis, thereby creating a gain under Section 357(c). Consequently, under Section 358, the shareholders wound up with zero basis and thus could not deduct any S corporate losses.

3. Contrast Section 1367's rules discussed above with the partnership rules regarding debt. (See Chapter 9.10.A.2 for an illustration of this point.)

E. Payment of Shareholder's Debt, or How to Convert Ordinary Income into Capital Gains

When an S corporation repays a shareholder's debt, generally, no gain or loss is recognized to the corporation. However, if the S corporation pays the debt with property, Reg. Section 1.1001-2 and Rev. Rul. 70-271[7] prescribe that gain or loss will be recognized on the difference between the corporation's basis in the property and its fair market value (which will give rise to gain being passed through to the shareholders pursuant to Section 1366 et seq.)

As to the shareholder, a taxable transaction will result upon the repayment of the debt by the corporation, depending upon whether the debt is evidenced by a note or not. If the debt is evidenced by a note, Section 1271(a)(1) provides that the retirement of a "debt instrument"[8] is treated as an exchange that will generally create capital gains. However, if the debt is not evidenced by a note, the income generated on its collection because no debt instrument exists is treated as ordinary income.[9]

If the shareholder's loan basis has been reduced, but not to zero, a corporate payment to the shareholder of the loan cannot be applied solely to the basis portion; rather, Rev. Rul. 64-162[10] and Rev. Rul. 68-537[11] prescribe that payment must be allocated proportionately so that there is a return of basis and taxable income to the shareholders.

When there are several debts owed to a shareholder-creditor at the time of repayment, the Tax Court has held in *Sam Novell*[12] that a portion of the payment shall be recognized into income pursuant to a formula. The formula used is as follows:

> We think that the fraction of any payments in 1964 which represents income should have as its numerator the difference between the face amount of the total indebtedness to the shareholder and the shareholder's basis therein, and as its denominator the total indebtedness. By "total indebtedness" we mean the aggregate of the balance of Accounts No. 1 and No. 2 at the time of such payments. Para. 70,031 P-H Memo T.C. at 111.

TAX POINTER

> There is always the risk that debt could be classified as equity. See, for example, *Harbour Properties, Inc.*[13] See also the discussion at Chapter 2.9.B.

7.3 TIMING OF BASIS DETERMINATIONS

Although Section 1366(d) is not entirely clear on this point, it appears that income items will increase basis before loss items are taken. If a shareholder sells stock during a year, and the S corporation incurs a loss for the year, the shareholder's basis on the date of sale will be determinative. Further, a shareholder can apply losses against basis in stock even if the stock has been sold during the year. An example will illustrate:

EXAMPLE 7-8

A, Inc., a calendar year S corporation, has two shareholders, B and C, who are brothers. In 19X7, B sells his shares to D, a permitted S shareholder, for $10,000. B basis in his stock on 1/1/X7 is $10,000. Prior to the sale, B lends the corporation $2,000 by a note. The corporation does not close its books on B's sale pursuant to Section 1362(e)(3). (See discussion at Chapter 10.7.A.2.) It is determined that A, Inc., had a loss for 19X7 and that B's share of the loss is $11,000 for the period B held his stock. B has sufficient basis to take the loss—$10,000 of stock and $1,000 of loan. Because B has no basis in his stock due to the allocation of the $10,000 of loss for the year 19X7, B will have a gain of $10,000 arising from the sale of stock ($10,000 − zero basis). (As to the tax consequence that will occur when A, Inc., pays B's debt of $2,000, see Chapter 7.2.E.) D's basis in the stock is $10,000, the cost basis for the stock.

A.   The Mechanics of the Basis Computations

In terms of the mechanics of the rules to compute basis, Reg. Section 1.1376-2(a)(3), adopted under former Section 1376, the predecessor to Section 1367, prescribes that basis reduction is made as of the close of the year for stock held at year end, and if the stock has been sold before the end of the year, the reduction is made as of the day before the stock is sold. Similarly, items of income, loss, and so on are generally allocated on a per share, per day basis as discussed generally in Chapter 10.8 to the point of sale. As to losses, Reg. Section 1.1376-2(a)(2) prescribes that the basis of each share is reduced by the shareholder's portion of losses and reductions attributable to each share. If the same number of shares are held by the shareholder during the year, then the calculation is relatively simple. An example will illustrate:

EXAMPLE 7-9

A, Inc., a calendar year S corporation is composed of two equal shareholders, X and Y, who own 50 shares each. Both shareholders have equal basis in their shares, to wit, $20 per share. In the first year of operation A, Inc., had a loss of $300, or $3 per share. Thus, X and Y's individual basis is $850 each ($20 − $3) × 50.

It becomes complicated when a shareholder has different batches of stock during the year. The example found at Reg. Section 1.1376-2(a)(2)(ii), which is set forth below, offers an illustration:

EXAMPLE 7-10

A's pro-rata share of the corporation's net operating loss for the taxable year is $100. This amount is attributable to three shares of stock held by A during the taxable year; one of which was owned by him during the entire year and the other two of which were acquired by him in the middle of the year. The amount of the pro-rata share of the loss attributable to each share is as follows:

Share No. 1 (owned for the entire year)	$50
Share No. 2 (owned for one-half year)	25
Share No. 3 (owned for one-half year)	25

The reduction in basis of share No. 1 is $50, and the reduction in basis of shares No. 2 and No. 3 is $25 each. Assume that the adjusted basis of the three shares of stock prior to this reduction is as follows:

Share No. 1	$40
Share No. 2	45
Share No. 3	35

After the reduction in basis by the amount of the loss attributable to each share, the basis of the shares is as follows:

Share No. 1	$ 0
Share No. 2	20
Share No. 3	10

The $10 excess of the basis reduction allocable to share No. 1 over the basis of that share is applied to reduce the basis of shares No. 2 and No. 3 in proportion to their remaining basis. Therefore, $6.67 of such excess reduces the basis of share No. 2, and $3.33 of such excess reduces the basis of share No. 3. After this reduction the shares have the following basis:

Share No. 1	$ 0
Share No. 2	13.33
Share No. 3	6.67

With respect to debt and the stock reduction rules set forth in Reg. Section 1.1376-2, they have no interchange except that Section 1367(b)(2) prescribes that debt cannot supply basis until after stock basis is exhausted. Furthermore, if debt is not done on a pro-rata basis by the shareholders, besides running the risk of a second class of stock classification if the debt is not incurred correctly (see Chapter 2.9.B), one shareholder could obtain losses and the other not. An example will illustrate:

EXAMPLE 7-11

A, Inc., is composed of two equal shareholders, B and C, both brothers. In 19X7 B lends A, Inc., $8,000 pursuant to the safe harbor rules set forth in Section 1361(c)(5). (See Chapter 2.9.B.2 for a description of the safe harbor rules.) B's stock basis, due to acquiring stock at various times during the year is $10,000 and C's basis is $9,000. In 19X7 A, Inc., had a loss of $24,000 that is allocable to B pursuant to Reg. Section 1.1376-2(b) in the amount of $11,000 and C $13,000. C will be only able to deduct $9,000, with $4,000 of loss being carried over ($13,000 − $9,000 of stock basis); B, however, will be able to deduct the entire $11,000 of loss ($10,000 of stock basis + $1,000 of debt basis). If the shareholders had lent the corporation $4,000 each, then C would have sufficient basis to deduct the loss.

7.4   THE SECTION 1366(d) RULES

A.   Section 1366(d)(1)—Losses Cannot Exceed Basis in Stock and Debt

Section 1366(d)(1) prescribes that the aggregate amount of losses and deductions that a shareholder can basically take in a tax year cannot exceed the shareholder's adjusted basis in stock and debt. If the loss exceeds the shareholder's adjusted basis in stock and debt, then it is carried over to the next year as per Section 1366(d)(2). (See Chapter 7.4.B.)

B.   Section 1366(d)(2)—Carryover Losses

Section 1366(d)(2) prescribes that if a loss is not used in one year because of insufficient basis in stock and debt, it is to be treated as incurred in the following year, and if it cannot be used in that following year, then it is to be carried over indefinitely so long as the S corporate election remains in effect. As to what occurs with losses after the S election terminates, see Section 1366(d)(3). (See Chapter 7.4.C.) An example will illustrate the effect of carryover losses:

EXAMPLE 7-12

A, Inc., was formed on 1/1/87 and elected S status. It has one shareholder, Laurie, who acquired stock for $10,000. At the end of the first year of operation, A, Inc., had an ordinary loss of $13,000. Laurie, pursuant to Section 1366(d)(1), took a deduction of an ordinary loss of $10,000 on her Form 1040, the amount of her basis in A, Inc.'s stock carrying over the $3,000 to 19X8 pursuant to Section 1366(d)(2). (No distributions were made during the year.) In 19X8, A, Inc., broke even, however, Laurie lent $3,000 to A, Inc. Laurie, pursuant to Sections 1366(d)(2) and 1367 will report an ordinary loss of $3,000 in 19X8.

C.   Section 1366(d)(3)—Carryover of Disallowed Losses in Posttermination Years

Section 1366(d)(3) prescribes that if an S corporation has unused losses or deductions when the S election terminates, such losses or deductions will be treated as if they were incurred by the shareholder on the last day of the S corporation's "posttermination transition period" (defined at Chapter 7.4.C.1), however, the losses and deductions are to be allowed only to the extent the losses and deductions reduce basis in stock (not loans) to zero. Further, Section 1366(d)(3) prescribes that if any losses or deductions are not so used, they are lost forever.

1.   Posttermination Transition Period—Section 1371(e)

Section 1371(e) defines a posttermination transition period as the 1-year period after the date of termination (see Chapter 10 generally for a definition of termination of S status) or 120 days after a determination is made on audit that the election had involuntarily terminated. See Chapter 8.6 for a more detailed discussion of this point.

7.5 IDENTITY OF PASS-THROUGH LOSSES

Chapter 5 detailed the deductions that passed through to shareholders as well as discussed the characterization that might occur (e.g., the hobby loss rules of Section 183 discussed at Chapter 5.11). Besides the normal problems of deductions for expenses and losses (i.e., is an item an expense or capital expenditure), there is the problem as to how to characterize losses in excess of basis. An example will illustrate:

EXAMPLE 7-13

B is the sole shareholder in A, Inc., and has $1,000 of basis in stock. A, Inc., in 19X7 has the following: an ordinary loss of $2,000 and a capital loss of $6,000.

Unfortunately, the Code offers no specific guidance as to allocation of these losses; however, practitioners usually follow the partnership rules set forth in Reg. Section 1.704-1(d) in regard to this problem. Reg. Section 1.704-1(d) allocates the losses pro rata. Thus, in Example 7-13, B would take $250 of ordinary loss—($2,000/[$6,000 + $2,000]) × $1,000—and $750 of capital loss—($6,000/[$6,000 + $2,000]) × $1,000.

As to the balance of unused losses—to wit, $1,750 of ordinary loss ($2,000 − $250) and $5,250 of capital loss ($6,000 − $750)—these losses are carried forward pursuant to Section 1366(d)(2) until basis is acquired. Further, their character will remain the same, that is, $5,250 of capital losses and $1,750 of ordinary losses.

TAX POINTER

It is important that accurate records be kept to establish basis. For instance, there have been cases where a taxpayer was unable to deduct the loss because of his inability to prove his basis for his S corporate stock. See, for example, *Donald J. Sauvigne*.[14]

7.6 SECTIONS 165(g) AND 166(d)'S RULES—SECTION 1367(b)(3)

Section 1367(b)(3) prescribes that the basis rules of Section 1366 that limit the deduction of losses to the amount of shareholder's basis are applied first before the application of Section 165(g) and 166(d) to any taxable year of the shareholder in which the stock or debt of the S corporation becomes worthless. Section 165(g) prescribes that if stock, which is a capital asset, becomes worthless during the taxable year, the loss is a capital loss. Section 166(d) prescribes that if a nonbusiness bad debt[15] becomes worthless, the loss is a capital loss. The example below will illustrate the effect of Section 1367(b)(3):

EXAMPLE 7-14

A, Inc., a calendar year S corporation has one shareholder, D. D's beginning basis in stock in 19X7 is $10,000. During 19X7, A, Inc., has an operating loss of $8,000 and goes bankrupt. The loss for D is computed as follows:

Stock basis before loss	$10,000
Deductible net operating loss	8,000
Stock basis	2,000
Capital loss due to stock becoming worthless	2,000
Stock basis	$–0–

7.7 HOW TO CREATE BASIS SO THAT CURRENT LOSSES CAN BE DEDUCTIBLE

While Section 1366(d)(2) allows S corporate losses to be carried over if a shareholder has insufficient basis in stock and/or debt, obviously, as a general rule, it is better to deduct S corporate losses currently rather than defer. Thus, care should be taken to review the S corporation books prior to the end of the taxable year to determine if it is operating at a gain or loss, and if it is operating at a loss, determine if the shareholders have enough basis in their stock and/or debt to take the loss. If there is not sufficient basis, the shareholders can undertake several steps to correct the problem; namely, if there is sufficient time, try to generate additional income to counteract the loss or contribute funds or property before the end of the year to establish basis. As to the second alternative, care must be exercised. Initially, the shareholder(s) may not have the funds to "pump into" the S corporation to take the losses. Thus, the shareholders may wish to "cut their losses" and leave the S corporation in limbo or terminate the S election, thereby creating a C corporation with future net operating (i.e., it will incur losses in C years) losses that can be marketed as a "loss corporation." Assuming that the shareholders have the funds and the desire to place them in the S corporation, the question to resolve is how to make this additional input—loan or acquire additional stock. As discussed at Chapter 2.9.B.1, the shareholders may wish to be creditors rather than just mere shareholders and lend money to the corporation to obtain basis. However, as Chapter 2.9.B, Example 7-11, and so on, illustrate, being the creditor of an S corporation could cause adverse tax consequences. As to guaranteeing a corporate debt, substitution of a shareholder's note for the S corporate note, and so on, to create basis, these points were discussed at Chapter 7.2.C.

There have been a number of cases, rulings, and so on in the area regarding the creation of basis and the reader is directed to consult these cases, rulings, and so on, for application to a particular situation.

7.8 PREPARER PENALTIES AND BASIS

In *Meyer Papermaster* v. *U.S.*,[16] a tax return preparer (a CPA and an attorney) had a preparer penalty imposed against him for negligence when he deducted an S corporate loss in excess of the shareholder's basis in stock in violation of Section 1374(c).

7.9 PASSIVE INCOME AND LOSSES

A. Introduction

The thrust of the TRA is to prevent taxpayers from using both net losses from passive activities and credits arising from passive activities to offset other income to reduce tax attributable to other activities. To accomplish this objective, Congress adopted or amended a number of provisions, with one major provision being Section 469, "Passive Activity Losses and Credit Limited," which is effective for taxable years beginning after 12/31/86.

While it is beyond the scope of this book to provide a detailed discussion of Section 469, a brief general discussion as it applies to S corporations and its shareholders is set forth below. It is to be noted that because an S corporation can be a limited partner as well as involved in real estate ventures, discussion is briefly made of these areas. Because the discussion is cursory, the reader is referred to the Senate and Conference Committee Reports and the General Explanation of the Tax Reform Act of 1986 prepared by the Staff of the Joint Committee on Taxation (hereinafter referred to as the "Blue Book") issued in connection with the TRA and the regulations to be promulgated for a fuller discussion of this area.

Under the passive loss rules, Section 469(e) places all income into three categories:

1. Active income (e.g., salary, bonuses, etc.).
2. Portfolio income (e.g., dividends, interest) (for the definition of portfolio income, see Chapter 7.9.C).
3. Income from passive activities (e.g., a limited partner's interest in a partnership).

Losses from passive activities, generally, can be used to offset only passive income, with any unused losses carried forward to future years and applied against passive income.[17] In the event that the taxpayer disposes of his or her or its entire interest in the passive activities, unused losses are allowed in full.[18]

In the event that tax credits are generated from the passive activity (other than foreign tax credits), they can only offset the tax payable on passive income.[19]

1.   Taxpayers Subject to the Rules

The passive loss rules of Section 469(a)(1) apply to individuals, estates, trusts, personal service corporations, and closely held corporations.[20] Thus, shareholders of S corporations are subject to the passive loss rules.

2.   Exceptions to the Passive Loss Rules

Sections 469(c)(3) and 469(c)(4) prescribe that a working interest[21] in an oil or gas property is not classified as a passive activity regardless of the participation of the taxpayer. Thus, losses and credits that are generated from a working interest in oil or gas property can be used in toto to offset taxpayer's income from other activities. However, Section 469(c)(3)(A) prescribes that if one is to take advantage of this exception to the general rule regarding passive losses, the taxpayer must hold the working interest directly or through an entity that will not limit his liability in regard to the activity involved. It remains to be seen if Section 469(c)(3) and Section 469(c)(4)'s exception applies to a shareholder in an S corporation that owns a working interest where the shareholder materially participates in the corporation.

3.   Examples of How the Passive Loss Rules Generally Work

Examples illustrating how the passive loss rules generally work are set forth below.

EXAMPLE 7-15

19X1

Taxpayer as a limited partner in 19X1 is involved in two tax shelters— shelter A produces $10,000 losses and shelter B produces $4,000 of income. Taxpayer's $4,000 of income is sheltered by $4,000 of losses. The $6,000 of unused losses is carried forward to future tax years.

19X2

Taxpayer as a limited partner still has an investment in the two tax shelters except that shelter A has no income or loss and shelter B the same $4,000 of income. Taxpayer applies the $6,000 of carryforward passive loss to the $4,000 of income, thereby leaving remaining as a carryforward $2,000 of losses.

4. Definition of Passive Activities

Section 469(c) defines two types of passive activities that produce passive income and loss:

1. Any trade or business, or to the extent as defined in the regulations, any activity conducted for profit, in which the taxpayer does not materially participate (Section 469(c)(1))

2. Any rental activity whether or not the taxpayer materially participates (Section 469(c)(2))

a. *Material Participation*

As the above description of passive activities indicates, Section 469(c)(1) contains material participation in its definition. Material participation is defined in Section 469(h) as involvement in the operation of the activity on a regular, continuous, and substantial basis. In regard to material participation the following should be noted:

1. The material participation standard is applied to a taxpayer (or his or her spouse) who owns an interest in the business as a proprietor, general partner, or S corporate shareholder.

2. The regular, continuous, and substantial standard applies both to individuals who own an interest in a trade or business directly and to those who own an interest in an activity conducted by a pass-through entity (such as an S corporate shareholder). Thus, within an S corporation, there could be shareholders who materially participate and whose income thus will be active and those that do not materially participate and whose income will be classified as passive. Likewise, presumably, the S corporation is subject to the material participation standards regarding classification of income. Thus, if the S corporation is a limited partner in a partnership, the income or loss received from the venture presumably will be treated as passive (see discussion below about limited partnership interest). If the S corporation is engaged in rental real estate activities, then by Section 469(c)(2) presumptively the income received from the venture will be passive.

3. The taxpayer's material participation in an activity is determined separately for each year.[22] Thus, the characterization of income and loss in an S corporation shareholder's Form K-1 will depend on the participation of the shareholder in the S corporation.

4. Temporary Passive Loss Regulations Section 1.469-5T issued on February 19, 1988 further clarified material participation by establishing three tests—A quantitative test based on the number of hours the taxpayer participates in the activity, a qualitative test based on prior performance before the passive loss rules took effect and a facts and circumstances test. In regard to the quantitative test of participation there are four types, all based on hours of participation. For instance, Temp. Reg. Section 1.469-5T(a)(2) states that a taxpayer will be deemed to materially participate if he or she participates in the activity (which is undefined) for more than 500 hours during the tax year. As to the qualitative test, Temp. Reg. Section 1.469-5T(a)(5) prescribes that a taxpayer will be deemed to materially participate if the taxpayer materially participates in the activity for any five of the preceding ten years. For purposes of the facts and circumstances test, future regulations will define this area; however, the fact that a taxpayer satisfies other participation standards such as Code Section 1402's standard for self-employment tax generally is not considered in determining whether a taxpayer materially participates for Section 469. Further, if the taxpayer does not participate in an activity for more than a hundred hours during the tax year, the taxpayer cannot satisfy the facts and circumstances test for the year.

Besides the Temporary Regulations defining material participation, the Regulations also create a new category, "significant participation." Temp. Reg. Section 1.469-2T(f)(2) defines "significant participation" as an activity (other than a rental activity) where the taxpayer participates more than 100 hours. If one significantly participates in an activity then the portion which is deemed significant participation is treated as not being from a passive activity. So, a taxpayer who is shareholder in an S corporation will be able to report S corporate income and loss as active if the shareholders during the tax year participate in the activity for over 500 hours.

In regard to determining whether income or loss allocated by an S corporation or partnership to a shareholder or partner is passive, Temp. Reg. Section 1.469-2T(e)(1) provides that participation is determined for the tax year of the entity, not the taxpayer's. An example will illustrate:

Example 7–16

A, a calendar year individual, is a shareholder in an S corporation that has a taxable year ending on January 31, 1988. During its taxable year ending on January 31, 1988, the S corporation engages in a single trade or business activity. For the period from February 1, 1987 through January

31, 1988, A does not materially participate in this activity. In A's calendar year 1988 return, A's distributive share of the S corporation's gross income and deductions from the activity must be treated as a passive activity gross income and passive activity deductions, without regard to A's participation in the activity from February 1, 1988, through December 31, 1988.

5. Temp. Reg. Section 1.469-5T(e) provides that if a taxpayer is both a general limited partner in a partnership, providing the taxpayer is deemed to be materially participating as a partner, then, the taxpayer will be deemed to materially participate throughout despite the fact that the taxpayer owns a limited partnership interest. Thus, if an S corporation owns a general and limited partnership interest in a partnership, and it materially participates as a partner, then all of its income and loss from the partnership will be active income or loss. Note also, that Temp. Reg. Section 1.469-5T(e) states that despite the tenor of Section 469, a limited partner can still materially participate if the limited partner participates in the activity for more than 500 hours during the tax year, or satisfies other tests set forth in the Regulations.

TAX POINTER

Providing legal, tax, or accounting services as an independent contractor (or as an employee thereof), or what the taxpayer commonly provides as an independent contractor, would not ordinarily constitute material participation in an activity other than the activity providing the services to the public. Thus, for example, a member of a law firm who provides legal services to an S corporation engaged in research and development is not, if the lawyer invests in such an S corporation, treated as materially participating in the research and development activity by reason of such legal services.

The fact that a taxpayer utilizes employees or contract services to perform daily functions in running the business does not prevent such a taxpayer from qualifying as materially participating. However, the activities of such agents are not attributed to the taxpayer, and the taxpayer must still personally perform sufficient services to establish material participation.[23]

b. *Material Participation by Entities*

As discussed in Chapter 7.9.A.1, estates and trusts are subject to the passive loss rules. Thus, since as discussed in Chapter 2.3.B, estates and certain types of trusts can be S shareholders, the characterization of income from an S corporation will presumably depend on the material participation of the fiduciary (i.e., the executor of the estate and the trustee of the trust).[24] (Note: Regulations will define material participation trusts and estates.)

B.   Operation of the Passive Loss Rules

Provided that the taxpayer is deemed to be not materially insignificantly participating, the passive loss rules do not disallow losses and credits from a passive activity. Rather, they determine how and when the losses and credits can be claimed by a taxpayer. The determination of whether a loss is suspended under the passive loss rule is made after the application of the "at-risk" rules[25] and other rules for determining loss. Generally, Section 469(d)(1) provides that the losses from a passive loss activity are deductible only against income from that or another passive activity. Thus, if a doctor has incurred losses as a limited partner in a computer leasing deal, he or she could not offset these losses against the salary the doctor receives as a member of the hospital staff or against any portfolio income.

If passive losses exceed passive income, the disallowed losses pursuant to Section 469(b) are carried forward indefinitely and are treated as losses from passive activity in succeeding years.

TAX POINTERS

1. If a taxpayer (i.e., an S corporate shareholder) is engaged in more than one passive activity in a taxable year, Section 469(j)(4) provides that passive activity loss and credit are to be allocated among and within the activity on a pro-rata basis pursuant to regulations to be issued (the Senate Report provides that the portion of the losses that are suspended and carried forward is determined according to the ratio of net losses from an activity to the total net losses from all passive activities for the year).[26]

2. As discussed in Chapter 7.9.M, the rules regarding interest limitation have priority over the deduction for passive losses during the phase in period.

C.   Portfolio Income and Expenses

As discussed in Chapter 7.9.A, portfolio income expense, gain, and loss are excluded from passive income treatment. Thus, proper definition is required so that correct reporting can occur. Section 469(e)(1) provides special rules to determine portfolio income. Excluded from the passive loss rules are the following:

1. Gross income of the activity from interest, dividends, annuities, or royalties not derived in the ordinary course of a trade or a business.

2. Gain or loss attributable to the disposition of the property producing the interest, dividends, annuities, or royalties or held for investment.

Sections 469(e)(1)(A)(i)(II) and (III) provide that certain types of expenses are excluded in calculating passive income—those that are clearly and directly allocable to gross income in the above categories and all interest properly allocable to such interest.

In regard to portfolio income and expense the following should be noted:

1. The Senate and Conference Committee Reports offer further definition of portfolio income: portfolio dividends are dividends on C corporation stock, REIT dividends, and regulated investment company dividends. (Excluded from this definition are income from an S corporation and general or limited partnership, a lease of property, and income from a grantor trust.)[27]

2. No exception is provided for the treatment of portfolio income arising from working capital (i.e., amounts set aside for the reasonable needs of business). Although setting aside such amounts may be necessary to the trade or business, earning portfolio income with respect to such amounts is investment related and not a part of trade or business itself. Under this rule, for example, interest earned on funds set aside by an S corporation operating a shopping mall, for the purpose of expanding the mall, is treated as portfolio income and is not taken into account in determining passive income or loss from the activity of operating the shopping mall.[28] Thus, in the area of S corporations, the S corporation on the Form 1120S, K-1 will break out the portfolio income and expense separately from the corporation's passive income and loss. Likewise, an S corporate shareholder will segregate his, her, or its passive income and loss from portfolio income and expense.

3. In regard to equity-financed lending activities (i.e., where taxpayers become passive investors in partnerships or S corporations that engage in the trade or business of lending equity funds contributed by the taxpayers), for tax years beginning after 1987, Temp. Reg. Section 1.469-11T(a)(2)(i) prescribes that if the entity meets certain tests, the taxpayers will treat the income or loss realized as nonpassive.

1. Self-charged Interest

Where an individual receives interest income on debt of a pass-through entity in which he or she owns an interest, under certain circumstances, the interest may essentially be "self-charged" and thus lack economic significance.

For example, assume that a taxpayer, X, charges $100 of interest on a loan to an S corporation that is engaged in 100% passive activities. Taxpayer, besides being the creditor of this S corporation, is the sole shareholder. In form, the transaction could be viewed as giving rise to offsetting payments of interest income and pass-through interest expense, although in economic substance, the taxpayer has paid the interest to himself, herself, or itself.

Under these circumstances, it is not appropriate to treat the transaction as giving rise to portfolio interest income to the S corporation shareholder and passive interest expense for the S corporation. Rather, to the extent that a taxpayer receives interest income with respect to a loan to a pass-through entity in which he, she, or it has an ownership interest, such income should be allowed to offset the interest expense passed through to the taxpayer from the activity for the same taxable year. Thus, in respect to a situation set forth above where X reports the $100 interest income as passive income, X would either net this interest income against the passive loss received from the S corporation or add it to the passive income received by the shareholder from the S corporation.[29]

TAX POINTER

In connection with the loans, the taxpayer should consult the temporary regulations issued under Section 163 to insure proper reporting as either consumer debt, or investment interest, and so forth.

D.   Rental Activities

Rental activities subject to six exceptions found at Temp. Reg. Section 1.469-ST(j) generally are deemed passive. Section 469(j)(8) defines rental activities as any activities in which payments are principally for the use of tangible property. The Blue Book, however, exempts from passive income taxation rental activities where substantial services are performed. Accordingly, the operation of a hotel, motel, or other similar transient lodging facilities is not subject to Section 469's passive income standards unless the operator of the lodging facility is owned by owners who do not meet the material participation test. Examples of rental income activity subject to Section 469 would be long-term rentals of apartments, office equipment, automobiles, bare-boat charters, and net leases of property.

TAX POINTER

In regard to real estate activities, Section 469(i)(6) provides that for losses to be taken by a taxpayer against ordinary income, that taxpayer does not have to participate materially; rather, the taxpayer has to "participate actively." Active participation is defined as something less than material participation.[30]

E. Distinguishing Among Activities

In some situations, an activity could have both active and passive components (e.g., an S corporation could be operating a hotel and renting a building on a triple net lease). Or the venture could go from one activity to the next (e.g., an S corporation could be involved in a bare-boat rental charter for part of the year, then sell off the charter and buy rental real estate, and so on. In the first instance the difficulty is to determine how much of the activity represents passive income and loss and how much not. For instance, expenses have to be allocated to each activity—salaries, pension costs, and so on—and it may be difficult to pigeon hole the exact amounts to each activity. In the latter instance unused passive losses may be triggered by the disposition of one venture into the next. (See Chapter 7.9.G for discussion of taxable disposition.) Presumably, the Service will issue regulations so that proper allocations can be made.

F. Tax Credits

As stated previously in Chapter 7.9.A, tax credits generated by passive activities can only be used against a tax attributable to such activities. Unused credit can basically be carried forward indefinitely (not carried back). Once a credit becomes allowable under the passive loss rules, it is aggregated with the other credits (i.e., the credits arising from nonpassive activities) for purposes of determining whether it is subject to other limitations. If the aggregate credits (passive and nonpassive) cannot be used in a taxable year in which they arise, they can be applied against future income tax with all the credits staying aggregated as one, subject to the general rules regarding credits, including carryovers.

G. Taxable Dispositions

Section 469(g)(1) provides that any suspended passive losses carried forward and any losses on the sale are deductible against income when the entire interest is sold to an unrelated third party in an arm's-length taxable transaction.

Section 469(g)(3) prescribes that if an installment sale is used to sell a passive asset, passive losses are recognized as payments are made pursuant to the terms of the sale.

With respect to credits, the Code provides that the taxpayers may make a special election to adjust basis to increase it by the amount of credit suspended by the passive loss rules up to the amount of the original basis. There are certain changes that will not trigger the recognition of loss, such as a like kind exchange of the passive loss asset, except to the extent of taxable boot, a change in the form of ownership (e.g., converting from a C corporation to an S corporation), and so on. Other points to be noted are as follows:

1. If the taxpayer abandons a passive asset reporting the tax consequences (e.g., an S shareholder's stock is deemed worthless and the stockholder reports the loss pursuant to Section 165), then the taxpayer can deduct suspended passive losses.[31]

2. Section 469(g)(1)(A) prescribes a pecking order (set forth below) as to how to apply the suspended passive losses and the losses arising from disposition of the asset against income.

   a. Income or gain from the passive activity for the taxable year (including any gain recognized on the disposition)
   b. Net income or gain for the taxable year from all passive activities
   c. Any other income or gain

3. If an S corporation conducts two separate activities, and a fully taxable disposition by the corporation of all the assets used or created in one activity occurs, this sale is deemed a disposition of the S shareholder's entire interest in the activity.[32]

H. Conversion of Activities

When an activity is converted from a passive to an active one, it does not trigger the suspended passive losses from prior years; rather, Section 469(f)(1) provides that the suspended passive losses in regard to the activity are allowed against the income from that activity (or tax liability in respect to credits) to the extent of such income or tax liability even though the activity and its income are no longer passive.

TAX POINTER

Wash sales, sham transactions, and the like that are truly not sales will not trigger the recognition of suspended passive losses.[33]

I. Death of a Taxpayer

When a taxpayer dies, Section 469(g)(2) prescribes that any suspended passive losses remaining at the date of death in excess of basis in the hands of a transferee over its basis in the hands of the taxpayer are generally allowed as deductions on the taxpayer's final return.

J. Gifts of Passive Loss Property

When a taxpayer makes a gift of his or her entire interest in a passive activity, Section 469(j)(6) prescribes that the donee's basis is increased by any suspended losses, and basically the donee steps into the shoes of the donor. The gift does not trigger suspended losses[34] (although the suspended passive losses are added to the donee's basis), and the donee's basis for purposes of determining loss in a subsequent transaction cannot exceed the fair market value of the gift at the time the donee received it.[35] If the taxpayer gives away less than all the taxpayer's interest in the passive loss property, an allocable portion of any suspended loss is added to the donee's basis.

K. Nonrecognition Exchanges Under Sections 351, 721, or 1031

Section 469(g) implies that an exchange under Sections 351, 721, or 1031 does not trigger suspended passive losses; rather, the suspended passive losses continue to be treated as such in the hands of the transferee. Thus, if an individual, X, transfers his limited partnership interest in ABC, Co., to X, Inc., an S corporation in a Section 351 transaction, X, Inc., will basically step into X's shoes taking into basis X's suspended passive losses, and the like. If gain is recognized on the transaction (e.g., boot in a Section 351 transaction), the suspended passive losses are applied to offset any gain recognized.[36]

L. Phase-in Rules

Generally the passive loss rules apply to tax years beginning after December 31, 1986. However, for passive activities held on the Tax Reform Act of 1986 enactment date (October 22, 1986), Section 469(1) prescribes a phase-in rule in regard to limiting the amount of losses that a taxpayer can take against income.[37] For taxable years beginning 1987, 35% of passive losses and credits from pre-1987 passive activities is subject to disallowance. For 1988, 1989, and 1990, the following losses are disallowed:

1988, 40%; 1989, 80%; 1990, 90%

For 1991 and thereafter, 100% of the passive losses and credits will be disallowed. An example will illustrate:

EXAMPLE 7-17

Mr. Taxpayer is involved in a computer lease deal that he acquired on 1/1/86. In 1987 the lease deal produces losses of $100,000. Taxpayer will only be able to deduct on his tax return $65,000: $100,000 − ($100,000 × 35%). With respect to the $35,000 of disallowed losses, Taxpayer will carry these forward to later years to the extent there is either net passive income or the passive asset is sold or disposed of in a taxable transaction.

M. Investment Income Expense

As sort of a "double whammie," Section 163(d)(4)(E) prescribes that generally investment income of a taxpayer for any tax year where the taxpayer is taking losses subject to Section 469(1)'s phase-in rule with respect to passive losses, the taxpayer's investment income is to be reduced by the amount of the passive activity loss the taxpayer is permitted to take. An example will illustrate:

EXAMPLE 7-18

Taxpayer acquired a limited partnership interest in a movie tax shelter in 1985 that produced losses of $10,000 in 1987. Additionally, in 1987 taxpayer had portfolio income of $20,000. For 1987, taxpayer will report $6,500 of losses from the tax shelter [$10,000 − ($10,000 × 35%)] and use $13,500 of portfolio income ($20,000 − $6,500) for investment interest purposes.

TAX POINTERS

1. Section 163(d)(4)(E)'s rule does not apply to any passive losses attributable to rental real estate, providing that the taxpayer actively participates, as that term is defined.[38] Thus, in Example 7-18 if the taxpayer was an active participant in the real estate venture instead of a limited partner in a movie deal, taxpayer would still report $6,500 of loss but $20,000 of portfolio income.

2. See also the discussion at Chapter 5.2.

N. Disposition of Interest in Partnerships and S Corporations

Generally, for federal income tax purposes, a disposition of an interest in an S corporation or partnership (a "pass-through entity") is treated as a disposition of such interest, rather than as a disposition of such interest in each of the entities' assets. Temp. Reg. Section 1.469-2T(e)(3)(ii) prescribes that a holder's gain or loss from a disposition of an interest in a pass-through entity is to be allocated among the activities of the pass-through entity in proportion to the amount of gain or loss, respectively, that would have been allocated to the holder by the pass-through entity with respect to each of the entity's activities if the entity had sold its interest in such activities on the applicable valuation date. The Preamble to the Temporary Regulations at pages 39–40 prescribes that:

> Generally, the passthrough entity may select either the beginning of the taxable year of the passthrough entity in which the holder's disposition occurs or the date of such disposition as the applicable valuation date. The date of the holder's disposition of an interest in the passthrough entity must be used as the applicable valuation date; however, if since the beginning of the entity's taxable year the entity has sold a significant amount of the property used in any activity or the holder has contributed a significant amount of substantially appreciated or substantially depreciated property to the passthrough entity. For purposes of this rule, property is substantially appreciated if its fair market value exceeds 120 percent of its adjusted basis, and property is substantially depreciated if its adjusted basis exceeds 120 percent of its fair market value.
>
> Under Section 1.469-2T(e)(e)(iii), gain from a holder's disposition of an interest in a passthrough entity that is allocated to a passive activity under the general rule will nonetheless be treated as gain that is not from a passive activity if (a) gain that would be treated as gain that is not from a passive activity under Section 1.469-2T(c)(2)(iii) would have been allocated to the holder if all of the property used in the activity had been sold, and (b) the amount of that gain exceeds 10 percent of the holder's gain from the disposition that is allocated to the activity under the general rule. This rule is designed to prevent taxpayers from using passthrough entities to structure dispositions of property in a manner that generates passive income in situations where such income would otherwise be treated as not from a passive activity under Section 1.469-2T(c)(2)(iii).
>
> Section 1.469-2T(e)(3)(iv) provides a transitional rule for dispositions of interests in a passthrough entity that occur during any taxable year of the entity beginning prior to February 19, 1988. Under this transitional rule, gain or loss from a qualifying disposition of an interest in the entity may be allocated among the activities of the entity under any reasonable method that the entity selects. This transitional rule does not apply to any sale of an interest in a passthrough entity that occurs after February 19, 1988, if the holder contributes certain substantially appreciated property to the entity after that date.

ENDNOTES FOR CHAPTER 7

1. 1981-2 C.B. 167.

2. 1970-1 C.B. 178.

3. 57 AFTR 2d 464 (11th Cir. 1985).

4. 1975-1 C.B. 277.

5. 1969-1 C.B. 207.

6. 59 T.C. 777, aff'd per curiam, 32 AFTR 2d 6181 (8th Cir. 1973).

7. 1970-1 C.B. 166.

8. See Section 1275(a)(1) for the definition of a "debt instrument."

9. See, e.g., *Bernard Barr,* Para. 80,003 P-H Memo T.C. (1980) (payment of an open account debt generated ordinary income not capital gains).

10. 1964-1 (Pt. 1) C.B. 304.

11. 1968-2 C.B. 372.

12. Para. 70,031 P-H Memo T.C. (1970).

13. Para. 73,134 P-H Memo T.C. 1973 (debt of an S corporation reclassified as stock for purposes of Sections 301 and 351, but not for second class of stock for former Section 1371).

14. Para. 71,030 P-H Memo T.C. (1971).

15. A nonbusiness bad debt is any debt except one created or acquired in a taxpayer's trade or business, or one involving loss proximately related to the trade or business in which the taxpayer is engaged when the debt becomes worthless.

16. 79-C-710 (E.D., Wis. Apr. 21, 1980), aff'd by unpublished order No. 80-1612 (7th Cir., June 25, 1982).

17. General Explanation of the Tax Reform Act of 1986 the Blue Book (hereinafter the Blue Book), p. 215.

18. Section 469(g). Note also at the death of an individual taxpayer, any suspended losses remaining at death are generally allowed as a deduction on the taxpayer's final return. See discussion at Chapter 7.9.I.

19. Blue Book, p. 215.

20. For the special rules that apply to closely held corporations, see Section 469(e)(2) and the Blue Book, pp. 215–235.

21. A working interest in oil or gas property is defined as interest that is burdened with the cost of development and operation of the property, Blue Book, p. 251.

22. Blue Book, p. 236.

23. Id. at 240.

24. Id.

25. Id. at 223.

26. Id. at 222.

27. Id. at 231. It is to be noted that dividends paid by an S corporation that was formerly a C corporation that are treated as derived from earnings and profits from a C corporation year under Section 1368, are treated as portfolio income, even though the income or loss passed through to the S corporation shareholders would otherwise be treated as passive.

28. Id. at 233.

29. Id. at 233-234.
30. Id. at 244.
31. Id. at 227.
32. Id. at 226.
33. Id. at 227.
34. Id. at 229.
35. Id.
36. Id.
37. Id. at 252-254. The Blue Book provides a further clarification as to when the phase-in rules apply. For instance, the Report states that "a rental activity has commenced when rental property has been placed in service."
38. For a definition of active participation see the Tax Pointer at Chapter 7.9.D.

8

Distributions and the Accumulated Adjustment Account

8.1   INTRODUCTION

As this book has indicated so far, there are two types of S corporations: those with earnings and profits[1] and those without. Chapter 8 will introduce two more types of S corporations: an S corporation with earnings and profits plus previously taxed income (PTI) (see Chapter 8.4 for a definition of the term PTI) and an S corporation without earnings and profits, but with PTI. The type of S corporation (i.e., does it have earnings and profits, PTI, etc.?) will have a bearing on the taxation of the distribution to the S corporate shareholders. As set forth in Chapter 1.1, S corporations basically allow the S corporation and the shareholders to pay a single level of tax on corporate income. Chapters 4 and 5 detailed how income, loss, and so on are reported by the S corporate shareholders. Chapter 7 detailed how the items of income, loss, and so on are passed through to an S shareholder and how an S shareholder determines basis. Chapter 8 will now complete the picture by detailing the taxation of distributions from the S corporation to the S corporate shareholders. The categories of S corporations to be discussed are S corporations without earnings and profits (Chapter 8.2), S corporations with earnings and profits (Chapter 8.3), S corporations without earnings and profits but PTI, and S corporations with earnings and profits and previously taxed income (Chapter 8.4).

8.2   DISTRIBUTIONS WITHIN S CORPORATIONS WITHOUT EARNINGS AND PROFITS—SECTION 1368(b)

An S corporation without earnings and profits could be created after the Subchapter S Revision Act of 1982 (SSRA) and thus pursuant to Section 1371(c)(1) can have no earnings and profits by definition. (See discussion at Chapter 4.9.) Or, it could have been created pre–SSRA but never had any earnings or profits. Alternately, the S corporation could have formerly been a C corporation that either had no earnings and profits at the time of conversion and never acquired them since or did have earnings and profits and eliminated them by the procedure set forth in Section 1368(e)(3). (See Chapter 6.4.K.)

Section 1368(b) establishes a two-tier system for distributions from these types of corporations: first, Section 1368(b)(1) states that distributions are tax free to the extent of shareholder's basis in the stock of the S corporation;

second, if the distribution exceeds the adjusted basis of the stock, such excess shall be treated as gain from the sale or exchange of property (i.e., capital gain). In terms of priority, Section 1368(d)(1) generally prescribes that basis increases and decreases for stock occur before the distribution rules of Section 1368 apply. Thus, if the S corporation has a loss and makes a distribution in the same year, the loss will pass through to the shareholder under Section 1366(a)(1), basis will be reduced by Section 1367(a)(2), and then any distribution in excess of basis will be taxed according to Section 1368(b). One area of prime difficulty would be if the S corporation has a different year from that of the shareholders (see Example 8-5 for an illustration of this point).

TAX POINTER

If the corporation is deemed a collapsible one under Section 341, then the capital gain would be converted to ordinary income.

Examples illustrating the operation of Section 1368(b) are as follows:

EXAMPLE 8-1

A, Inc., a calendar year S corporation, is composed of one shareholder, B, and was formed on 1/1/X7. B, a bachelor, contributed $10,000 for the stock interest in the S corporation. By definition of Section 1371(c)(1), A, Inc., has no earnings and profits because it was formed after 1982. At the end of A, Inc.'s first year of operation, it had ordinary income (Form 1120S, page 1, line 21) of $30,000. B materially participated in A, Inc. During the year, A, Inc., made a distribution to B of $46,000. The tax results that will be determined at the end of the S corporate year are as follows:

B has taxable income of $30,000 pursuant to Section 1366(a)(1)(B); B's basis is increased by $30,000 pursuant to Section 1367(a)(1)(B) thereby increasing B's stock basis to $40,000 ($10,000 original basis plus $30,000 income). B receives the $40,000 distribution tax free and B's basis is reduced tax free by $40,000 pursuant to Section 1368(b)(1) and the $6,000 is taxed as a capital gain (Section 1368(b)(2)). (As to the treatment of capital gain, see Chapter 8.2.A.)

EXAMPLE 8-2

Assume the same facts as in Example 8-1 except as modified below. A, Inc., a calendar year S corporation was formed on 1/1/X7. A, Inc., has no earnings and profits. A, Inc., has one shareholder, B, who made a capital contribution of $10,000. At the end of 19X7, A, Inc., has ordinary income of $12,000 and $18,000 of tax exempt income. During 19X7, A, Inc., made a distribution to B of $46,000. The tax results are as follows:

B had taxable income of $12,000 pursuant to Section 1366(a)(1)(B); B's basis is increased $30,000 pursuant to Section 1367(a)(1)(B) and (A), thereby increasing stock basis to $40,000 ($10,000 + $12,000 + $18,000). B's basis is reduced tax free by $40,000 pursuant to Section 1368(b)(1) and $6,000 is taxed as capital gain. (For an example illustrating the tax reporting of the above transactions on Form 1120S and the shareholder's tax return, see Appendix 6.)

EXAMPLE 8-3

Assume the same facts as in Example 8-1, except that A, Inc., does not distribute $46,000 to B until 19X8. Accordingly, B will still report $30,000 in income and have basis increased by $30,000. The taxability to B of the $46,000 distribution in 19X7 will depend upon the adjustments to B's basis pursuant to Section 1367(a) and (b). Assuming that B's basis did not change in 1988, the $46,000 distribution will cause B to receive a tax-free distribution pursuant to Section 1368(b)(1) of $40,000, have his basis reduced by $40,000 at the same time and $6,000 of capital gain pursuant to Section 1368(b)(2). (See Appendix 7 for an illustration as to how the above tax transaction will be reported on the corporation's tax return and the shareholder's tax return.)

EXAMPLE 8-4

A, Inc., is a calendar S corporation having one shareholder, B, who materially particpates in the corporation. A, Inc., was formed on 1/1/X7, and B's initial contribution to A, Inc., was $10,000. During 19X7, A, Inc., made a distribution of $2,000 to B. At the end of 1987, A, Inc., had ordinary income of $7,000. B reports $7,000 of income for 19X7 pursuant to Section 1366(a)(1), the $2,000 distribution is tax free to B pursuant to Section 1368(b)(1) and B's basis as of 12/31/X7 pursuant to Section 1368(d)(1) is $15,000: $10,000 + $7,000 − $2,000.

A. Distributions from S Corporations in Excess of Stock Basis, Long-Term or Short-Term Capital Gains

If a distribution is in excess of stock basis, Section 1368(b)(2) treats the excess distribution over stock basis as capital gain. The capital gain will be either long or short term, depending on how long the shareholder has held the stock. As to when the capital gain occurred, Section 1368 is unclear. However, it is presumed that the sale will be deemed to have occurred at the end of the S corporation's taxable year because a shareholder's basis pursuant to Section 1368(d)(1) is not adjusted for income or deductions until the S corporation's year end when these items can be determined. Further, it is unclear whether separate basis accounts must be maintained by the shareholders if they acquire stock at different times and for different amounts. Presumably, the S corporation follows the partnership rules and uses the aggregate approach for stock basis.

B. Fiscal Year S Corporations

As discussed at Chapter 1.4, an S corporation could have a taxable year different from that of its shareholders. However, as discussed at Chapter 8.2.A, Section 1368(d)(1) prescribes that the tax characteristics of a tax distribution cannot be determined until the end of the S corporation's taxable year. An example will illustrate the tax consequences:

EXAMPLE 8-5

A, Inc., an S corporation formed on 1/1/87, has a fiscal year ending 10/31/87. A, Inc, has one shareholder, B, an individual, whose stock basis on 11/1/87 is $10,000. On 12/31/87 A, Inc., makes a distribution to B of $25,000. The $25,000 distribution will have no effect on B's Form 1040 for 1987; rather, it will be reported on B's 1988 return when A, Inc.'s Form 1120S will be filed.

C. Section 1368 Distribution Rules and Debt

It is to be noted that Section 1368 distribution rules apply only to stock, not to debt. So, for instance, assume stock basis is reduced to zero pursuant to Section 1367(a)(2)(C) and Section 1368(b)(1), and there is still basis remaining in debt, then any future distributions will be against stock basis pursuant to Section 1368(b)(2). Examples of the application of Section 1368(b) and debt are set forth below:

EXAMPLE 8-6

19X7

A, Inc., is a calendar year S corporation having one shareholder, B, a bachelor who materially participates. It has no earnings or profits or PTI. For the year ending 19X7, the records indicate the following:

Stock basis, 1/1/X7	$10,000
B's loan to A, Inc., 1/1/X7	4,000
Distribution to B, 7/1/X7	8,000
Ordinary income for 19X7 (Form 1120S, page 1, line 21)	15,000

19X8

In 19X8, A, Inc., reported a loss of $21,000 on Form 1120S, page 1, line 21, and on 1/1/X8 made a distribution of $2,000 to B.

19X9

In 19X9, A, Inc., had ordinary income of $23,000, and on 12/31/X9 A, Inc., made a distribution of $27,000 to B. The tax results are reported as follows:

19X7

	Stock	Debt	Total
Basis, 1/1/X7	$10,000	$4,000	$14,000
Ordinary income	15,000		15,000
Distribution	(8,000)		(8,000)
Basis, 12/31/X7	$17,000	$4,000	$21,000

19X8

	Stock	Debt	Total
Basis, 1/1/X8	$17,000	$4,000	$21,000
$20,000 loss			
Stock: Section 1367(a)(2)(C)	(17,000)		(17,000)
Debt: Section 1367(b)(2)(A)		(3,000)	(3,000)
$2,000 distribution*	—		—
Basis, 12/31/X8	$ –0–	$1,000	$ 1,000

* Because B has no stock basis, the $2,000 distribution 1/1/X8 is treated as a capital gain per Section 1368(b)(2). (See Chapter 8.2.A for treatment of the capital gain.)

19X9

	Stock	Debt	Total
Basis, 1/1/X9	$ –0–	$1,000	$ 1,000
$23,000 ordinary income			
Applied to restore debt (Section 1367(b)(2)(B))	–0–	3,000	3,000
Applied to stock, (Section 1367(a)(1)(B))	$20,000		20,000
$27,000 distribution†			
to stock basis (Section 1368(b)(1))	(20,000)		(20,000)
Basis, 12/31/X9	$ –0–	$4,000	$ 4,000

† Because B has no stock basis, $7,000 of the distribution on 12/31/X9 ($27,000 − $20,000) is treated as capital gain pursuant to Section 1368(b)(2). (See Chapter 8.2.A for treatment of the capital gain.) (See Appendix 8 for a filled-in tax return for the shareholder and the S corporation illustrating the above example.)

8.3 DISTRIBUTION IN S CORPORATIONS WITH EARNINGS AND PROFITS

As discussed at various points in this book, an S corporation could have earnings and profits (see, for example, the discussion at Chapter 4.9 and 10.4). If the S corporation is engaged in passive investment income activities, earnings and profits, as Chapter 4.9.B details, could cause tax consequences and possible loss of S status. However, if the S corporation is not engaged in any passive investment income activities (e.g., is a personal service business or is engaged in manufacturing), earnings and profits may not be a concern to the shareholders since the S corporation will never run afoul of Sections 1375 (Chapter 6.4) and 1362(d)(3) (Chapter 10.4) as long as it engages in nonpassive investment income activities. However, the S shareholders might be myopic in that the corporate activities could change, causing the S corporation to engage in passive investment income activities. If the S corporation begins to engage in passive investment income activities, the S corporation's earnings and profits will come back to haunt the shareholders.

A. Means to Eliminate Earnings and Profits

There are basically two means to eliminate earnings and profits: the procedure set forth in Section 1368(e)(3)(Chapter 6.4.K) and a dividend distribution under Section 1368 (discussed on page 169). Earnings and profits can also be reduced in the event of liquidations (Chapter 10.10) and redemptions (Chapter 10.9) per Section 1371(c)(2), or because taxes paid at the shareholder level for investment tax credit recapture (see Chapter 6.3), per Section 1371(d)(3).

TAX POINTER

It should be noted that under Section 1371(c)(1) an S corporation cannot make any adjustment to earnings and profits. Presumably, then, earnings and profits will always be overstated if there are timing differences due to the method of accounting employed by the corporation that generated the earnings and profits. For instance, assume that a C corporation converted to S status. Before conversion, it purchased an asset and depreciated the asset using accelerated cost recovery system; however, for earnings and profits purposes, the corporation must use straight-line depreciation. Thus, earnings and profits will be overstated from the point of conversion.

B. The Accumulated Adjustments Account (AAA)— Section 1368(e)(1)

To deal with an S corporation that could be operating with earnings and profits, Congress adopted the AAA concept to provide a means generally to allow the earnings of the S corporation to be distributed tax free, but imposing a tax on dividends and distributions in regard to any earnings and profits. (As to how PTI distributions are handled, see Chapter 8.4.) Section 1368(e)(1)(A) and (2) defines AAA as a corporate account that is adjusted for the period the corporation operates under S status similar to the adjustments made to basis under Section 1367, except that no adjustments shall be made for tax-exempt income and related expenses. In other words, the AAA, in a simplified definition, means the earnings of the corporation during its S years (other than tax-exempt income) while it has earnings and profits, less any amount of these earnings distributed to the shareholders. AAA is a corporate account like earnings and profits—in contrast, basis is a shareholder's account. Further, distributions that reduce AAA also reduce stock basis. The operation of the AAA can be illustrated as follows:

Beginning balance	By definition the AAA starts at zero on the first day of the S corporation's first taxable year beginning after 1982
Increase	Separately and nonseparately stated items as set forth in Section 1367(a)(1) with the exception of tax-exempt income, that is, ordinary income, separately stated items of income (e.g., capital gains, Section 1231 gains), excess of the deduction of depreciation over the basis of property subject to depletion.*
Decrease	Items set forth at Section 1367(a)(2)(B)–(E) with the exception of any expense related to tax-exempt income, that is, operating losses, penalties, fines, Section 1231 losses, and the amount of the shareholder's deductions for the depletion of oil and gas wells under Section 611.*
	Distributions that are not includible in the shareholder's income, such as distribution of prior year's AAA.

---

* For a discussion of how these increases and decreases apply, see the discussion at Chapters 7.2.B.2 and 7.2.B.3.

1.   Treatment of Tax-Exempt Income and Expense

Section 1368(e)(1)(A) specifically excludes an adjustment in the AAA for tax-exempt income and expense. Accordingly, tax exempt income bonds should not be run through S corporations. (See Chapter 9.20 for other reasons why S corporations should not own tax-exempt bonds.) An example will illustrate:

EXAMPLE 8-7

In 19X6, A, Inc., incorporated as a C corporation having one shareholder, F. In 19X7, A, Inc., elected S status; however, at the time of its election to S status, it had $100 of earnings and profits. In 19X7, A, Inc., had $50 of ordinary income and $10 of tax-exempt interest. A, Inc., in 19X7 distributed $60 to F. F's stock basis pursuant to Section 1367(a)(1) was increased by $60; however, A, Inc.'s AAA only increased by $50 pursuant to Section 1368(e)(1)(A). Therefore, $50 of the distribution will be tax-free pursuant to Section 1368(c)(1), with the balance of $10 taxable to F pursuant to Section 1368(c)(2) as a dividend. (For a discussion of the distribution rules as they pertain to AAA, see the material below.).

TAX POINTER

It is important to note that S corporations without earnings and profits should also not consider tax-exempt income since the inability to increase the AAA may affect posttermination distributions under Section 1371(e). (For a discussion of posttermination distributions, see Chapter 8.6.)

2.   AAA May Be Reduced Below Zero

Because the AAA is a corporate account, it can be reduced below zero and have a negative basis because of S corporate losses.

3.   AAA Transferable and Not Affected by Stock Transfers

Because AAA is a corporate account, it is transferable by definition and not affected by corporate transfers caused by sale of stock, gifts, and so on.[2]

4.   Redemptions Under Sections 302(a) and 303(a)—Section 1368(e)(1)(B)

Section 1368(e)(1)(B) prescribes that in the case of redemptions of S corporate stock that is treated as an exchange under Sections 302(a) and 303(a) to pay death taxes, the AAA is decreased by the balance in the account times the percentage of shares redeemed. The following will illustrate:

EXAMPLE 8-8

A, Inc., is a calendar year S corporation composed of two shareholders, B and C, two bachelors, who are not related. B owns 30% of A, Inc., and C, 70%. On 1/1/X7 A, Inc.'s AAA was $50,000. On 6/1/X7, B redeemed all his stock in A, Inc. On 12/31/X7, A, Inc.'s books reflect the following as of 12/31/X7—ordinary income (Form 1120S, page 1, line 21) $20,000. A, Inc.'s AAA as of 12/31/X7 is $49,000 computed as follows:

AAA balance, 1/1/X7	$50,000
Addition: ordinary income	20,000
	$70,000
Less: redemptions (30% × 70,000)	21,000
AAA balance, 12/31/X7	$49,000

5. Investment Tax Credit Recapture

Chapter 9.14 basically detailed how investment tax credit recapture could occur with S corporations. If an S corporation elected to take full investment tax credit on an asset, that asset's basis was decreased by one-half the investment tax credit. If investment tax credit recapture arose on the disposal of the asset, the asset's basis is increased by one-half of the recapture. Because stock basis was adjusted under Section 1367(a) for investment tax credit items, likewise AAA is adjusted for investment tax credit recapture.

6. An Example of the AAA Computation

Set forth below is an example of how to determine an S corporation's AAA.

EXAMPLE 8-9

A, Inc., was incorporated on 1/1/86 as a calendar year S corporation with F as a sole shareholder. F was a material participant. F's basis in A, Inc.'s stock as of incorporation was $1,600. A, Inc., had the following transaction for 1986 reflected on its books:

Tax-exempt interest	$ 200
Long-term capital gain	1,000
Charitable contributions	500
Payroll tax penalties	300
Ordinary income, Form 1120S, page 1, line 21	20,000
Distributions to F	15,000

The 19X7 transactions are reflected on A, Inc.'s tax returns as follows:

	AAA	Basis
Balance, 1/1/X7	$ –0–	$ 1,600
Income:		
Ordinary income	20,000	20,000
Long-term capital gains	1,000	1,000
Tax-exempt interest	–0–	200
Decrease:		
Charitable contributions	(500)	(500)
Payroll tax penalties	(300)	(300)
Balance before distribution	20,200	22,000
Distribution	15,000	15,000
Balance, 12/31/X7	$ 5,200	$ 7,000

(See Appendix 9, which details how this example is reflected on the S corporate tax return and the individual's Form 1040.)

C. The Order Applying Distributions If the S Corporation Has Earnings and Profits—Section 1368(c)

Section 1368(c) prescribes the following order for making distributions if the S corporation has earnings and profits:

First: Distributions are tax free to the extent of the AAA (Section 1368(c)(1)).

Second: Dividend is payable to the extent of the S corporation's earnings and profits (Section 1368(c)(2)).

Third: Distributions are tax free to the extent of the shareholder's basis in stock of the S corporation (Section 1368(b)(1)).

Fourth: A taxable gain (capital gain) to the extent the distribution exceeds the basis in stock (Section 1368(b)(2)).

1. Classification of the Gain, Distribution Rules, Fiscal Year S Corporation, Priority Rules, and So On

The rules of long-term versus short-term capital gain, the distribution rules, and so on, discussed with respect to S corporations without earnings and profits in Chapter 8.2, likewise apply to S distributions when the S corporation has earnings and profits.

2. An Example of the Distribution Rules

Set forth on page 173 is an example to show the distribution rules. See Appendix 10 to see how this information is reflected on the tax return.

EXAMPLE 8-10

A, Inc., is an S corporation composed of one shareholder F, a bachelor. F acquired his stock basis in 19X1 for $55,000. F is a material participant. In 19X7, A, Inc., broke even and has as of 12/31/X7 the following items on its books: AAA, $50,000; earnings and profits, $20,000. On 12/31/X7 A, Inc., makes a distribution of $87,000 to F. The tax consequences are as follows:

	Total Distribution	Non-taxable	Earnings and Profits	Capital Gain
Balance, 1/1/X7		$55,000	$20,000	—
$87,000 Distribution:				
AAA and basis reduction, Section 1368(c)(1)*	$50,000	(50,000)		
Dividends, Section 1368(c)(2)	20,000		(20,000)	
Basis reduction, Section 1368(b)(2)	5,000	5,000		
Capital gain, Section 1368(b)(2)	12,000			12,000
Total	$87,000	$ –0–	$ –0–	$12,000

* As discussed in the introductory part of Chapter 8.3.B, distributions that reduce AAA also reduce basis.

	Balances		Earnings and Profits
	Basis	AAA	
Beginning balance	$55,000	$50,000	$20,000
AAA	(50,000)	(50,000)	
Dividend			(20,000)
Basis reduction	(5,000)		
Total	$ –0–	$ –0–	$ –0–

The S corporation would furnish F with the following information on the Form 1120S, K-1, and Form 1099-DIV.

Nondividend (K-1)	67,000
Dividend (Form 1099-DIV)	20,000

F would then apply the K-1 information against his basis:

K-1 nondividend distribution	67,000
Less: stock basis	55,000
Capital gain†	12,000

† The classification of long-term or short-term capital gain will depend on how long F held his stock. Note, if F's basis was different than on the tax

return because he acquired stock by sale, death, and so on, there may or may not be a capital gain reported on F's Form 1040.

D.   AAA Can Be Less than Zero

Section 1368(e)(1)(A) prescribes that losses can reduce AAA below zero, whereas Section 1367 prescribes that stock (and debt) basis cannot be reduced below zero. If distributions are made when AAA is negative and earnings and profits are positive, a dividend will result to the shareholder due to the pecking order set forth in Section 1368(c). (See Chapter 8.3.C.) An example will illustrate:

EXAMPLE 8-11

A, Inc., is a calendar year S corporation composed of one shareholder, B. On 1/1/X7, A, Inc., had the following on its books and records $2,000 of AAA and $20,000 of earnings and profits. On 12/31/X7, A, Inc., reported an ordinary loss of $5,000 and a distribution to B of $9,000. B, who materially participates in the organization, reports an ordinary loss of $5,000 and a dividend on $9,000 computed as follows:

	AAA	Earnings and Profits
Balance, 1/1/X7	$ 2,000	$20,000
Loss	(5,000)	
Balance before distribution	(3,000)	20,000
Distribution		9,000
Balance, 12/31/X7	$(3,000)	$11,000

The consequence of Example 8-11 is that until AAA is restored to zero by S corporate income, any distributions from the S corporation will be a dividend to the shareholders until the earnings and profits are drawn down to zero.

TAX POINTER

To avoid the situation set forth in Example 8-11, the S corporation should lend the shareholder money rather than make a distribution to the shareholder. (See discussion at Chapter 9.15 for the proper interest rate to be charged.)

E.   AAA Is Transferable

As discussed at Chapter 8.3.B, AAA is a corporate account. It is also transferable to a new shareholder. Thus, if a shareholder acquires stock, any distributions to a new shareholder qualify as a nontaxable return of capital treatment to the extent that the distribution is out of the corporation's AAA.

F. AAA Is Included in Distributions Pro Rata

Section 1368(c)(3) provides that, except to the extent provided in the regulations, if the distribution during the taxable year exceeds the amount of AAA at the close of the taxable year, the balance of the AAA is to be distributed pro rata. Obviously, if there is no change of stock ownership during the taxable year, Section 1368(c)(3) has no effect, but, if there is a change of ownership during the taxable year, there could be tax consequences. An example will illustrate:

EXAMPLE 8-12

A, Inc., a calendar year S corporation, is composed of two shareholders, B and C, both sisters who own stock equally. In 19X7, A, Inc., has the following on its books after income was posted to them: AAA of $10,000 and earnings and profits of $5,000. On 4/1/X7 and 9/1/X7, $7,500 was distributed to the shareholders. On 9/1/X7, C sold 10% of her shares to D, a permitted S corporate shareholder. The shareholders report the distributions as follows:

	4/1X7		9/1/X7		
	AAA	Earnings and Profits	AAA	Earnings and Profits	Total
B	$2,500	$1,250	$2,500	$1,250	$ 7,500
C	2,500	1,250	2,250	1,125	7,125
D			250	125	375
				Total	$15,000

G. Operation of Section 1368(e)(3) Election

As discussed at Chapter 6.4.K, the shareholders of an S corporation can make an election to reduce earnings and profits of the S corporation before taking a distribution from AAA. The shareholders may consider this where a tax will be faced under Section 1375 (see generally Chapter 6.4) or loss of election under Section 1362(d)(3). (See Chapter 10.4.) Appendix 5 sets forth the form to make this election. Set forth below is an example illustrating the operation of the election under Section 1368(c)(3):

EXAMPLE 8-13

A, Inc., a calendar year S corporation is composed of two shareholders, A and B, brothers. In 19X7, A, Inc., makes a distribution to the two brothers of $10,000 each. On 12/31/X7, before giving effect to the distributions, A, Inc.'s earnings and profits account is $20,000, the AAA is $35,000, and the shareholder's basis is $40,000. The brothers, because the corporation will face a tax under Section 1375 for passive investment income, decide to file an election under Section 1368(e)(3) with respect to the $20,000 distribution. The effect of the Section 1368(e)(3) election will be to reduce the $20,000 of earnings and profits to zero and thus prevent the imposition of tax under Section 1375. The brothers would realize ordinary income of $20,000 from the dividend.

1. Reasons Why a Shareholder Would Want to Make a Section 1368(e)(3) Election

At first blush, it may seem strange that an S shareholder in a situation where Section 1375 and Section 1362(d)(3) have no effect would want to make a Section 1368(e)(3) election to incur a dividend rather than have a tax-free distribution under AAA. However, the S shareholder may have a substantial personal net operating loss in the taxable year that cannot otherwise be utilized. Alternatively, the shareholder may need investment income for purposes of the investment interest limitation of Section 163(d). Thus, the shareholder would make the election under Section 1368(e)(3). An example will illustrate:

EXAMPLE 8-14

Assume the same facts as in Example 8-13, except the S corporation is not facing a tax under Section 1375. The shareholders, because of Section 163(d), need investment income of $10,000 each. They file the Section 1368(e)(3) election to have $10,000 distributed to them in 19X7 as a dividend.

TAX POINTER

Note, if the S corporation does not completely distribute the earnings and profits in the first year it elects under Section 1368(e)(3) and wants to make the election in a different year, it must file this election form again and obtain the necessary consents.

8.4 DISTRIBUTIONS IN S CORPORATIONS WITH PTI

If an S corporation was in existence prior to the Subchapter S Revision Act of 1982 (SSRA), it could have previous taxable income (PTI). It is beyond the scope of this book to offer a detailed discussion of PTI; however, the following should be noted. PTI represents taxable income of an S corporation pre–1/1/83 that was not distributed to the shareholders. PTI is a personal item to the shareholders—it is not transferable as is AAA. Under prior law PTI increased the basis of stock.

In regard to distributions involving PTI, Section 1368 does not specifically address this point. However, I.R.S. Publication 589, "Tax Information on S Corporation" (1986) at page 10-12, sets forth distribution rules. If the S corporation does not have earnings and profits, the distribution from the S corporation is made in the following order:

1. AAA

2. PTI

3. Nontaxable return of capital to the extent of remaining basis

4. Taxable disposition of stock

If the S corporation does have earnings and profits as well as PTI, the order of distribution is as follows:

1. AAA

2. PTI

3. Dividend to the extent of earnings and profits

4. Nontaxable return of capital to the extent of remaining basis

5. Taxable disposition of stock

In regard to the distribution of PTI, Section 1379(c) basically states that PTI is to be distributed in accordance with former Sections 1375(d) and (f). Examples illustrating distributions involving PTI are set forth below:

EXAMPLE 8-15

A, Inc., a calendar year S corporation, is composed of one shareholder, B. A, Inc., was incorporated in 1978. In 1987, it has the following items on its balance sheet: AAA, $5,000; PTI, $10,000. B's stock basis is $1,500. In 1987, A, Inc., distributed a total of $17,000 to B—$8,000 in June and $9,000 in October. The tax treatment is as follows:

Source of Distribution	Distribution	Nontaxable	Taxable Distribution: Capital Gains
Total distribution	$17,000		
From AAA	(5,000)	$ 5,000	
Balance	$12,000		
From PTI	(10,000)	10,000	
Balance	$ 2,000		
From stock basis	1,500	1,500	
Balance	$ 500		
Capital gains	(500)		$500
Total	$ –0–	$16,500	$500

EXAMPLE 8-16

M has been a shareholder in an S corporation since 1978. At the end of 1986 the basis of M's stock basis is $15,500. This $15,500 basis is divided as follows:

1. AAA	$ 5,000
2. PTI	10,000
3. Balance of basis	500
	$15,500

During 1986 M received distributions of $8,000 in June and $9,000 in October from the S corporation. M's share of earnings and profits of the S corporation was $500. The tax treatment of the distribution is figured as follows:

Source of Distribution	Distribution	Nontaxable	Taxable Distribution — Dividend	Taxable Distribution — Capital Gains
Total distribution	$17,000			
From AAA	(5,000)	$ 5,000		
Balance	$12,000			
From PTI	(10,000)	10,000		
Balance	$ 2,000			
From earnings and profits	(500)		$500	
Balance	$ 1,500			
From balance of stock basis	(500)	500		
Balance	$ 1,000			
Gain from a sale or exchange	1,000			$1,000
Total	$ –0–	$15,500	$500	$1,000

Since the distributions of $17,000 exceed the balance in the AAA at the close of the tax year, the $5,000 must be allocated proportionately between the June distribution of $8,000 and the October distribution of $9,000 or $2,353 and $2,647, respectively. Therefore, M's basis in her stock is $0 because her beginning adjusted basis in the stock was $15,500 and $15,500 of the distributions is treated as a return of her basis in the stock. Also, in addition to her share of the separately stated items and the nonseparately computed income, M must report a $500 dividend and a $1,000 long-term capital gain on her personal income tax return as a result of the distributions.

8.5   PROPERTY DISTRIBUTIONS—SECTION 1363(d)

Section 1363(d) prescribes that if the S corporation makes a distribution of appreciated property (other than its own obligations) to a shareholder, gain is recognized to the S corporate shareholder just as if the S corporation sold the property to the S shareholder at its fair market value. (For a discussion of the general rules of Section 1363(d); see Chapter 4.8.A.) If the S corporation makes a distribution to its shareholder of the property whose fair market value is equal to or less than the property's basis on the S corporation's tax return, then there is no gain or loss at the corporate level, and the S shareholder is deemed to have received a distribution equal to the fair market value of the property with the order of distribution rules set forth in Chapters 8.2 and 8.3 to apply. However, Section 267(a)(1) may disallow a loss if the S shareholder owns more than 50% in value of the S corporate stock either outright or by the Section 267 rules of attribution. (See Chapter 5.12.)

A.   The Effect of Complete Liquidations and Reorganizations on Property Distributions Under Sections 1363(d) and (e)

Section 1363(e) prescribes that if a property distribution to a shareholder arises in connection with a complete liquidation of the corporation or in a corporate reorganization where property is distributed to Sections 354, 355, or 356, Section 1363(d)'s distribution rules do not apply.

B.   The Characterization of the Gain Realized, Shareholders Basis, and the Effect That the Property Distribution Will Have on the S Corporation Under Sections 1374 and 1375

The gain recognized by the S corporation will generally reflect the property's character in the hands of S corporation. Thus, if appreciated inventory is distributed to the S corporate shareholders, the S corporation will have ordinary income equal to the difference between the inventory's fair market value and the basis on the S corporation's books. In regard to the S corporate shareholder, the shareholder takes the fair market value as his, her, or its basis for the property distributed pursuant to Section 301(d). If depreciable property is distributed to an S corporate shareholder and the shareholder owns more than 50% in value of the S corporate stock, Section 1239 prescribes that for distributions in taxable years after October 22, 1986, the S corporation will have ordinary income instead of capital gains. The consequence of Section

1239's recharacterization of gain is that because income is passed through proportionally to all shareholders, shareholders owning less than a 50% interest in the S corporation will have ordinary income. While this recharacterization may not have too much effect on the shareholders due to the elimination by the TRA of the capital gain deduction, it still has some effect on individuals (for instance, a shareholder may want to "wash" capital losses against capital gains, and if Section 1239 recharacterizes the gain, then this recharacterization deprives the individual of the needed capital gain). (For an additional discussion of Section 1239, see Chapter 4.7.) Further, Sections 1245, 1250, and so on, investment tax credit recapture, and so on, could come into play at the corporate level depending on the type of property distributed.

If the S corporation is subject to Section 1374 (old and new), the distribution of appreciated property will generate tax under this provision (see discussion at Chapters 6.2 and 6.7); if the property being distributed will generate passive investment income (e.g., stock in another corporation) (Chapter 6.4), then Section 1375's tax will be imposed on the distribution.

C. Tax Planning Under Section 1363(d)

By definition, it is obvious that if Section 1363(d) only applies to appreciated property, it does not make sense to distribute property whose fair market value is less than the adjusted basis on the S corporate books since no loss deduction will result. Likewise, by definition, care should be exercised when money and appreciated property are to be distributed if the S corporation wants to eliminate earnings and profits. Examples will illustrate:

EXAMPLE 8-17

A, Inc., a calendar year S corporation, has one shareholder, B. On 12/31/X7, A, Inc., has the following on its books: AAA, $15,000; earnings and profits, $10,000; a stock investment in ABC, Inc., cost basis $7,000, fair market value $67,000. B's stock basis is $12,000, and in 19X7 A, Inc., broke even. On 12/31/X7, A, Inc., distributes $60,000 in cash to B. The tax consequences to B is that B receives a tax-free distribution of $27,000 ($15,000 of AAA and $12,000 as a reduction in stock basis), a dividend of $10,000 from earnings and profits, and $23,000 of capital gain (total $60,000).

EXAMPLE 8-18

Assume the same facts as in Example 8-16 except that A, Inc., distributes the stock in ABC, Inc., to B instead of cash. The following occurs: B has a capital gain of $60,000 ($67,000 − $7,000); A, Inc.'s AAA is first increased to $75,000 ($15,000 + $60,000) and then this is reduced to $8,000 ($75,000

− $67,000); B's stock basis is at first increased to $72,000 ($60,000 + $12,000), and this is reduced to $5,000 by the distribution of stock in ABC, Inc. ($72,000 −$67,000).

Also, if the asset is depreciable, the shareholders may have other adverse tax consequences. For instance, Section 179(d)(2)(A) prescribes that the asset will not be subject to Section 179 expensing if the shareholder owns more than 50% of the stock, or the shareholder pursuant to Section 168(e)(4)(A)(i) could be prohibited from using accelerated cost recovery system for depreciation purposes.

D. AAA and Earnings and Profits

It is to be noted that distributions of depreciated property under AAA and earnings and profits are treated differently. Under AAA, Section 1368 prescribes that distributions of appreciated property reduce the account by fair market value, but Section 312(a)(3) prescribes that if appreciated property is distributed, it can only reduce earnings and profits by the property's basis.

8.6 POSTTERMINATION DISTRIBUTIONS

As discussed at Chapters 10.1–10.4, an S corporation could be terminated. Section 1371(e)(1) basically allows the S corporation to distribute tax-free money from the S corporation to the shareholders to be applied against stock basis to the extent of AAA, providing the money is distributed within the posttermination transition period. Section 1377(b)(1) defines the posttermination period as the period commencing on the day after the last day of the corporation's last taxable year as an S corporation and ends on the later of

- the day that is one year after such last day or the due date for filing the S corporate return for such last year, including extensions, whichever is later (Section 1377(b)(1)(A)), and
- the end of the 120-day period beginning on the day of the determination that the S corporation's election had terminated for a previous taxable year under Section 1362(a) (Section 1377(b)(1)(B)).

Section 1377(b)(2) defines "determination" for purposes of Section 1377(b)(1)(B) as

- A court decision that becomes final
- A closing agreement

• An agreement between the corporation and the Service that the corporation failed to qualify as an S corporation

Examples illustrating the effect of Section 1371(e)(1) are as follows:

EXAMPLE 8-19

A, Inc., is a calendar year S corporation composed of one shareholder, Belmont. On 1/1/X7, A, Inc., revokes its S status pursuant to Section 1362(d)(1). (See Chapter 10.2.) At the time A, Inc., revoked its status, the basis of Belmont's stock is $25,000. A, Inc., had the following on its books: AAA, $5,000; earnings and profits, $25,000. On 10/30/X7 A, Inc., distributed $17,000 to Belmont. The effect per Section 1371(e)(1) is that $5,000 will be received tax free by Belmont and $12,000 will be treated as a dividend.

EXAMPLE 8-20

Assume the same facts as in Example 8-19, except the distribution was made on 2/15/X9. The entire $17,000 distribution will give rise to dividend income since the distribution was not within the posttermination period.

A. Dividend Election Under Section 1371(e)(2)

After the termination of S corporate status, the shareholders can, under Section 1371(e)(2), elect to have the distribution of the earnings from the S corporation treated as a dividend instead of tax free under Section 1371(e)(1). The shareholders may want to consider this alternative if the shareholders fear that the C corporation, which will emerge after the S corporation status is terminated, will have an exposure to either Section 531's accumulative earnings tax or Section 541's personal holding company tax. The election is made by the corporation attaching a statement to its Form 1120 for the C short year to show that the Section 1371(e)(1) treatment is not to apply to any distributions.

ENDNOTES FOR CHAPTER 8

1. For a definition of earnings and profits, see Chapter 4.9.
2. S. Rep. No. 640, 97th Cong., 2d Sess. 20.

9

Income and Estate Tax Planning for S Corporations, Audit Procedures, and Statute of Limitations Problems

9.1 TAX PLANNING FOR S CORPORATIONS

Although Congress throughout the years has restricted income and estate tax planning opportunities for S corporations (e.g., eliminating the Clifford Trust as an S corporation shareholder in the Tax Reform Act of 1986, hereinafter, the TRA), there are still numerous ways to use S corporations in income and estate tax planning scenarios. Below are briefly set forth some planning opportunities.

9.2 PROVIDING FUNDS FOR THE ELDERLY

As alluded to in Chapter 1, the S corporation can assist an adult child to provide funds for parents. An example will illustrate the problem:

EXAMPLE 9-1

Taxpayer's parents, Alvin and Harriet, are retired and living on social security. Taxpayer, because of his high income, is in the 33% bracket. Thus, for every $1 he gives his parents, it cost him 33 cents in federal taxes, thereby leaving a net to his parents of 67 cents. If the adult child made his parents S corporate shareholders in his corporation, the "middleman," "Uncle Sam," would be eliminated and thus Taxpayer would effectively be able to give more money to his parents since the money would come directly to them from the S corporation. The reason for this savings is that his parents would pay tax on the income at their low bracket (15%) instead of the taxpayer's high bracket (33%), thereby providing more funds to the parents: 18% (33% − 15%) times whatever funds are paid to the parents from the S corporation, subject to them exceeding the 15% bracket. (Note: This example assumes certain facts, namely, that the adult child is not supporting the parents and taking them as exemptions on his tax return, that Section 1366(e)'s family reallocation rules do not apply, etc.)

9.3 PROVIDING FUNDS FOR CHILDREN—THE EFFECT THAT THE "KIDDIE TAX" HAS ON INCOME TAX PLANNING WITH S CORPORATIONS

Parents are always seeking means to have Uncle Sam assist them in raising their children. The TRA has seriously hampered parents in having Uncle Sam foot the bill for children after 1986 because of the imposition of

185

the "kiddie tax" as set forth in Section 1 of the Code. The "kiddie tax" generally provides that the unearned income of children under the age of 14 is to be taxed at the parent's highest tax rate, regardless of the source of the child's unearned income. While it is beyond the scope of this book to discuss in detail the "kiddie tax," a brief discussion is set forth below. An example will illustrate the operation of the rule.

EXAMPLE 9-2

Grandma Hannah in 19X1 established in her will that her stock in XYZ, Inc., an S corporation, was to go to her grandson, Charles on her death. Grandma died in 1987 when her grandson Charles was 2 years old. Charles's 1987 Form K-1 from XYZ, Inc., set forth $10,000 in income to him. Charles will be taxed at his parents' highest tax rate. In 1987, Charles's parents tax rate is 28%. Thus, Charles will be taxed on the $10,000 of income from XYZ, Inc., at 28%.

If the child is over the age of 14, the "kiddie tax" does not apply, and thus a parent can utilize the teenager for tax planning, providing that Section 1366(e)'s family reallocation rules are not breached. An example of the use would be the situation set forth with taxpayer's parents in Example 9-1.

TAX POINTER

Care has to be taken in that, if income of an S corporation is received by a child, that the income is not used to satisfy a parent's support obligation. If it is, the parent will be taxed on the income.[1]

9.4 PROVIDING FUNDS FOR OTHER RELATIVES

A taxpayer may be providing funds to a relative (e.g., a brother, sister). In accordance with the discussion in Chapter 9.2, a taxpayer can use his or her S corporation as a means to provide the funds, thereby saving the taxpayer money.

9.5 RETIREMENT PLAN AND FRINGE BENEFITS

As discussed at Chapters 5.6 and 5.7, an S corporation can establish fringe benefits and retirement plans for its employees, but there are certain restrictions in regard to certain shareholder employees with respect to fringe benefits. Likewise, there are restrictions for shareholder-employees in retirement plans. However, retirement plans may be the only option for shareholder-employees to accumulate funds "tax free."

A. Employee Stock Ownership Trusts Cannot Be Holders of S Corporate Stock

As discussed at Chapter 2.3.A, ESOPs cannot be shareholders in an S corporation because an ESOP is not a permitted trust.

B. Retirement Plans Are Subject to Creditor Attack

Creditors have been able to, in a number of instances, mount successful challenges and to seize a participant's assets in a company's retirement plan. Thus, care should be undertaken before becoming a participant in a plan, since, if the participant has credit problems, all the participant's accrued benefits could be lost.[2]

9.6 SOCIAL SECURITY BENEFITS AND S CORPORATIONS

Generally, once an individual begins drawing social security benefits, he or she is limited to how much benefits they can draw. However, according to a recent unreported decision, *Gonzales* v. *Heckler,*[3] an S corporation provides a means to overcome this social security situation. In *Gonzales,* the social security recipient was a 50% shareholder in an S corporation; however, instead of taking out funds from the S corporation, the recipient's profits were left in the company to allow the company to grow. On these facts, the court held that the shareholder was permitted to draw social security benefits.

9.7 DISTRIBUTIONS OF EARNINGS GENERALLY NOT SUBJECT TO SELF-EMPLOYMENT TAX

As discussed at Chapter 5.16, distributions of income received by a shareholder from an S corporation generally are not subject to self-employment tax, thereby permitting a savings of tax for shareholders in closely held S corporations since the distribution is coming "payroll tax free."

TAX POINTER

As discussed at Chapter 5.16, naturally, since the distribution of income from the S corporation is not subject to self-employment tax, likewise, it will not accrue any benefits under the Social Security Act.

9.8   SHAREHOLDERS' AGREEMENT

Chapter 10.2 indicates that an S corporation can revoke its status if more than 50% of the shareholders of the corporation consent to the revocation. However, it is possible for one shareholder, although not a 50% or more shareholder, to terminate an S election. The method is simple—all the shareholder has to do to break the S corporate election is to transfer the shareholder's stock to an entity that is not a permitted shareholder (e.g., a C corporation controlled by the shareholder, a nonresident alien).[4] Therefore, to protect against this contingency, a shareholders' agreement is required to be established among the shareholders with language inserted to guard against the inadvertent termination detailed herein. (Note, a shareholders' agreement will not be deemed a second class of stock.[5]) Examples of such language are set forth in the Appendix 11.

In addition, a shareholders' agreement also provides other benefits, such as a means of establishing a basis for valuation of the stock for estate tax purposes, orderly transition if a shareholder wants to sell a stock interest, limitation of the shareholder's ability to give away the stock. A shareholders' agreement also protects the company if a shareholder is convicted of a crime, by forcing the convicted shareholder to sell his or her stock.

In regard to the importance of a shareholders' agreement in estate tax planning situations, see Chapter 9.11.A.1.a.

9.9   S CORPORATION CAN BE A SHAREHOLDER IN A C CORPORATION

By definition, an S corporation can be a shareholder of a C corporation, but if its stock interest results in the C corporation becoming a subsidiary for purposes of Section 1361(b)(2), then the S election will be lost. As to the amount of stock that the S corporation can own in a C corporation, it can be as high as 79%. (See Chapter 2.5 et seq. for further discussion of this topic.)

A.   Reasons Why an S Corporation Wants to Be a Shareholder in a C corporation

An S corporation may want to acquire stock in a C corporation to take advantage of the dividend received deduction provisions of Section 243. Another reason would be to take advantage of items unique to C corporate status (e.g., the accumulated earnings credit of Section 535, NOLs).

9.10 S CORPORATION CAN BE A PARTNER IN A PARTNERSHIP

By definition, partnership taxation is different from S corporate taxation. Because of these differences, S corporations may want to be a partner in a partnership. Some of the reasons why an S corporation wants to be a partner are set forth below.

For an example of when an S corporation was a partner in a partnership, see *Selig* v. *U.S.*[6]

A. Reasons Why an S Corporation Wants to Be a Partner

1. Section 704

Section 704 allows a partnership to allocate its income among its partners pursuant to an agreement, providing the allocation has substantial economic effect. In contrast, S corporations can basically distribute the income in two ways: distributions pursuant to stock interests or by means of salary to its shareholder-employees.

2. Partnership Basis Rules

The partnership basis rules are different from S basis rules in that partnership debt can be used to create bases for purposes of loss deductions. The simplified examples set forth below illustrate this point:

EXAMPLE 9-3

AB Company is a general partnership formed on 1/1/X7 composed of two equal partners, A and B. Both partners contribute $5,000 in cash as their capital contribution. On 1/1/X7 AB Company buys residential building and land costing $380,000, which is allocated $100,000 to land and $280,000 to building. To pay for the land and building, AB Company borrows $370,000 from the bank. AB Company proceeds to rent the building, depreciating it over 27.5 years. In the first 5 years of operation, the partnership losses are $10,000 each year. Each partner reports subject to the passive loss rules as his or her distribution of losses $5,000 each year for the first 5 years of operation.

EXAMPLE 9-4

Assume the same facts as in Example 9-3, but instead of AB Company being a partnership, it is an S corporation. A and B would only be able to deduct $5,000 of losses in the first year since that is the extent of their basis in the stock. As to the remaining $20,000 of losses for each shareholder, this could only be deducted by them when and if they have basis and after they satisfy the passive loss rules. (See Chapter 7 for discussion of how the shareholders would obtain basis.)

TAX POINTER

As discussed at the tax pointer in Chapter 2.2.A.1, if the Service detects an attempt to subvert the 35 shareholder limit by having S corporations composed of 35 shareholders each enter into ventures in partnership situations, the Service could strike them down.

9.11   ESTATE AND GIFT TAX PLANNING

A.   Estate Tax

When an S shareholder dies, general tax principles allow the stock basis of deceased shareholders to be stepped up to fair market value, at death, or the alternate valuation value, if the alternate valuation date is chosen. As discussed at Chapter 2.3.B.1, estates can be shareholders in an S corporation. An example to illustrate the effect that death will have in regard to the S corporation is set forth below:

EXAMPLE 9-5

P is the sole shareholder of A, Inc., an S corporation. At the time of P's death, his stock basis is zero because of all the losses passed through to him due to A, Inc.'s. operations; however, for purposes of estate tax valuation on the Form 706, P's basis for his stock is $300. P leaves all his assets to his sister, D. D's basis in her stock for sale of stock or taking losses in A, Inc., from operations is $300.

1.   Estate Tax Planning

As discussed at Chapter 2.3.B et seq., only certain types of testamentary trusts can be S shareholders. For instance, a QTIP trust (a qualified terminal interest property trust established under Section 2056(b)(7)) can be an S shareholder, but a testamentary trust, where the trustee has the right to accumulate income, cannot. Thus, to solve the problem where a prohibited testamentary trust could become a shareholder, as discussed at Chapter 2.3.B.1, the executor of the estate attempts to keep the estate, which is a permitted shareholder, in existence as long as possible before funding the trust, which will cause the S corporate election to be terminated pursuant to Section 1361(c)(2)(A)(iii) 60 days after the trust is funded with the S corporate stock.

Rather than have this termination of S status pursuant to Section 1362(d)(2)(Chapter 10.3), proper tax planning would be to ensure that the S corporate stock does not pass in a situation that would cause loss of S status. Thus, for instance in the case of a QTIP trust, care has to be taken in regard to who will receive the remainder portion of the trust so that the 35 shareholder limit of Section 1361(b)(1)(A) will not be breached; that wills are reviewed to ensure that proper testamentary trusts are provided if S corporate stock is an estate asset, and so on.

a. The Shareholders' Agreement

The shareholders' agreement as discussed at Chapter 9.9 provides an orderly means of transition of stock at death, lifetime transfers, and so on. It also provides a means for valuing the stock of the S corporation when a shareholder dies so that the uncertainty of valuation can be eliminated. Various means can be used to accomplish this valuation, for instance, a certificate of value, valuation based on the book value of the corporation, or a multiple earnings approach. As to what method should be used, it depends on the particular business in which the S corporation is engaged, and the reader is respectfully requested to consult the case law dealing with estate tax and shareholders' agreement to determine the proper valuation formula for the respective business involved.

b. Private Annuities

A private annuity is one planning device used to reduce estate taxes. Basically, the mechanics of the annuity are that an individual (a "parent") transfers assets to another individual (a "child") in return for the child's promise to support the parent for the parent's life pursuant to actuarial formulas and tables. An example will illustrate the tax effect of an annuity:

EXAMPLE 9-6

Arthur, a widower, is a 50% shareholder in an S corporation, XYZ, Inc. The other shareholder of XYZ, Inc., is Bob, Arthur's son. Arthur's estate is composed mainly of stock in XYZ, Inc., which is worth in excess of $600,000. In an effort to reduce his taxable estate, in 1986 Arthur enters into a private annuity with his daughter, Dorothy, a permitted S corporate shareholder, and funds the annuity with some of his S corporate stock in XYZ, Inc. By doing this, Arthur reduces his estate to $500,000. Shortly after entering into this annuity with his daughter, Arthur dies in a plane crash in 1987. Because Arthur's estate is below $600,000, there will be no estate tax. In regard to Dorothy, she acquires this stock in XYZ, Inc., estate tax free because of the annuity contract.

c. The Cain Redemption

As an alternative to the private annuity discussed in Chapter 9.11.A.1.b, a *Cain*[7] redemption can be done. In *Cain*, the decedent redeemed, without reservation or contingency, stock in a family-owned corporation for $150,000. The corporation was to pay $6,000 at the time the stock was transferred and $1,000 per month for 12 years or until the decedent's death, whichever occurred first. Prior to the decedent's redemption of her stock, the corporation had 1,600 shares issued and outstanding, of which the decedent owned 600 shares; her son, the president of the corporation, owned 600 shares; and her son's wife owned 400 shares.

The $1,000 monthly payments were made pursuant to a note, which provided that the note was payable without interest, except that any installment that became delinquent would carry 6% interest from the scheduled date of payment until it was actually paid. At the time the decedent died, the balance of the unpaid note was $44,135.

The court in *Cain* sustained the stock redemption and excluded the balance of the unpaid note from the decedent's estate. Thus, the family was able to reduce the decedent's estate tax in a manner similar to that produced in an annuity transaction. However, unlike an annuity but similar to an installment sale, an interest deduction was created for the buyer (i.e., the corporation). Thus, in the case of a corporate redemption, taxpayers might consider adopting the approach used in *Cain* to accomplish their objectives. (For a discussion of redemptions, see Chapter 10.9.A.)

TAX POINTER

> The Omnibus Budget Reconciliation Act (OBRA), Section 203G(c) has prescribed that sales between family members are suspect where potential appreciation of the assets is involved. Accordingly, care should be exercised in connection with family annuities such as the *Cain* situation.

B. Gift Tax

A shareholder during life may decide to reduce his or her holdings by making gifts of S corporate stock to take advantage of the $10,000 annual exclusion as prescribed in Section 2503(b), the unified credit of Section 2010, or just on general principles. Care must be exercised when gifts are made with S corporate stock to ensure the requirements of Section 1361 are not breached in that the stock will not be transferred to nonpermitted shareholders or that the numerical limit of 35 shareholders is not exceeded. Further, if a shareholders' agreement is in place, then the gift of the S corporate stock must comply with the terms of the agreement.

TAX POINTER

If sufficient stock is transferred and the S corporation owns investment tax credit property, investment tax credit recapture could occur (see discussion at Chapter 9.14) or the books of the S corporation have to be closed (see Chapter 10.7.C.).

9.12 SALE OF THE S CORPORATE BUSINESS

A. Introduction

At sometime during the S corporation's history, the shareholders may want to sell the business. Prior to the Tax Reform Act of 1986, the shareholders had a number of choices to accomplish their objectives (e.g., Section 337 liquidation, a sale of assets at the corporate level, or a sale of stock). Now that the TRA has made Section 337 a prohibitive undertaking (Chapter 10.10), the S shareholders basically have two choices to sell the business: either an asset sale at the corporate level or a sale of corporate stock. For an excellent discussion of how to sell a business, see *Tax Guide for Buying and Selling a Business* by Stanley Hagendorf (Prentice-Hall) (in the process of being revised to reflect the TRA). The discussion below outlines pertinent points in regard to the sale of an S corporate business after the TRA.

B. Sale of Assets

If an S corporation has been one since inception, or has no C corporate assets, then sale of the business assets at the corporate level becomes an easy undertaking, with a gain or loss from the sale of the assets being passed through to the shareholders pursuant to Section 1366. (See discussion at Chapter 4.) Because of the fact that assets are being sold instead of stock, a buyer should be easily found to purchase the business since the buyer will be assuming little risk in purchasing these assets. (As to the risks in purchasing stock, see the discussion at Chapter 10.8.C.) One of the reasons why a buyer usually likes to purchase assets rather than stock in acquiring a business is that the buyer can easily obtain a stepped-up basis for the assets that would be basically prohibitive in a stock acquisition. (See Chapter 10.8.C.4 as to step-up in basis for assets when S stock is acquired.)

1. The Effect That C Corporate Assets Will Have on the Sale— Section 1374

If the S corporation has C corporate assets because it acquired them in a merger or a spin-off, or was formerly a C corporation, sale of the assets becomes complicated because of the fact of Section 1374. (See Chapters 6.2 and 6.7.) Thus, shareholders will probably give serious consideration to a stock sale to sell the corporate business. (See discussion at Chapter 10.8.)

2.   Tax Consequences of Sale of S Corporate Assets

a.   *Investment Tax Credit Recapture*

As discussed in Chapter 9.14, if there remains investment tax credit with respect to assets sold or disposed of by the S corporation, the S corporate shareholders will have investment tax credit recapture.

b.   *What to Do with Unwanted Assets Not Needed by the Purchaser of the Corporate Business*

When a purchaser acquires corporate assets of a business, the purchaser may not want all the assets. For instance, the purchaser may not want a shareholder-employee's car, desk, or obsolete assets. Alternatively, the S corporate shareholder in selling the assets of the business may not want to sell certain assets, for example, cash, accounts receivable, and so on. The shareholders have various means to solve the problem of the unwanted assets—liquidating the corporation (see general discussion at Chapter 10.10), distributing the assets to the shareholders (Chapter 10.9.A), or keeping the assets in corporate name. (This last alternative may not be a viable one if the S corporation is in a state that does not recognize S corporate status and imposes a minimum franchise tax; see Appendix 4.) To determine the best course to follow, the S shareholders will have to investigate each situation determining the tax effect.

C.   Sale of Stock

As discussed at Chapter 10.8, it may be difficult to sell S corporate stock because of the risks involved. However, as discussed at Chapter 10.8.E, the sale of S corporate stock may be the only viable alternative to dispose of the business in certain circumstances.

D.   Reorganizations—Mergers, Recapitalizations, and So On

Rather than pursue the sale of corporate stock or S corporate assets that would produce a taxable situation, the shareholders may consider the tax-free reorganization sections under Section 368 as a means of corporate transition. For a discussion of reorganizations, see Chapter 10.11.

9.13 SECTION 1244 ELECTION

As discussed at various places in this book, the TRA eliminated the capital gains deduction described in Section 1202, but basically left intact the capital loss rules (i.e., the $3,000 annual loss limitation, except that now, long-term losses offset ordinary income on a one-to-one basis). If an S corporation does not elect Section 1244 status for its stock, then the individuals on sale of the stock, liquidation of the corporation, and so on where the disposition produces a loss for the shareholder will be subject to the TRA's new rules on capital losses. However, if the S corporation elects Section 1244 treatment for its stock, then the shareholders, when a loss is created in connection with their stock pursuant to Section 1244(b), can take each year a maximum of $50,000 of ordinary loss if the taxpayer is single and $100,000 if the taxpayer is married and a joint return is filed. Section 1244 sets forth a number of requirements for the corporation to qualify for the stock. For instance, Section 1244(d)(4) states that estates and trusts do not qualify for Section 1244 treatment. It is beyond the scope of this book to offer a detailed discussion of Section 1244; accordingly, the reader is requested to review Section 1244 to see if it applies to specific situations facing the S corporation shareholder.

9.14 INVESTMENT TAX CREDIT RECAPTURE

Under prior law, when an S corporation acquired property other than in a Section 351 nontaxable exchange, the investment tax credit was taken by the shareholders. Similarly, when the S corporation disposed of or sold the property in a taxable situation prior to the expiration of the asset's useful life, Section 47 prescribed that investment tax credit recapture would be reported by the shareholders, akin to the method that an individual would use to report the investment tax credit recapture if the individual purchased and later sold the assets. In addition, Reg. Section 1.47-4(a) prescribes that when an S shareholder's stock interest is reduced below two-thirds of what it was when the investment tax credit was passed through, there is investment tax credit recapture to the extent of the interest conveyed. The disposition of stock to generate the recapture could arise in a number of ways—gift or sale of stock, liquidation of the corporation, and so on. Examples of a disposition of the investment tax credit property at the corporate level that would generate recapture would be a sale, involuntary conversion, trade-in, converting a business asset to a personal asset, and so on. As the examples on page 196 indicate, there are ways to eliminate the harsh effects of investment tax credit recapture.

EXAMPLE 9-7

A and B, two brothers, are equal shareholders in C, Inc., a calendar year S corporation. Each shareholder owns 100 shares of this stock in the corporation. In early 1985, C, Inc., bought 5-year property for $100,000. Each shareholder reported $50,000 as the purchase on their Form 3468, taking a credit of $5,000 each (10% × $50,000). In 1987, A sold 60 shares of its stock in C, Inc., to X, a qualified S corporate shareholder. A will have investment tax credit of $3,000 (60% × $5,000) reported on his Form 1040 using Form 4255.

EXAMPLE 9-8

Assume the same facts as in Example 9-7, but that A instead of selling the stock to X, gives it to him instead, filing a Form 709. A would still be required to report the investment tax credit recapture in 1987 of $3,000.[8]

EXAMPLE 9-9

Assume the same facts as in Example 9-8, but instead of disposing of 60 shares, A only disposes of 30 shares in 1987. No investment tax credit recapture can occur since A did not reduce his stock interest in C, Inc., below two-thirds of what it was when the credit was passed through to him.

There is also another special rule set forth in Reg. Section 1.47-4 regarding S stock reduction in that once there is recapture with respect to a particular property, no additional recapture as to that property can occur unless stock ownership is further reduced to less than one-third of what it was at the time of the credit pass-through. An example will illustrate.

EXAMPLE 9-10

Assume the same facts as in Example 9-8. In 1987, A disposes of 5 more shares, bringing his stock interest down to 35 shares from his original 100 share holding. Because A did not dispose of sufficient amount of shares, there is no more investment tax credit recapture with respect to these 5 shares.

TAX POINTERS

1. As discussed at Chapter 10.8.C.3, while stock disposition triggers investment tax credit recapture, it will not trigger depreciation recapture under Sections 1245, 1250, et seq.

2. Pursuant to Reg. Section 1.47-4(d), termination of S status will not trigger S status recapture. (See discussion at Chapter 10.7.B.1.c.)

9.15 BELOW-MARKET LOANS—SECTION 7872

Section 7872 was enacted to deal with situations where inadequate interest was being charged for the loan. These types of loans are commonly referred to as "below-market loans." In the context of S corporations, below-market loans could arise in two situations: loans from a shareholder to the shareholder's S corporation, and vice versa. The discussion below briefly outlines both situations and the tax consequences that might arise. It is to be noted that if the loans by shareholders are not pro rata or are made pursuant to Section 1361(c)(5)'s safe harbor rules, the S status could be lost. (See Chapter 2.9.B for a discussion about this loss of status.) Also, the tracing Rules set forth in the Temporary Regulations under Section 163 have to be followed in regard to the loan(s).

A. Loans from Shareholders to S Corporations

By definition, if a shareholder makes a below-market loan to an S corporation, the shareholder will be deemed to make a contribution to capital for the amount of the below-market loan interest that will increase the shareholder's basis. On the other side, the corporation will be deemed to have made an interest payment to the shareholder for the amount of the below-market interest that will cause the shareholder to report interest income equal to this amount. However, the shareholder will be able to offset this interest income by the amount of the corporation's interest deduction to the shareholder allowable pursuant to the rules discussed in Chapter 7.

B. Loans from the S Corporation to the S Shareholder

Section 7872 prescribes two different types of loans: a below-market loan or a compensation-related loan. Basically, the transaction between the S corporation and the shareholder will be a wash; however, adverse tax consequences could possibly develop if the shareholder's accumulated adjustment account has a zero balance at the time the below-market or compensation related loan is occurring.

TAX POINTER

> To avoid running afoul of Section 7872, proper interest should be charged on all loans between the corporation and the S shareholder.

9.16 OTHER AREAS OF TAX PLANNING

Discussions of various tax planning possibilities will be found throughout the text. For instance, Chapter 3.6 discusses tax considerations with respect to C corporations converting to S corporate status. The reader is referred to the index and table of contents of this book to find these tax planning situations.

9.17 STATUTE OF LIMITATIONS

Statute of limitations problems could arise in a number of situations—at the corporate level, shareholder level, or the unified determination levels of Sections 6221–6233. (See Chapter 9.18.) It is beyond the scope of this book to offer a detailed discussion of this area. Accordingly, only significant points will be discussed. It is to be noted that the Code has a specific section dealing with S corporations, Section 6037, and the reader should consult it when reviewing problems concerning the statute of limitations.

A. Statute of Limitations at Corporate Level—Section 6037

The filing of the Form 1120S by the corporation will start the running of the statute of limitations. This running of the statute of limitations is important for the corporation if it is liable for taxes under Sections 1371(d)(2), 1374, or 1375, or if the S corporation's election has terminated. Section 6501(a) prescribes that the number of years that the Service has to access a deficiency is 3 years from the later on the due date of the return or the actual date the return is filed. Reg. Section 1.6037-1(b) prescribes that the Form 1120S must be filed on or before the fifteenth day of the third month following the close of the taxable year. Reg. Section 1.6037-1(c) prescribes that filing of the Form 1120S will cause the statute of limitations to start to run even though it may be determined at a later date that the S corporation lost its status and should have filed Form 1120.

TAX POINTER

See discussion at Chapter 3.4, which details that the filing of a Form 1120S for many years does not stop the Service from raising the issue of an initial improper election.

1. Filing Tax Court Petition

In regard to tax deficiencies arising from S transactions, there is no requirement that the notice of deficiency be mailed to the corporation, unless the deficiency concerns itself with taxation at the corporate level (e.g., tax under Sections 1374, 1375, and so on).[9]

B. Statute of Limitations—Shareholder Level

Basically, the statute of limitations runs separately for each shareholder. So, based on a filed Form 1120S, one shareholder could be subject to a 3-year statute of limitations, while another, who omitted income, could be subject by Section 6501(e) to the 6-year statute of limitations.

C. Unified Determinations

As discussed at Chapter 9.18, the Tax Equity and Fiscal Responsibility Act of 1982 (TEFRA) established complex rules for auditing partnerships, which Congress implied are to apply to S corporations. As the discussion in Chapter 9.18 indicates, statute of limitations for assessing a deficiency fluctuates depending on what procedural step is reached in the audit process and the reader is respectfully referred to Chapter 9.18 for a discussion of this topic.

9.18 AUDIT OF S CORPORATIONS

Prior to the Subchapter S Revision Act of 1982 (SSRA), it was possible to have several different audits regarding S corporate transactions for the same year. The SSRA simplified the procedure by establishing Sections 6241–6245. With respect to Section 6242, it requires a shareholder to "treat a Subchapter S item in a manner which is consistent with the treatment of such item on the corporate return unless the shareholder notifies the Secretary [at the time and in the manner prescribed by the Regulations] of the inconsistency." To notify the Service of the inconsistency, the shareholder is required to use Form 8082 for this purpose (Appendix 12).

A. Unified Determinations

The Tax Equity and Fiscal Responsibility Act of 1982 (TEFRA) imposed new rules regarding audits of partnerships generally after 1982 (Sections 6221–6233) in an effort to standardize them and adopt a more uniform procedure. Congress in the SSRA implied that these partnership rules apply to S corporations. It is beyond the scope of this book to offer a detailed discussion about this area; however, significant portions are mentioned below:

1. There are two different rules that apply to refund and deficiencies.
2. Section 6231(a)(1)(B) exempts from the Sections 6221–6233 rules partnerships that have 10 or fewer partners, unless the partners wish

to have the special rules apply. Presumably, the same rule applies to S corporations.

3. Various statutes of limitation are prescribed in Sections 6221–6233. For instance, Section 6229(a) prescribes that the period for assessing any tax should not expire before the date that is 3 years after the later of (a) the date on which the S corporate return for such taxable year was filed or (b) the last day for filing such return for such year (determined without regard to extensions). However, before the Service can assess the tax, Section 6226 prescribes that one or more shareholders can request judicial review with the period of limitations of assessment suspended until 1 year after the judicial review becomes final.

9.19   SHAREHOLDER DEBT—PROS AND CONS

Chapter 2.9.B.1 discussed the nontax reason for debt in an S corporation. As discussed at Chapter 7.2.E, if the shareholder's debt is evidenced by a written note, then when the note is repaid, when basis is zero, Section 1271(a)(1) prescribes that capital gain will result. If the debt is an open account, that is, just a book entry, then ordinary income will result. While under the TRA this might not have any bearing since, as discussed throughout this book, capital gain is taxed basically the same as ordinary income, it would have a bearing in the future if capital gains are taxed differently from ordinary income. Therefore, S shareholders, if they are lending money to their S corporation, should do so by means of a note to preserve their tax position, should the law change. There are also risks in the use of debt in an S corporation. For instance, see the Tax Pointer at Chapter 7.2.E, where debt was reclassified as equity. Pursuant to the Section 1366(d)(3) rules as discussed at Chapter 7.4.C, unused losses or deductions that are in existence with the S election terminates can only be applied against stock basis, not loans.

9.20   THE DANGER OF HAVING THE S CORPORATION OWNING TAX-EXEMPT BONDS AND STOCK AND SECURITIES

A.   Tax-Exempt Bonds

At first blush, it may appear that because an S corporation, per the discussion at Chapter 4.1, generally passes income through to its shareholders, there should be no problem in having the S corporation hold tax-exempt bonds. However, on several grounds, this is dangerous. As discussed at Chapter 8.3.B.1, having the S corporation own tax-exempt bonds when it has earnings and profits could lead to the recharacterization of the tax-exempt income as taxable.

Under Section 1363(d)'s rules discussed at Chapter 4.8, if the tax-exempt bonds are in excess of book value and they are distributed to the shareholders, gain will be realized by the shareholders on the distribution in an amount equal to the difference between fair market value at the time of distribution and the S corporation's basis. Likewise, when the S corporation liquidates under Section 337, the shareholders will have to report gain on the difference between fair market value and shareholder's basis in his, her, or its stock in the S corporation.

B. Stock and Securities

Stock and securities also pose a problem for S corporate shareholders. The problem generated by stock and securities is the same one that plagues tax-exempt bonds as outlined in the last two sentences of Chapter 9.20.A.

ENDNOTES FOR CHAPTER 9

1. See, e.g., *Braun,* T.C. Memo 1984, 285.

2. See, e.g., *St. Paul Fire and Marine Ins. Co.* v. *Cox,* 752 F. 2d 550 (11th Cir. 1985).

3. U.S.D.C., (S.D., Fla.), 83 Civ. 8199 (1985).

4. For example of how this can be done, see *T. J. Henry Associates,* 80 T.C. 886 (1983) discussed at Chapter 10.3.

5. See, e.g., Ltr. Rul. 8411057.

6. 565 F. Supp. 524 (E.D., Wis. 1983), aff'd 740 F. 2d 572 (7th Cir. 1984) (a partnership involving the Milwaukee Brewers, which was a limited partnership, having the Milwaukee Brewers Baseball Club, Inc., an S corporation, as a partner).

7. 37 T.C. 185.

8. *Charbonnet* v. *U.S.,* 29 AFTR 2d 633 (5th Cir. 1972).

9. *Robert L. Bunnel,* 50 T.C. 837 (1968).

10

Revocation and Termination of S Status;

Tax Consequences on Sale of S Corporate Stock;

Redemptions, Partial Liquidations, Liquidations, and Reorganizations Under Section 368(a)

10.1 TERMINATION AND REVOCATION OF S STATUS—STATUTORY GROUNDS

An S corporation can lose its S status in any of three different ways: a voluntary revocation of status pursuant to Section 1362(d)(1)(Chapter 10.2), the S corporation ceasing to be an S corporation pursuant to Section 1362(d)(2) by flunking one of the statutory standards to be an S corporation (e.g., acquiring 36 shareholders)(Chapter 10.3), or the S corporation having passive investment income in excess of 25% of gross receipts for three consecutive taxable years where the S corporation has Subchapter C corporate earnings and profits pursuant to Section 1362(d)(3). (See Chapter 10.4.)

When termination occurs other than at the beginning or end of the S corporation's taxable year, this causes the taxable year to be split into two parts: the first, a short S taxable year, and the second, a short C taxable year. Adverse tax consequences could arise if proper planning does not occur with respect to termination. (For a discussion of the tax aspects in connection with termination, see Chapter 10.7.) Because termination could be accidental, there is a provision in the Code, Section 1362(f), whereby the Service can waive inadvertent terminations. (See Chapter 10.5.) And, assuming that the termination was deliberate, there is even a procedure for reelection of S status after the termination of S status (Section 1362(g)). (See Chapter 10.6.)

10.2 VOLUNTARY REVOCATION OF S STATUS—SECTION 1362(d)(1)

Section 1362(d)(1) prescribes that an S corporation can voluntarily revoke its status. The revocation is accomplished by shareholders holding more than one-half of the stock of the corporation on the date revocation is made simply consenting to the revocation. Temp. Reg. Section 18.1362-3 provides that the "revocation shall be made by the corporation filing a statement that the corporation revokes" its S election. No official form for the revocation is prescribed or has been issued by the Service. (A copy of an unofficial form is found in Appendix 13.) Temp. Reg. Section 18.1362-3 lists some other requirements, namely,

- The statement shall be signed by any person authorized to sign the return required to be filed under Section 6037 and shall be filed with the Service center where the election was properly filed.

- There shall be attached to the statement of revocation a statement of consent signed by each shareholder who consents to the revocation stating the number of issued and outstanding shares of stock (including nonvoting stock) that is held by each such shareholder at the time the revocation is made.

TAX POINTERS

1. Care must be exercised in revoking S status since there are a number of Private Letter Rulings which state that once an S corporation files its statement of revocation, the Service will not allow it to be rescinded.[1]
2. If an S corporation revokes its status under Section 1362(d)(1), Section 1362(f)(1) prescribes that it cannot seek relief under Section 1362(f) to restore its S election.

A. Reasons for Revoking S Status

There are many reasons for revoking S status, tax and nontax. Nontax reasons might be that the S corporation wants to have corporations and partnerships as shareholders, wants more than 35 shareholders, and so on. A tax reason might be that the corporation has turned profitable. As discussed in Chapter 1.3, a prime reason for electing S status is to pass start-up losses directly through to the shareholders. Once the S corporation is profitable, there may not be a reason to maintain S status (i.e., to take advantage of lower corporate income tax rates). However, in view of the changes to Section 337, the corporate alternative minimum tax, and so on, it is doubtful that once S status is elected, many corporations will opt C status for tax reasons. (See discussion at Chapters 10.10 and 1.2.E.)

B. Effective Date of Revocation—Sections 1362(d)(1)(C) and (D)

1.   Section 1362(d)(1)(C)

Various dates can be chosen for revoking S status. For instance, Section 1362(d)(1)(C)(i) prescribes that a revocation made within the first 2 months and 15 days of the S corporation tax year is retroactive and in effect for the entire tax year. Thus revocation would mean that there would not be any S corporate year if a revocation is made under Section 1362(d)(1)(C)(i). However, Section 1362(d)(1)(C)(ii) prescribes that a revocation made during a taxable year but after the fifteenth day of the first 2 months of the taxable year will cause the revocation to be effective on the first day of the following tax year.

2.   Section 1362(d)(1)(D)

Overriding the revocation specified in Section 1362(d)(1)(C) is Section 1362(d)(1)(D)'s general statement that "[i]f the revocation specifies a date for revocation which is on or after the day on which the revocation is made, the revocation shall be effective on and after the date so specified." Thus, shareholders holding more than 50% of the stock (see Section 1362(d)(1)(B) for the requirement of how many shareholders are required to revoke S status) could elect a date of revocation to be the date the revocation is made or any date thereafter. Examples will illustrate:

EXAMPLE 10-1

A, Inc., an S corporation is formed on 1/1/X7 and has one shareholder, L. It files its tax return on a calendar year basis. On 2/15/X7, L, the sole shareholder, decides to revoke the S corporate status. A, Inc., will file as a calendar year corporation for 19X7 pursuant to Section 1362(d)(1)(C)(i).

EXAMPLE 10-2

Assume the same facts as in Example 10-1, but L revokes the S status on 4/1/X7 not specifying when the revocation will go into effect. Pursuant to Section 1362(d)(1)(C)(ii), A, Inc., will file as an S corporation for 19X7, but as of 1/1/X8, it will file as a C corporation.

EXAMPLE 10-3

Assume the same facts as in Example 10-2, but in filing the revocation on 4/1/X7 L specifies that the revocation pursuant to Section 1362(d)(1)(D) shall go into effect on 7/1/X7. The effect is that A, Inc., will be an S corporation for a 6-month period 1/1–6/30/X7 and a C corporation for the rest of its life subject to A, Inc., reelecting S status pursuant to Section 1362(g). Further, A, Inc., will file two short returns: one for the period 1/1–6/30/X7 as an S corporation and the other for the period 7/1–12/31/X7 as a C corporation. (For discussion of the tax effects in connection with having two short returns in the same year and how to determine the number of days in each short year, see Chapter 10.7.)

TAX POINTERS

1. It is to be noted that the filing of Form 1120 instead of Form 1120S may be determined as a sufficient statement to cause a revocation of S status, especially if the corporation has only one shareholder.[2]

2. Another means to effect elimination of S status is for a 50% or more shareholder (i.e., a father) to transfer more than 50%

of the stock to another shareholder (i.e., himself, as custodian of his children) and refuse to consent to S status.[3]

C. Revocation of an Intentional Termination Under Section 1362(d)(1)(D) or Section 1362(d)(1)(C)(ii)

After revocation is made under Sections 1362(d)(1)(D) or 1362(d)(1)(C)(ii), the shareholders of the S corporation opting for revocation may wish to change their minds before the effective date for the revocation of S status. Unfortunately, there is no specific statutory authority allowing a revocation of an intentional termination. However, by logic, it would seem that the shareholders who filed for the revocation should be able to withdraw it by notifying the Service before the effective date of the revocation.

10.3   FAILURE TO REMAIN AS AN S CORPORATION—SECTION 1362(d)(2)

Electing S corporate status is not a one-time event; it is an continuing process, and once the S corporation fails to meet one of the requirements discussed in Chapter 2 set forth in Section 1361 (e.g., having a nonresident alien shareholder, having a corporation as an S shareholder), the corporation will lose its status. For taxable years beginning after 1982, Section 1362(d)(2)(B) prescribes that the S corporation loses its S status on the date of the terminating event. An example will illustrate:

EXAMPLE 10-4

A, Inc., is a calendar year S corporation. On July 1, it acquired a nonresident alien as a shareholder, Gloria, thereby terminating its S status pursuant to Section 1361(b)(1)(C) on July 1.

Because the S corporation in Example 10-4 ceased to be such on a date other than the beginning and end of its taxable year, it will be forced to file two tax returns: one for the period 1/1–6/30, which will be on Form 1120S, and one for the period 7/1–12/31, which will be on Form 1120. Thereafter, as discussed in Chapter 10.1, unless the corporation can show that its termination was inadvertent or it applies for reelection under Section 1362(g), it will file a Form 1120 for the rest of its existence. (See Chapter 10.7 for the tax consequences that arise on the termination of the S election.)

As to how to terminate the S election effectively under Section 1362(d)(2), the termination could be done deliberately or inadvertently. *T. J. Henry Associates, Inc.,*[4] offers a means of how to do an intentional termination under

Section 1362(d)(2) rather than under Section 1362(d)(1). As to inadvertent termination, this could arise in a number of circumstances: for instance, the corporation failing to keep track of the number of shareholders it has and thus having 36 shareholders at one juncture instead of 35.

In regard to some terminating events under Section 1362(d)(2), the corporation can take steps to prevent them from occurring by entering into a shareholders' agreement with its shareholders proscribing certain events, for example, transferring stock to a shareholder who would cause the loss of the election. (For an example of language that could be used in a shareholders' agreement, see Appendix 12 as well as the discussion at Chapter 9.8.) In the event that there is a terminating event under Section 1362(d)(2), the shareholders can follow the procedure of Sections 1362(f) and (g) to regain the election. (See Chapters 10.5 and 10.6 for a discussion of these topics.)

A. Notification of Termination

Under prior law, Reg. Section 1.1372-4(b)(3) adopted under former Section 1372, required the S corporation to notify the Service about the termination. With the passage of the Subchapter S Revision Act of 1982, which revised Section 1372, the Service did not adopt a regulation requiring notification, so presumably the S corporation, if a termination occurs under Section 1362(d)(2), does not have to notify the Service.

10.4 S CORPORATION HAVING SUBCHAPTER C EARNINGS AND PROFITS AND DERIVING MORE THAN 25% OF ITS GROSS RECEIPTS FROM PASSIVE INVESTMENT INCOME FOR THREE CONSECUTIVE YEARS—SECTION 1362(d)(3)

One danger in operating an S corporation with Subchapter C earnings and profits from a C corporation (see Chapter 10.4.A for a definition of "Subchapter C earnings and profits") is that the S corporation could pay a tax under Section 1375 if it has "gross receipts" more than 25% of which are passive investment income. (See Chapter 6.4 et seq. for a discussion of this topic and the definition of the other related terms found herein.) The other danger is that if the S corporation meets the requirements set forth in the preceding sentence for 3 consecutive years (i.e., has Subchapter C earnings and profits and 25% or more of passive investment income), pursuant to Section 1362(d)(3)(A)(ii) and (iii) it can lose its S status. If the S corporation meets the test set forth in Section 1362(d)(3)(A)(ii) and (iii), it will lose its S status pursuant to Section 1362(d)(3)(A) on the first day of the first taxable year beginning after the third consecutive year in which the S corporation has excessive passive investment income.

In connection with the above, the following should be noted:

1. The test for termination under Section 1362(d)(3) is multifaceted so that if one part of the test can be flunked (e.g., having gross receipts less than 25% from passive income for one of the counting years), the S status will not be lost.

2. Section 1362(d)(3) by definition is designed to prevent an inadvertent termination because of failure to monitor the S corporation for one year. To prevent difficulty, prudent advice would be to take steps to remove the Subchapter C earnings and profits from the corporation. (See Chapter 6.4.K for a discussion of this topic.)

An example will illustrate the mechanics of Section 1362(d)(3)(A)(ii):

EXAMPLE 10-5

A, Inc., converted to S status on 1/1/87 having one shareholder, R. At the time of its conversion, it had $1 of Subchapter C earnings and profits. In its first two years of operation as an S corporation, its gross receipts consisted of 100% of passive investment income. A, Inc., paid a tax under Section 1375 on its passive investment income for the 2 years involved. In year 3, A, Inc., had no passive investment income. A, Inc., will not lose its S status under Section 1362(d)(3)(A)(ii) because, even though it has Subchapter C earnings and profits, it did not have passive investment income exceeding 25% of gross receipts for 3 consecutive years. Thus, the 3-year counting period commences again.

A. Definition of Subchapter C Earnings and Profits

For an S corporation to be taxed under Section 1375 or to lose its S status under Section 1362(d)(3), it must have "Subchapter C earnings and profits." Section 1362(d)(3)(B) defines Subchapter C earnings and profits as earnings and profits arising from a period when the corporation was not an S corporation. In regard to a definition of earnings and profits, see Sections 312 and 316. (See also discussion at Chapter 4.9.)

B. Elimination of Subchapter C Earnings and Profits— Section 1368(e)(3)

As discussed at Chapter 6.4.K, Section 1368(e)(3) prescribes a method to eliminate earnings and profits, thereby eliminating the problem for termination of S corporate status under Section 1362(d)(3).

10.5 WAIVER OF TERMINATION—SECTION 1362(f)

To prevent unwarranted tax results arising from termination, Congress has prescribed some ameliorative relief in Section 1362(f). If the following occurs,

1. The S corporation loses its election pursuant to Section 1362(d)(2) (Chapter 10.3) or Section 1362(d)(3) (Chapter 10.4),

2. The Service deems the termination was inadvertent,

3. The corporation, within a reasonable time after discovering the termination of election, takes steps to restore S status,

4. The corporation and all persons who were shareholders during the effective period, agree to make whatever adjustments are required by the Service,

the S status will be restored pursuant to Section 1362(f).

In regard to the above, it should be noted that Section 1362(f) is devoid as to prescribing what types of inadvertent terminations are covered. The Senate Finance Committee Report to the Subchapter S Revision Act of 1982 (hereinafter, the SSRA Senate Finance Committee Report) states that the Service should grant waivers and restore S status when no tax avoidance will result.[5] Examples of what the SSRA Senate Finance Committee Report felt would not be tax avoidance would be inadvertent breaches of the one class of stock requirements of Section 1361(b)(1)(D) (Chapters 2.1 and 2.2) and inadvertent violations of the passive income rules of Section 1362(d)(3) (Chapter 10.4) if the shareholders agreed to treat any additional income from C corporate years arising from audit, as a dividend. Further examples are found in the Private Letter Rulings, and the reader is directed to consult these rulings for the types of terminations where a waiver has been issued. (In regard to consulation of Private Letter Rulings, the Private Letter Ruling Services frequently have an index by Code sections to assist the reader in locating a particular topic.) In connection with same, one particular Private Letter Ruling is noted, Private Letter Ruling 8523097. In Private Letter Ruling 8523097, an attorney advised a major shareholder of an S corporation that he would not cause the S status of the corporation to terminate if he transferred a portion of his stock to two trusts established for the benefit of the shareholder's children. The attorney who rendered this advice was also the attorney for the S corporation. In fact, the attorney's advice was wrong, and the trusts were not permitted shareholders under Section 1361. In the year subsequent to termination, under Section 1362(d)(2), a new attorney discovered that the S corporation terminated in the prior year when the trusts became shareholders.

When the new attorney learned about the termination in the prior year, steps were taken to transfer the stock held by the trusts to permitted shareholders. The Service, under Section 1362(f), restored the S status retroactive to the terminating event.

TAX POINTER

> It is to be noted that Section 1362(f) does not cover revocation under Section 1362(d)(1). (See Chapter 10.2.B for discussions of revocations under Section 1362(d)(1).) Consequently, if an S corporation revokes its status under Section 1362(d)(1), and it wants to have its S status restored, it will have to do so under Section 1362(g). (See discussion under Chapter 10.6.)

10.6   ELECTION AFTER TERMINATION—SECTION 1362(g)

If an S corporation loses its S status under the grounds specified in Section 1362(d), Section 1362(g) provides for a procedure to restore the election. Section 1362(g) lists a number of requirements that must be satisfied, namely, that the corporation and any successor corporation must wait 5 years to reelect S status unless the Service consents earlier. As to what a successor corporation is, Section 1362(g) does not define the term; rather, Reg. Section 1.1372-5(b) adopted under former Section 1372, the predecessor to Section 1362(g), prescribes that the successor corporation means

any corporation

1. 50 percent or more of the stock of which is owned, directly or indirectly, by the same persons who at any time during the first taxable year for which such termination was effective, owned 50 percent or more of the stock of the small business corporation with respect to which the election was terminated, and,
2. (i) [w]hich acquires a substantial portion of the assets of such small business corporation, or
    (ii) [a] substantial portion of the assets of which were assets of such small business corporation.

In regard to reelecting the S status, the following should be noted:

1. Section 1362(g) applies only to corporations that lost their S election. If the corporation filed an invalid election, Section 1362(g) can never apply, since the corporation never was an S corporation. Thus the corporation can elect S status at any time.[6]
2. As the requirements of Section 1362(g) detailed above indicate, the S corporation that has lost its S status has a choice: it can wait the

full 5-year waiting period and then reelect S status, or it can request reapplication with the Service's permission during the 5-year waiting period with the burden on the corporation to convince the Service to allow reelection. Reg. Section 1.1372-5(a), adopted under former Section 1372, lists grounds for reelection of S status:

a. If there is a change of stock ownership of more than 50% in the corporation after the year of termination, this will tend to establish consent should be granted.

b. The events causing the termination were not reasonably within the control of the corporation or shareholders having a substantial interest in the corporation and these substantial shareholders were not participating in the plan to terminate the election.

A number of Revenue Rulings and Private Letter Rulings have been issued in connection with Section 1362(g), and the reader is directed to review them for application to a particular S corporate termination situation. Examples of where permission has been granted are Rev. Rul. 78-275[7] (permission granted because recession caused a drop in sales and bank required a deposit that caused disqualifying interest); Rev. Rul. 78-333[8] (permission granted where a corporation's assets were leased to another party while shareholder-manager was temporarily disabled and no replacement manager could be found); and Ltr. Rul. 8351065 (permission granted where a real estate downturn caused lack of sales of homes and investment income caused termination).

TAX POINTER

An S corporation, if it loses its S status under Section 1362(d)(2) and (3), should also consider reelecting S status under Section 1362(f). (See discussion at Chapter 10.5.)

10.7   THE TAX EFFECTS OF TERMINATION

When an S corporation terminates its S status, various tax effects occur. If the termination is intentional, that is, there is a revocation under Section 1362(d)(1)(D) or under the *T. J. Henry Associates*[9] rationale, some tax planning can occur. The discussion below will detail the consequences of termination plus options available to minimize the adverse tax consequences.

A.   The S Termination Year

As illustrated in Chapter 10.2.B.2, if an S corporation terminates at a point other than at the beginning or end of the taxable year, the taxable year is divided into two segments: an S year (hereinafter "S short year") and a C year (hereinafter "C short year"). Section 1362(e)(1)(A) prescribes that the S short year ends on the day before the occurrence of the terminating event and the C short year begins on the terminating date. As a general rule, Section 1362(e)(2) prescribes that items of income, loss, deduction, or credit are allocated to the C and S short years on a pro-rata basis based on a number of days of each year. There are exceptions to the general rule; namely,

1. Section 1362(e)(6)(D) prescribes that the Section 1362(e)(2)'s pro-rata allocation rules cannot be used if there is a sale or exchange of 50% or more of the S stock during an S termination year.

2. Section 1362(e)(3)(B) prescribes that if all persons who held stock in the corporation at any time during the S short year and those who were shareholders on the first day of the C short year unanimously consent, the shareholders can have the items of income, loss, and so on reported in each short taxable year under "normal tax accounting rules" (this method is called the "book method"). (See Appendix 14 for a sample form to make this election.)

3. Section 1362(e)(6)(C) prescribes that if a corporation acquires the S corporation under a Section 338 election procedure, the pro-rata allocation rules will not apply.

As to the C short year, Section 1362(e)(5) prescribes that the tax for the C short year is determined on an annualized basis. An example indicating the effect of the 2 short years is set forth below:

EXAMPLE 10-6

B, Inc., is a calendar year S corporation having one shareholder F. On 7/1/X7, pursuant to Section 1362(d)(1)(D), the S status terminated, thereby dividing the taxable year of the corporation into two segments: the S short year 1/1–6/30/X7 and the C short year 7/1–12/31/X7. Income, losses, and so on for the calendar year 19X7 will be prorated between the S and C short years on a daily basis pursuant to Section 1362(e)(2), unless shareholders pursuant to Section 1362(e)(3) elect to report the taxable income on each return on the basis of income or loss shown on its permanent records.

1. When Tax Returns Are Due for S and C Short Years— Section 1362(e)(6)(B)

Section 1362(e)(6)(B) prescribes that the due date for filing the tax returns for the S short year is the same date as that for the C short year, including extensions.

2. Overlap Between Sections 1362(e)(3) and 1377(a)(2), the Mechanics of the Section 1362(e)(3) Election

As discussed at Chapter 10.8(d)(1), the books of the S corporation can be closed pursuant to Section 1377(a)(2) when an S shareholder's stock holding in an S corporation terminates. It is possible that the closing of the books under Section 1377(a)(2) could overlap with the special election to use the book method under Section 1362(e)(3). This overlap could arise if an S shareholder sells stock to a nonpermitted shareholder under Section 1361(b)(1)(B), which causes the S termination. In regard to the overlap, it is to be noted that an election under Section 1362(e)(3) closes the books on the day before the termination of S status, and Section 1377(a)(2) election closes the books on the date of termination of a shareholder's stock interest. As to the mechanics of making a Section 1362(e)(3) election to close the books, see the instructions for the form set forth in Appendix 14.

TAX POINTER

Because the book method computes income and expense in the S short year on the basis of transactions that occur up to the last day of the S short year, tax planning might be possible if the shareholders were to remain the same in the C corporation as they were in the S corporation. An example will illustrate:

EXAMPLE 10-7

A, Inc., a calendar year cash basis S corporation, terminates its status on 7/1/X7. At the time of the termination, A, Inc., was operating at a loss; however, it was projected that in the C short year (7/1–12/31/X7), the company would operate profitably. Based on the accounting analysis for 19X7, it was projected that if the pro-rata method was used, a profit would be shown in both the S and C short years. However, if the book method were used, the S short year would show a loss and C year would show income. If the shareholders have basis in their S stock, they may consider electing the book method as a very desirable alternative since they can reduce their Form 1040 taxable income from the S short year. (Because the C corporate's income is not passed through to them, it will not affect the shareholders' Form 1040s.) Thus, the shareholders likely will make an election under Section 1362(e)(3).

3. Distribution of Money by the Corporation with Respect to Its Stock During a Posttermination Period

As discussed in Chapter 8.6, Section 1371(e) provides that a corporation can distribute income that has been taxed but not previously distributed to the shareholders as a reduction in basis rather than as a dividend to the shareholders.

B.   The Tax Consequences to the C Corporation in the C Short Year and Thereafter

When the S corporate election terminates and the C corporation begins, certain tax consequences will occur to the C corporation. The discussion here can be divided into two segments: S corporations that were never C corporations and S corporations that were C corporations at one point in their existence.

1.   Tax Consequences Shared by Both Types of C Corporations

C status bestows certain tax consequences to the former S corporation. Some of the tax consequences are

a.   *Borrowing from the Retirement Plan*

If the S corporation had a retirement plan, when C corporate status commences, the shareholder-employee can borrow from the plan. However, the benefit of this borrowing may be sharply curtailed. (See Tax Pointer at Chapter 5.7.B for a discussion of this topic.)

b.   *Members of a Controlled Group*

For purposes of Section 1651 et seq., when the S corporation becomes a C corporation, it becomes subject to the controlled group rules for purposes of the corporate rates under Section 11 (see Chapter 2.6), accumulated earnings credit under Section 535, and so on.

c.   *Investment Tax Credit Recapture*

For those S corporations that were subject to investment tax credit provisions under pre–Tax Reform Act of 1986, termination of S status pursuant to Reg. Section 1.47-4(a)(1) does not trigger investment tax credit recapture. However, Reg. Section 1.47-4(a)(2) prescribes that a subsequent disposition of S corporate stock may trigger investment tax credit recapture of the assets acquired during S status (for a general discussion of this area, see Chapter 9.14).

d.   *Estimated Taxes*

Because there may be taxable income under Section 11 for the C corporation, the C corporation will be liable for estimated taxes.

2. S Corporations That Have C Corporate Attributes

As discussed in Chapter 3.6.H, a C corporation, when it elects S status basically keeps in limbo its C corporate attributes, namely, net operating losses (NOLs). When the S corporation becomes a C corporation, the former C corporate attributes come into play. Thus, for example, assume that when a C corporation becomes an S one, it had in the year of the S election an NOL of $10,000. The corporation remained as such for 5 years and then terminated its S status. At the time the corporation regained its C status, it will lose 5 years of the NOL carryover period.

C. Closing the Books Under Section 1362(e)(6)(D)

If a 50% or more change of ownership occurs during the S corporation taxable year, Section 1362(e)(6)(D) prescribes that the pro-rata allocation rules for the S termination year as set forth in Section 1362(e)(2) shall not apply; rather, the books are closed on the date of sale. Accordingly, the shareholders should take necessary steps in advance of the change of ownership to prevent any adverse tax consequences from occurring due to the sale.

10.8 TAX EFFECTS OF S SHAREHOLDERS SELLING STOCK INTERESTS

Because of the changes to Sections 336, 337, et seq., it is doubtful that there will be many liquidations of S corporations. (For a discussion of Section 337, see Chapter 10.10.) Rather, sales of S corporate stock will be in vogue. Further, in the course of the S corporation, a shareholder may sell his, her, or its stock interest. If care is not practiced, certain inadvertent tax consequences as discussed below could develop. (As to redemption of stock and partial liquidations, see generally Chapter 10.9 et seq.)

A. Computation of Seller's Gain and Loss

An S shareholder's gain or loss on the sale of S corporate stock is computed under Section 1001(a) just as if stock in a C corporation was sold. Gain or loss is determined by the difference between the amount received for the stock less the seller's basis. As discussed generally in Chapters 4 through 8, a shareholder's basis in an S corporation is adjusted for the amount of income and loss passed through to the shareholders plus the amount of certain distributions. If the sale occurs other than at the beginning or end of the S corporate taxable year, adverse tax consequences could develop, because the S corporate selling shareholder will not know exactly his, her, or its basis. The reason for this lack of knowledge of basis is that, as discussed at Chapter 7.2 et seq., a shareholder does not know his, her, or its basis until the end of the S corporation's taxable year. Thus, the selling shareholder is "flying blind" with respect to sales of stock "midyear" as to whether gain or loss will be recognized on the transaction. However, as discussed below, certain steps can be taken to minimize the tax consequences.

TAX POINTER

Before setting forth an example of adverse tax consequences that could result from a sale of stock, it is important to note that most likely there will be a shareholders' agreement in place restricting the sales of stock as well as handling the effects of the sale, namely, the Section 1377(a)(2) election to close the S corporate books on the day of sale (discussed at Chapter 10.8.D.1). For purposes of the example set forth below, it is assumed that there is no shareholders' agreement restricting the situation.

EXAMPLE 10-8

A, Inc., is a calendar year S corporation composed of three sisters who are equal shareholders, A, B, and C. On 3/1/X7, C sells her stock to D, a qualified S corporate shareholder. A and B refuse to consent to the Section 1377(a)(2) election to close the S corporate books; however, C is confident that a capital loss will result on the sale. At the time of the sale, C projects that her basis at $100 will produce a capital loss, since D is only paying $75 for the stock. At the end of the year when the income and loss of A, Inc., is determined, it is found that C's basis at the time of sale was $65 instead of $100 due to the fact that A, Inc., operated at a loss for 19X7 and C's share of loss to the point of the sale was $35 based on the pro-rata method of Section 1362(e)(2). Thus, C realizes a $10 gain on the sale instead of a $25 projected loss.

B.   Character of Seller's Gain or Loss

In regard to the character of the gain or loss from the sale, Section 1222 will generally treat the sale as a capital transaction. However, if the stock is subject to Section 341, Section 1244 (see Chapter 9.13 regarding the tax advantages to have Section 1244 stock), and so on, the results will be different according to general tax principles.

C.   The Tax Consequences of the Sale

A sale of S corporate stock could also generate the tax consequences discussed on page 219.

1. Risks in Sale of Stock

If stock of an S corporation is sold, the buyer of the stock is assuming a risk in that if the corporation has a problem, whether it is a tax or nontax problem, the buyer risks losing his, her or its investment. An example will illustrate:

EXAMPLE 10-9

B formed XYZ, Inc., in 1981. Through inadvertence, the S election for XYZ, Inc., was never filed, although B believed that it was. A purchased all B's stock in XYZ, Inc., in 19X7, relying on the tax returns that A saw for the prior years of operation for XYZ, Inc., which showed that the corporation filed tax returns using Form 1120S. After A purchased the stock, the Service commenced an audit of XYZ, Inc., and found that the corporation had never elected S status. When A sued B for the tax consequences that resulted from the loss of S status, B went bankrupt, thereby depriving A of any recovery for damages.

While it is possible to minimize the risks of stock sales by (1) having the seller of the stock indemnify and hold the buyer harmless in case of losses, (2) having the buyer purchase the stock with long-term notes that contain the right of set-off in the event that the representations of the seller in the sales agreement prove untrue, or (3) having the seller guarantee and warrant that the representations contained in the contract are true, and so on, there is still the risk that claims will be made that will exceed the indemnity, set-off, guarantee, and so on. Accordingly, buyers of stock should consider the risks very carefully before purchasing the stock of S corporations.

2. Investment Tax Credit Recapture

Reg. Section 1.47-4(a)(2) prescribes that a sale of more than a third of a shareholder's stock interest in the S corporation will trigger recapture of the investment tax credit for any S corporate property for the unused portion equal to the amount of change of stock ownership computed pursuant to a formula. Note, however, by definition, the sale of S corporate stock should not trigger any investment tax credit recapture of C corporate property that existed when a C corporation converted to S status. An example will illustrate:

EXAMPLE 10-10

A, Inc., is an S corporation that has two equal shareholders: C and D. In prior years, A, Inc., as an S corporation, purchased property subject to investment tax credit. On 1/1/X7 C sold 50% of his stock interest to E, a qualified S corporate shareholder. At the time of the sale, C had $1,000 of credit from basis in eligible investment property. C will be required to file Form 4255 to recapture investment tax credit on $500 of property (50% × $1,000).

TAX POINTER

While termination of S status does not cause investment tax credit recapture, sale of S corporate stock after termination can result in investment tax credit recapture.[10]

3. Depreciation Recapture—Sections 1245, 1250, et seq.

While sale of S corporate stock may trigger investment tax credit recapture, there appears to be no statutory provision requiring recapture of depreciable property under Sections 1245, 1250, et seq. Thus, a seller of S corporate stock could leave an unsophisticated buyer of stock with an untenable situation. An example will clarify:

EXAMPLE 10-11

A, Inc., a calendar year S corporation, has one shareholder, H. In 1970, A, Inc., purchased $500,000 of Section 1231 assets that, on the date of sale of H's stock to L, a qualified S corporate shareholder, had been completely depreciated. H sold the stock in A, Inc., to L for $500,000 on 1/1/X7, with the $500,000 representing the fair market value of A, Inc., at the time. At the time of the sale of stock, A, Inc., had no assets other than the Section 1231 assets purchased in 1970. In 19X7, A, Inc., disposed of all of A, Inc.'s Section 1231 assets for $600,000. L would have depreciation recapture of $500,000 on the sale of the Section 1231 assets.

EXAMPLE 10-12

Assume the same facts as in Example 10-11, but instead of buying A, Inc.'s stock from H, L bought the Section 1231 assets from A, Inc., for $500,000 and then disposed of them in 19X7. H has the $500,000 of depreciation recapture, not L. L upon obtaining A, Inc.'s assets sold them immediately for $600,000. L only has $100,000 of income.

4. No Step-up in Basis of Assets Unless Section 338 Is Elected

As Example 10-11 indicates, when S corporate stock is acquired, the buyer basically does not obtain a step-up in basis for the assets. Thus, in Example 10-11, L owns a corporation that is worth $500,000, but if the corporation sells the assets, depreciation recapture will be generated for a maximum of $500,000. Further, L cannot obtain a depreciation deduction from A, Inc.'s assets because they are completely depreciated. If L could step-up A, Inc.'s assets to their fair market value, $500,000, then L could obtain depreciation for his, her, or its investment, thereby minimizing the tax consequences of any disposition of A, Inc.'s assets. However, the only statutory method to step-up A, Inc.'s assets when a stock acquisition is made is to use Section 338, which by definition under Section 1361 will cause the S election to be terminated at the time of the Section 338 election. Further, as discussed at Chapter 10.10.B.1.a, the TRA makes acquisitions of stock under Section 338 prohibitive from a tax point of view. Thus, it is improbable that individuals will be making acquisitions of S corporate stock to step-up basis; rather, because of the complexities of the Code, they will acquire assets to obtain a step-up in basis.

D. Reasons Why a Seller of S Corporate Stock Wants a Section 1377(a)(2) Election to Close the Books and Steps to Be Taken to Obtain the Closure

As discussed at chapter 10.8.A, a seller of less than a 50% interest in S corporate stock could be faced with a situation that unless the books are closed pursuant to Section 1377(a)(2) at the time of sale, adverse tax consequences could develop completely beyond the control of the seller. In regard to the sale or a change of ownership of 50% or more interest in an S corporation, the books have to be closed pursuant to Section 1362(e)(6)(D). (For a discussion of the closure rules under Section 1362(e)(6)(D), see Chapter 10.7.C; the procedure to close the books under Section 1377(a)(2) is outlined at Chapter 10.8.D.1.) To prevent adverse tax results, shareholders of S corporations should, when they adopt the shareholders' agreement, provide that there shall be a closing of the books when a shareholder sells his, her, or its stock interest and all the shareholders will consent to this election. (Note, while state law may recognize the agreement, the Service may not.) When a Section 1377(a)(2) election is made, two short taxable years will result: one for the period including the selling shareholder and one for the period including the purchasing shareholder. An example will illustrate:

EXAMPLE 10-13

A, Inc., a calendar year S corporation, is composed of three sisters who are equal shareholders: A, B, and C. On 4/1/X7, C sells her interest to D, a qualified S shareholder. At the time of the sale, all the shareholders of the S corporation elect under Section 1377(a)(2) to close the books of the corporation on 4/1/X7. Thus, C will report all items of income passed through that are actually realized or incurred during the tax period 1/1–4/1/X7. If the Section 1377(a)(2) election was not made, C would report items of income, expense, and so on that are passed through to her for the entire year of 19X7 on the basis of the number of days C was a shareholder in the corporation.

If the seller of the S corporate stock cannot have the books of the S corporation closed, pursuant to Section 1377(a)(2) election, the following could occur:

1. The S corporation could change its method of accounting (with the consent of the Service), which could affect the seller's income for the period.
2. As discussed at Chapter 10.8.A, the seller of S corporate stock is at the mercy of the new and remaining shareholders for the balance of the taxable year in regard to the tax treatment of the S corporation's operating results for the selling shareholder's tenure in the corporation (i.e., they could create a loss or taxable income for the S corporation by controlling sales, expenses, and so on).

1.   The Steps to Be Taken to Make the Section 1377(a)(2) Election

In regard to how the Section 1377(a)(2) election is made, the following should be noted:

1. the Section 1377(a)(2) election can only be made if the selling shareholder terminates his, her, or its entire interest in the S corporation and all the other shareholders consent.
2. Temp. Reg. Section 18.1377-1 provides specific requirements that must be made if the election is to occur, for example, that a statement must be filed with the S corporation's tax returns for the year when the election is made (see Appendix 15 for a sample form), that the S shareholders must sign a consent (see Appendix 16 for the sample consent form), and so on.

TAX POINTER

There is a potential overlap in regard to a termination of the S corporation under Section 1362 and termination of an S shareholder's interest under Section 1377(a)(2). (See Chapter 10.7.A.2 for discussion about this topic.)

E.   Reasons Why a Stock Sale Is Desired

As would be expected, there may be situations where a stock sale may be the only way to proceed, even though there may be risks in purchasing the stock of the S corporation as set forth at Chapter 10.8.C.1 et seq. Set forth on page 223 are situations that might make a stock sale advantageous.

1. Situations Involving Assets Subject to Section 453C

The TRA and OBRA have prescribed various rules to limit the use of installment reporting in connection with the sale of real estate. To avoid these problems found in Section 453A, S corporation shareholders will sell stock in the corporation under the installment method rather than assets. An example will illustrate:

EXAMPLE 10-14

A, Inc., an S corporation has one shareholder, Philip. When A, Inc. was incorporated, Philip acquired all its stock for $10 million. A, Inc. used the $10 million to acquire a piece of land which it rents out to third parties. In 19X8, A, Inc. has been approached by a buyer to purchase the land for $25 million using the installment method where A, Inc. will receive a mortgage to secure the debt. The property will be sold pursuant to a balloon mortgage with the terms being nothing down, $25 million due ten years from the date of sale, interest at two points above prime on the $25 million.

If the S corporation sells the asset through the corporation, the corporation has the problem of Section 453A. However, if Philip could sell his stock in A, Inc. to the buyer, securing the installment sale of the stock with the property, by definition, Section 453A will not apply. (Note, however, that if the buyer buys the stock of corporation instead of the property, the buyer will not obtain a stepped-up basis; but, the buyer may be willing to take this approach if payment for the stock can be done pursuant to a balloon mortgage as set forth in this example).

To cover situations where the buyer does not wish to purchase certain assets of the corporation when the buyer purchases the stock of the corporation, the shareholders can use a *Zenz* v. *Quinlivan*,[11] redemption to eliminate the problem of the unwanted assets. Basically, a *Zenz* v. *Quinlivan* redemption occurs at the time of the sale with the shareholder redeeming stock equivalent to the unwanted assets and the buyer buying the stock for the wanted assets. An example will illustrate:

EXAMPLE 10-15

Assume the same facts as in Example 10–14, except that A, Inc. besides having the land on its balance sheet also has $1 million of cash. Further, the total capital stock issued to Philip is 26 shares of common stock. The buyer has indicated to Philip that if the buyer purchases Philip's stock that the buyer only wants to buy the corporation with its sole asset being the land. Accordingly, Philip at the time he sells the stock to the buyer will do it as follows: he will sell 25 shares of stock to the buyer for the buyer's $25 million note and will redeem one share of stock for the million dollars in cash pursuant to the *Zenz* v. *Quinlivan* rationale.

2. The Assets on S Corporate Books Have a Shorter Depreciation Life than If the Purchaser Bought the Assets Outright

The TRA has basically lengthened the lives of assets subject to depreciation. For instance, real estate has gone from 19 years to 27.5 years for residential property and 31.5 years for nonresidential property. If an S corporation purchased nonresidential real estate in 1986 and decided to sell it in 1987, it may pay for the purchaser to acquire the stock of the S corporation rather than the building since the purchaser as a successor shareholder (providing the buyer was a permitted shareholder) could step into the shoes of the selling shareholder and obtain the higher level of depreciation (i.e., 19 years instead of 31.5 years). By definition, the purchaser would not consider this option unless the book value for the building and the other tax advantages associated with the purchase were approximately equal to the purchase price.

TAX POINTERS

1. A nonpermitted shareholder could purchase the stock of the S corporation thereby terminating the S status. The resulting C corporation in the above discussion would then be able to take advantage of the higher level of depreciation.

2. Owning real estate in S corporate name may not be wise. (See discussion at Examples 9-3 and 9.4.)

F. Selling More than a 50% Interest—Closing of the Books Under Section 1362(e)(6)(D)

As set forth at Chapter 10.7.C, Section 1362(e)(6)(D) requires that the S corporate books be closed when there is a sale involving 50% or more of a stock interest in the corporation.

G. How S Shareholders Report Income, Loss, and So On, If There Has Been a Change of S Corporate Stock Ownership During the Year Less than 50% and the Books of the S Corporation Are Not Closed Pursuant to Section 1377(a)(2)

Section 1362(e)(3)(D) (Chapter 10.8.F) discussed the rules if there is a change of stock ownership of 50% or more. Section 1377(a)(1) prescribes the rules for reporting income where less than a 50% change of ownership occurs. For a discussion of Section 1377(a)(1)'s rules, see Chapter 7.1.A.2, in particular, Example 7-2.

10.9 REDEMPTION OF AN S SHAREHOLDER'S INTEREST IN THE CORPORATION, PARTIAL LIQUIDATIONS

A. Redemptions

Under pre–TRA law, an S corporate shareholder could redeem his, her, or its stock in the corporation under Section 302 and receive capital gains treatment. An S corporate shareholder would consider a redemption under the following circumstances:

1. One of the shareholder's wishes to terminate his, her, or its interest in the S corporation, and there is no purchaser willing to pay the price desired for the stock, but the corporation has sufficient assets to make the acquisition.

2. The shareholders are selling their stock in the S corporation and the buyer(s) do not want certain assets. Thus, under the *Zenz* v. *Quinlivan*[12] rationale, the selling shareholder(s) will redeem a pro-rata portion of his, her, or its stock for the S corporate assets not wanted by the buyer(s) of the S corporate shares. Likewise, the *Zenz* v. *Quinlivan* rationale could be used where the S corporation is selling its assets under Section 337 and the buyer of the assets does not want certain assets of the corporation.

Under pre–TRA, if the redeeming shareholder does not satisfy the requirements under Section 302, the redemption would be subject to the rules under Section 301 (i.e., ordinary income treatment instead of capital gains). As to what the tax effect will be on redemptions that do not satisfy Section 302 under the TRA, at this stage it is premature to say, since the TRA has eliminated the capital gains deduction. (For a discussion of the accumulated adjustments account in regard to redemptions, see Chapter 8.3.B.4.) It is to be noted, however, that the entire amount redeemed will be treated as income, not the difference between the consideration paid for the shares and the shareholder's basis. An example will illustrate:

EXAMPLE 10-16

Laurie and Charles are unrelated shareholders in B, Inc., a calender year S corporation. Each owns 100 shares in the corporation. On 12/31/X7, Laurie redeems 1 share of stock from the corporation receiving $100 for the stock. Her basis is $40 in the stock. Since this was not a disproportionate redemption under Section 302, Laurie will have $100 of income from the redemption. If the redemption had been disproportionate, then Laurie would have only reported $60 of income ($100–$40).

B. Partial Liquidations

Under pre–TRA, an S corporation could engage in a partial liquidation. One classic example of a partial liquidation is the case of *Joseph W. Imler,*[13] which involved a non–S corporation. In *Imler,* the distribution of unused fire insurance proceeds in redemption of stock was treated as a partial liquidation, thereby yielding capital gains treatment to the shareholders. The corporation decided not to rebuild floors destroyed by fire and discontinued operations carried out in part on these floors.

As to what will be the tax effect of partial liquidations after the TRA, it is difficult to project at this time because of the elimination of the capital gains deduction. (See Chapter 10.10 for a further discussion of these points.)

10.10 LIQUIDATIONS OF S CORPORATION UNDER SECTIONS 337, 338, 333, AND 332

A. Section 337 Liquidations

Under pre–TRA S corporations could sell their assets under Section 337 and realize capital gains treatment for their shareholders.[14] The S corporation would consider this means of disposition of assets under the following circumstances:

1. To avoid the capital gains tax under old Section 1374.
2. To take advantage of Section 337's bulk sale rule regarding inventory.
3. To defer recognition of gain at the shareholder level for one year.

The TRA changed the law tremendously with respect to Section 337 treatment in liquidations for tax years beginning after 12/31/86 by imposing a double tax on the appreciation. Examples will illustrate:

EXAMPLE 10-17

A, Inc., a C corporation, all of whose shares are owned by B, liquidates in 1986 under Section 337 by selling all its assets to X. At the time of the sale, A, Inc.'s balance sheet was as follows: land, cost basis $20,000; fair market value, $70,000. B's stock basis was $1,000. X pays $70,000 for the land. B will pay a tax on the $69,000 gain realized ($70,000 proceeds from the land less $1,000 stock basis).

EXAMPLE 10-18

Assume the same facts as in Example 10-15 except that A, Inc., is liquidated in 1990. The tax consequences would be that A, Inc., would pay a tax on

$50,000 ($70,000 proceeds less $20,000 cost basis). Assume the tax on $50,000 is $7,500 (15% × $50,000). Thus B would receive $62,500 from the sale ($70,000 − $7,500 corporate tax). B would now pay a tax on the difference between $62,500 and $1,000 (B's basis in A, Inc.'s stock). The consequence is that B pays a double tax on the liquidation.

TAX POINTER

In connection with a liquidation, Ltr. Rul. 8609052 prescribes that payment of a bonus to a shareholder-employee did not affect the liquidation. Thus, a corporation could possibly limit the double taxation effect of Section 337 by declaring a bonus to a shareholder-employee.

1. The Ameliorative Relief Prescribed in Section 633 of the TRA

To ease the harsh effects of the changes made to Section 337 by the TRA, Congress in Section 633 of the TRA prescribed various effective dates for the new law regarding liquidation as well as grandfathered certain liquidations. Section 337 liquidations that have been grandfathered are

1. Liquidations completed before 1/1/87.
2. Liquidations of a corporation if a majority of the voting stock is acquired on or after 8/1/86 under a written binding contract in effect before 8/1/86, providing the liquidation is completed before 1988.
3. Liquidation under a liquidation plan adopted before 8/1/86 and completed before 1/1/88.

In regard to ameliorative relief, TRA Section 633(d) prescribes that the old rules regarding Section 337 apply for liquidating sales or distributions occurring before 1/1/89 for certain closely held corporations. For a corporation to qualify as a "closely held one" for the special relief set forth in TRA Section 633(d), the fair market value of the corporation's stock generally must, on the date of the plan of complete liquidation, be less than $5,000,000. If the value of the stock is between $5,000,000 and $10,000,000 on the date the plan is adopted TRA Section 633(d)(3) prescribes a phase-in rule. Further, to qualify for special relief set forth in TRA Section 633(d), TRA Section 633(d)(5) prescribes that the corporation must have for the period 8/1/86 until liquidation, more than 50% by value of its stock held by 10 or fewer qualified persons. A qualified person is an individual, estate, or trust set forth in Section 1361(c)(2)(A)(ii) or (iii).

As to the correlation between TRA Section 633(d) and Section 1374, see TRA Section 633(d)(8). (Section 1374 is discussed in Chapter 6.)

B.   Section 338 Liquidations

Under pre–TRA, the acquiring corporation of the target's stock would basically not pay a tax on liquidation of the target except for depreciation recapture and so on; however, under the TRA, the acquiring corporation would pay a tax on the liquidation of the target similar to the double tax situation under Section 337 illustrated above.

Grandfathered, however, are deemed liquidations under Section 338 or actual liquidations of corporations that are acquired under a binding contract entered into before 8/1/86, if the deemed or actual liquidation occurs before 1/1/88.

In regard to S corporations and Section 338, it is important to note that S corporations by the provisions of Section 1361(b)(2)(A) cannot engage in them since the S corporation will lose its S status; rather, if an S corporation is to engage in a Section 338 transaction, it must do the transaction as a C corporation and then elect S status after the transaction is completed.

C.   Section 333 Liquidations

Alternatively, an S corporation may desire to liquidate under Section 333. The Service in Rev. Rul. 76-347[15] has prescribed that an S corporation can avail itself of a Section 333 liquidation. The TRA, however, has legislated Section 333 out of existence unless the corporation can avail itself of the transitory relief prescribed in TRA 633(d).[16] Under the TRA transitory rules, if the S corporation stock has a fair market value of $5,000,000 or less, and more than 50% of the stock by value for the period 8/1/86 until liquidation is owned by 10 or fewer qualified persons, the corporation can avail itself of Section 333 liquidation treatment, under the rules in existence pre–TRA if the liquidating distribution occurs before 1/1/89. If the fair market value of the stock of the corporation is between $5,000,000 and $10,000,000, then under TRA Section 633 there is a phase-out of the relief available.

For an S corporation to liquidate under Section 333, at least 80% of the shareholders must consent to the liquidation by filing timely elections using Form 964, the corporation cannot be collapsible under Section 341, and the corporation must liquidate within one calendar month. If the S corporation meets all the liquidation requirements under Section 333, then gain will be recognized to the greater of earnings and profits or cash. It is because S corporations have either no or low accumulated earnings and profits that make them attractive candidates for Section 333 liquidations.

In regard to the mechanics of the liquidation, the following should be noted:

1. The normal mechanics of Section 333 liquidation apply to determine a shareholder's gain or loss in the liquidation.

2. Section 337(c)(1)(B) prescribes that if Section 333 applies, Section 337 cannot. Thus, the S corporation's normal operating gain or loss should pass through to the shareholders without being affected by the Section 333 liquidation.[17]

3. Distribution of depreciable assets to the shareholders that generate recapture under Section 1245, 1250, and so on should have no effect on the liquidation since the income generated on the distribution is recognized by the shareholders as ordinary income.

4. Because the amount of the corporation's cash will generate income to the shareholders, steps should be taken prior to adopting the liquidation to reduce it, such as paying expenses in connection with the property being distributed (i.e., repairs).

D.   Section 332 Liquidations

By definition, under Section 1361, since an S corporation cannot have a corporate shareholder, it cannot avail itself of a Section 332 liquidation.

10.11   REORGANIZATIONS

A.   Introduction

One primary benefit for operating in the S corporate form is that the corporation and its shareholders can avail themselves of the tax-free reorganization sections of Section 368 to accomplish various objectives (partnerships have basically no such comparable provisions). However, because of the mechanisms of certain reorganization provisions under Section 368 (e.g., a B or C type reorganization), reorganizations under these sections may not be practical for an S corporation, particularly if an S corporation is to be the surviving corporation. The discussion below is a general one, and while it is not intended to be exhaustive, it will include a discussion of each type of reorganization as it pertains to S corporations and some of the problems and situations encountered. The field of tax-free reorganizations is a highly technical one, and in reading the text, it is assumed that the reader has some familiarity with the six basic types of reorganizations and the two hybrid types plus the shorthand terms used to describe the reorganizations, such as an "A merger" for a merger under Section 368(a)(1)(A).

In terms of any reorganization involving S corporations, the key is Section 1371(a)(1). Section 1371(a)(1) provides that Subchapter C (which contains the reorganization Section 368) shall apply to S corporations except to the extent it is inconsistent with S corporate taxation. Thus, an S corporation can be the acquiring corporation in an A merger and keep its status after the merger providing the acquired corporation's shareholders are permitted S shareholders, there will be less than 35 shareholders after the merger, and so on, but if the acquiring corporation in the merger is a C corporation, the S election will be terminated as of the date of the merger. To prevent unwarranted tax results, the shareholders of the S corporation should consider the consequences if the S status is lost in terms of investment tax credit recapture, distributions, flow-through of income and loss in the terminating year, and so on (discussed below).

B.   Statutory Merger and Consolidations—Section 368(a)(1)(A)

In a statutory merger under Section 368(a)(1)(A), a corporation is merged ("the acquired corporation") into a surviving one, and in a consolidation, two corporations are consolidated into a new one.

In a merger, if the S corporation is the acquiring corporation, usually the S status is retained, unless the acquired corporation causes the S corporation to lose its S status, for example, by having a nonpermitted shareholder. To prevent the loss of S status by the acquiring corporation, steps should be undertaken prior to the merger by the corporation to be acquired to eliminate the problem by reducing the number of shareholders so that there will be 35 shareholders in total after the merger, or eliminating the nonpermitted shareholders by having these shareholders who would destroy the S status after the merger redeem their shares prior to the merger or sell their shares to permitted shareholders, and so on. However, if a C corporation is going to be the acquiring corporation, Section 1362(d)(2)(B) prescribes that the termination will occur on the date of the merger. (See Chapter 10.3 for a discussion of the tax consequences of termination.) In regard to reorganizations under Section 368(a)(1)(A), a number of situations can arise. For instance, two C corporations could merge and then elect S status, or the acquiring corporation could be a C corporation that previously had an S election that was lost, and so on. Again, careful tax planning before the reorganization is required so that no adverse tax consequences will develop.

1.   Reelection of S Status After the Merger

If the S status is lost after the reorganization under Section 368(a)(1)(A), the acquiring corporation may want to reelect S status under Section 1362.

(See Chapter 10.6 for a discussion on how to reelect S status.) However, because a reorganization under Section 368 is a voluntary event, conceptually, the corporation that lost its S status cannot say it was inadvertent, and so on under Section 1362(f). Thus, the S corporation that lost its S status in the merger will have to wait the 5-year waiting period prescribed in Section 1362(g), unless the secretary of the treasury is willing to waive all or part of the 5-year statutory period.

2. Investment Tax Credit Recapture

As discussed in Chapter 9.14, investment tax credit recapture occurs when an S shareholder's stock interest is reduced by more than a third. This reduction of stock interest could occur in a merger under Section 368(a)(1)(A) where the S corporation is the acquiring corporation and the stock interest of the shareholders in the acquiring corporation is reduced due to the fact of the shareholders of the acquired corporation acquiring stock in the acquiring corporation. An example will illustrate the consequences of a merger and subsequent investment tax credit recapture.

EXAMPLE 10-19

A, Inc., is an S corporation and owned entirely by B. As of 1/1/87 it had $10,000 of property that was still subject to investment tax credit recapture, with the amount of the investment tax credit equaling $500. On 1/1/87, A, Inc., merged with F, Inc., another S corporation, in a Section 368(a)(1)(A) merger, where A, Inc., was the survivor. As a consequence of the merger, B's interest in A, Inc., was decreased to 55%. B will have investment tax credit recapture on 45% of the property (100 − 55) because of B's reduction in stock interest below one-third.

3. Postmerger Distributions

For a discussion of postmerger distributions where S status is terminated, see Chapter 8.6.

C. Sections 368(a)(1)(B) and (C) Reorganizations

Because of the provisions of the Code as they pertain to these types of reorganizations, if the S corporation enters into them, S status basically will be lost, which will generate 2 tax years, posttermination distributions, and so on. (See, in general, the discussion of A mergers found at Chapter 10.11.B regarding the consequences when the S corporation loses its status.)

D. Section 368(a)(1)(D) Reorganizations

There are basically two different types of situations that qualify as a Section 368(a)(1)(D) reorganization: a divisive and a nondivisive reorganization. In regard to a nondivisive D reorganization it can take two forms: a merger or a nonmerger situation. Nondivisive D reorganizations can be done with S corporations; however, S status may be lost by the S corporation participating in the situations.

As to the divisive situations, Section 368(a)(1)(D) prescribes that, if a corporation transfers part of its assets to another corporation, immediately thereafter the transferor corporation controls the transferee, and the transferor corporation distributes stock or securities of the controlled corporation to one or more of its shareholders, the result will be tax free. As can be seen, if the transferor corporation is an S corporation, it technically will lose its S status after it acquires 80% control of the transferee corporation. However, the Service has ruled that momentary control of a wholly owned subsidiary for the purposes of a D reorganization followed immediately by a distribution of the subsidiary's stock will not trigger a termination of the transferor's S status.[18] An example of where an S corporation would undertake a divisive reorganization is found in the factual situation of Rev. Rul. 72-230[19] set forth below:

EXAMPLE 10-20

Z corporation, an S corporation, was owned by four brothers, M, N, O, and P, who were all equal shareholders. The corporation was engaged in the manufacture of heavy construction equipment. The corporation had a division in California, which was operated by M and N, and another in New York, which was operated by O and P. Disputes broke out among the four brothers, with M and N looking for expansion and O and P not. To solve the dispute, pursuant to Section 368(a)(1)(D), Z corporation created a subsidiary, Y, Inc., and transferred all the assets of the New York division to Y, Inc., subject to its liabilities, taking back all the stock and then immediately transferring all the stock of Y, Inc., to O and P in exchange for their stock in Z corporation.

1. Business Purpose

To have a D reorganization, Reg. Section 1.355-2(c) states that it must satisfy a business purpose. The reader is advised to consult the case law for situations where a business purpose has been found to sustain the D reorganization.

2. Reelection of S Status for the Spun-off Corporation

In Example 10-20, Y, Inc., was spun off to O and P. The question to be asked now is, Can Y, Inc., elect S status? Most likely, since the spin-off was a voluntary act, Y, Inc., would have to wait the 5-year period prescribed in Section 1362(g) (see Chapter 10.6 for a discussion of reelections under Section 1362(g)) to elect S status.

E. Recapitalizations—Section 368(a)(1)(E)

In a typical recapitalization under Section 368(a)(1)(E), stock and/or securities in a corporation is exchanged for new stock and/or securities in the same corporation. If an S corporation is undertaking an E reorganization, it will not lose its S status unless two or more classes of stock result after the reorganization. Examples of where a recapitalization will be used in connection with S corporations would be one where an exchange of old debt was done for new stock and old stock for new stock (the exchange of old stock for new stock might be taken by a C corporation that has several classes of stock. The exchange that might be undertaken would be to exchange the several classes of stock for one class of stock so that the corporation would then qualify for S status.). The "estate freeze" recapitalization to create two classes of stock, preferred and common, to bring in favored employees as shareholders at little or no cost to them is by definition not available to S corporations, because the one class of stock requirement of Section 1361(b)(1)(D) would be breached.

F. F Reorganizations—Section 368(a)(1)(F)

Section 368(a)(1)(F) prescribes that an F reorganization occurs where there is a "mere change in identity, form or place or organization of one corporation, however effected." A type F reorganization can resemble an A, C, or D reorganization. An example of a type A and F reorganization is found in Rev. Rul. 64-250.[20] An example illustrating the reasons for a reorganization under Rev. Rul. 64-250 is set forth below.

EXAMPLE 10-21

A formed AB, Inc., in state Y and elected S status on formation. A also qualified the corporation to do business in state X. Over time, AB, Inc.'s operations changed, and it solely did business in state X. To avoid having to pay tax to both states X and Y for future operations since states X and Y did not recognize S status, A incorporated AB, Inc., in state X and merged AB, Inc., of state Y into AB, Inc., of state X.

G. Hybrid Mergers—Sections 368(a)(2)(D) and (E)

Section 368(a) prescribes two types of mergers that technically qualify as A mergers: the forward triangle merger under Section 368(a)(2)(D) and the reverse triangle merger under Section 368(a)(2)(E). However, because of the unique requirements of these two types of mergers, an S corporation cannot basically participate in them without losing S status.

ENDNOTES FOR CHAPTER 10

1. See, e.g., Ltr. Rul. 8336033, 8336014.

2. *Alfred N. Hoffman*, 47 T.C. 218 (1966), aff'd per curiam, 391 F. 2d 930 (5th Cir. 1968), but see *Frank E. Poulter*, Para. 67,220 P-H Memo T.C. (1967), aff'd per curiam, 397 F. 2d 415 (4th Cir. 1968).

3. *T. J. Henry Associates, Inc.*, 80 T.C. 886 (1983) (a father, a principal shareholder in an S corporation, transferred stock to himself as custodian for his four children and as such a custodian refused to consent to continue S status thereby terminating the S election). Note, the Service acquiesced in this decision, 1984-1 C.B. 2.

4. Id.

5. S. Rep. No. 640, 97th Cong., 2d Sess. 12 (1982).

6. Rev. Rul. 71-549, 1971-2 C.B. 319 (adopted under former Section 1372).

7. 1978-2 C.B. 221.

8. 1978-2 C.B. 224.

9. Endnote 3.

10. *Estate of C. A. Diecks*, 65 T.C. 117 (1975), acq. 1978-1 C.B. 1.

11. 213 F. 2d 914 (6th Cir. 1954).

12. Id.

13. 11 T.C. 836, acq. 1949-1 C.B. 2.

14. It is to be noted that there was some discussion that Section 337 under prior law did not apply to S corporations; however, the general consensus was that it did apply. Authority that Section 337 treatment applied to S corporations is found in Reg. Section 1.1372-1 (c) adopted under former Section 1372, which states that Section 331 specifically applies to S corporations. By inference, Section 337, which incorporates Section 331, has to apply to S corporations. See also Rev. Rul. 78-89, 1978-1 C.B. 272.

15. 1976-2 C.B. 253.

16. Rev. Rul. 87-4, IRB 1987-2.

17. Rev. Rul. 76-347, 1976-2 C.B. 253 (undistributed taxable income under prior law passed through in the year of a Section 333 liquidation).

18. Rev. Rul. 72-230, 1972-1 C.B. 270; see also Ltr. Rul. 8529037.

19. 1972-1 C.B. 270.

20. 1964-2 C.B. 333.

Appendices

CAUTION

In using the material found in the appendices, the reader is directed to consult the law of the jurisdiction where this material will be used. For instance, with respect to the sample provisions regarding the shareholders' agreement (Appendix 11), the state law where the S corporation is incorporated should be consulted to determine if the language contained is proper in the jurisdiction and a restriction on shareholders.

Appendix 1
Form 2553

For a discussion of this form, see Chapter 3.1.

238

Election by a Small Business Corporation

(Under section 1362 of the Internal Revenue Code)
▶ **For Paperwork Reduction Act Notice, see page 1 of Instructions.**
▶ **See separate Instructions.**

Note: *This election, to be treated as an "S corporation," can be approved only if all the tests in Instruction B are met.*

Part I Election Information

Name of corporation (see instructions)	Employer identification number (see instructions)	Principal business activity and principal product or service (see instructions)
Number and street		Election is to be effective for tax year beginning (month, day, year)
City or town, state and ZIP code		Number of shares issued and outstanding (see instructions)

Is the corporation the outgrowth or continuation of any form of predecessor? . . . ☐ **Yes** ☐ **No** | Date and place of incorporation

If "Yes," state name of predecessor, type of organization, and period of its existence ▶ . . . .

A If this election takes effect for the first tax year the corporation exists, enter the earliest of the following: (1) date the corporation first had shareholders, (2) date the corporation first had assets, or (3) date the corporation began doing business. ▶

B Selected tax year: Annual return will be filed for tax year ending (month and day) ▶ . . . .

See instructions before entering your tax year. If the tax year ends any date other than December 31, you must complete Part II or Part IV on back. You may want to complete Part III to make a back-up request.

C Name of each shareholder, person having a community property interest in the corporation's stock, and each tenant in common, joint tenant, and tenant by the entirety. (A husband and wife (and their estates) are counted as one shareholder in determining the number of shareholders without regard to the manner in which the stock is owned.)	D Shareholders' Consent Statement. We, the undersigned shareholders, consent to the corporation's election to be treated as an "S corporation" under section 1362(a). (Shareholders sign and date below.)*	E Stock owned		F Social security number (employer identification number for estates or trust)	G Tax year ends (month and day)
		Number of shares	Dates acquired		

*For this election to be valid, the consent of each shareholder, person having a community property interest in the corporation's stock, and each tenant in common, joint tenant, and tenant by the entirety must either appear above or be attached to this form. (See instructions for Column D, if continuation sheet or a separate consent statement is needed.)

Under penalties of perjury, I declare that I have examined this election, including accompanying schedules, and statements, and to the best of my knowledge and belief, it is true, correct, and complete.

Signature and Title of Officer ▶ _____   Date ▶ _____

See Parts II, III, and IV on back.

Form **2553** (Rev. 2-87)

Appendix 2
Consent to Election to Be Treated
as an S Corporation

The undersigned shareholder hereby consents to the election of [name of corpora-tion, address, and Employer Identification Number] to be treated as an S corporation under Section 1362(a) of the Internal Revenue Code of 1986.

Name and address of consenting shareholder:

Number of shares owned:

Date(s) shares were acquired:

Social Security Number of consenting shareholder or Employer Identification Num-ber:

Month and day on which shareholder's taxable year ends:

Date: (Signature)

Consent of Spouse*

The shares listed above are community property. I hereby consent to the election of [Name of Corporation] to be treated as an S corporation under Section 1362(a) of the Internal Revenue Code of 1986.

Date: (Signature)

Spouse's Name:
Address:
Social Security No.:
Taxable Year:

* To be used only in community property states.

For a discussion of this form, see Chapter 3.1.

Appendix 3
Transmittal Letter for Form 2553

Certified Mail No.:*
Return Receipt Requested
Internal Revenue Service Center
[Address]

RE: Corporate Name, Employer Identification Number†

Enclosed for filing is a Form 2553 to elect S corporation status for [Name of Corporation]. Please acknowledge receipt of this letter by stamping and returning the enclosed copy of this letter, returning it to the undersigned in the enclosed preaddressed envelope.

Very truly yours,

[Corporation Name]

By: _____
[Name, Title]

Enclosures: Copy of Letter
             Form 2553

For a discussion of this form, see Chapter 3.4.

* This number is to be inserted after first preparing the envelope to mail to the Service.

† Note, if the Employee Identification Number is pending at the time the Form 2553 is being filed, then this letter and the Form 2553 should state "Application Pending."

Appendix 4
State Taxation of S Corporations

The chart below details the requirement for the various states in regard to S corporations specifying whether the state recognizes S corporations or not. Further, the chart details the restrictions and conditions that are placed upon S corporations by each state. Because a state may change its laws regarding the taxation of S corporations the reader is requested to consult the laws of the state where the S corporation is formed to determine the exact requirements that have to be met. No discussion is set forth as to the consequences regarding an S corporation doing business multistate.

State	Tax Treatment	Election	Restrictions and Conditions
Alabama	No tax	State	Nonresident shareholders must pay tax. Corporations with gross sales over $10 million may make election.
Alaska	No tax	Federal	Shareholders must file information returns.
Arizona	No tax	Federal	—
Arkansas	No tax	State	Nonresident shareholders must pay state tax.
California	Taxable	—	—
Colorado	No tax	Federal	—
Connecticut	Taxable	—	—
Delaware	No tax	Federal	Corporations are taxed on shares allocable to nonresident shareholder.
District of Columbia	Taxable	—	Nonresident shareholder not subject to state tax.
Florida	No tax	Federal	Shareholders have three options for taxation of corporate income.

For a discussion of this appendix, see Chapters 5.4A, 5.16, and 6.6.

State	Tax Treatment	Election	Restrictions and Conditions
Georgia	No tax	Federal	All Georgia's shareholders and nonresident shareholders must pay state tax.
Hawaii	No tax	Federal	Nonresident and elderly shareholders must pay state tax. Election lost if over 80% of receipts from out of state.
Idaho	No tax	Federal	Corporations are taxed on compensation dividends not reported by nonresident shareholders.
Illinois	No tax	Federal	Corporations are subject to state personal property replacement tax.
Indiana	No tax	State	Corporations taxed on certain capital gains. Nonresident shareholders must pay state tax.
Iowa	No tax	Federal	Nonresident shareholders must pay state tax.
Kansas	No tax	Federal	Nonresident shareholders must pay state tax.
Kentucky	No tax	Federal	Corporations are taxed on capital gains over $25,000.
Louisiana	Taxable	—	—
Maine	No tax	Federal	—
Maryland	No tax	Federal	—
Massachusetts	Taxable	—	—
Michigan	Taxable	—	—
Minnesota	No tax	Federal	Corporations must withhold tax on distributions to shareholders.
Mississippi	No tax	State	Information return required. Nonresident shareholders must pay state tax.
Missouri	No tax	Federal	Nonresident shareholders must pay state tax.
Montana	No tax	State	—

State	Tax Treatment	Election	Restrictions and Conditions
Nebraska	No tax	Federal	Nonresident shareholders must pay state tax or corporations must remit 10% of their distributive share.
Nevada	—	—	Has no state income tax.
New Hampshire	Taxable	—	—
New Jersey	Taxable	—	—
New Mexico	No tax	Federal	—
New York	No tax	State	—
North Carolina	Taxable	—	—
North Dakota	No tax	Federal	Election is optional. Corporations can pay North Dakota tax and shareholders can deduct federal tax paid on corporate income received.
Ohio	Taxable	—	—
Oklahoma	No tax	Federal	Nonresident shareholders must pay state tax.
Oregon	Taxable	—	Corporations pay excise tax only.
Pennsylvania	No tax	State	Election is optional. Corporations must file information return.
Rhode Island	No tax	Federal	Nonresidential shareholders must pay state tax.
South Carolina	Taxable	—	—
South Dakota	—	—	Has no state income tax.
Tennessee	Taxable	—	—
Texas	—	—	Has no state income tax.
Utah	No tax	Federal	Corporations are taxed on ratio of stock owned by nonresidents.
Vermont	Taxable	—	Corporations are taxed only on stock allocable to nonresident shareholders.
Virginia	No tax	State	Nonresident shareholders must pay state tax.

245

State	Tax Treatment	Election	Restrictions and Conditions
Washington	—	—	Has no state income tax.
West Virginia	No tax	Federal	Corporations must file information return.
Wisconsin	No tax	State	Nonresident shareholders must pay state tax.
Wyoming	—	—	Has no state tax.

Appendix 5
Section 1368(e)(3) Election to Distribute Accumulated Earnings and Profits Before Accumulated Adjustments Account

CERTIFIED MAIL
RETURN RECEIPT REQUESTED
Internal Revenue Service Center
[Address]

[Corporation Name, Address, Identification Number] hereby elects under Section 1368(e)(3) to treat those distributions not exceeding accumulated adjustments accounts during the taxable year as distributions out of accumulated earnings and profits rather than distributions from the accumulated adjustments accounts. This election applies only to distributions made during the taxable year ending (date).

Dated:

[Corporate Name]

By: _____
[Name, Title]

Consent of Shareholders

The undersigned being all the shareholders of [Corporation Name] receiving a distribution during the taxable year ending [Date] hereby consent to the above election under Section 1368(e)(3) being made by the corporation with the respect to distributions made during the taxable year.

| | Shareholder | |
Name of Shareholder	Identification No.	
_____	_____	_____
		Date
_____	_____	_____
_____		Date

For a discussion of this form, see Chapters 6.4.K and 8.3.G.

Appendix 6
Filled-in Return—Distributions
Where S Corporation Has No
Earnings and Profits

The facts for this problem are found at Example 8.2.

Schedule L **Balance Sheets**	Beginning of tax year		End of tax year	
Assets	**(a)**	**(b)**	**(c)**	**(d)**
1 Cash				
2 Trade notes and accounts receivable				
a Less allowance for bad debts				
3 Inventories				
4 Federal and state government obligations				
5 Other current assets (attach schedule)				
6 Loans to shareholders				
7 Mortgage and real estate loans				
8 Other investments (attach schedule)				
9 Buildings and other depreciable assets				
a Less accumulated depreciation				
10 Depletable assets				
a Less accumulated depletion				
11 Land (net of any amortization)				
12 Intangible assets (amortizable only)				
a Less accumulated amortization				
13 Other assets (attach schedule)				
14 Total assets				
Liabilities and Shareholders' Equity				
15 Accounts payable				
16 Mortgages, notes, bonds payable in less than 1 year				
17 Other current liabilities (attach schedule)				
18 Loans from shareholders				
19 Mortgages, notes, bonds payable in 1 year or more				
20 Other liabilities (attach schedule)				
21 Capital stock				10,000
22 Paid-in or capital surplus				
23 Accumulated adjustments account			⟨16,000⟩	
24 Other adjustments account				
25 Shareholders' undistributed taxable income previously taxed				
26 Other retained earnings (see instructions). Check this box if the corporation has subchapter C earnings and profits at the close of the tax year ▶ ☐ (see instructions)				
27 Total retained earnings per books—Combine amounts on lines 23 through 26, columns (a) and (c) (see instructions)				⟨16,000⟩
28 Less cost of treasury stock		( )		( )
29 Total liabilities and shareholders' equity				

The facts for this problem are found at example 8-2

Schedule M **Analysis of Accumulated Adjustments Account, Other Adjustments Account, and Shareholders' Undistributed Taxable Income Previously Taxed** (If Schedule L, column (c), amounts for lines 23, 24, or 25 are not the same as corresponding amounts on line 9 of Schedule M, attach a schedule explaining any differences. See instructions.)

	Accumulated adjustments account	Other adjustments account	Shareholders' undistributed taxable income previously taxed
1 Balance at beginning of year	0		
2 Ordinary income from page 1, line 21	12,000		
3 Other additions		18,000	
4 Total of lines 1, 2, and 3	12,000	18,000	
5 Distributions other than dividend distributions	⟨28,000⟩	⟨18,000⟩	
6 Loss from page 1, line 21			
7 Other reductions			
8 Add lines 5, 6, and 7	⟨28,000⟩	⟨18,000⟩	
9 Balance at end of tax year—Subtract line 8 from line 4	⟨16,000⟩	0	

☆U.S. GOVERNMENT PRINTING OFFICE: 1987—183-209

Shareholder's Share of Income, Credits, Deductions, etc.

For calendar year 1987 or tax year

beginning _____, 1987, and ending _____, 19___

▶ **For Paperwork Reduction Act Notice, see page 1 of Instructions for Form 1120S.**

OMB No. 1545-0130

1987

Shareholder's identifying number ▶	Corporation's identifying number ▶
Shareholder's name, address, and ZIP code	Corporation's name, address, and ZIP code
B	A, INC.

A (1) Shareholder's percentage of stock ownership for tax year (see instructions for Schedule K-1) . . . . . ▶ _____ %

  (2) Number of shares owned by shareholder at tax year end . . . . ▶

B Internal Revenue Service Center where corporation filed its return ▶

C Tax shelter registration number (see Instructions for Schedule K-1) . . . . ▶

D Did the shareholder materially participate in the trade or business activity(ies) of the corporation? (See instructions for Schedule K-1. Leave the check boxes blank if there are no trade or business activities.) . . . . [X] Yes [ ] No

E Did the shareholder actively participate in the rental real estate activity(ies) of the corporation? (See instructions for Schedule K-1. Leave the check boxes blank if there are no rental real estate activities.) . . . . [ ] Yes [ ] No

F If (1) question D is checked "No" or income or loss is reported on line 2 or 3 and (2) the shareholder acquired corporate stock after 10/22/86, check here ▶ [ ] and enter the shareholder's weighted percentage increase in stock ownership for 1987 (see instructions for Schedule K-1) . . . . ▶ _____ %

G If question D is checked "No" and any activity referred to in question D was started or acquired by the corporation after 10/22/86, check here ▶ [ ] and enter the date of start up or acquisition in the date space on line 1. Also, if an activity for which income or loss is reported on line 2 or 3 was started after 10/22/86, check the box and enter the start up date in the date space on line 2 or 3.

H If the short tax year shown above was a result of a change in tax year required by section 1378, check here . . . . ▶ [ ]

Caution: *Refer to Shareholder's Instructions for Schedule K-1 before entering information from Schedule K-1 on your tax return.*

	(a) Distributive share items	(b) Amount	(c) Form 1040 filers enter the amount in column (b) on:
Income (Losses) and Deductions	**1** Ordinary income (loss) from trade or business activity(ies). Date: _____	12,000	See Shareholder's Instructions for Schedule K-1 (Form 1120S).
	2 Income or loss from rental real estate activity(ies). Date: _____		
	3 Income or loss from rental activity(ies) other than line 2 above. Date: _____		
	4 Portfolio income (loss):		
	a Interest		Sch. B, Part I, line 2
	b Dividends		Sch. B, Part II, line 4
	c Royalties		Sch. E, Part I, line 5
	d Net short-term capital gain (loss)		Sch. D, line 5, col. (f) or (g)
	e Net long-term capital gain (loss)		Sch. D, line 12, col. (f) or (g)
	f Other portfolio income (loss).		(Enter on applicable line of your return.)
	5 Net gain (loss) under section 1231 (other than due to casualty or theft).		Form 4797, line 1
	6 Other income (loss) (attach schedule)		(Enter on applicable line of your return.)
	7 Charitable contributions.		See Form 1040 Instructions.
	8 Section 179 expense deduction (attach schedule) . . .		See Shareholder's Instructions for Schedule K-1 (Form 1120S).
	9 Deductions related to portfolio income (loss) (attach schedule) . .		
	10 Other deductions (attach schedule)		
Credits	**11a** Jobs credit		Form 5884
	b Low-income housing credit		Form 8586, line 8
	c Qualified rehabilitation expenditures related to rental real estate activity(ies) (attach schedule)		
	d Credits related to rental real estate activity(ies) other than on lines 11b and 11c (attach schedule)		See Shareholder's Instructions for Schedule K-1 (Form 1120S).
	e Credits related to rental activity(ies) other than on lines 11b, c, and d (attach schedule)		
	12 Other credits (attach schedule)		
Tax Preference and Adjustment Items	**13a** Accelerated depreciation of real property placed in service before 1987		Form 6251, line 5a
	b Accelerated depreciation of leased personal property placed in service before 1987.		Form 6251, line 5b
	c Depreciation adjustment on property placed in service after 1986 . .		Form 6251, line 4g
	d Depletion (other than oil and gas)		Form 6251, line 5h
	e (1) Gross income from oil, gas, or geothermal properties		See Form 6251 Instructions.
	(2) Gross deductions allocable to oil, gas, or geothermal properties . .		See Shareholder's Instructions for Schedule K-1 (Form 1120S).
	f Other items (attach schedule)		

(a) Distributive share items	(b) Amount	(c) Form 1040 filers enter the amount in column (b) on:
14a Interest expense on investment debts		Form 4952, line 1
b (1) Investment income included on Schedule K-1, lines 4a through 4f .		See Shareholder's Instructions for Schedule K-1 (Form 1120S).
(2) Investment expenses included on Schedule K-1, line 9		
15a Type of income ▶		Form 1116, Check boxes
b Name of foreign country or U.S. possession ▶		Form 1116, Check boxes
c Total gross income from sources outside the U.S. (attach schedule) . .		Form 1116, Part I
d Total applicable deductions and losses (attach schedule).		Form 1116, Part I
e Total foreign taxes (check one): ▶ ☐ Paid ☐ Accrued		Form 1116, Part II
f Reduction in taxes available for credit (attach schedule)		Form 1116, Part III
g Other (attach schedule)		See Form 1116 Instructions.
16 Property distributions (including cash) other than dividend distributions reported to you on Form 1099-DIV	*46,00*	See Shareholder's Instructions for Schedule K-1 (Form 1120S)
17 Amount of loan repayments for "Loans from Shareholders"		

18 Properties:	A	B	C	
a Description of property (State whether recovery or non-recovery property. If recovery property, state whether regular percentage method or section 48(q) election used.).				
b Date placed in service .				Form 4255, top
c Cost or other basis . .				Form 4255, line 2
d Class of recovery property or original estimated useful life .				Form 4255, line 3
e Date item ceased to be investment credit property				Form 4255, line 4
				Form 4255, line 8

19 Supplemental information for lines 1 through 18 that is required to be reported separately to each shareholder (attach additional schedules if more space is needed):

Property Subject to Recapture of Investment Credit

Supplemental Schedules

Form **1040** Department of the Treasury—Internal Revenue Service
U.S. Individual Income Tax Return **1987** (O)

For the year Jan.–Dec. 31, 1987, or other tax year beginning , 1987, ending , 19 | OMB No. 1545-0074

Label

Use IRS label.
Otherwise,
please print or
type.

Your first name and initial (if joint return, also give spouse's name and initial) | Last name | **Your social security number**

Present home address (number and street or rural route). (If you have a P.O. Box, see page 6 of Instructions.) | **Spouse's social security number**

City, town or post office, state, and ZIP code | For Privacy Act and Paperwork Reduction Act Notice, see Instructions.

Presidential Election Campaign

▶ Do you want $1 to go to this fund? . . . . | Yes | No
If joint return, does your spouse want $1 to go to this fund?. . | Yes | No

Note: *Checking "Yes" will not change your tax or reduce your refund.*

Filing Status

Check only
one box.

1 ☐ Single
2 ☐ Married filing joint return (even if only one had income)
3 ☐ Married filing separate return. Enter spouse's social security no. above and full name here. _____
4 ☐ Head of household (with qualifying person). (See page 7 of Instructions.) If the qualifying person is your child but not your dependent, enter child's name here. _____
5 ☐ Qualifying widow(er) with dependent child (year spouse died ▶ 19). (See page 7 of Instructions.)

Exemptions

(See
Instructions
on page 7.)

If more than 7
dependents, see
Instructions on
page 7.

Caution: If you can be claimed as a dependent on another person's tax return (such as your parents' return), do not check box 6a. But be sure to check the box on line 32b on page 2.

6a ☐ Yourself   6b ☐ Spouse

c Dependents (1) Name (first, initial, and last name)	(2) Check if under age 5	(3) If age 5 or over, dependent's social security number	(4) Relationship	(5) No. of months lived in your home in 1987
		:		
		:		
		:		
		:		
		:		

No. of boxes
checked on 6a
and 6b ▶ ☐

No. of children
on 6c who lived
with you ▶ ☐

No. of children
on 6c who didn't
live with you due
to divorce or
separation ▶ ☐

No. of parents
listed on 6c ▶ ☐

No. of other
dependents
listed on 6c ▶ ☐

d If your child didn't live with you but is claimed as your dependent under a pre-1985 agreement, check here . ▶☐
e Total number of exemptions claimed (also complete line 35) . . . .

Add numbers
entered in
boxes above ▶ ☐

Income

Please attach
Copy B of your
Forms W-2, W-2G,
and W-2P here.

If you do not have
a W-2, see
page 6 of
Instructions.

Please
attach check
or money
order here.

7	Wages, salaries, tips, etc. (attach Form(s) W-2)	7	
8	**Taxable** interest income (also attach Schedule B if over $400) . . .	8	
9	Tax-exempt interest income (see page 10). DON'T include on line 8 9	18,000	
10	Dividend income (also attach Schedule B if over $400)	10	
11	Taxable refunds of state and local income taxes, if any, from worksheet on page 11 of Instructions . .	11	
12	Alimony received	12	
13	Business income or (loss) (attach Schedule C)	13	
14	Capital gain or (loss) (attach Schedule D)	14	6,000
15	Other gains or (losses) (attach Form 4797)	15	
16a	Pensions, IRA distributions, annuities, and rollovers. Total received 16a		
b	Taxable amount (see page 11)	16b	
17	Rents, royalties, partnerships, estates, trusts, etc. (attach Schedule E) . . .	17	12,000
18	Farm income or (loss) (attach Schedule F)	18	
19	Unemployment compensation (insurance) (see page 11) . . .	19	
20a	Social security benefits (see page 12) 20a		
b	Taxable amount, if any, from the worksheet on page 12 . . .	20b	
21	Other income (list type and amount—see page 12) _____	21	
22	Add the amounts shown in the far right column for lines 7, 8, and 10–21. This is your **total income** ▶	22	18,000

Adjustments to Income

(See
Instructions
on page 12.)

23	Reimbursed employee business expenses from Form 2106 . .	23	
24a	Your IRA deduction, from applicable worksheet on page 13 or 14	24a	
b	Spouse's IRA deduction, from applicable worksheet on page 13 or 14 . .	24b	
25	Self-employed health insurance deduction, from worksheet on page 14 .	25	
26	Keogh retirement plan and self-employed SEP deduction . .	26	
27	Penalty on early withdrawal of savings	27	
28	Alimony paid (recipient's last name _____ and social security no. _____) .	28	
29	Add lines 23 through 28. These are your **total adjustments** . . . . ▶	29	

Adjusted Gross Income

30 Subtract line 29 from line 22. This is your **adjusted gross income.** *If this line is less than $15,432 and a child lived with you, see "Earned Income Credit" (line 56) on page 18 of the Instructions. If you want IRS to figure your tax, see page 15 of the Instructions* . . . ▶ | 30 | |

SCHEDULE D
(Form 1040)

Department of the Treasury
Internal Revenue Service (O)

Capital Gains and Losses
and Reconciliation of Forms 1099-B

▶ Attach to Form 1040.   ▶ See Instructions for Schedule D (Form 1040).

For Paperwork Reduction Act Notice, see Form 1040 Instructions.

OMB No. 1545-0074

1987

Attachment
Sequence No. **12**

Name(s) as shown on Form 1040

Your social security number

1 Report here, the total sales of stocks, bonds, etc., reported for 1987 by your broker to you on Form(s) 1099-B or an equivalent substitute statement(s). If this amount differs from the total of lines 2b and 9b, column (d), attach a statement explaining the difference. See the Instructions for line 1 for examples. Do not include real estate transactions reported to you on a Form 1099-B on line 1, 2a, or 9a **1**

Part I Short-term Capital Gains and Losses—Assets Held Six Months or Less

(a) Description of property (Example, 100 shares 7% preferred of "Z" Co.)	(b) Date acquired (Mo., day, yr.)	(c) Date sold (Mo., day, yr.)	(d) Sales price (see Instructions)	(e) Cost or other basis (see Instructions)	(f) LOSS If (e) is more than (d), subtract (d) from (e)	(g) GAIN If (d) is more than (e), subtract (e) from (d)
2a Form 1099-B Transactions (Sales of Stocks, Bonds, etc.):		(Do not report real estate transactions here. See the instructions for lines 2a and 9a.)				
2b Total (add column (d)) . . . . ▶						
2c Other Transactions:						

3 Short-term gain from sale or exchange of a principal residence from Form 2119, lines 8 or 14 **3**

4 Short-term gain from installment sales from Form 6252, lines 23 or 31 . . . **4**

5 Net short-term gain or (loss) from partnerships, S corporations, and fiduciaries . **5**

6 Short-term capital loss carryover **6**

7 Add all of the transactions on lines 2a and 2c and lines 3 through 6 in columns (f) and (g) . . . **7** (   )

8 Net short-term gain or (loss), combine columns (f) and (g) of line 7 . . . . **8**

Part II Long-term Capital Gains and Losses—Assets Held More Than Six Months

(a)	(b)	(c)	(d)	(e)	(f)	(g)
9a Form 1099-B Transactions (Sales of Stocks, Bonds, etc.):		(Do not report real estate transactions here. See the instructions for lines 2a and 9a.)				
9b Total (add column (d)) . . . . ▶						
9c Other Transactions:						
Distribution in excess of Basis S-Corp.						6,000

10 Long-term gain from sale or exchange of a principal residence from Form 2119, lines 8, 10, or 14 **10**

11 Long-term gain from installment sales from Form 6252, lines 23 or 31 . . . . **11**

12 Net long-term gain or (loss) from partnerships, S corporations, and fiduciaries . **12**

13 Capital gain distributions. **13**

14 Enter gain from Form 4797, line 7 or 9 . . . . **14**

15 Long-term capital loss carryover **15**

16 Add all of the transactions on lines 9a and 9c and lines 10 through 15 in columns (f) and (g) . . **16** (   )

17 Net long-term gain or (loss), combine columns (f) and (g) of line 16 . . . . **17** 6,000

Schedule D (Form 1040) 1987

Attachment Sequence No. **13** Page **2**

Name(s) as shown on Form 1040. (Do not enter name and social security number if shown on other side.)	Your social security number
	⋮ ⋮

Part II Income or (Loss) from Partnerships and S Corporations

If you report a loss below and have amounts invested in that activity for which you are **not at risk**, you MUST check "Yes" in column (e) and attach Form 6198. Otherwise, you must check "No." See Instructions.

	(a) Name	(b) Enter **P** for partnership; **S** for S Corporation	(c) Check if foreign partnership	(d) Employer identification number	(e) Not at-Risk? Yes	No
A	A, INC.	S		11 - 111111	✓	
B						
C						
D						
E						

	Passive Activities		Nonpassive Activities		
	(f) Passive loss allowed from Form 8582	(g) Passive income from Schedule K–1	(h) Nonpassive loss from Schedule K–1	(i) Section 179 deduction	(j) Nonpassive income from Schedule K–1
A					12,000
B					
C					
D					
E					
30a Totals					12,000
b Totals					

31	Add amounts in columns (g) and (j), line 30a. Enter total income here	31	12,000	
32	Add amounts in columns (f), (h), and (i), line 30b. Enter total here	32	(	)
33	Total partnership and S corporation income or (loss). Combine amounts on lines 31 and 32. Enter the total here and include in line 42 below	33	12,000	

Part III Income or (Loss) from Estates and Trusts

	(a) Name	(b) Employer identification number
A		
B		
C		

	Passive Activities		Nonpassive Activities	
	(c) Passive deduction or loss allowed from Form 8582	(d) Passive income from Schedule K–1	(e) Deduction or loss from Schedule K–1	(f) Other income from Schedule K–1
A				
B				
C				
34a Totals				
b Totals				

35	Add amounts in columns (d) and (f), line 34a. Enter total income here	35		
36	Add amounts in columns (c) and (e), line 34b. Enter total (loss) here	36	(	)
37	Total estate and trust income or (loss). Combine amounts on lines 35 and 36. Enter the total here and include in line 42 below	37		

Part IV Income or (Loss) from Real Estate Mortgage Investment Conduits (REMICs)—Residual Holder

	(a) Name	(b) Employer identification number	(c) Excess inclusion from Schedules Q, line 2c (see Instructions)	(d) Taxable income (net loss) from Schedules Q, line 1b	(e) Income from Schedules Q, line 3b

38	Combine columns (d) and (e) only. Enter the total here and include in line 42 below	38	

Part V Windfall Profit Tax Summary

39	Windfall profit tax credit or refund received in 1987 (see Instructions)	39		
40	Windfall profit tax withheld in 1987 (see Instructions)	40	(	)
41	Combine amounts on lines 39 and 40. Enter the total here and include in line 42 below	41		

Part VI Summary

42	TOTAL income or (loss). Combine lines 29, 33, 37, 38, and 41. Enter total here and on Form 1040, line 17 . . . . ▶	42	12,000
43	Farmers and fishermen: Enter your share of GROSS FARMING AND FISHING INCOME applicable to Parts I, II, and III (see Instructions) . . . **43**		

Appendix 7
Filled-in Return—Distributions Where S Corporation Has No Earnings and Profits

---

The facts for this problem are found at Example 8.3.

Schedule L   Balance Sheets

Assets	Beginning of tax year		End of tax year	
	(a)	(b)	(c)	(d)
1 Cash				
2 Trade notes and accounts receivable				
a Less allowance for bad debts				
3 Inventories		*THE FACTS FOR THIS PROBLEM*		
4 Federal and state government obligations		*ARE FOUND AT EXAMPLE 8-3*		
5 Other current assets (attach schedule)				
6 Loans to shareholders				
7 Mortgage and real estate loans				
8 Other investments (attach schedule)				
9 Buildings and other depreciable assets				
a Less accumulated depreciation				
10 Depletable assets				
a Less accumulated depletion				
11 Land (net of any amortization)				
12 Intangible assets (amortizable only)				
a Less accumulated amortization				
13 Other assets (attach schedule)				
14 Total assets				40,000
Liabilities and Shareholders' Equity				
15 Accounts payable				
16 Mortgages, notes, bonds payable in less than 1 year				
17 Other current liabilities (attach schedule)				
18 Loans from shareholders				
19 Mortgages, notes, bonds payable in 1 year or more				
20 Other liabilities (attach schedule)				
21 Capital stock				10,000
22 Paid-in or capital surplus				
23 Accumulated adjustments account			12,000	
24 Other adjustments account			18,000	
25 Shareholders' undistributed taxable income previously taxed				
26 Other retained earnings (see instructions)				
Check this box if the corporation has subchapter C earnings and profits at the close of the tax year ▶ ☐ (see instructions)				
27 Total retained earnings per books—Combine amounts on lines 23 through 26, columns (a) and (c) (see instructions)				30,000
28 Less cost of treasury stock		( )		( )
29 Total liabilities and shareholders' equity				40,000

Schedule M   Analysis of Accumulated Adjustments Account, Other Adjustments Account, and Shareholders' Undistributed Taxable Income Previously Taxed (If Schedule L, column (c), amounts for lines 23, 24, or 25 are not the same as corresponding amounts on line 9 of Schedule M, attach a schedule explaining any differences. See instructions.)

	Accumulated adjustments account	Other adjustments account	Shareholders' undistributed taxable income previously taxed
1 Balance at beginning of year	0	0	
2 Ordinary income from page 1, line 21	12,000		
3 Other additions		18,000	
4 Total of lines 1, 2, and 3	12,000	18,000	
5 Distributions other than dividend distributions			
6 Loss from page 1, line 21			
7 Other reductions			
8 Add lines 5, 6, and 7			
9 Balance at end of tax year—Subtract line 8 from line 4	12,000	18,000	

SCHEDULE K-1 (Form 1120S)	Shareholder's Share of Income, Credits, Deductions, etc.	OMB No. 1545-0130
Department of the Treasury Internal Revenue Service	For calendar year 1987 or tax year beginning _____ , 1987, and ending _____ , 19 ____ ▶ For Paperwork Reduction Act Notice, see page 1 of Instructions for Form 1120S.	1987

Shareholder's identifying number ▶	Corporation's identifying number ▶
Shareholder's name, address, and ZIP code	Corporation's name, address, and ZIP code

A (1) Shareholder's percentage of stock ownership for tax year (see instructions for Schedule K-1) . . . . ▶ _____ %

(2) Number of shares owned by shareholder at tax year end . . . . ▶

B Internal Revenue Service Center where corporation filed its return ▶

C Tax shelter registration number (see Instructions for Schedule K-1) . . . . ▶

D Did the shareholder materially participate in the trade or business activity(ies) of the corporation? (See instructions for Schedule K-1. Leave the check boxes blank if there are no trade or business activities.) . . . . ☒ Yes ☐ No

E Did the shareholder actively participate in the rental real estate activity(ies) of the corporation? (See instructions for Schedule K-1. Leave the check boxes blank if there are no rental real estate activities.) . . . . ☐ Yes ☐ No

F If (1) question D is checked "No" or income or loss is reported on line 2 or 3 and (2) the shareholder acquired corporate stock after 10/22/86, check here ▶ ☐ and enter the shareholder's weighted percentage increase in stock ownership for 1987 (see instructions for Schedule K-1) . . . . ▶ _____ %

G If question D is checked "No" and any activity referred to in question D was started or acquired by the corporation after 10/22/86, check here ▶ ☐ and enter the date of start up or acquisition in the date space on line 1. Also, if an activity for which income or loss is reported on line 2 or 3 was started after 10/22/86, check the box and enter the start up date in the date space on line 2 or 3.

H If the short tax year shown above was a result of a change in tax year required by section 1378, check here . . . . . . ▶ ☐

Caution: *Refer to Shareholder's Instructions for Schedule K-1 before entering information from Schedule K-1 on your tax return.*

	(a) Distributive share items	(b) Amount	(c) Form 1040 filers enter the amount in column (b) on:
Income (Losses) and Deductions	**1** Ordinary income (loss) from trade or business activity(ies). Date:_____	12,000	} See Shareholder's Instructions for Schedule K-1 (Form 1120S).
	2 Income or loss from rental real estate activity(ies). Date: _____		
	3 Income or loss from rental activity(ies) other than line 2 above. Date: _____		
	4 Portfolio income (loss):		
	a Interest		Sch. B, Part I, line 2
	b Dividends		Sch. B, Part II, line 4
	c Royalties		Sch. E, Part I, line 5
	d Net short-term capital gain (loss)		Sch. D, line 5, col. (f) or (g)
	e Net long-term capital gain (loss)		Sch. D, line 12, col. (f) or (g)
	f Other portfolio income (loss).		(Enter on applicable line of your return.)
	5 Net gain (loss) under section 1231 (other than due to casualty or theft).		Form 4797, line 1
	6 Other income (loss) (attach schedule)		(Enter on applicable line of your return.)
	7 Charitable contributions		See Form 1040 Instructions.
	8 Section 179 expense deduction (attach schedule) . . .		} See Shareholder's Instructions for Schedule K-1 (Form 1120S).
	9 Deductions related to portfolio income (loss) (attach schedule) . . .		
	10 Other deductions (attach schedule)		
Credits	**11a** Jobs credit		Form 5884
	b Low-income housing credit		Form 8586, line 8
	c Qualified rehabilitation expenditures related to rental real estate activity(ies) (attach schedule)	/////////	} See Shareholder's Instructions for Schedule K-1 (Form 1120S).
	d Credits related to rental real estate activity(ies) other than on lines 11b and 11c (attach schedule)	/////////	
	e Credits related to rental activity(ies) other than on lines 11b, c, and d (attach schedule)	/////////	
	12 Other credits (attach schedule)		
Tax Preference and Adjustment Items	**13a** Accelerated depreciation of real property placed in service before 1987	/////////	Form 6251, line 5a
	b Accelerated depreciation of leased personal property placed in service before 1987		Form 6251, line 5b
	c Depreciation adjustment on property placed in service after 1986 . .		Form 6251, line 4g
	d Depletion (other than oil and gas)		Form 6251, line 5h
	e (1) Gross income from oil, gas, or geothermal properties		} See Form 6251 Instructions.
	(2) Gross deductions allocable to oil, gas, or geothermal properties . .		See Shareholder's Instructions for Schedule K-1 (Form 1120S).
	f Other items (attach schedule)		

	(a) Distributive share items	(b) Amount	(c) Form 1040 filers enter the amount in column (b) on:
Investment Interest	**14a** Interest expense on investment debts		Form 4952, line 1
	b **(1)** Investment income included on Schedule K-1, lines 4a through 4f .		See Shareholder's Instructions for Schedule K-1 (Form 1120S).
	(2) Investment expenses included on Schedule K-1, line 9		
Foreign Taxes	**15a** Type of income ▶		Form 1116, Check boxes
	b Name of foreign country or U.S. possession ▶		Form 1116, Part I
	c Total gross income from sources outside the U.S. (attach schedule) . .		Form 1116, Part I
	d Total applicable deductions and losses (attach schedule)		Form 1116, Part I
	e Total foreign taxes (check one): ▶ ☐ Paid ☐ Accrued		Form 1116, Part II
	f Reduction in taxes available for credit (attach schedule)		Form 1116, Part III
	g Other (attach schedule)		See Form 1116 Instructions.
Other Items	**16** Property distributions (including cash) other than dividend distributions reported to you on Form 1099-DIV		See Shareholder's Instructions for Schedule K-1 (Form 1120S).
	17 Amount of loan repayments for "Loans from Shareholders"		

	18 Properties:	A	B	C	
Property Subject to Recapture of Investment Credit	**a** Description of property (State whether recovery or non-recovery property. If recovery property, state whether regular percentage method or section 48(q) election used.)				Form 4255, top
	b Date placed in service .				Form 4255, line 2
	c Cost or other basis . .				Form 4255, line 3
	d Class of recovery property or original estimated useful life .				Form 4255, line 4
	e Date item ceased to be investment credit property				Form 4255, line 8

19 Supplemental information for lines 1 through 18 that is required to be reported separately to each shareholder (attach additional schedules if more space is needed):

TAX-EXEMPT INCOME $18,000

Supplemental Schedules

Form 1040

Department of the Treasury—Internal Revenue Service

U.S. Individual Income Tax Return 1987 (O)

For the year Jan.–Dec. 31, 1987, or other tax year beginning _____ , 1987, ending _____ , 19 ___ | OMB No. 1545-0074

Label

Use IRS label. Otherwise, please print or type.

Your first name and initial (if joint return, also give spouse's name and initial) | Last name | **Your social security number**

Present home address (number and street or rural route). (If you have a P.O. Box, see page 6 of Instructions.) | **Spouse's social security number**

City, town or post office, state, and ZIP code | For Privacy Act and Paperwork Reduction Act Notice, see Instructions.

Presidential Election Campaign

▶ Do you want $1 to go to this fund? . . . . | Yes ☐ | No ☐ | **Note:** Checking "Yes" will not change your tax or reduce your refund.

If joint return, does your spouse want $1 to go to this fund?. . | Yes ☐ | No ☐

Filing Status

Check only one box.

1 ☐ Single

2 ☐ Married filing joint return (even if only one had income)

3 ☐ Married filing separate return. Enter spouse's social security no. above and full name here. _____

4 ☐ Head of household (with qualifying person). (See page 7 of Instructions.) If the qualifying person is your child but not your dependent, enter child's name here. _____

5 ☐ Qualifying widow(er) with dependent child (year spouse died ▶ 19 ___). (See page 7 of Instructions.)

Exemptions

(See Instructions on page 7.)

Caution: If you can be claimed as a dependent on another person's tax return (such as your parents' return), do not check box 6a. But be sure to check the box on line 32b on page 2.

6a ☐ Yourself   6b ☐ Spouse

| No. of boxes checked on 6a and 6b ▶ ☐ |

c Dependents

(1) Name (first, initial, and last name)	(2) Check if under age 5	(3) If age 5 or over, dependent's social security number	(4) Relationship	(5) No. of months lived in your home in 1987
_____		: :		
_____		: :		
_____		: :		
_____		: :		
_____		: :		
_____		: :		
_____		: :		

No. of children on 6c who lived with you ▶ ☐

No. of children on 6c who didn't live with you due to divorce or separation ▶ ☐

No. of parents listed on 6c ▶ ☐

No. of other dependents listed on 6c ▶ ☐

If more than 7 dependents, see Instructions on page 7.

d If your child didn't live with you but is claimed as your dependent under a pre-1985 agreement, check here . ▶ ☐

e Total number of exemptions claimed (also complete line 35)

Add numbers entered in boxes above ▶ ☐

Income

Please attach Copy B of your Forms W-2, W-2G, and W-2P here.

If you do not have a W-2, see page 6 of Instructions.

7	Wages, salaries, tips, etc. (attach Form(s) W-2)	7	
8	**Taxable** interest income (also attach Schedule B if over $400) .	8	
9	**Tax-exempt** interest income (see page 10). DON'T include on line 8	9	18,000	
10	Dividend income (also attach Schedule B if over $400)	10	
11	Taxable refunds of state and local income taxes, if any, from worksheet on page 11 of Instructions .	11	
12	Alimony received	12	
13	Business income or (loss) (attach Schedule C).	13	
14	Capital gain or (loss) (attach Schedule D).	14	
15	Other gains or (losses) (attach Form 4797)	15	
16a	Pensions, IRA distributions, annuities, and rollovers. Total received	16a	
b	Taxable amount (see page 11)	16b	
17	Rents, royalties, partnerships, estates, trusts, etc. (attach Schedule E)	17	12,006
18	Farm income or (loss) (attach Schedule F)	18	
19	Unemployment compensation (insurance) (see page 11)	19	
20a	Social security benefits (see page 12)	20a	
b	Taxable amount, if any, from the worksheet on page 12	20b	
21	Other income (list type and amount—see page 12) _____	21	
22	Add the amounts shown in the far right column for lines 7, 8, and 10–21. This is your **total income** ▶	22	12,000

Please attach check or money order here.

Adjustments to Income

(See Instructions on page 12.)

23	Reimbursed employee business expenses from Form 2106 .	23	
24a	Your IRA deduction, from applicable worksheet on page 13 or 14	24a	
b	Spouse's IRA deduction, from applicable worksheet on page 13 or 14 . .	24b	
25	Self-employed health insurance deduction, from worksheet on page 14 .	25	
26	Keogh retirement plan and self-employed SEP deduction . .	26	
27	Penalty on early withdrawal of savings	27	
28	Alimony paid (recipient's last name _____ and social security no. _____) .	28	
29	Add lines 23 through 28. These are your **total adjustments** . . . . ▶	29	

Adjusted Gross Income

| 30 | Subtract line 29 from line 22. This is your **adjusted gross income**. If this line is less than $15,432 and a child lived with you, see "Earned Income Credit" (line 56) on page 18 of the Instructions. If you want IRS to figure your tax, see page 15 of the Instructions . . ▶ | 30 | 12,000 |

Name(s) as shown on Form 1040. (Do not enter name and social security number if shown on other side.) | **Your social security number**

Part II Income or (Loss) from Partnerships and S Corporations

If you report a loss below and have amounts invested in that activity for which you are **not at risk**, you MUST check "Yes" in column (e) and attach Form 6198. Otherwise, you must check "No." See Instructions.

	(a) Name	(b) Enter P for partnership; S for S Corporation	(c) Check if foreign partnership	(d) Employer identification number	(e) Not at-Risk? Yes | No
A	A, Inc.	S		11-111111	✓
B					
C					
D					
E					

	Passive Activities		Nonpassive Activities		
	(f) Passive loss allowed from Form 8582	(g) Passive income from Schedule K-1	(h) Nonpassive loss from Schedule K-1	(i) Section 179 deduction	(j) Nonpassive income from Schedule K-1
A					12,000
B					
C					
D					
E					
30a Totals					12,000
b Totals					

31 Add amounts in columns (g) and (j), line 30a. Enter total income here **31** 12,000
32 Add amounts in columns (f), (h), and (i), line 30b. Enter total here . . . . . . **32** ( )
33 Total partnership and S corporation income or (loss). Combine amounts on lines 31 and 32. Enter the total here and include in line 42 below **33** 12,000

Part III Income or (Loss) from Estates and Trusts

	(a) Name	(b) Employer identification number
A		
B		
C		

	Passive Activities		Nonpassive Activities	
	(c) Passive deduction or loss allowed from Form 8582	(d) Passive income from Schedule K-1	(e) Deduction or loss from Schedule K-1	(f) Other income from Schedule K-1
A				
B				
C				
34a Totals				
b Totals				

35 Add amounts in columns (d) and (f), line 34a. Enter total income here **35**
36 Add amounts in columns (c) and (e), line 34b. Enter total (loss) here . . . . . **36** ( )
37 Total estate and trust income or (loss). Combine amounts on lines 35 and 36. Enter the total here and include in line 42 below **37**

Part IV Income or (Loss) from Real Estate Mortgage Investment Conduits (REMICs)—Residual Holder

(a) Name	(b) Employer identification number	(c) Excess inclusion from Schedules Q, line 2c (see Instructions)	(d) Taxable income (net loss) from Schedules Q, line 1b	(e) Income from Schedules Q, line 3b

38 Combine columns (d) and (e) only. Enter the total here and include in line 42 below **38**

Part V Windfall Profit Tax Summary

39 Windfall profit tax credit or refund received in 1987 (see Instructions) **39**
40 Windfall profit tax withheld in 1987 (see Instructions) . . . . **40** ( )
41 Combine amounts on lines 39 and 40. Enter the total here and include in line 42 below . . . **41**

Part VI Summary

42 TOTAL income or (loss). Combine lines 29, 33, 37, 38, and 41. Enter total here and on Form 1040, line 17 . . . . ▶ **42** 12,000
43 Farmers and fishermen: Enter your share of GROSS FARMING AND FISHING INCOME applicable to Parts I, II, and III (see Instructions) . . . **43**

☆ U.S.G.P.O.: 1987 - 183-104

Schedule L   Balance Sheets

Assets	Beginning of tax year (a)	(b)	End of tax year (c)	(d)
1 Cash				
2 Trade notes and accounts receivable				
a Less allowance for bad debts				
3 Inventories				
4 Federal and state government obligations				
5 Other current assets (attach schedule)				
6 Loans to shareholders				
7 Mortgage and real estate loans				
8 Other investments (attach schedule)				
9 Buildings and other depreciable assets				
a Less accumulated depreciation				
10 Depletable assets				
a Less accumulated depletion				
11 Land (net of any amortization)				
12 Intangible assets (amortizable only)				
a Less accumulated amortization				
13 Other assets (attach schedule)				
14 Total assets		40,000		
Liabilities and Shareholders' Equity				
15 Accounts payable				
16 Mortgages, notes, bonds payable in less than 1 year				
17 Other current liabilities (attach schedule)				
18 Loans from shareholders				
19 Mortgages, notes, bonds payable in 1 year or more				
20 Other liabilities (attach schedule)				
21 Capital stock		10,000		10,000
22 Paid-in or capital surplus				
23 Accumulated adjustments account	12,000		⟨16,000⟩	
24 Other adjustments account	18,000		-0-	
25 Shareholders' undistributed taxable income previously taxed				
26 Other retained earnings (see instructions)				
Check this box if the corporation has subchapter C earnings and profits at the close of the tax year ▶ ☐ (see instructions)				
27 Total retained earnings per books—Combine amounts on lines 23 through 26, columns (a) and (c) (see instructions)		30,000		⟨16,000⟩
28 Less cost of treasury stock		( )		( )
29 Total liabilities and shareholders' equity		40,000		

Schedule M   Analysis of Accumulated Adjustments Account, Other Adjustments Account, and Shareholders' Undistributed Taxable Income Previously Taxed (If Schedule L, column (c), amounts for lines 23, 24, or 25 are not the same as corresponding amounts on line 9 of Schedule M, attach a schedule explaining any differences. See instructions.)

	Accumulated adjustments account	Other adjustments account	Shareholders' undistributed taxable income previously taxed
1 Balance at beginning of year	12,000	18,000	
2 Ordinary income from page 1, line 21			
3 Other additions			
4 Total of lines 1, 2, and 3	12,000	18,000	
5 Distributions other than dividend distributions	⟨28,000⟩	⟨18,000⟩	
6 Loss from page 1, line 21			
7 Other reductions			
8 Add lines 5, 6, and 7	⟨28,000⟩	⟨18,000⟩	
9 Balance at end of tax year—Subtract line 8 from line 4	⟨16,000⟩	-0-	

SCHEDULE K-1
(Form 1120S)

Department of the Treasury
Internal Revenue Service

Shareholder's Share of Income, Credits, Deductions, etc.

For calendar year 1987 or tax year

beginning _____, 1987, and ending _____, 19 ____

▶ **For Paperwork Reduction Act Notice, see page 1 of Instructions for Form 1120S.**

OMB No. 1545-0130

19 x 8

~~1987~~ **87**

Shareholder's identifying number ▶	Corporation's identifying number ▶
Shareholder's name, address, and ZIP code	Corporation's name, address, and ZIP code

A (1) Shareholder's percentage of stock ownership for tax year (see instructions for Schedule K-1) . . . . ▶ _____ %

    (2) Number of shares owned by shareholder at tax year end . . . . ▶

B Internal Revenue Service Center where corporation filed its return ▶

C Tax shelter registration number (see Instructions for Schedule K-1) . . . . ▶

D Did the shareholder materially participate in the trade or business activity(ies) of the corporation? (See instructions for Schedule K-1. Leave the check boxes blank if there are no trade or business activities.) . . . . ☒ Yes ☐ No

E Did the shareholder actively participate in the rental real estate activity(ies) of the corporation? (See instructions for Schedule K-1. Leave the check boxes blank if there are no rental real estate activities.) . . . . ☐ Yes ☐ No

F If (1) question D is checked "No" or income or loss is reported on line 2 or 3 and (2) the shareholder acquired corporate stock after 10/22/86, check here ▶ ☐ and enter the shareholder's weighted percentage increase in stock ownership for 1987 (see instructions for Schedule K-1) . . . . ▶ %

G If question D is checked "No" and any activity referred to in question D was started or acquired by the corporation after 10/22/86, check here ▶ ☐ and enter the date of start up or acquisition in the date space on line 1. Also, if an activity for which income or loss is reported on line 2 or 3 was started after 10/22/86, check the box and enter the start up date in the date space on line 2 or 3.

H If the short tax year shown above was a result of a change in tax year required by section 1378, check here . . . . . . ▶ ☐

Caution: *Refer to Shareholder's Instructions for Schedule K-1 before entering information from Schedule K-1 on your tax return.*

	(a) Distributive share items	**(b)** Amount	**(c)** Form 1040 filers enter the amount in column (b) on:
1	Ordinary income (loss) from trade or business activity(ies). Date:_____	- O -	See Shareholder's Instructions for Schedule K-1 (Form 1120S).
2	Income or loss from rental real estate activity(ies). Date: _____		
3	Income or loss from rental activity(ies) other than line 2 above. Date: _____		
4	Portfolio income (loss):		
a	Interest		Sch. B, Part I, line 2
b	Dividends		Sch. B, Part II, line 4
c	Royalties		Sch. E, Part I, line 5
d	Net short-term capital gain (loss)		Sch. D, line 5, col. (f) or (g)
e	Net long-term capital gain (loss)		Sch. D, line 12, col. (f) or (g)
f	Other portfolio income (loss).		(Enter on applicable line of your return.)
5	Net gain (loss) under section 1231 (other than due to casualty or theft).		Form 4797, line 1
6	Other income (loss) (attach schedule)		(Enter on applicable line of your return.)
7	Charitable contributions		See Form 1040 Instructions.
8	Section 179 expense deduction (attach schedule)		See Shareholder's Instructions for Schedule K-1 (Form 1120S).
9	Deductions related to portfolio income (loss) (attach schedule) . .		
10	Other deductions (attach schedule)		
11a	Jobs credit		Form 5884
b	Low-income housing credit		Form 8586, line 8
c	Qualified rehabilitation expenditures related to rental real estate activity(ies) (attach schedule)	/////	See Shareholder's Instructions for Schedule K-1 (Form 1120S).
d	Credits related to rental real estate activity(ies) other than on lines 11b and 11c (attach schedule)	/////	
e	Credits related to rental activity(ies) other than on lines 11b, c, and d (attach schedule)	/////	
12	Other credits (attach schedule)		
13a	Accelerated depreciation of real property placed in service before 1987	/////	Form 6251, line 5a
b	Accelerated depreciation of leased personal property placed in service before 1987		Form 6251, line 5b
c	Depreciation adjustment on property placed in service after 1986 . .		Form 6251, line 4g
d	Depletion (other than oil and gas)		Form 6251, line 5h
e	**(1)** Gross income from oil, gas, or geothermal properties		See Form 6251 Instructions.
	(2) Gross deductions allocable to oil, gas, or geothermal properties . .		See Shareholder's Instructions for Schedule K-1 (Form 1120S).
f	Other items (attach schedule)		

Income (Losses) and Deductions — *Credits* — *Tax Preference and Adjustment Items*

	(a) Distributive share items	(b) Amount	(c) Form 1040 filers enter the amount in column (b) on:
Investment Interest	**14a** Interest expense on investment debts		Form 4952, line 1
	b (1) Investment income included on Schedule K-1, lines 4a through 4f .		See Shareholder's Instructions for Schedule K-1 (Form 1120S).
	(2) Investment expenses included on Schedule K-1, line 9		
Foreign Taxes	**15a** Type of income ▶		Form 1116, Check boxes
	b Name of foreign country or U.S. possession ▶		Form 1116, Part I
	c Total gross income from sources outside the U.S. (attach schedule) . .		Form 1116, Part I
	d Total applicable deductions and losses (attach schedule)		Form 1116, Part I
	e Total foreign taxes (check one): ▶ ☐ Paid ☐ Accrued		Form 1116, Part II
	f Reduction in taxes available for credit (attach schedule)		Form 1116, Part III
	g Other (attach schedule)		See Form 1116 Instructions.
Other Items	**16** Property distributions (including cash) other than dividend distributions reported to you on Form 1099-DIV	*46,000*	See Shareholder's Instructions for Schedule K-1 (Form 1120S).
	17 Amount of loan repayments for "Loans from Shareholders"		

	18 Properties:	A	B	C	
Property Subject to Recapture of Investment Credit	**a** Description of property (State whether recovery or non-recovery property. If recovery property, state whether regular percentage method or section 48(q) election used.)				Form 4255, top
	b Date placed in service .				Form 4255, line 2
	c Cost or other basis . .				Form 4255, line 3
	d Class of recovery property or original estimated useful life .				Form 4255, line 4
	e Date item ceased to be investment credit property				Form 4255, line 8

19 Supplemental information for lines 1 through 18 that is required to be reported separately to each shareholder (attach additional schedules if more space is needed):

Supplemental Schedules

_____

_____

_____

_____

_____

_____

_____

_____

_____

_____

Form 1040

Department of the Treasury—Internal Revenue Service

U.S. Individual Income Tax Return ~~1987~~ 1987 (O) 19X8

For the year Jan.–Dec. 31, 1987, or other tax year beginning _____, 1987, ending _____, 19___. OMB No. 1545-0074

Label

Use IRS label. Otherwise, please print or type.

Your first name and initial (if joint return, also give spouse's name and initial) | Last name

Your social security number

Present home address (number and street or rural route). (If you have a P.O. Box, see page 6 of Instructions.)

Spouse's social security number

City, town or post office, state, and ZIP code

For Privacy Act and Paperwork Reduction Act Notice, see Instructions.

Presidential Election Campaign

▶ Do you want $1 to go to this fund? . . . . | Yes ☐ | No ☐

If joint return, does your spouse want $1 to go to this fund? . . | Yes ☐ | No ☐

Note: Checking "Yes" will not change your tax or reduce your refund.

Filing Status

Check only one box.

1 ☐ Single

2 ☐ Married filing joint return (even if only one had income)

3 ☐ Married filing separate return. Enter spouse's social security no. above and full name here. _____

4 ☐ Head of household (with qualifying person). (See page 7 of Instructions.) If the qualifying person is your child but not your dependent, enter child's name here. _____

5 ☐ Qualifying widow(er) with dependent child (year spouse died ▶ 19___). (See page 7 of Instructions.)

Exemptions

(See Instructions on page 7.)

If more than 7 dependents, see Instructions on page 7.

Caution: If you can be claimed as a dependent on another person's tax return (such as your parents' return), do not check box 6a. But be sure to check the box on line 32b on page 2.

6a ☐ Yourself   6b ☐ Spouse

No. of boxes checked on 6a and 6b ▶ ☐

c Dependents (1) Name (first, initial, and last name)	(2) Check if under age 5	(3) If age 5 or over, dependent's social security number	(4) Relationship	(5) No. of months lived in your home in 1987
		: :		
		: :		
		: :		
		: :		
		: :		

No. of children on 6c who lived with you ▶ ☐

No. of children on 6c who didn't live with you due to divorce or separation ▶ ☐

No. of parents listed on 6c ▶ ☐

No. of other dependents listed on 6c ▶ ☐

d If your child didn't live with you but is claimed as your dependent under a pre-1985 agreement, check here . ▶ ☐

e Total number of exemptions claimed (also complete line 35) . . . .

Add numbers entered in boxes above ▶ ☐

Income

Please attach Copy B of your Forms W-2, W-2G, and W-2P here.

If you do not have a W-2, see page 6 of Instructions.

Please attach check or money order here.

7	Wages, salaries, tips, etc. (attach Form(s) W-2)	7	
8	**Taxable** interest income (also attach Schedule B if over $400) . . .	8	
9	**Tax-exempt** interest income (see page 10). DON'T include on line 8	9	
10	Dividend income (also attach Schedule B if over $400)	10	
11	Taxable refunds of state and local income taxes, if any, from worksheet on page 11 of Instructions .	11	
12	Alimony received	12	
13	Business income or (loss) (attach Schedule C).	13	
14	Capital gain or (loss) (attach Schedule D)	14	6,000
15	Other gains or (losses) (attach Form 4797)	15	
16a	Pensions, IRA distributions, annuities, and rollovers. Total received	16a	
b	Taxable amount (see page 11)	16b	
17	Rents, royalties, partnerships, estates, trusts, etc. (attach Schedule E) . .	17	
18	Farm income or (loss) (attach Schedule F)	18	
19	Unemployment compensation (insurance) (see page 11)	19	
20a	Social security benefits (see page 12)	20a	
b	Taxable amount, if any, from the worksheet on page 12	20b	
21	Other income (list type and amount—see page 12) _____	21	
22	Add the amounts shown in the far right column for lines 7, 8, and 10–21. This is your **total income** ▶	22	6,000

Adjustments to Income

(See Instructions on page 12.)

23	Reimbursed employee business expenses from Form 2106 . .	23	
24a	Your IRA deduction, from applicable worksheet on page 13 or 14	24a	
b	Spouse's IRA deduction, from applicable worksheet on page 13 or 14 . .	24b	
25	Self-employed health insurance deduction, from worksheet on page 14	25	
26	Keogh retirement plan and self-employed SEP deduction . .	26	
27	Penalty on early withdrawal of savings	27	
28	Alimony paid (recipient's last name _____ and social security no. _____) .	28	
29	Add lines 23 through 28. These are your **total adjustments** . . . . . ▶	29	

Adjusted Gross Income

30 Subtract line 29 from line 22. This is your **adjusted gross income.** If this line is less than $15,432 and a child lived with you, see "Earned Income Credit" (line 56) on page 18 of the Instructions. If you want IRS to figure your tax, see page 15 of the Instructions . . . ▶ | 30 | 6,000

SCHEDULE D
(Form 1040)

Department of the Treasury
Internal Revenue Service   (O)

Capital Gains and Losses
and Reconciliation of Forms 1099-B

▶ Attach to Form 1040.   ▶ See Instructions for Schedule D (Form 1040).

For Paperwork Reduction Act Notice, see Form 1040 Instructions.

OMB No. 1545-0074

1987

Attachment
Sequence No. **12**

Name(s) as shown on Form 1040

Your social security number

---

1   Report here, the total sales of stocks, bonds, etc., reported for 1987 by your broker to you on Form(s) 1099-B or an equivalent substitute statement(s). If this amount differs from the total of lines 2b and 9b, column (d), attach a statement explaining the difference. See the Instructions for line 1 for examples. Do not include real estate transactions reported to you on a Form 1099-B on line 1, 2a, or 9a **1**

Part I   Short-term Capital Gains and Losses—Assets Held Six Months or Less

(a) Description of property (Example, 100 shares 7% preferred of "Z" Co.)	(b) Date acquired (Mo., day, yr.)	(c) Date sold (Mo., day, yr.)	(d) Sales price (see Instructions)	(e) Cost or other basis (see Instructions)	(f) LOSS If (e) is more than (d), subtract (d) from (e)	(g) GAIN If (d) is more than (e), subtract (e) from (d)
2a Form 1099-B Transactions (Sales of Stocks, Bonds, etc.): (Do not report real estate transactions here. See the instructions for lines 2a and 9a.)						
2b Total (add column (d)) . . . . ▶						
2c Other Transactions:						

3   Short-term gain from sale or exchange of a principal residence from Form 2119, lines 8 or 14   **3**

4   Short-term gain from installment sales from Form 6252, lines 23 or 31   . . .   **4**

5   Net short-term gain or (loss) from partnerships, S corporations, and fiduciaries   .   **5**

6   Short-term capital loss carryover **6**

7   Add all of the transactions on lines 2a and 2c and lines 3 through 6 in columns (f) and (g)   . . .   **7** ( )

8   Net short-term gain or (loss), combine columns (f) and (g) of line 7 . . . .   **8**

Part II   Long-term Capital Gains and Losses—Assets Held More Than Six Months

(a)	(b)	(c)	(d)	(e)	(f)	(g)
9a Form 1099-B Transactions (Sales of Stocks, Bonds, etc.): (Do not report real estate transactions here. See the instructions for lines 2a and 9a.)						
9b Total (add column (d)) . . . . ▶						
9c Other Transactions:						
DISTRIBUTION IN						6,000
EXCESS OF BASIS						
S- Corp						

10   Long-term gain from sale or exchange of a principal residence from Form 2119, lines 8, 10, or 14   **10**

11   Long-term gain from installment sales from Form 6252, lines 23 or 31   . . . .   **11**

12   Net long-term gain or (loss) from partnerships, S corporations, and fiduciaries   .   **12**

13   Capital gain distributions **13**

14   Enter gain from Form 4797, line 7 or 9 . . . .   **14**

15   Long-term capital loss carryover **15**

16   Add all of the transactions on lines 9a and 9c and lines 10 through 15 in columns (f) and (g)   . .   **16** ( )

17   Net long-term gain or (loss), combine columns (f) and (g) of line 16 . . . .   **17**   6,000

Schedule D (Form 1040) 1987

Appendix 8
Filled-in Return—Distributions Where S Corporation Has No Earnings and Profits

The facts for this problem are found at Example 8.6.

Schedule L	Balance Sheets	Beginning of tax year		End of tax year	
Assets		**(a)**	**(b)**	**(c)**	**(d)**
1 Cash					
2 Trade notes and accounts receivable					
a Less allowance for bad debts			*THE FACTS FOR THIS PROBLEM*		
3 Inventories			*ARE FOUND AT EXAMPLE 8-6*		
4 Federal and state government obligations					
5 Other current assets (attach schedule)					
6 Loans to shareholders					
7 Mortgage and real estate loans					
8 Other investments (attach schedule)					
9 Buildings and other depreciable assets					
a Less accumulated depreciation					
10 Depletable assets					
a Less accumulated depletion					
11 Land (net of any amortization)					
12 Intangible assets (amortizable only)					
a Less accumulated amortization					
13 Other assets (attach schedule)					
14 Total assets					*21,000*
Liabilities and Shareholders' Equity					
15 Accounts payable					
16 Mortgages, notes, bonds payable in less than 1 year					
17 Other current liabilities (attach schedule)					
18 Loans from shareholders					*4,000*
19 Mortgages, notes, bonds payable in 1 year or more					
20 Other liabilities (attach schedule)					
21 Capital stock					
22 Paid-in or capital surplus					*10,000*
23 Accumulated adjustments account				*7,000*	
24 Other adjustments account					
25 Shareholders' undistributed taxable income previously taxed					
26 Other retained earnings (see instructions). Check this box if the corporation has subchapter C earnings and profits at the close of the tax year ▶ ☐ (see instructions)					
27 Total retained earnings per books—Combine amounts on lines 23 through 26, columns (a) and (c) (see instructions)					*7,000*
28 Less cost of treasury stock		(	)	(	)
29 Total liabilities and shareholders' equity					*21,000*

Schedule M	Analysis of Accumulated Adjustments Account, Other Adjustments Account, and Shareholders' Undistributed Taxable Income Previously Taxed (If Schedule L, column (c), amounts for lines 23, 24, or 25 are not the same as corresponding amounts on line 9 of Schedule M, attach a schedule explaining any differences. See instructions.)

	Accumulated adjustments account	Other adjustments account	Shareholders' undistributed taxable income previously taxed
1 Balance at beginning of year			
2 Ordinary income from page 1, line 21	*15,000*		
3 Other additions			
4 Total of lines 1, 2, and 3	*15,000*		
5 Distributions other than dividend distributions	*8,000*		
6 Loss from page 1, line 21			
7 Other reductions			
8 Add lines 5, 6, and 7	*8,000*		
9 Balance at end of tax year—Subtract line 8 from line 4	*7,000*		

SCHEDULE K-1	Shareholder's Share of Income, Credits, Deductions, etc.	OMB No. 1545-0130
(Form 1120S)	For calendar year 1987 or tax year	**1987**
Department of the Treasury Internal Revenue Service	beginning _____, 1987, and ending _____, 19 ____ ▶ For Paperwork Reduction Act Notice, see page 1 of Instructions for Form 1120S.	

Shareholder's identifying number ▶	Corporation's identifying number ▶
Shareholder's name, address, and ZIP code	Corporation's name, address, and ZIP code

A (1) Shareholder's percentage of stock ownership for tax year (see instructions for Schedule K-1) . . . .▶ _____ %
   (2) Number of shares owned by shareholder at tax year end . . . . ▶ _____

B Internal Revenue Service Center where corporation filed its return ▶

C Tax shelter registration number (see Instructions for Schedule K-1) . . . . ▶

D Did the shareholder materially participate in the trade or business activity(ies) of the corporation? (See instructions for Schedule K-1. Leave the check boxes blank if there are no trade or business activities.) . . . . ☒ Yes ☐ No

E Did the shareholder actively participate in the rental real estate activity(ies) of the corporation? (See instructions for Schedule K-1. Leave the check boxes blank if there are no rental real estate activities.) . . . . ☐ Yes ☐ No

F If (1) question D is checked "No" or income or loss is reported on line 2 or 3 and (2) the shareholder acquired corporate stock after 10/22/86, check here ▶ ☐ and enter the shareholder's weighted percentage increase in stock ownership for 1987 (see instructions for Schedule K-1) . . . . ▶ _____ %

G If question D is checked "No" and any activity referred to in question D was started or acquired by the corporation after 10/22/86, check here ▶ ☐ and enter the date of start up or acquisition in the date space on line 1. Also, if an activity for which income or loss is reported on line 2 or 3 was started after 10/22/86, check the box and enter the start up date in the date space on line 2 or 3.

H If the short tax year shown above was a result of a change in tax year required by section 1378, check here . . . . . . ▶ ☐

Caution: *Refer to Shareholder's Instructions for Schedule K-1 before entering information from Schedule K-1 on your tax return.*

		(a) Distributive share items	(b) Amount	(c) Form 1040 filers enter the amount in column (b) on:
Income (Losses) and Deductions	1	Ordinary income (loss) from trade or business activity(ies). Date:_____	15,000	See Shareholder's Instructions for Schedule K-1 (Form 1120S).
	2	Income or loss from rental real estate activity(ies). Date: _____		
	3	Income or loss from rental activity(ies) other than line 2 above. Date: _____		
	4	Portfolio income (loss):		
	a	Interest		Sch. B, Part I, line 2
	b	Dividends		Sch. B, Part II, line 4
	c	Royalties.		Sch. E, Part I, line 5
	d	Net short-term capital gain (loss)		Sch. D, line 5, col. (f) or (g)
	e	Net long-term capital gain (loss)		Sch. D, line 12, col. (f) or (g)
	f	Other portfolio income (loss).		(Enter on applicable line of your return.)
	5	Net gain (loss) under section 1231 (other than due to casualty or theft).		Form 4797, line 1
	6	Other income (loss) (attach schedule)		(Enter on applicable line of your return.)
	7	Charitable contributions.		See Form 1040 Instructions.
	8	Section 179 expense deduction (attach schedule) . .		See Shareholder's Instructions for Schedule K-1 (Form 1120S).
	9	Deductions related to portfolio income (loss) (attach schedule) . . .		
	10	Other deductions (attach schedule)		
Credits	11a	Jobs credit		Form 5884
	b	Low-income housing credit		Form 8586, line 8
	c	Qualified rehabilitation expenditures related to rental real estate activity(ies) (attach schedule)	////////	See Shareholder's Instructions for Schedule K-1 (Form 1120S).
	d	Credits related to rental real estate activity(ies) other than on lines 11b and 11c (attach schedule)	////////	
	e	Credits related to rental activity(ies) other than on lines 11b, c, and d (attach schedule)	////////	
	12	Other credits (attach schedule)		
Tax Preference and Adjustment Items	13a	Accelerated depreciation of real property placed in service before 1987	////////	Form 6251, line 5a
	b	Accelerated depreciation of leased personal property placed in service before 1987		Form 6251, line 5b
	c	Depreciation adjustment on property placed in service after 1986 . .		Form 6251, line 4g
	d	Depletion (other than oil and gas)		Form 6251, line 5h
	e	(1) Gross income from oil, gas, or geothermal properties		See Form 6251 Instructions.
		(2) Gross deductions allocable to oil, gas, or geothermal properties . .		
	f	Other items (attach schedule)		See Shareholder's Instructions for Schedule K-1 (Form 1120S)

	(a) Distributive share items	(b) Amount	(c) Form 1040 filers enter the amount in column (b) on:
Investment Interest	**14a** Interest expense on investment debts		Form 4952, line 1
	b **(1)** Investment income included on Schedule K-1, lines 4a through 4f .		See Shareholder's Instructions for Schedule K-1 (Form 1120S).
	(2) Investment expenses included on Schedule K-1, line 9		
Foreign Taxes	**15a** Type of income ▶		Form 1116, Check boxes
	b Name of foreign country or U.S. possession ▶		Form 1116, Part I
	c Total gross income from sources outside the U.S. (attach schedule) . .		Form 1116, Part I
	d Total applicable deductions and losses (attach schedule)		Form 1116, Part I
	e Total foreign taxes (check one): ▶ ☐ Paid ☐ Accrued		Form 1116, Part II
	f Reduction in taxes available for credit (attach schedule)		Form 1116, Part III
	g Other (attach schedule)		See Form 1116 Instructions.
Other Items	**16** Property distributions (including cash) other than dividend distributions reported to you on Form 1099-DIV	*8,000*	See Shareholder's Instructions for Schedule K-1 (Form 1120S).
	17 Amount of loan repayments for "Loans from Shareholders"		

	18 Properties:	A	B	C	
Property Subject to Recapture of Investment Credit	**a** Description of property (State whether recovery or non-recovery property. If recovery property, state whether regular percentage method or section 48(q) election used.).				Form 4255, top
	b Date placed in service .				Form 4255, line 2
	c Cost or other basis . .				Form 4255, line 3
	d Class of recovery property or original estimated useful life .				Form 4255, line 4
	e Date item ceased to be investment credit property				Form 4255, line 8

19 Supplemental information for lines 1 through 18 that is required to be reported separately to each shareholder (attach additional schedules if more space is needed):

Supplemental Schedules

Form **1040**   Department of the Treasury—Internal Revenue Service

U.S. Individual Income Tax Return **1987** (O)

For the year Jan.–Dec. 31, 1987, or other tax year beginning   , 1987, ending   , 19 | OMB No. 1545-0074

Label

Use IRS label. Otherwise, please print or type.

Your first name and initial (if joint return, also give spouse's name and initial)	Last name	**Your social security number**
Present home address (number and street or rural route). (If you have a P.O. Box, see page 6 of Instructions.)		**Spouse's social security number**
City, town or post office, state, and ZIP code		For Privacy Act and Paperwork Reduction Act Notice, see Instructions.

Presidential Election Campaign ▶

Do you want $1 to go to this fund? . . . .   Yes ☐   No ☐

If joint return, does your spouse want $1 to go to this fund?. .   Yes ☐   No ☐

Note: *Checking "Yes" will not change your tax or reduce your refund.*

Filing Status

Check only one box.

1 ☐ Single

2 ☐ Married filing joint return (even if only one had income)

3 ☐ Married filing separate return. Enter spouse's social security no. above and full name here. _____

4 ☐ Head of household (with qualifying person). (See page 7 of Instructions.) If the qualifying person is your child but not your dependent, enter child's name here. _____

5 ☐ Qualifying widow(er) with dependent child (year spouse died ▶ 19___). (See page 7 of Instructions.)

Exemptions

(See Instructions on page 7.)

Caution: If you can be claimed as a dependent on another person's tax return (such as your parents' return), do not check box 6a. But be sure to check the box on line 32b on page 2.

6a ☐ Yourself   6b ☐ Spouse

c Dependents	(2) Check if under age 5	(3) If age 5 or over, dependent's social security number	(4) Relationship	(5) No. of months lived in your home in 1987
(1) Name (first, initial, and last name)				
		: :		
		: :		
		: :		
		: :		
		: :		
		: :		

If more than 7 dependents, see Instructions on page 7.

d If your child didn't live with you but is claimed as your dependent under a pre-1985 agreement, check here . ▶ ☐

e Total number of exemptions claimed (also complete line 35) . . . .

No. of boxes checked on 6a and 6b ▶ ☐

No. of children on 6c who lived with you ▶ ☐

No. of children on 6c who didn't live with you due to divorce or separation ▶ ☐

No. of parents listed on 6c ▶ ☐

No. of other dependents listed on 6c ▶ ☐

Add numbers entered in boxes above ▶ ☐

Income

Please attach Copy B of your Forms W-2, W-2G, and W-2P here.

If you do not have a W-2, see page 6 of Instructions.

Please attach check or money order here.

7	Wages, salaries, tips, etc. (attach Form(s) W-2)	7	
8	**Taxable** interest income (also attach Schedule B if over $400) .	8	
9	**Tax-exempt** interest income (see page 10). DON'T include on line 8 9		
10	Dividend income (also attach Schedule B if over $400)	10	
11	Taxable refunds of state and local income taxes, if any, from worksheet on page 11 of Instructions .	11	
12	Alimony received	12	
13	Business income or (loss) (attach Schedule C).	13	
14	Capital gain or (loss) (attach Schedule D)	14	
15	Other gains or (losses) (attach Form 4797)	15	
16a	Pensions, IRA distributions, annuities, and rollovers. Total received 16a		
b	Taxable amount (see page 11)	16b	
17	Rents, royalties, partnerships, estates, trusts, etc. (attach Schedule E)	17	*15,000*
18	Farm income or (loss) (attach Schedule F)	18	
19	Unemployment compensation (insurance) (see page 11)	19	
20a	Social security benefits (see page 12) 20a		
b	Taxable amount, if any, from the worksheet on page 12	20b	
21	Other income (list type and amount—see page 12) _____	21	
22	Add the amounts shown in the far right column for lines 7, 8, and 10–21. This is your **total income** ▶	22	*15,000*

Adjustments to Income

(See Instructions on page 12.)

23	Reimbursed employee business expenses from Form 2106 .	23		
24a	Your IRA deduction, from applicable worksheet on page 13 or 14	24a		
b	Spouse's IRA deduction, from applicable worksheet on page 13 or 14 . .	24b		
25	Self-employed health insurance deduction, from worksheet on page 14 .	25		
26	Keogh retirement plan and self-employed SEP deduction. .	26		
27	Penalty on early withdrawal of savings	27		
28	Alimony paid (recipient's last name _____ and social security no. _____) .	28		
29	Add lines 23 through 28. These are your **total adjustments** . . . . ▶	29		

Adjusted Gross Income

30 Subtract line 29 from line 22. This is your **adjusted gross income.** If this line is less than $15,432 and a child lived with you, see "Earned Income Credit" (line 56) on page 18 of the Instructions. If you want IRS to figure your tax, see page 15 of the Instructions . . . ▶ | 30 | *15,000*

Name(s) as shown on Form 1040. (Do not enter name and social security number if shown on other side.)   **Your social security number**

Part II   Income or (Loss) from Partnerships and S Corporations

If you report a loss below and have amounts invested in that activity for which you are **not at risk**, you MUST check "Yes" in column (e) and attach Form 6198. Otherwise, you must check "No." See Instructions.

	(a) Name	(b) Enter **P** for partnership; **S** for S Corporation	(c) Check if foreign partnership	(d) Employer identification number	(e) Not at-Risk? Yes | No
A	A, Inc.	S		11-111111	✓ |
B					
C					
D					
E					

	Passive Activities		Nonpassive Activities		
	(f) Passive loss allowed from Form 8582	(g) Passive income from Schedule K–1	(h) Nonpassive loss from Schedule K–1	(i) Section 179 deduction	(j) Nonpassive income from Schedule K–1
A					15,000
B					
C					
D					
E					
30a Totals					15,000
b Totals					

31	Add amounts in columns (g) and (j), line 30a. Enter total income here	31	15,000
32	Add amounts in columns (f), (h), and (i), line 30b. Enter total here	32 (	)
33	Total partnership and S corporation income or (loss). Combine amounts on lines 31 and 32. Enter the total here and include in line 42 below	33	15,000

Part III   Income or (Loss) from Estates and Trusts

	(a) Name	(b) Employer identification number
A		
B		
C		

	Passive Activities		Nonpassive Activities	
	(c) Passive deduction or loss allowed from Form 8582	(d) Passive income from Schedule K–1	(e) Deduction or loss from Schedule K–1	(f) Other income from Schedule K–1
A				
B				
C				
34a Totals				
b Totals				

35	Add amounts in columns (d) and (f), line 34a. Enter total income here	35	
36	Add amounts in columns (c) and (e), line 34b. Enter total (loss) here	36 (	)
37	Total estate and trust income or (loss). Combine amounts on lines 35 and 36. Enter the total here and include in line 42 below	37	

Part IV   Income or (Loss) from Real Estate Mortgage Investment Conduits (REMICs)—Residual Holder

(a) Name	(b) Employer identification number	(c) Excess inclusion from Schedules Q, line 2c (see Instructions)	(d) Taxable income (net loss) from Schedules Q, line 1b	(e) Income from Schedules Q, line 3b

38	Combine columns (d) and (e) only. Enter the total here and include in line 42 below	38	

Part V   Windfall Profit Tax Summary

39	Windfall profit tax credit or refund received in 1987 (see Instructions)	39	
40	Windfall profit tax withheld in 1987 (see Instructions)	40 (	)
41	Combine amounts on lines 39 and 40. Enter the total here and include in line 42 below	41	

Part VI   Summary

42	TOTAL income or (loss). Combine lines 29, 33, 37, 38, and 41. Enter total here and on Form 1040, line 17 . . . . ▶	42	15,000
43	Farmers and fishermen: Enter your share of GROSS FARMING AND FISHING INCOME applicable to Parts I, II, and III (see Instructions) . . .	43	

☆ U.S.G.P.O.: 1987 – 183-104

Schedule L — Balance Sheets

Assets	Beginning of tax year (a)	(b)	End of tax year (c)	(d)
1 Cash				
2 Trade notes and accounts receivable		*THE FACTS FOR THIS PROBLEM*		
a Less allowance for bad debts		*ARE FOUND AT EXAMPLE 8-6*		
3 Inventories				
4 Federal and state government obligations				
5 Other current assets (attach schedule)				
6 Loans to shareholders				
7 Mortgage and real estate loans				
8 Other investments (attach schedule)				
9 Buildings and other depreciable assets				
a Less accumulated depreciation				
10 Depletable assets				
a Less accumulated depletion				
11 Land (net of any amortization)				
12 Intangible assets (amortizable only)				
a Less accumulated amortization				
13 Other assets (attach schedule)				
14 Total assets		21,000		
Liabilities and Shareholders' Equity				
15 Accounts payable				
16 Mortgages, notes, bonds payable in less than 1 year				
17 Other current liabilities (attach schedule)				
18 Loans from shareholders		4,000		4,000
19 Mortgages, notes, bonds payable in 1 year or more				
20 Other liabilities (attach schedule)				
21 Capital stock		10,000		10,000
22 Paid-in or capital surplus				
23 Accumulated adjustments account	7,000		⟨15,000⟩	
24 Other adjustments account				
25 Shareholders' undistributed taxable income previously taxed				
26 Other retained earnings (see instructions). Check this box if the corporation has subchapter C earnings and profits at the close of the tax year ▶ ☐ (see instructions)				
27 Total retained earnings per books—Combine amounts on lines 23 through 26. columns (a) and (c) (see instructions)		7000 ( )		⟨15,000⟩ ( )
28 Less cost of treasury stock		( )		( )
29 Total liabilities and shareholders' equity		21,000		

Schedule M — Analysis of Accumulated Adjustments Account, Other Adjustments Account, and Shareholders' Undistributed Taxable Income Previously Taxed

(If Schedule L, column (c), amounts for lines 23, 24, or 25 are not the same as corresponding amounts on line 9 of Schedule M, attach a schedule explaining any differences. See instructions.)

	Accumulated adjustments account	Other adjustments account	Shareholders' undistributed taxable income previously taxed
1 Balance at beginning of year	7,000		
2 Ordinary income from page 1, line 21			
3 Other additions			
4 Total of lines 1, 2, and 3	7,000		
5 Distributions other than dividend distributions	2,000		
6 Loss from page 1, line 21	20,000		
7 Other reductions			
8 Add lines 5, 6, and 7	22,000		
9 Balance at end of tax year—Subtract line 8 from line 4	⟨15,000⟩		

SCHEDULE K-1
(Form 1120S)

Department of the Treasury
Internal Revenue Service

Shareholder's Share of Income, Credits, Deductions, etc.

For calendar year 1987 or tax year
beginning _____, 1987, and ending _____, 19 ___
▶ For Paperwork Reduction Act Notice, see page 1 of Instructions for Form 1120S.

OMB No. 1545-0130

1987

Shareholder's identifying number ▶

Corporation's identifying number ▶

Shareholder's name, address, and ZIP code

Corporation's name, address, and ZIP code

A (1) Shareholder's percentage of stock ownership for tax year (see instructions for Schedule K-1) . . . . ▶ _____ %
    (2) Number of shares owned by shareholder at tax year end . . . . ▶

B Internal Revenue Service Center where corporation filed its return ▶

C Tax shelter registration number (see Instructions for Schedule K-1) . . . . ▶

D Did the shareholder materially participate in the trade or business activity(ies) of the corporation? (See instructions for Schedule K-1. Leave the check boxes blank if there are no trade or business activities.) . . . . ☒ Yes ☐ No

E Did the shareholder actively participate in the rental real estate activity(ies) of the corporation? (See instructions for Schedule K-1. Leave the check boxes blank if there are no rental real estate activities.) . . . . ☐ Yes ☐ No

F If (1) question D is checked "No" or income or loss is reported on line 2 or 3 and (2) the shareholder acquired corporate stock after 10/22/86, check here ▶ ☐ and enter the shareholder's weighted percentage increase in stock ownership for 1987 (see instructions for Schedule K-1) . . . . ▶ _____ %

G If question D is checked "No" and any activity referred to in question D was started or acquired by the corporation after 10/22/86, check here ▶ ☐ and enter the date of start up or acquisition in the date space on line 1. Also, if an activity for which income or loss is reported on line 2 or 3 was started after 10/22/86, check the box and enter the start up date in the date space on line 2 or 3.

H If the short tax year shown above was a result of a change in tax year required by section 1378, check here . . . . . . ▶ ☐

Caution: *Refer to Shareholder's Instructions for Schedule K-1 before entering information from Schedule K-1 on your tax return.*

		(a) Distributive share items	(b) Amount	(c) Form 1040 filers enter the amount in column (b) on:
Income (Losses) and Deductions	1	Ordinary income (loss) from trade or business activity(ies). Date: _____	⟨20,000⟩	See Shareholder's Instructions for Schedule K-1 (Form 1120S).
	2	Income or loss from rental real estate activity(ies). Date: _____		
	3	Income or loss from rental activity(ies) other than line 2 above. Date: _____		
	4	Portfolio income (loss):		
	a	Interest		Sch. B, Part I, line 2
	b	Dividends		Sch. B, Part II, line 4
	c	Royalties		Sch. E, Part I, line 5
	d	Net short-term capital gain (loss)		Sch. D, line 5, col. (f) or (g)
	e	Net long-term capital gain (loss)		Sch. D, line 12, col. (f) or (g)
	f	Other portfolio income (loss).		(Enter on applicable line of your return.)
	5	Net gain (loss) under section 1231 (other than due to casualty or theft).		Form 4797, line 1
	6	Other income (loss) (attach schedule)		(Enter on applicable line of your return.)
	7	Charitable contributions.		See Form 1040 Instructions.
	8	Section 179 expense deduction (attach schedule)		See Shareholder's Instructions for Schedule K-1 (Form 1120S).
	9	Deductions related to portfolio income (loss) (attach schedule) . . .		
	10	Other deductions (attach schedule)		
Credits	11a	Jobs credit		Form 5884
	b	Low-income housing credit		Form 8586, line 8
	c	Qualified rehabilitation expenditures related to rental real estate activity(ies) (attach schedule)	/////////	See Shareholder's Instructions for Schedule K-1 (Form 1120S).
	d	Credits related to rental real estate activity(ies) other than on lines 11b and 11c (attach schedule)	/////////	
	e	Credits related to rental activity(ies) other than on lines 11b, c, and d (attach schedule)	/////////	
	12	Other credits (attach schedule)		
Tax Preference and Adjustment Items	13a	Accelerated depreciation of real property placed in service before 1987	/////////	Form 6251, line 5a
	b	Accelerated depreciation of leased personal property placed in service before 1987.		Form 6251, line 5b
	c	Depreciation adjustment on property placed in service after 1986 . .		Form 6251, line 4g
	d	Depletion (other than oil and gas)		Form 6251, line 5h
	e	(1) Gross income from oil, gas, or geothermal properties		See Form 6251 Instructions.
		(2) Gross deductions allocable to oil, gas, or geothermal properties . .		
	f	Other items (attach schedule)		See Shareholder's Instructions for Schedule K-1 (Form 1120S).

	(a) Distributive share items	(b) Amount	(c) Form 1040 filers enter the amount in column (b) on:
Investment Interest	**14a** Interest expense on investment debts		Form 4952, line 1
	b **(1)** Investment income included on Schedule K-1, lines 4a through 4f .		See Shareholder's Instructions for Schedule K-1 (Form 1120S).
	(2) Investment expenses included on Schedule K-1, line 9		
Foreign Taxes	**15a** Type of income ▶		Form 1116, Check boxes
	b Name of foreign country or U.S. possession ▶		Form 1116, Part I
	c Total gross income from sources outside the U.S. (attach schedule) . .		Form 1116, Part I
	d Total applicable deductions and losses (attach schedule)		Form 1116, Part I
	e Total foreign taxes (check one): ▶ ☐ Paid ☐ Accrued		Form 1116, Part II
	f Reduction in taxes available for credit (attach schedule)		Form 1116, Part III
	g Other (attach schedule)		See Form 1116 Instructions.
Other Items	**16** Property distributions (including cash) other than dividend distributions reported to you on Form 1099-DIV	2,000	See Shareholder's Instructions for Schedule K-1 (Form 1120S).
	17 Amount of loan repayments for "Loans from Shareholders"		

	18 Properties:	A	B	C	
Property Subject to Recapture of Investment Credit	**a** Description of property (State whether recovery or non-recovery property. If recovery property, state whether regular percentage method or section 48(q) election used.).				Form 4255, top
	b Date placed in service .				Form 4255, line 2
	c Cost or other basis . .				Form 4255, line 3
	d Class of recovery property or original estimated useful life .				Form 4255, line 4
	e Date item ceased to be investment credit property				Form 4255, line 8

19 Supplemental information for lines 1 through 18 that is required to be reported separately to each shareholder (attach additional schedules if more space is needed):

Supplemental Schedules

Form 1040

Department of the Treasury—Internal Revenue Service

U.S. Individual Income Tax Return 1987 (O)

For the year Jan.–Dec. 31, 1987, or other tax year beginning _____ , 1987, ending _____ , 19 ____ .

OMB No. 1545-0074

Label

Use IRS label. Otherwise, please print or type.

Your first name and initial (if joint return, also give spouse's name and initial) | Last name

Your social security number

Present home address (number and street or rural route). (If you have a P.O. Box, see page 6 of Instructions.)

Spouse's social security number

City, town or post office, state, and ZIP code

For Privacy Act and Paperwork Reduction Act Notice, see Instructions.

Presidential Election Campaign ▶

Do you want $1 to go to this fund? . . . . ▢ Yes ▨ ▢ No

If joint return, does your spouse want $1 to go to this fund?. . ▢ Yes ▨ ▢ No

Note: Checking "Yes" will not change your tax or reduce your refund.

Filing Status

Check only one box.

1 ▢ Single
2 ▢ Married filing joint return (even if only one had income)
3 ▢ Married filing separate return. Enter spouse's social security no. above and full name here. _____
4 ▢ Head of household (with qualifying person). (See page 7 of Instructions.) If the qualifying person is your child but not your dependent, enter child's name here. _____
5 ▢ Qualifying widow(er) with dependent child (year spouse died ▶ 19 ____). (See page 7 of Instructions.)

Exemptions

(See Instructions on page 7.)

Caution: If you can be claimed as a dependent on another person's tax return (such as your parents' return), do not check box 6a. But be sure to check the box on line 32b on page 2.

6a ▢ Yourself   6b ▢ Spouse

No. of boxes checked on 6a and 6b ▶ ▢

c Dependents

(1) Name (first, initial, and last name)	(2) Check if under age 5	(3) If age 5 or over, dependent's social security number	(4) Relationship	(5) No. of months lived in your home in 1987
		:		
		:		
		:		
		:		
		:		
		:		
		:		

No. of children on 6c who lived with you ▶ ▢

No. of children on 6c who didn't live with you due to divorce or separation ▶ ▢

No. of parents listed on 6c ▶ ▢

No. of other dependents listed on 6c ▶ ▢

If more than 7 dependents, see Instructions on page 7.

d If your child didn't live with you but is claimed as your dependent under a pre-1985 agreement, check here . ▶ ▢

e Total number of exemptions claimed (also complete line 35) . . . .

Add numbers entered in boxes above ▶ ▢

Income

Please attach Copy B of your Forms W-2, W-2G, and W-2P here.

If you do not have a W-2, see page 6 of Instructions.

7	Wages, salaries, tips, etc. (attach Form(s) W-2)	7
8	**Taxable** interest income (also attach Schedule B if over $400)	8
9	**Tax-exempt** interest income (see page 10). DON'T include on line 8 9	
10	Dividend income (also attach Schedule B if over $400) . . .	10
11	Taxable refunds of state and local income taxes, if any, from worksheet on page 11 of Instructions . .	11
12	Alimony received	12
13	Business income or (loss) (attach Schedule C).	13
14	Capital gain or (loss) (attach Schedule D)	14 2000
15	Other gains or (losses) (attach Form 4797)	15
16a	Pensions, IRA distributions, annuities, and rollovers. Total received 16a	
b	Taxable amount (see page 11)	16b
17	Rents, royalties, partnerships, estates, trusts, etc. (attach Schedule E)	17 <20,000>
18	Farm income or (loss) (attach Schedule F)	18
19	Unemployment compensation (insurance) (see page 11) . . .	19
20a	Social security benefits (see page 12) 20a	
b	Taxable amount, if any, from the worksheet on page 12 . . .	20b
21	Other income (list type and amount—see page 12) _____	21
22	Add the amounts shown in the far right column for lines 7, 8, and 10–21. This is your **total income** ▶	22 <18,000>

Please attach check or money order here.

Adjustments to Income

(See Instructions on page 12.)

23	Reimbursed employee business expenses from Form 2106 .	23
24a	Your IRA deduction, from applicable worksheet on page 13 or 14	24a
b	Spouse's IRA deduction, from applicable worksheet on page 13 or 14 . .	24b
25	Self-employed health insurance deduction, from worksheet on page 14	25
26	Keogh retirement plan and self-employed SEP deduction . .	26
27	Penalty on early withdrawal of savings	27
28	Alimony paid (recipient's last name _____ and social security no. _____) .	28
29	Add lines 23 through 28. These are your **total adjustments** . . . . ▶	29

Adjusted Gross Income

30 Subtract line 29 from line 22. This is your **adjusted gross income.** If this line is less than $15,432 and a child lived with you, see "Earned Income Credit" (line 56) on page 18 of the Instructions. If you want IRS to figure your tax, see page 15 of the Instructions . . . ▶ | 30 <18,000>

SCHEDULE D (Form 1040) Department of the Treasury Internal Revenue Service (O)	**Capital Gains and Losses and Reconciliation of Forms 1099-B** ▶ Attach to Form 1040. ▶ See Instructions for Schedule D (Form 1040). For Paperwork Reduction Act Notice, see Form 1040 Instructions.	OMB No. 1545-0074 19**87** Attachment Sequence No. **12**

Name(s) as shown on Form 1040	Your social security number

1 Report here, the total sales of stocks, bonds, etc., reported for 1987 by your broker to you on Form(s) 1099-B or an equivalent substitute statement(s). If this amount differs from the total of lines 2b and 9b, column (d), attach a statement explaining the difference. See the Instructions for line 1 for examples. Do not include real estate transactions reported to you on a Form 1099-B on line 1, 2a, or 9a **1**

Part I Short-term Capital Gains and Losses—Assets Held Six Months or Less

(a) Description of property (Example, 100 shares 7% preferred of "Z" Co.)	(b) Date acquired (Mo., day, yr.)	(c) Date sold (Mo., day, yr.)	(d) Sales price (see Instructions)	(e) Cost or other basis (see Instructions)	(f) LOSS If (e) is more than (d), subtract (d) from (e)	(g) GAIN If (d) is more than (e), subtract (e) from (d)
2a Form 1099-B Transactions (Sales of Stocks, Bonds, etc.): (Do not report real estate transactions here. See the instructions for lines 2a and 9a.)						
2b Total (add column (d)) . . . . ▶						
2c Other Transactions:						

3	Short-term gain from sale or exchange of a principal residence from Form 2119, lines 8 or 14	**3**	
4	Short-term gain from installment sales from Form 6252, lines 23 or 31 . . .	**4**	
5	Net short-term gain or (loss) from partnerships, S corporations, and fiduciaries .	**5**	
6	Short-term capital loss carryover	**6**	
7	Add all of the transactions on lines 2a and 2c and lines 3 through 6 in columns (f) and (g) . . .	**7** ( )	
8	Net short-term gain or (loss), combine columns (f) and (g) of line 7	**8**	

Part II Long-term Capital Gains and Losses—Assets Held More Than Six Months

(a)	(b)	(c)	(d)	(e)	(f)	(g)
9a Form 1099-B Transactions (Sales of Stocks, Bonds, etc.): (Do not report real estate transactions here. See the instructions for lines 2a and 9a.)						
9b Total (add column (d)) . . . . . . ▶						
9c Other Transactions:						
DISTRIBUTION IN EXCESS OF BASIS - S Corp						*2000*

10	Long-term gain from sale or exchange of a principal residence from Form 2119, lines 8, 10, or 14	**10**	
11	Long-term gain from installment sales from Form 6252, lines 23 or 31	**11**	
12	Net long-term gain or (loss) from partnerships, S corporations, and fiduciaries .	**12**	
13	Capital gain distributions	**13**	
14	Enter gain from Form 4797, line 7 or 9	**14**	
15	Long-term capital loss carryover	**15**	
16	Add all of the transactions on lines 9a and 9c and lines 10 through 15 in columns (f) and (g) . .	**16** ( )	
17	Net long-term gain or (loss), combine columns (f) and (g) of line 16	**17** *2000*	

Schedule D (Form 1040) 1987

Name(s) as shown on Form 1040. (Do not enter name and social security number if shown on other side.)

Your social security number

Part II Income or (Loss) from Partnerships and S Corporations

If you report a loss below and have amounts invested in that activity for which you are **not at risk**, you MUST check "Yes" in column (e) and attach Form 6198. Otherwise, you must check "No." See Instructions.

	(a) Name	(b) Enter **P** for partnership; **S** for S Corporation	(c) Check if foreign partnership	(d) Employer identification number	(e) Not at-Risk? Yes / No
A	A, Inc.	S		11 - 111111	✓
B					
C					
D					
E					

	Passive Activities		Nonpassive Activities		
	(f) Passive loss allowed from Form 8582	(g) Passive income from Schedule K–1	(h) Nonpassive loss from Schedule K–1	(i) Section 179 deduction	(j) Nonpassive income from Schedule K–1
A			20,000		
B					
C					
D					
E					
30a Totals					
b Totals			20,000		

31 Add amounts in columns (g) and (j), line 30a. Enter total income here **31**

32 Add amounts in columns (f), (h), and (i), line 30b. Enter total here **32** (20,000)

33 Total partnership and S corporation income or (loss). Combine amounts on lines 31 and 32. Enter the total here and include in line 42 below . . . . . **33** ⟨20,000⟩

Part III Income or (Loss) from Estates and Trusts

	(a) Name	(b) Employer identification number
A		
B		
C		

	Passive Activities		Nonpassive Activities	
	(c) Passive deduction or loss allowed from Form 8582	(d) Passive income from Schedule K–1	(e) Deduction or loss from Schedule K–1	(f) Other income from Schedule K–1
A				
B				
C				
34a Totals				
b Totals				

35 Add amounts in columns (d) and (f), line 34a. Enter total income here **35**

36 Add amounts in columns (c) and (e), line 34b. Enter total (loss) here . . . . **36** ( )

37 Total estate and trust income or (loss). Combine amounts on lines 35 and 36. Enter the total here and include in line 42 below **37**

Part IV Income or (Loss) from Real Estate Mortgage Investment Conduits (REMICs)—Residual Holder

(a) Name	(b) Employer identification number	(c) Excess inclusion from Schedules Q, line 2c (see Instructions)	(d) Taxable income (net loss) from Schedules Q, line 1b	(e) Income from Schedules Q, line 3b

38 Combine columns (d) and (e) only. Enter the total here and include in line 42 below **38**

Part V Windfall Profit Tax Summary

39 Windfall profit tax credit or refund received in 1987 (see Instructions) **39**

40 Windfall profit tax withheld in 1987 (see Instructions) . . . . **40** ( )

41 Combine amounts on lines 39 and 40. Enter the total here and include in line 42 below **41**

Part VI Summary

42 TOTAL income or (loss). Combine lines 29, 33, 37, 38, and 41. Enter total here and on Form 1040, line 17 . . . . ▶ **42** ⟨20,000⟩

43 Farmers and fishermen: Enter your share of GROSS FARMING AND FISHING INCOME applicable to Parts I, II, and III (see Instructions) . . . **43**

☆ U.S.G.P.O.: 1987 - 183-104

Schedule L Balance Sheets

Assets	Beginning of tax year		End of tax year	
	(a)	(b)	(c)	(d)
1 Cash				
2 Trade notes and accounts receivable . . .				
a Less allowance for bad debts		*THE FACTS FOR THIS PROBLEM*		
3 Inventories		*ARE FOUND AT EXAMPLE 8-6*		
4 Federal and state government obligations . .				
5 Other current assets (attach schedule) . . .				
6 Loans to shareholders				
7 Mortgage and real estate loans . . .				
8 Other investments (attach schedule) . .				
9 Buildings and other depreciable assets . . .				
a Less accumulated depreciation				
10 Depletable assets				
a Less accumulated depletion				
11 Land (net of any amortization)				
12 Intangible assets (amortizable only) . . .				
a Less accumulated amortization . . .				
13 Other assets (attach schedule) . . .				
14 Total assets		- 0 -		
Liabilities and Shareholders' Equity				
15 Accounts payable		1,000		
16 Mortgages, notes, bonds payable in less than 1 year				
17 Other current liabilities (attach schedule) . .				
18 Loans from shareholders		4,000		4,000
19 Mortgages, notes, bonds payable in 1 year or more				
20 Other liabilities (attach schedule) . . .				
21 Capital stock		10,000		10,000
22 Paid-in or capital surplus				
23 Accumulated adjustments account	⟨15,000⟩		⟨19,000⟩	
24 Other adjustments account				
25 Shareholders' undistributed taxable income previously taxed				
26 Other retained earnings (see instructions) . .				
Check this box if the corporation has subchapter C earnings and profits at the close of the tax year ▶ ☐ (see instructions)				
27 Total retained earnings per books—Combine amounts on lines 23 through 26, columns (a) and (c) (see instructions)		⟨15,000⟩		⟨19,000⟩
28 Less cost of treasury stock		( )		( )
29 Total liabilities and shareholders' equity . .		0		

Schedule M

Analysis of Accumulated Adjustments Account, Other Adjustments Account, and Shareholders' Undistributed Taxable Income Previously Taxed (If Schedule L, column (c), amounts for lines 23, 24, or 25 are not the same as corresponding amounts on line 9 of Schedule M, attach a schedule explaining any differences. See instructions.)

	Accumulated adjustments account	Other adjustments account	Shareholders' undistributed taxable income previously taxed
1 Balance at beginning of year	⟨15,000⟩		
2 Ordinary income from page 1, line 21 . . .	23,000		
3 Other additions			
4 Total of lines 1, 2, and 3	8,000		
5 Distributions other than dividend distributions	27,000		
6 Loss from page 1, line 21			
7 Other reductions			
8 Add lines 5, 6, and 7	27,000		
9 Balance at end of tax year—Subtract line 8 from line 4	⟨19,000⟩		

SCHEDULE K-1
(Form 1120S)

Department of the Treasury
Internal Revenue Service

Shareholder's Share of Income, Credits, Deductions, etc.

For calendar year 1987 or tax year

beginning _____, 1987, and ending _____, 19 ____

▶ **For Paperwork Reduction Act Notice, see page 1 of Instructions for Form 1120S.**

OMB No. 1545-0130

1987

Shareholder's identifying number ▶	Corporation's identifying number ▶
Shareholder's name, address, and ZIP code	Corporation's name, address, and ZIP code

A (1) Shareholder's percentage of stock ownership for tax year (see instructions for Schedule K-1) . . . . ▶ _____ %

    (2) Number of shares owned by shareholder at tax year end . . . . ▶ _____

B Internal Revenue Service Center where corporation filed its return ▶

C Tax shelter registration number (see Instructions for Schedule K-1) . . . . ▶

D Did the shareholder materially participate in the trade or business activity(ies) of the corporation? (See instructions for Schedule K-1. Leave the check boxes blank if there are no trade or business activities.) . . . . ☒ Yes ☐ No

E Did the shareholder actively participate in the rental real estate activity(ies) of the corporation? (See instructions for Schedule K-1. Leave the check boxes blank if there are no rental real estate activities.) . . . . ☐ Yes ☐ No

F If (1) question D is checked "No" or income or loss is reported on line 2 or 3 and (2) the shareholder acquired corporate stock after 10/22/86, check here ▶ ☐ and enter the shareholder's weighted percentage increase in stock ownership for 1987 (see instructions for Schedule K-1) . . . . ▶ _____ %

G If question D is checked "No" and any activity referred to in question D was started or acquired by the corporation after 10/22/86, check here ▶ ☐ and enter the date of start up or acquisition in the date space on line 1. Also, if an activity for which income or loss is reported on line 2 or 3 was started after 10/22/86, check the box and enter the start up date in the date space on line 2 or 3.

H If the short tax year shown above was a result of a change in tax year required by section 1378, check here . . . . . . ▶ ☐

Caution: *Refer to Shareholder's Instructions for Schedule K-1 before entering information from Schedule K-1 on your tax return.*

		(a) Distributive share items	(b) Amount	(c) Form 1040 filers enter the amount in column (b) on:
Income (Losses) and Deductions	1	Ordinary income (loss) from trade or business activity(ies). Date: _____	23,000	See Shareholder's Instructions for Schedule K-1 (Form 1120S).
	2	Income or loss from rental real estate activity(ies). Date: _____		
	3	Income or loss from rental activity(ies) other than line 2 above. Date: _____		
	4	Portfolio income (loss):		
	a	Interest		Sch. B, Part I, line 2
	b	Dividends		Sch. B, Part II, line 4
	c	Royalties		Sch. E, Part I, line 5
	d	Net short-term capital gain (loss)		Sch. D, line 5, col. (f) or (g)
	e	Net long-term capital gain (loss)		Sch. D, line 12, col. (f) or (g)
	f	Other portfolio income (loss).		(Enter on applicable line of your return.)
	5	Net gain (loss) under section 1231 (other than due to casualty or theft).		Form 4797, line 1
	6	Other income (loss) (attach schedule) . .		(Enter on applicable line of your return.)
	7	Charitable contributions		See Form 1040 Instructions.
	8	Section 179 expense deduction (attach schedule)		See Shareholder's Instructions for Schedule K-1 (Form 1120S).
	9	Deductions related to portfolio income (loss) (attach schedule) . . .		
	10	Other deductions (attach schedule)		
Credits	11a	Jobs credit		Form 5884
	b	Low-income housing credit		Form 8586, line 8
	c	Qualified rehabilitation expenditures related to rental real estate activity(ies) (attach schedule)		
	d	Credits related to rental real estate activity(ies) other than on lines 11b and 11c (attach schedule)		See Shareholder's Instructions for Schedule K-1 (Form 1120S).
	e	Credits related to rental activity(ies) other than on lines 11b, c, and d (attach schedule) . . .		
	12	Other credits (attach schedule)		
Tax Preference and Adjustment Items	13a	Accelerated depreciation of real property placed in service before 1987		Form 6251, line 5a
	b	Accelerated depreciation of leased personal property placed in service before 1987		Form 6251, line 5b
	c	Depreciation adjustment on property placed in service after 1986 . .		Form 6251, line 4g
	d	Depletion (other than oil and gas)		Form 6251, line 5h
	e	(1) Gross income from oil, gas, or geothermal properties		See Form 6251 Instructions.
		(2) Gross deductions allocable to oil, gas, or geothermal properties . .		
	f	Other items (attach schedule)		See Shareholder's Instructions for Schedule K-1 (Form 1120S).

	(a) Distributive share items	(b) Amount	(c) Form 1040 filers enter the amount in column (b) on:
Investment Interest	**14a** Interest expense on investment debts		Form 4952, line 1
	b (1) Investment income included on Schedule K-1, lines 4a through 4f .		See Shareholder's Instructions for Schedule K-1 (Form 1120S).
	(2) Investment expenses included on Schedule K-1, line 9		
Foreign Taxes	**15a** Type of income ▶		Form 1116, Check boxes
	b Name of foreign country or U.S. possession ▶		Form 1116, Part I
	c Total gross income from sources outside the U.S. (attach schedule) . .		Form 1116, Part I
	d Total applicable deductions and losses (attach schedule)		Form 1116, Part I
	e Total foreign taxes (check one): ▶ ☐ Paid ☐ Accrued		Form 1116, Part II
	f Reduction in taxes available for credit (attach schedule)		Form 1116, Part III
	g Other (attach schedule)		See Form 1116 Instructions.
Other Items	**16** Property distributions (including cash) other than dividend distributions reported to you on Form 1099-DIV	*27,000*	See Shareholder's Instructions for Schedule K-1 (Form 1120S).
	17 Amount of loan repayments for "Loans from Shareholders"		

	18 Properties:	**A**	**B**	**C**	
Property Subject to Recapture of Investment Credit	**a** Description of property (State whether recovery or non-recovery property. If recovery property, state whether regular percentage method or section 48(q) election used.)				Form 4255, top
	b Date placed in service .				Form 4255, line 2
	c Cost or other basis . .				Form 4255, line 3
	d Class of recovery property or original estimated useful life .				Form 4255, line 4
	e Date item ceased to be investment credit property				Form 4255, line 8

19 Supplemental information for lines 1 through 18 that is required to be reported separately to each shareholder (attach additional schedules if more space is needed):

Supplemental Schedules

19x9

Form **1040** Department of the Treasury—Internal Revenue Service
U.S. Individual Income Tax Return **1987** (O)

For the year Jan.–Dec. 31, 1987, or other tax year beginning   , 1987, ending   , 19   . | OMB No. 1545-0074

Label

Use IRS label. Otherwise, please print or type.

Your first name and initial (if joint return, also give spouse's name and initial)	Last name	Your social security number
Present home address (number and street or rural route). (If you have a P.O. Box, see page 6 of Instructions.)		Spouse's social security number
City, town or post office, state, and ZIP code		For Privacy Act and Paperwork Reduction Act Notice, see Instructions.

Presidential Election Campaign

▶ Do you want $1 to go to this fund? . . . . Yes ▨ No
If joint return, does your spouse want $1 to go to this fund?. . Yes ▨ No

Note: Checking "Yes" will not change your tax or reduce your refund.

Filing Status

Check only one box.

1 ☐ Single
2 ☐ Married filing joint return (even if only one had income)
3 ☐ Married filing separate return. Enter spouse's social security no. above and full name here. _____
4 ☐ Head of household (with qualifying person). (See page 7 of Instructions.) If the qualifying person is your child but not your dependent, enter child's name here. _____
5 ☐ Qualifying widow(er) with dependent child (year spouse died ▶ 19   ). (See page 7 of Instructions.)

Exemptions

(See Instructions on page 7.)

Caution: If you can be claimed as a dependent on another person's tax return (such as your parents' return), do not check box 6a. But be sure to check the box on line 32b on page 2.

6a ☐ Yourself   6b ☐ Spouse

c Dependents (1) Name (first, initial, and last name)	(2) Check if under age 5	(3) If age 5 or over, dependent's social security number	(4) Relationship	(5) No. of months lived in your home in 1987
_____		:		
_____		:		
_____		:		
_____		:		
_____		:		
_____		:		
_____		:		

	No. of boxes checked on 6a and 6b ▶ ☐
	No. of children on 6c who lived with you ▶ ☐
	No. of children on 6c who didn't live with you due to divorce or separation ▶ ☐
	No. of parents listed on 6c ▶ ☐
	No. of other dependents listed on 6c ▶ ☐

If more than 7 dependents, see Instructions on page 7.

d If your child didn't live with you but is claimed as your dependent under a pre-1985 agreement, check here . . ▶ ☐

e Total number of exemptions claimed (also complete line 35) . . . . Add numbers entered in boxes above ▶ ☐

Income

Please attach Copy B of your Forms W-2, W-2G, and W-2P here.

If you do not have a W-2, see page 6 of Instructions.

7	Wages, salaries, tips, etc. (attach Form(s) W-2)	7	
8	**Taxable** interest income (also attach Schedule B if over $400)	8	
9	**Tax-exempt** interest income (see page 10). DON'T include on line 8 9 ▨		
10	Dividend income (also attach Schedule B if over $400)	10	
11	Taxable refunds of state and local income taxes, if any, from worksheet on page 11 of Instructions .	11	
12	Alimony received	12	
13	Business income or (loss) (attach Schedule C).	13	
14	Capital gain or (loss) (attach Schedule D)	14	7,000
15	Other gains or (losses) (attach Form 4797)	15	
16a	Pensions, IRA distributions, annuities, and rollovers. Total received 16a		
b	Taxable amount (see page 11)	16b	
17	Rents, royalties, partnerships, estates, trusts, etc. (attach Schedule E)	17	23,000
18	Farm income or (loss) (attach Schedule F)	18	
19	Unemployment compensation (insurance) (see page 11)	19	
20a	Social security benefits (see page 12) 20a		
b	Taxable amount, if any, from the worksheet on page 12	20b	
21	Other income (list type and amount—see page 12) _____	21	
22	Add the amounts shown in the far right column for lines 7, 8, and 10–21. This is your **total income** ▶	22	30,000

Please attach check or money order here.

Adjustments to Income

(See Instructions on page 12.)

23	Reimbursed employee business expenses from Form 2106 .	23	
24a	Your IRA deduction, from applicable worksheet on page 13 or 14	24a	
b	Spouse's IRA deduction, from applicable worksheet on page 13 or 14 . . .	24b	
25	Self-employed health insurance deduction, from worksheet on page 14 .	25	
26	Keogh retirement plan and self-employed SEP deduction. . .	26	
27	Penalty on early withdrawal of savings	27	
28	Alimony paid (recipient's last name _____ and social security no. _____) .	28	
29	Add lines 23 through 28. These are your **total adjustments** . . . . ▶	29	

Adjusted Gross Income

30 Subtract line 29 from line 22. This is your **adjusted gross income**. If this line is less than $15,432 and a child lived with you, see "Earned Income Credit" (line 56) on page 18 of the Instructions. If you want IRS to figure your tax, see page 15 of the Instructions . . . ▶ | 30 | 30,000

SCHEDULE D (Form 1040)	Capital Gains and Losses and Reconciliation of Forms 1099-B	OMB No. 1545-0074
Department of the Treasury Internal Revenue Service (O)	▶ Attach to Form 1040. ▶ See Instructions for Schedule D (Form 1040). For Paperwork Reduction Act Notice, see Form 1040 Instructions.	1987 Attachment Sequence No. 12

Name(s) as shown on Form 1040 | Your social security number

1 Report here, the total sales of stocks, bonds, etc., reported for 1987 by your broker to you on Form(s) 1099-B or an equivalent substitute statement(s). If this amount differs from the total of lines 2b and 9b, column (d), attach a statement explaining the difference. See the Instructions for line 1 for examples. Do not include real estate transactions reported to you on a Form 1099-B on line 1, 2a, or 9a **1**

Part I Short-term Capital Gains and Losses—Assets Held Six Months or Less

(a) Description of property (Example, 100 shares 7% preferred of "Z" Co.)	(b) Date acquired (Mo., day, yr.)	(c) Date sold (Mo., day, yr.)	(d) Sales price (see Instructions)	(e) Cost or other basis (see Instructions)	(f) LOSS If (e) is more than (d), subtract (d) from (e)	(g) GAIN If (d) is more than (e), subtract (e) from (d)
2a Form 1099-B Transactions (Sales of Stocks, Bonds, etc.):		(Do not report real estate transactions here. See the instructions for lines 2a and 9a.)				
2b Total (add column (d)) . . . . ▶						
2c Other Transactions:						

3	Short-term gain from sale or exchange of a principal residence from Form 2119, lines 8 or 14	**3**	
4	Short-term gain from installment sales from Form 6252, lines 23 or 31 . . .	**4**	
5	Net short-term gain or (loss) from partnerships, S corporations, and fiduciaries .	**5**	
6	Short-term capital loss carryover	**6**	
7	Add all of the transactions on lines 2a and 2c and lines 3 through 6 in columns (f) and (g) . . .	**7** ( )	
8	Net short-term gain or (loss), combine columns (f) and (g) of line 7	**8**	

Part II Long-term Capital Gains and Losses—Assets Held More Than Six Months

9a Form 1099-B Transactions (Sales of Stocks, Bonds, etc.): (Do not report real estate transactions here. See the instructions for lines 2a and 9a.)

(a)	(b)	(c)	(d)	(e)	(f)	(g)
9b Total (add column (d)) . . . . ▶						
9c Other Transactions:						
DISTRIBUTION IN EXCESS OF BASIS - S Corp.						7,000

10	Long-term gain from sale or exchange of a principal residence from Form 2119, lines 8, 10, or 14	**10**	
11	Long-term gain from installment sales from Form 6252, lines 23 or 31	**11**	
12	Net long-term gain or (loss) from partnerships, S corporations, and fiduciaries .	**12**	
13	Capital gain distributions	**13**	
14	Enter gain from Form 4797, line 7 or 9	**14**	
15	Long-term capital loss carryover	**15**	
16	Add all of the transactions on lines 9a and 9c and lines 10 through 15 in columns (f) and (g) . .	**16** ( )	
17	Net long-term gain or (loss), combine columns (f) and (g) of line 16	**17** 7,000	

Schedule D (Form 1040) 1987

Name(s) as shown on Form 1040. (Do not enter name and social security number if shown on other side.) | **Your social security number**

Part II   Income or (Loss) from Partnerships and S Corporations

If you report a loss below and have amounts invested in that activity for which you are **not at risk**, you MUST check "Yes" in column (e) and attach Form 6198. Otherwise, you must check "No." See Instructions.

	(a) Name	(b) Enter **P** for partnership; **S** for S Corporation	(c) Check if foreign partnership	(d) Employer identification number	(e) Not at-Risk? Yes | No
A					
B					
C					
D					
E					

	Passive Activities		Nonpassive Activities		
	(f) Passive loss allowed from Form 8582	(g) Passive income from Schedule K–1	(h) Nonpassive loss from Schedule K–1	(i) Section 179 deduction	(j) Nonpassive income from Schedule K–1
A					23,000
B					
C					
D					
E					
30a Totals					23 000
b Totals					

31	Add amounts in columns (g) and (j), line 30a. Enter total income here	**31**	23,000
32	Add amounts in columns (f), (h), and (i), line 30b. Enter total here	**32**	( )
33	Total partnership and S corporation income or (loss). Combine amounts on lines 31 and 32. Enter the total here and include in line 42 below	**33**	23,000

Part III   Income or (Loss) from Estates and Trusts

	(a) Name	(b) Employer identification number
A		
B		
C		

	Passive Activities		Nonpassive Activities	
	(c) Passive deduction or loss allowed from Form 8582	(d) Passive income from Schedule K–1	(e) Deduction or loss from Schedule K–1	(f) Other income from Schedule K–1
A				
B				
C				
34a Totals				
b Totals				

35	Add amounts in columns (d) and (f), line 34a. Enter total income here	**35**	
36	Add amounts in columns (c) and (e), line 34b. Enter total (loss) here	**36**	( )
37	Total estate and trust income or (loss). Combine amounts on lines 35 and 36. Enter the total here and include in line 42 below	**37**	

Part IV   Income or (Loss) from Real Estate Mortgage Investment Conduits (REMICs)—Residual Holder

(a) Name	(b) Employer identification number	(c) Excess inclusion from Schedules Q, line 2c (see Instructions)	(d) Taxable income (net loss) from Schedules Q, line 1b	(e) Income from Schedules Q, line 3b

38	Combine columns (d) and (e) only. Enter the total here and include in line 42 below	**38**	

Part V   Windfall Profit Tax Summary

39	Windfall profit tax credit or refund received in 1987 (see Instructions)	**39**	
40	Windfall profit tax withheld in 1987 (see Instructions)	**40**	( )
41	Combine amounts on lines 39 and 40. Enter the total here and include in line 42 below	**41**	

Part VI   Summary

42	TOTAL income or (loss). Combine lines 29, 33, 37, 38, and 41. Enter total here and on Form 1040, line 17 . . . . ▶	**42**	23,000
43	Farmers and fishermen: Enter your share of GROSS FARMING AND FISHING INCOME applicable to Parts I, II, and III (see Instructions) . . .	**43**	

Appendix 9
Filled-in Return—Distributions Where S Corporation Has Earnings and Profits

The facts for this problem are found at Example 8.9.

Schedule L	**Balance Sheets**	Beginning of tax year		End of tax year	
	Assets	(a)	(b)	(c)	(d)
1	Cash				
2	Trade notes and accounts receivable . . .				
a	Less allowance for bad debts		THE FACTS FOR THIS PROBLEM			
3	Inventories		FOUND AT EXAMPLE 8-9			
4	Federal and state government obligations . .				
5	Other current assets (attach schedule) . . .				
6	Loans to shareholders				
7	Mortgage and real estate loans				
8	Other investments (attach schedule) . . .				
9	Buildings and other depreciable assets . . .				
a	Less accumulated depreciation				
10	Depletable assets				
a	Less accumulated depletion				
11	Land (net of any amortization)				
12	Intangible assets (amortizable only)				
a	Less accumulated amortization				
13	Other assets (attach schedule)				
14	Total assets				7,000
	Liabilities and Shareholders' Equity				
15	Accounts payable				
16	Mortgages, notes, bonds payable in less than 1 year				
17	Other current liabilities (attach schedule) . .				
18	Loans from shareholders				
19	Mortgages, notes, bonds payable in 1 year or more				
20	Other liabilities (attach schedule)				
21	Capital stock				1600
22	Paid-in or capital surplus				
23	Accumulated adjustments account			5500	
24	Other adjustments account			·<100>	
25	Shareholders' undistributed taxable income previously taxed				
26	Other retained earnings (see instructions) . .				
	Check this box if the corporation has sub-chapter C earnings and profits at the close of the tax year ▶ ☐ (see instructions)				
27	Total retained earnings per books—Combine amounts on lines 23 through 26, columns (a) and (c) (see instructions)				5400
28	Less cost of treasury stock		( )		( )
29	Total liabilities and shareholders' equity . .				7000

Schedule M	**Analysis of Accumulated Adjustments Account, Other Adjustments Account, and Shareholders' Undistributed Taxable Income Previously Taxed** (If Schedule L, column (c), amounts for lines 23, 24, or 25 are not the same as corresponding amounts on line 9 of Schedule M, attach a schedule explaining any differences. See instructions.)

		Accumulated adjustments account	Other adjustments account	Shareholders' undistributed taxable income previously taxed
1	Balance at beginning of year	0	0	
2	Ordinary income from page 1, line 21 . . .	20,000		
3	Other additions	1,000	200	
4	Total of lines 1, 2, and 3	21,000	200	
5	Distributions other than dividend distributions	15,000		
6	Loss from page 1, line 21			
7	Other reductions	500	300	
8	Add lines 5, 6, and 7	15,500	300	
9	Balance at end of tax year—Subtract line 8 from line 4	5,500	<100>	

SCHEDULE K-1
(Form 1120S)

Department of the Treasury
Internal Revenue Service

Shareholder's Share of Income, Credits, Deductions, etc.

For calendar year 1987 or tax year
beginning _____, 1987, and ending _____, 19 ____
▶ **For Paperwork Reduction Act Notice, see page 1 of Instructions for Form 1120S.**

1987

Shareholder's identifying number ▶	Corporation's identifying number ▶
Shareholder's name, address, and ZIP code	Corporation's name, address, and ZIP code
F	A, INC.

A (1) Shareholder's percentage of stock ownership for tax year (see instructions for Schedule K-1) . . . . ▶ _____ %
  (2) Number of shares owned by shareholder at tax year end . . . . ▶

B Internal Revenue Service Center where corporation filed its return ▶

C Tax shelter registration number (see Instructions for Schedule K-1) . . . . ▶

D Did the shareholder materially participate in the trade or business activity(ies) of the corporation? (See instructions for Schedule K-1. Leave the check boxes blank if there are no trade or business activities.) . . . . ☒ Yes ☐ No

E Did the shareholder actively participate in the rental real estate activity(ies) of the corporation? (See instructions for Schedule K-1. Leave the check boxes blank if there are no rental real estate activities.) . . . . ☐ Yes ☐ No

F If (1) question D is checked "No" or income or loss is reported on line 2 or 3 and (2) the shareholder acquired corporate stock after 10/22/86, check here ▶ ☐ and enter the shareholder's weighted percentage increase in stock ownership for 1987 (see instructions for Schedule K-1) . . . . ▶ %

G If question D is checked "No" and any activity referred to in question D was started or acquired by the corporation after 10/22/86, check here ▶ ☐ and enter the date of start up or acquisition in the date space on line 1. Also, if an activity for which income or loss is reported on line 2 or 3 was started after 10/22/86, check the box and enter the start up date in the date space on line 2 or 3.

H If the short tax year shown above was a result of a change in tax year required by section 1378, check here . . . . . . ▶ ☐

Caution: *Refer to Shareholder's Instructions for Schedule K-1 before entering information from Schedule K-1 on your tax return.*

		(a) Distributive share items	**(b)** Amount	**(c)** Form 1040 filers enter the amount in column (b) on:
Income (Losses) and Deductions	**1**	Ordinary income (loss) from trade or business activity(ies). Date: _____	20,000	See Shareholder's Instructions for Schedule K-1 (Form 1120S).
	2	Income or loss from rental real estate activity(ies). Date: _____		
	3	Income or loss from rental activity(ies) other than line 2 above. Date: _____		
	4	Portfolio income (loss):		
	a	Interest		Sch. B, Part I, line 2
	b	Dividends		Sch. B, Part II, line 4
	c	Royalties		Sch. E, Part I, line 5
	d	Net short-term capital gain (loss)		Sch. D, line 5, col. (f) or (g)
	e	Net long-term capital gain (loss)	1,000	Sch. D, line 12, col. (f) or (g)
	f	Other portfolio income (loss).		(Enter on applicable line of your return.)
	5	Net gain (loss) under section 1231 (other than due to casualty or theft).		Form 4797, line 1
	6	Other income (loss) (attach schedule) . . .		(Enter on applicable line of your return.)
	7	Charitable contributions.	500	See Form 1040 Instructions.
	8	Section 179 expense deduction (attach schedule)		See Shareholder's Instructions for Schedule K-1 (Form 1120S).
	9	Deductions related to portfolio income (loss) (attach schedule) . . .		
	10	Other deductions (attach schedule)		
Credits	**11a**	Jobs credit		Form 5884
	b	Low-income housing credit		Form 8586, line 8
	c	Qualified rehabilitation expenditures related to rental real estate activity(ies) (attach schedule)	////////	See Shareholder's Instructions for Schedule K-1 (Form 1120S).
	d	Credits related to rental real estate activity(ies) other than on lines 11b and 11c (attach schedule)	////////	
	e	Credits related to rental activity(ies) other than on lines 11b, c, and d (attach schedule)	////////	
	12	Other credits (attach schedule)		
Tax Preference and Adjustment Items	**13a**	Accelerated depreciation of real property placed in service before 1987		Form 6251, line 5a
	b	Accelerated depreciation of leased personal property placed in service before 1987 . . .	////////	Form 6251, line 5b
	c	Depreciation adjustment on property placed in service after 1986 . .		Form 6251, line 4g
	d	Depletion (other than oil and gas)		Form 6251, line 5h
	e	(1) Gross income from oil, gas, or geothermal properties		See Form 6251 Instructions.
		(2) Gross deductions allocable to oil, gas, or geothermal properties . .		
	f	Other items (attach schedule)		See Shareholder's Instructions for Schedule K-1 (Form 1120S).

	(a) Distributive share items	**(b)** Amount	**(c)** Form 1040 filers enter the amount in column (b) on:
Investment Interest	**14a** Interest expense on investment debts		Form 4952, line 1
	b (1) Investment income included on Schedule K-1, lines 4a through 4f .		See Shareholder's Instructions for Schedule K-1 (Form 1120S).
	(2) Investment expenses included on Schedule K-1, line 9		
Foreign Taxes	**15a** Type of income ▶...	////////	Form 1116, Check boxes
	b Name of foreign country or U.S. possession ▶.................................	////////	Form 1116, Part I
	c Total gross income from sources outside the U.S. (attach schedule) . .		Form 1116, Part I
	d Total applicable deductions and losses (attach schedule)		Form 1116, Part I
	e Total foreign taxes (check one): ▶ ☐ Paid ☐ Accrued		Form 1116, Part II
	f Reduction in taxes available for credit (attach schedule)		Form 1116, Part III
	g Other (attach schedule)		See Form 1116 Instructions.
Other Items	**16** Property distributions (including cash) other than dividend distributions reported to you on Form 1099-DIV		See Shareholder's Instructions for Schedule K-1 (Form 1120S).
	17 Amount of loan repayments for "Loans from Shareholders"		

	18 Properties:	**A**	**B**	**C**	
Property Subject to Recapture of Investment Credit	**a** Description of property (State whether recovery or non-recovery property. If recovery property, state whether regular percentage method or section 48(q) election used.).				Form 4255, top
	b Date placed in service .				Form 4255, line 2
	c Cost or other basis . .				Form 4255, line 3
	d Class of recovery property or original estimated useful life .				Form 4255, line 4
	e Date item ceased to be investment credit property				Form 4255, line 8

19 Supplemental information for lines 1 through 18 that is required to be reported separately to each shareholder (attach additional schedules if more space is needed):

Supplemental Schedules

Form 1040

Department of the Treasury—Internal Revenue Service

U.S. Individual Income Tax Return 1987 (O)

For the year Jan.–Dec. 31, 1987, or other tax year beginning ____ , 1987, ending ____ , 19 ____ | OMB No. 1545-0074

Label

Use IRS label.
Otherwise,
please print or
type.

| Your first name and initial (if joint return, also give spouse's name and initial) | Last name | Your social security number |

| Present home address (number and street or rural route). (If you have a P.O. Box, see page 6 of Instructions.) | Spouse's social security number |

| City, town or post office, state, and ZIP code | For Privacy Act and Paperwork Reduction Act Notice, see Instructions. |

Presidential Election Campaign ▶

Do you want $1 to go to this fund? . . . . Yes ▢ No ▢

If joint return, does your spouse want $1 to go to this fund?. . Yes ▢ No ▢

Note: *Checking "Yes" will not change your tax or reduce your refund.*

Filing Status

Check only
one box.

1 ▢ Single

2 ▢ Married filing joint return (even if only one had income)

3 ▢ Married filing separate return. Enter spouse's social security no. above and full name here. ____

4 ▢ Head of household (with qualifying person). (See page 7 of Instructions.) If the qualifying person is your child but not your dependent, enter child's name here. ____

5 ▢ Qualifying widow(er) with dependent child (year spouse died ▶ 19 ____). (See page 7 of Instructions.)

Exemptions

(See Instructions on page 7.)

If more than 7 dependents, see Instructions on page 7.

Caution: If you can be claimed as a dependent on another person's tax return (such as your parents' return), do not check box 6a. But be sure to check the box on line 32b on page 2.

6a ▢ Yourself   6b ▢ Spouse

c Dependents (1) Name (first, initial, and last name)	(2) Check if under age 5	(3) If age 5 or over, dependent's social security number	(4) Relationship	(5) No. of months lived in your home in 1987

No. of boxes checked on 6a and 6b ▶ ▢

No. of children on 6c who lived with you ▶ ▢

No. of children on 6c who didn't live with you due to divorce or separation ▢

No. of parents listed on 6c ▶ ▢

No. of other dependents listed on 6c ▶ ▢

d If your child didn't live with you but is claimed as your dependent under a pre-1985 agreement, check here . ▶ ▢

e Total number of exemptions claimed (also complete line 35) . . . .

Add numbers entered in boxes above ▶ ▢

Income

Please attach Copy B of your Forms W-2, W-2G, and W-2P here.

If you do not have a W-2, see page 6 of Instructions.

Please attach check or money order here.

7	Wages, salaries, tips, etc. (attach Form(s) W-2)	7	
8	**Taxable** interest income (also attach Schedule B if over $400)	8	0
9	**Tax-exempt** interest income (see page 10). DON'T include on line 8	9	200	
10	Dividend income (also attach Schedule B if over $400)	10	
11	Taxable refunds of state and local income taxes, if any, from worksheet on page 11 of Instructions .	11	
12	Alimony received	12	
13	Business income or (loss) (attach Schedule C).	13	
14	Capital gain or (loss) (attach Schedule D)	14	1000
15	Other gains or (losses) (attach Form 4797)	15	
16a	Pensions, IRA distributions, annuities, and rollovers. Total received 16a		
b	Taxable amount (see page 11)	16b	
17	Rents, royalties, partnerships, estates, trusts, etc. (attach Schedule E)	17	2000
18	Farm income or (loss) (attach Schedule F)	18	
19	Unemployment compensation (insurance) (see page 11) . .	19	
20a	Social security benefits (see page 12) 20a		
b	Taxable amount, if any, from the worksheet on page 12 . . .	20b	
21	Other income (list type and amount—see page 12) ____	21	
22	Add the amounts shown in the far right column for lines 7, 8, and 10–21. This is your **total income** ▶	22	

Adjustments to Income

(See Instructions on page 12.)

23	Reimbursed employee business expenses from Form 2106 .	23	
24a	Your IRA deduction, from applicable worksheet on page 13 or 14	24a	
b	Spouse's IRA deduction, from applicable worksheet on page 13 or 14 . .	24b	
25	Self-employed health insurance deduction, from worksheet on page 14 .	25	
26	Keogh retirement plan and self-employed SEP deduction. .	26	
27	Penalty on early withdrawal of savings	27	
28	Alimony paid (recipient's last name ____ and social security no. ____) .	28	
29	Add lines 23 through 28. These are your **total adjustments** . . . . ▶	29	

Adjusted Gross Income

30 Subtract line 29 from line 22. This is your **adjusted gross income.** *If this line is less than $15,432 and a child lived with you, see "Earned Income Credit" (line 56) on page 18 of the Instructions. If you want IRS to figure your tax, see page 15 of the Instructions* . . . ▶ | 30 |

Schedule A—Itemized Deductions

(Schedule B is on back)

▶ Attach to Form 1040.   ▶ See Instructions for Schedules A and B (Form 1040).

OMB No. 1545-0074

1987

Attachment
Sequence No. **07**

Name(s) as shown on Form 1040

Your social security number

Medical and Dental Expenses (Do not include expenses reimbursed or paid by others.) (See Instructions on page 21.)	**1a** Prescription medicines and drugs, insulin, doctors, dentists, nurses, hospitals, insurance premiums you paid for medical and dental care, etc.	**1a**			
	b Transportation and lodging	**1b**			
	c Other (list—include hearing aids, dentures, eyeglasses, etc.) ▶	**1c**			
	2 Add lines 1a through 1c, and enter the total here	**2**			
	3 Multiply the amount on Form 1040, line 31, by 7.5% (.075)	**3**			
	4 Subtract line 3 from line 2. If zero or less, enter -0-. **Total** medical and dental ▶	**4**			
Taxes You Paid (See Instructions on page 22.)	**Note:** Sales taxes are no longer deductible.				
	5 State and local income taxes	**5**			
	6 Real estate taxes	**6**			
	7 Other taxes (list—include personal property taxes) ▶	**7**			
	8 Add the amounts on lines 5 through 7. Enter the total here. **Total** taxes ▶	**8**			
Interest You Paid (See Instructions on page 22.)	**Note:** If you borrowed any new amounts against your home **after** 8/16/86 and at any time in 1987 the total of **all** your mortgage debts was more than what you paid for your home plus improvements, attach Form 8598 and check here ▶ ☐				
	9a Deductible home mortgage interest you paid to financial institutions (report deductible points on line 10)	**9a**			
	b Deductible home mortgage interest you paid to individuals (show that person's name and address) ▶	**9b**			
	10 Deductible points	**10**			
	11 Deductible investment interest	**11**			
	12a Personal interest you paid (see page 22) . |**12a**|				
	b Multiply the amount on line 12a by 65% (.65). Enter the result	**12b**			
	13 Add the amounts on lines 9a through 11, and 12b. Enter the total here. **Total** interest ▶	**13**			
Contributions You Made (See Instructions on page 23.)	**14a** Cash contributions. (If you gave $3,000 or more to any one organization, report those contributions on line 14b.)	**14a**	500		
	b Cash contributions totaling $3,000 or more to any one organization. (Show to whom you gave and how much you gave.) ▶	**14b**			
	15 Other than cash. (You must attach Form 8283 if over $500.)	**15**			
	16 Carryover from prior year	**16**			
	17 Add the amounts on lines 14a through 16. Enter the total here. **Total** contributions ▶	**17**		500	
Casualty and Theft Losses	**18** Casualty or theft loss(es) (attach Form 4684). (See page 23 of the Instructions.) ▶	**18**			
Moving Expenses	**19** Moving expenses (attach Form 3903 or 3903F). (See page 24 of the Instructions.) ▶	**19**			
Miscellaneous Deductions Subject to 2% AGI Limit (See Instructions on page 24.)	**20** Unreimbursed employee business expenses (attach Form 2106)	**20**			
	21 Other expenses (list type and amount) ▶	**21**			
	22 Add the amounts on lines 20 and 21. Enter the total.	**22**			
	23 Multiply the amount on Form 1040, line 31, by 2% (.02). Enter the result here	**23**			
	24 Subtract line 23 from line 22. Enter the result (but not less than zero) ▶	**24**			
Other Miscellaneous Deductions	**25** Miscellaneous deductions not subject to 2% AGI limit (see page 24). (List type and amount.) ▶	**25**			
Total Itemized Deductions	**26** Add the amounts on lines 4, 8, 13, 17, 18, 19, 24, and 25. Enter the total here and on Form 1040, line 33a. ▶	**26**		500	

For Paperwork Reduction Act Notice, see Form 1040 Instructions.   ⋆ U.S. Government Printing Office: 1987 — 183-092   **Schedule A (Form 1040) 1987**

SCHEDULE D (Form 1040)	Capital Gains and Losses and Reconciliation of Forms 1099-B	OMB No. 1545-0074
Department of the Treasury Internal Revenue Service (O)	▶ Attach to Form 1040. ▶ See Instructions for Schedule D (Form 1040). For Paperwork Reduction Act Notice, see Form 1040 Instructions.	1987 Attachment Sequence No. 12

Name(s) as shown on Form 1040 | Your social security number

1 Report here, the total sales of stocks, bonds, etc., reported for 1987 by your broker to you on Form(s) 1099-B or an equivalent substitute statement(s). If this amount differs from the total of lines 2b and 9b, column (d), attach a statement explaining the difference. See the Instructions for line 1 for examples. Do not include real estate transactions reported to you on a Form 1099-B on line 1, 2a, or 9a **1**

Part I Short-term Capital Gains and Losses—Assets Held Six Months or Less

(a) Description of property (Example, 100 shares 7% preferred of "Z" Co.)	(b) Date acquired (Mo., day, yr.)	(c) Date sold (Mo., day, yr.)	(d) Sales price (see Instructions)	(e) Cost or other basis (see Instructions)	(f) LOSS If (e) is more than (d), subtract (d) from (e)	(g) GAIN If (d) is more than (e), subtract (e) from (d)
2a Form 1099-B Transactions (Sales of Stocks, Bonds, etc.):			(Do not report real estate transactions here. See the instructions for lines 2a and 9a.)			
2b Total (add column (d)) . . . . ▶						
2c Other Transactions:						

3 Short-term gain from sale or exchange of a principal residence from Form 2119, lines 8 or 14 | **3** |
4 Short-term gain from installment sales from Form 6252, lines 23 or 31 . . . | **4** |
5 Net short-term gain or (loss) from partnerships, S corporations, and fiduciaries . | **5** |
6 Short-term capital loss carryover . . . . | **6** |
7 Add all of the transactions on lines 2a and 2c and lines 3 through 6 in columns (f) and (g) . . . | **7** | (|) |
8 Net short-term gain or (loss), combine columns (f) and (g) of line 7 . . . . | **8** |

Part II Long-term Capital Gains and Losses—Assets Held More Than Six Months

(a) Description of property	(b) Date acquired	(c) Date sold	(d) Sales price	(e) Cost or other basis	(f) LOSS	(g) GAIN
9a Form 1099-B Transactions (Sales of Stocks, Bonds, etc.):			(Do not report real estate transactions here. See the instructions for lines 2a and 9a.)			
9b Total (add column (d)) . . . . ▶						
9c Other Transactions:						

10 Long-term gain from sale or exchange of a principal residence from Form 2119, lines 8, 10, or 14 | **10** |
11 Long-term gain from installment sales from Form 6252, lines 23 or 31 . . . . | **11** |
12 Net long-term gain or (loss) from partnerships, S corporations, and fiduciaries | **12** | *1000* |
13 Capital gain distributions . . . . | **13** |
14 Enter gain from Form 4797, line 7 or 9 . . . . | **14** |
15 Long-term capital loss carryover . . . . | **15** |
16 Add all of the transactions on lines 9a and 9c and lines 10 through 15 in columns (f) and (g) . | **16** | (|) |
17 Net long-term gain or (loss), combine columns (f) and (g) of line 16 . . . . | **17** | *1000* |

Schedule D (Form 1040) 1987

Name(s) as shown on Form 1040. (Do not enter name and social security number if shown on other side.) | **Your social security number**

Part II   Income or (Loss) from Partnerships and S Corporations

If you report a loss below and have amounts invested in that activity for which you are **not at risk**, you MUST check "Yes" in column (e) and attach Form 6198. Otherwise, you must check "No." See Instructions.

	(a) Name	(b) Enter **P** for partnership; **S** for S Corporation	(c) Check if foreign partnership	(d) Employer identification number	(e) Not at-Risk? Yes / No
A	A, Inc.	S		11-111111	✓
B					
C					
D					
E					

	Passive Activities		Nonpassive Activities		
	(f) Passive loss allowed from Form 8582	(g) Passive income from Schedule K-1	(h) Nonpassive loss from Schedule K-1	(i) Section 179 deduction	(j) Nonpassive income from Schedule K-1
A					20,000
B					
C					
D					
E					
30a Totals					20,000
b Totals					

31	Add amounts in columns (g) and (j), line 30a. Enter total income here	**31** 20,000
32	Add amounts in columns (f), (h), and (i), line 30b. Enter total here	**32** ( )
33	Total partnership and S corporation income or (loss). Combine amounts on lines 31 and 32. Enter the total here and include in line 42 below	**33** 20,000

Part III   Income or (Loss) from Estates and Trusts

	(a) Name	(b) Employer identification number
A		
B		
C		

	Passive Activities		Nonpassive Activities	
	(c) Passive deduction or loss allowed from Form 8582	(d) Passive income from Schedule K-1	(e) Deduction or loss from Schedule K-1	(f) Other income from Schedule K-1
A				
B				
C				
34a Totals				
b Totals				

35	Add amounts in columns (d) and (f), line 34a. Enter total income here	**35**
36	Add amounts in columns (c) and (e), line 34b. Enter total (loss) here	**36** ( )
37	Total estate and trust income or (loss). Combine amounts on lines 35 and 36. Enter the total here and include in line 42 below	**37**

Part IV   Income or (Loss) from Real Estate Mortgage Investment Conduits (REMICs)—Residual Holder

(a) Name	(b) Employer identification number	(c) Excess inclusion from Schedules Q, line 2c (see Instructions)	(d) Taxable income (net loss) from Schedules Q, line 1b	(e) Income from Schedules Q, line 3b

38	Combine columns (d) and (e) only. Enter the total here and include in line 42 below	**38**

Part V   Windfall Profit Tax Summary

39	Windfall profit tax credit or refund received in 1987 (see Instructions)	**39**
40	Windfall profit tax withheld in 1987 (see Instructions)	**40** ( )
41	Combine amounts on lines 39 and 40. Enter the total here and include in line 42 below	**41**

Part VI   Summary

42	TOTAL income or (loss). Combine lines 29, 33, 37, 38, and 41. Enter total here and on Form 1040, line 17 . . . . ▶	**42** 20,000
43	Farmers and fishermen: Enter your share of GROSS FARMING AND FISHING INCOME applicable to Parts I, II, and III (see Instructions) . . . **43**	

Appendix 10
Filled-in Return—Distributions Where S Corporation Has Earnings and Profits

The facts for this problem are found at Example 8.10.

Schedule L	Balance Sheets	Beginning of tax year		End of tax year	
	Assets	**(a)**	**(b)**	**(c)**	**(d)**
1	Cash				
2	Trade notes and accounts receivable				
a	Less allowance for bad debts		*THE FACTS FOR THIS PROBLEM*		
3	Inventories		*ARE FOUND AT EXAMPLE 8-10*		
4	Federal and state government obligations				
5	Other current assets (attach schedule)				
6	Loans to shareholders				
7	Mortgage and real estate loans				
8	Other investments (attach schedule)				
9	Buildings and other depreciable assets				
a	Less accumulated depreciation				
10	Depletable assets				
a	Less accumulated depletion				
11	Land (net of any amortization)				
12	Intangible assets (amortizable only)				
a	Less accumulated amortization				
13	Other assets (attach schedule)				
14	Total assets		125,000		38,000
	Liabilities and Shareholders' Equity				
15	Accounts payable				
16	Mortgages, notes, bonds payable in less than 1 year				
17	Other current liabilities (attach schedule)				
18	Loans from shareholders				
19	Mortgages, notes, bonds payable in 1 year or more				
20	Other liabilities (attach schedule)				
21	Capital stock		55,000		55,000
22	Paid-in or capital surplus				
23	Accumulated adjustments account	50,000		<17,000>	
24	Other adjustments account				
25	Shareholders' undistributed taxable income previously taxed				
26	Other retained earnings (see instructions)	20,000		0	
	Check this box if the corporation has subchapter C earnings and profits at the close of the tax year ▶ ☐ (see instructions)				
27	Total retained earnings per books—Combine amounts on lines 23 through 26, columns (a) and (c) (see instructions)		70,000		<17,000>
28	Less cost of treasury stock		( )		( )
29	Total liabilities and shareholders' equity		125,000		38000

Schedule M	Analysis of Accumulated Adjustments Account, Other Adjustments Account, and Shareholders' Undistributed Taxable Income Previously Taxed (If Schedule L, column (c), amounts for lines 23, 24, or 25 are not the same as corresponding amounts on line 9 of Schedule M, attach a schedule explaining any differences. See instructions.)

		Accumulated adjustments account	Other adjustments account	Shareholders' undistributed taxable income previously taxed
1	Balance at beginning of year	50000		
2	Ordinary income from page 1, line 21	- 0 -		
3	Other additions	0		
4	Total of lines 1, 2, and 3	50000		
5	Distributions other than dividend distributions	67,000		
6	Loss from page 1, line 21			
7	Other reductions			
8	Add lines 5, 6, and 7	67,000		
9	Balance at end of tax year—Subtract line 8 from line 4	<17,000>		

SCHEDULE K-1	Shareholder's Share of Income, Credits, Deductions, etc.	OMB No. 1545-0130
(Form 1120S)	For calendar year 1987 or tax year	
Department of the Treasury Internal Revenue Service	beginning _____, 1987, and ending _____, 19 ___ ► **For Paperwork Reduction Act Notice, see page 1 of Instructions for Form 1120S.**	**1987**

Shareholder's identifying number ►	Corporation's identifying number ►
Shareholder's name, address, and ZIP code	Corporation's name, address, and ZIP code

A (1) Shareholder's percentage of stock ownership for tax year (see instructions for Schedule K-1) . . . . ► _____ %

(2) Number of shares owned by shareholder at tax year end . . . . ►

B Internal Revenue Service Center where corporation filed its return ►

C Tax shelter registration number (see Instructions for Schedule K-1) . . . . ►

D Did the shareholder materially participate in the trade or business activity(ies) of the corporation? (See instructions for Schedule K-1. Leave the check boxes blank if there are no trade or business activities.) . . . . ☒ Yes ☐ No

E Did the shareholder actively participate in the rental real estate activity(ies) of the corporation? (See instructions for Schedule K-1. Leave the check boxes blank if there are no rental real estate activities.) . . . . ☐ Yes ☐ No

F If (1) question D is checked "No" or income or loss is reported on line 2 or 3 and (2) the shareholder acquired corporate stock after 10/22/86, check here ► ☐ and enter the shareholder's weighted percentage increase in stock ownership for 1987 (see instructions for Schedule K-1) . . . . ► %

G If question D is checked "No" and any activity referred to in question D was started or acquired by the corporation after 10/22/86, check here ► ☐ and enter the date of start up or acquisition in the date space on line 1. Also, if an activity for which income or loss is reported on line 2 or 3 was started after 10/22/86, check the box and enter the start up date in the date space on line 2 or 3.

H If the short tax year shown above was a result of a change in tax year required by section 1378, check here . . . . . . ► ☐

Caution: *Refer to Shareholder's Instructions for Schedule K-1 before entering information from Schedule K-1 on your tax return.*

		(a) Distributive share items	**(b)** Amount	**(c)** Form 1040 filers enter the amount in column (b) on:
Income (Losses) and Deductions	1	Ordinary income (loss) from trade or business activity(ies). Date: _____		See Shareholder's Instructions for Schedule K-1 (Form 1120S).
	2	Income or loss from rental real estate activity(ies). Date: _____		
	3	Income or loss from rental activity(ies) other than line 2 above. Date: _____		
	4	Portfolio income (loss):		
	a	Interest		Sch. B, Part I, line 2
	b	Dividends		Sch. B, Part II, line 4
	c	Royalties		Sch. E, Part I, line 5
	d	Net short-term capital gain (loss)		Sch. D, line 5, col. (f) or (g)
	e	Net long-term capital gain (loss)		Sch. D, line 12, col. (f) or (g)
	f	Other portfolio income (loss).		(Enter on applicable line of your return.)
	5	Net gain (loss) under section 1231 (other than due to casualty or theft).		Form 4797, line 1
	6	Other income (loss) (attach schedule)		(Enter on applicable line of your return.)
	7	Charitable contributions.		See Form 1040 Instructions.
	8	Section 179 expense deduction (attach schedule) . .		See Shareholder's Instructions for Schedule K-1 (Form 1120S).
	9	Deductions related to portfolio income (loss) (attach schedule) . . .		
	10	Other deductions (attach schedule)		
Credits	11a	Jobs credit		Form 5884
	b	Low-income housing credit		Form 8586, line 8
	c	Qualified rehabilitation expenditures related to rental real estate activity(ies) (attach schedule)	///	See Shareholder's Instructions for Schedule K-1 (Form 1120S).
	d	Credits related to rental real estate activity(ies) other than on lines 11b and 11c (attach schedule)	///	
	e	Credits related to rental activity(ies) other than on lines 11b, c, and d (attach schedule)	///	
	12	Other credits (attach schedule)		
Tax Preference and Adjustment Items	13a	Accelerated depreciation of real property placed in service before 1987	///	Form 6251, line 5a
	b	Accelerated depreciation of leased personal property placed in service before 1987		Form 6251, line 5b
	c	Depreciation adjustment on property placed in service after 1986 . .		Form 6251, line 4g
	d	Depletion (other than oil and gas)		Form 6251, line 5h
	e	(1) Gross income from oil, gas, or geothermal properties		See Form 6251 Instructions.
		(2) Gross deductions allocable to oil, gas, or geothermal properties . .		
	f	Other items (attach schedule)		See Shareholder's Instructions for Schedule K-1 (Form 1120S).

	(a) Distributive share items	(b) Amount	(c) Form 1040 filers enter the amount in column (b) on:
Investment Interest	**14a** Interest expense on investment debts		Form 4952, line 1
	b (1) Investment income included on Schedule K-1, lines 4a through 4f .		See Shareholder's Instructions for Schedule K-1 (Form 1120S).
	(2) Investment expenses included on Schedule K-1, line 9		
Foreign Taxes	**15a** Type of income ▶..		Form 1116, Check boxes
	b Name of foreign country or U.S. possession ▶.............................		Form 1116, Part I
	c Total gross income from sources outside the U.S. (attach schedule) . .		Form 1116, Part I
	d Total applicable deductions and losses (attach schedule)		Form 1116, Part I
	e Total foreign taxes (check one): ▶ ☐ Paid ☐ Accrued		Form 1116, Part II
	f Reduction in taxes available for credit (attach schedule)		Form 1116, Part III
	g Other (attach schedule)		See Form 1116 Instructions.
Other Items	**16** Property distributions (including cash) other than dividend distributions reported to you on Form 1099-DIV	*67,000*	See Shareholder's Instructions for Schedule K-1 (Form 1120S).
	17 Amount of loan repayments for "Loans from Shareholders"		

	18 Properties:	A	B	C	
Property Subject to Recapture of Investment Credit	**a** Description of property (State whether recovery or non-recovery property. If recovery property, state whether regular percentage method or section 48(q) election used.).				Form 4255, top
	b Date placed in service .				Form 4255, line 2
	c Cost or other basis . .				Form 4255, line 3
	d Class of recovery property or original estimated useful life .				Form 4255, line 4
	e Date item ceased to be investment credit property				Form 4255, line 8

19 Supplemental information for lines 1 through 18 that is required to be reported separately to each shareholder (attach additional schedules if more space is needed):

Supplemental Schedules

Form 1099-DIV (Copy 1)

9191 ☐ VOID ☐ CORRECTED — For Official Use Only

Type or machine print PAYER'S name, street address, city, state, and ZIP code	1 Gross dividends and other distributions on stock	OMB No. 1545-0110	
	$ 20,000	**1987** Statement for Recipients of	**Dividends and Distributions**

A, Inc.

PAYER'S Federal identification number	RECIPIENT'S identification number	2 Investment expenses included in Box 1 $	3 Capital gain distributions $	**Copy A For Internal Revenue Service Center**
Type or machine print RECIPIENT'S name (first, middle, last) F		4 Federal income tax withheld $	5 Nontaxable distributions (if determinable) $	For Paperwork Reduction Act Notice and instructions for completing this form, see Instructions for Forms 1099, 1098, 5498, 1096, and W-2G.
Street address		6 Foreign tax paid $	7 Foreign country or U.S. possession	
City, state, and ZIP code		**Liquidation Distributions**		
Account number (optional)		8 Cash $	9 Noncash (Fair market value) $	

Form **1099-DIV**   Do NOT Cut or Separate Forms on This Page   Department of the Treasury - Internal Revenue Service

---

9191 ☐ VOID ☐ CORRECTED — For Official Use Only

Type or machine print PAYER'S name, street address, city, state, and ZIP code	1 Gross dividends and other distributions on stock	OMB No. 1545-0110	
	$	**1987** Statement for Recipients of	**Dividends and Distributions**

PAYER'S Federal identification number	RECIPIENT'S identification number	2 Investment expenses included in Box 1 $	3 Capital gain distributions $	**Copy A For Internal Revenue Service Center**
Type or machine print RECIPIENT'S name (first, middle, last)		4 Federal income tax withheld $	5 Nontaxable distributions (if determinable) $	For Paperwork Reduction Act Notice and instructions for completing this form, see Instructions for Forms 1099, 1098, 5498, 1096, and W-2G.
Street address		6 Foreign tax paid $	7 Foreign country or U.S. possession	
City, state, and ZIP code		**Liquidation Distributions**		
Account number (optional)		8 Cash $	9 Noncash (Fair market value) $	

Form **1099-DIV**   Do NOT Cut or Separate Forms on This Page   Department of the Treasury - Internal Revenue Service

---

9191 ☐ VOID ☐ CORRECTED — For Official Use Only

Type or machine print PAYER'S name, street address, city, state, and ZIP code	1 Gross dividends and other distributions on stock	OMB No. 1545-0110	
	$	**1987** Statement for Recipients of	**Dividends and Distributions**

PAYER'S Federal identification number	RECIPIENT'S identification number	2 Investment expenses included in Box 1 $	3 Capital gain distributions $	**Copy A For Internal Revenue Service Center**
Type or machine print RECIPIENT'S name (first, middle, last)		4 Federal income tax withheld $	5 Nontaxable distributions (if determinable) $	For Paperwork Reduction Act Notice and instructions for completing this form, see Instructions for Forms 1099, 1098, 5498, 1096, and W-2G.
Street address		6 Foreign tax paid $	7 Foreign country or U.S. possession	
City, state, and ZIP code		**Liquidation Distributions**		
Account number (optional)		8 Cash $	9 Noncash (Fair market value) $	

Form **1099-DIV**   Department of the Treasury - Internal Revenue Service

Form 1040 — U.S. Individual Income Tax Return 1987 (O)

Department of the Treasury—Internal Revenue Service

For the year Jan.–Dec. 31, 1987, or other tax year beginning _____ , 1987, ending _____ , 19 ___ . | OMB No. 1545-0074

Label

Use IRS label. Otherwise, please print or type.

Your first name and initial (if joint return, also give spouse's name and initial) | Last name

Present home address (number and street or rural route). (If you have a P.O. Box, see page 6 of Instructions.)

City, town or post office, state, and ZIP code

Your social security number

Spouse's social security number

For Privacy Act and Paperwork Reduction Act Notice, see Instructions.

Presidential Election Campaign

▶ Do you want $1 to go to this fund? . . . . Yes ▢ No ▢

If joint return, does your spouse want $1 to go to this fund?. . Yes ▢ No ▢

Note: Checking "Yes" will not change your tax or reduce your refund.

Filing Status

Check only one box.

1. ▢ Single
2. ▢ Married filing joint return (even if only one had income)
3. ▢ Married filing separate return. Enter spouse's social security no. above and full name here. _____
4. ▢ Head of household (with qualifying person). (See page 7 of Instructions.) If the qualifying person is your child but not your dependent, enter child's name here. _____
5. ▢ Qualifying widow(er) with dependent child (year spouse died ▶ 19 ___). (See page 7 of Instructions.)

Exemptions

(See Instructions on page 7.)

Caution: If you can be claimed as a dependent on another person's tax return (such as your parents' return), do not check box 6a. But be sure to check the box on line 32b on page 2.

6a ▢ Yourself   6b ▢ Spouse

No. of boxes checked on 6a and 6b ▶ ▢

c Dependents (1) Name (first, initial, and last name)	(2) Check if under age 5	(3) If age 5 or over, dependent's social security number	(4) Relationship	(5) No. of months lived in your home in 1987
		: :		
		: :		
		: :		
		: :		
		: :		
		: :		
		: :		

If more than 7 dependents, see Instructions on page 7.

No. of children on 6c who lived with you ▶ ▢

No. of children on 6c who didn't live with you due to divorce or separation ▢

No. of parents listed on 6c ▶ ▢

No. of other dependents listed on 6c ▶ ▢

d If your child didn't live with you but is claimed as your dependent under a pre-1985 agreement, check here . . ▶ ▢

e Total number of exemptions claimed (also complete line 35) . . . .

Add numbers entered in boxes above ▶ ▢

Income

Please attach Copy B of your Forms W-2, W-2G, and W-2P here.

If you do not have a W-2, see page 6 of Instructions.

Please attach check or money order here.

7 Wages, salaries, tips, etc. (attach Form(s) W-2)	7	
8 **Taxable** interest income (also attach Schedule B if over $400) . .	8	
9 **Tax-exempt** interest income (see page 10). DON'T include on line 8 9		
10 Dividend income (also attach Schedule B if over $400) . . .	10	26,000
11 Taxable refunds of state and local income taxes, if any, from worksheet on page 11 of Instructions . .	11	
12 Alimony received	12	
13 Business income or (loss) (attach Schedule C)	13	
14 Capital gain or (loss) (attach Schedule D)	14	12,000
15 Other gains or (losses) (attach Form 4797)	15	
16a Pensions, IRA distributions, annuities, and rollovers. Total received 16a		
b Taxable amount (see page 11)	16b	
17 Rents, royalties, partnerships, estates, trusts, etc. (attach Schedule E) . .	17	- 0 -
18 Farm income or (loss) (attach Schedule F)	18	
19 Unemployment compensation (insurance) (see page 11) . . .	19	
20a Social security benefits (see page 12) 20a		
b Taxable amount, if any, from the worksheet on page 12 . . .	20b	
21 Other income (list type and amount—see page 12) _____	21	
22 Add the amounts shown in the far right column for lines 7, 8, and 10–21. This is your **total income** ▶	22	32,000

Adjustments to Income

(See Instructions on page 12.)

23 Reimbursed employee business expenses from Form 2106 .	23		
24a Your IRA deduction, from applicable worksheet on page 13 or 14	24a		
b Spouse's IRA deduction, from applicable worksheet on page 13 or 14 . .	24b		
25 Self-employed health insurance deduction, from worksheet on page 14 .	25		
26 Keogh retirement plan and self-employed SEP deduction. . .	26		
27 Penalty on early withdrawal of savings	27		
28 Alimony paid (recipient's last name _____ and social security no. _____) .	28		
29 Add lines 23 through 28. These are your **total adjustments** . . . . ▶	29		

Adjusted Gross Income

30 Subtract line 29 from line 22. This is your **adjusted gross income.** If this line is less than $15,432 and a child lived with you, see "Earned Income Credit" (line 56) on page 18 of the Instructions. If you want IRS to figure your tax, see page 15 of the Instructions . . . ▶ | 30 | 32,000

Name(s) as shown on Form 1040. (Do not enter name and social security number if shown on other side.)	Your social security number

Schedule B—Interest and Dividend Income   Attachment Sequence No. **08**

Part I Interest Income

(See Instructions on pages 9 and 24.)

Also complete Part III.

Note: If you received a Form 1099–INT or Form 1099–OID from a brokerage firm, enter the firm's name and the total interest shown on that form.

If you received more than $400 in taxable interest income, you must complete Part I and list ALL interest received. If you received, as a nominee, interest that actually belongs to another person, or you received or paid accrued interest on securities transferred between interest payment dates, see page 24.

Interest Income		Amount	
1 Interest income from seller-financed mortgages. (See Instructions and list name of payer.) ▶	1		
2 Other interest income (list name of payer) ▶			
	2		
3 Add the amounts on lines 1 and 2. Enter the total here and on Form 1040, line 8. ▶	3		

Part II Dividend Income

(See Instructions on pages 10 and 25.)

Also complete Part III.

Note: If you received a Form 1099-DIV from a brokerage firm, enter the firm's name and the total dividends shown on that form.

If you received more than $400 in gross dividends and/or other distributions on stock, complete Part II. If you received, as a nominee, dividends that actually belong to another person, see page 25.

Dividend Income		Amount	
4 Dividend income (list name of payer—include on this line capital gain distributions, nontaxable distributions, etc.) ▶			
DIVIDENDS - S. Corp		*20,000*	
	4		
5 Add the amounts on line 4. Enter the total here	5		
6 Capital gain distributions. Enter here and on line 13, Schedule D.*	6		
7 Nontaxable distributions. (See Schedule D Instructions for adjustment to basis.)	7		
8 Add the amounts on lines 6 and 7. Enter the total here	8		
9 Subtract line 8 from line 5. Enter the result here and on Form 1040, line 10 ▶	9	*20,000*	

*If you received capital gain distributions but do not need Schedule D to report any other gains or losses **or** to figure your tax (see the **Tax Tip** under **Capital gain distributions** on page 10), enter your capital gain distributions on Form 1040, line 14. Write "CGD" on the dotted line to the left of line 14.

Part III Foreign Accounts and Foreign Trusts

(See Instructions on page 25.)

If you received more than $400 of interest or dividends, OR if you had a foreign account or were a grantor of, or a transferor to, a foreign trust, you must answer both questions in Part III.   Yes   No

10 At any time during the tax year, did you have an interest in or a signature or other authority over a financial account in a foreign country (such as a bank account, securities account, or other financial account)? (See page 25 of the Instructions for exceptions and filing requirements for Form TD F 90-22.1.)

If "Yes," enter the name of the foreign country ▶

11 Were you the grantor of, or transferor to, a foreign trust which existed during the current tax year, whether or not you have any beneficial interest in it? If "Yes," you may have to file Forms 3520, 3520-A, or 926.

For Paperwork Reduction Act Notice, see Form 1040 Instructions.   **Schedule B (Form 1040) 1987**

SCHEDULE D	Capital Gains and Losses	OMB No. 1545-0074

SCHEDULE D
(Form 1040)

Department of the Treasury
Internal Revenue Service   (0)

**Capital Gains and Losses
and Reconciliation of Forms 1099-B**

▶ Attach to Form 1040.   ▶ See Instructions for Schedule D (Form 1040).

For Paperwork Reduction Act Notice, see Form 1040 Instructions.

OMB No. 1545-0074

1987

Attachment
Sequence No. **12**

Name(s) as shown on Form 1040

Your social security number

1 Report here, the total sales of stocks, bonds, etc., reported for 1987 by your broker to you on Form(s) 1099-B or an equivalent substitute statement(s). If this amount differs from the total of lines 2b and 9b, column (d), attach a statement explaining the difference. See the Instructions for line 1 for examples. Do not include real estate transactions reported to you on a Form 1099-B on line 1, 2a, or 9a **1**

Part I   Short-term Capital Gains and Losses—Assets Held Six Months or Less

(a) Description of property (Example, 100 shares 7% preferred of "Z" Co.)	(b) Date acquired (Mo., day, yr.)	(c) Date sold (Mo., day, yr.)	(d) Sales price (see Instructions)	(e) Cost or other basis (see Instructions)	(f) LOSS If (e) is more than (d), subtract (d) from (e)	(g) GAIN If (d) is more than (e), subtract (e) from (d)
2a Form 1099-B Transactions (Sales of Stocks, Bonds, etc.): (Do not report real estate transactions here. See the instructions for lines 2a and 9a.)						
2b Total (add column (d)) . . . . . . ▶						
2c Other Transactions:						

3 Short-term gain from sale or exchange of a principal residence from Form 2119, lines 8 or 14	**3**		
4 Short-term gain from installment sales from Form 6252, lines 23 or 31 . . .	**4**		
5 Net short-term gain or (loss) from partnerships, S corporations, and fiduciaries .	**5**		
6 Short-term capital loss carryover	**6**		
7 Add all of the transactions on lines 2a and 2c and lines 3 through 6 in columns (f) and (g) . .	**7** (	)	
8 Net short-term gain or (loss), combine columns (f) and (g) of line 7	**8**		

Part II   Long-term Capital Gains and Losses—Assets Held More Than Six Months

(a)	(b)	(c)	(d)	(e)	(f)	(g)
9a Form 1099-B Transactions (Sales of Stocks, Bonds, etc.): (Do not report real estate transactions here. See the instructions for lines 2a and 9a.)						
9b Total (add column (d)) . . . . ▶						
9c Other Transactions:						
DISTRIBUTION IN EXCESS OF BASIS—S CORP.						12,000

10 Long-term gain from sale or exchange of a principal residence from Form 2119, lines 8, 10, or 14	**10**		
11 Long-term gain from installment sales from Form 6252, lines 23 or 31	**11**		
12 Net long-term gain or (loss) from partnerships, S corporations, and fiduciaries .	**12**		
13 Capital gain distributions	**13**		
14 Enter gain from Form 4797, line 7 or 9	**14**		
15 Long-term capital loss carryover	**15**		
16 Add all of the transactions on lines 9a and 9c and lines 10 through 15 in columns (f) and (g) . .	**16** (	)	
17 Net long-term gain or (loss), combine columns (f) and (g) of line 16	**17**	12,000	

Schedule D (Form 1040) 1987

Name(s) as shown on Form 1040. (Do not enter name and social security number if shown on other side.) | **Your social security number**

Part II   Income or (Loss) from Partnerships and S Corporations

If you report a loss below and have amounts invested in that activity for which you are **not at risk**, you MUST check "Yes" in column (e) and attach Form 6198. Otherwise, you must check "No." See Instructions.

	(a) Name	(b) Enter P for partnership; S for S Corporation	(c) Check if foreign partnership	(d) Employer identification number	(e) Not at-Risk? Yes | No
A	A, INC.	S		11-111111	✓
B					
C					
D					
E					

	Passive Activities		**Nonpassive Activities**		
	(f) Passive loss allowed from Form 8582	(g) Passive income from Schedule K-1	(h) Nonpassive loss from Schedule K-1	(i) Section 179 deduction	(j) Nonpassive income from Schedule K-1
A		0			0
B					
C					
D					
E					
30a Totals		0			0
b Totals					

31 Add amounts in columns (g) and (j), line 30a. Enter total income here . . . . | 31 | 0
32 Add amounts in columns (f), (h), and (i), line 30b. Enter total here . . . . | 32 | ( )
33 Total partnership and S corporation income or (loss). Combine amounts on lines 31 and 32. Enter the total here and include in line 42 below . . . . | 33 | 0

Part III   Income or (Loss) from Estates and Trusts

	(a) Name	(b) Employer identification number
A		
B		
C		

	Passive Activities		**Nonpassive Activities**	
	(c) Passive deduction or loss allowed from Form 8582	(d) Passive income from Schedule K-1	(e) Deduction or loss from Schedule K-1	(f) Other income from Schedule K-1
A				
B				
C				
34a Totals				
b Totals				

35 Add amounts in columns (d) and (f), line 34a. Enter total income here . . . . | 35 |
36 Add amounts in columns (c) and (e), line 34b. Enter total (loss) here . . . . | 36 | ( )
37 Total estate and trust income or (loss). Combine amounts on lines 35 and 36. Enter the total here and include in line 42 below . . . . | 37 |

Part IV   Income or (Loss) from Real Estate Mortgage Investment Conduits (REMICs)—Residual Holder

(a) Name	(b) Employer identification number	(c) Excess inclusion from Schedules Q, line 2c (see Instructions)	(d) Taxable income (net loss) from Schedules Q, line 1b	(e) Income from Schedules Q, line 3b

38 Combine columns (d) and (e) only. Enter the total here and include in line 42 below . . . . . | 38 |

Part V   Windfall Profit Tax Summary

39 Windfall profit tax credit or refund received in 1987 (see Instructions) . . . . | 39 |
40 Windfall profit tax withheld in 1987 (see Instructions) . . . . | 40 | ( )
41 Combine amounts on lines 39 and 40. Enter the total here and include in line 42 below . . . . | 41 |

Part VI   Summary

42 TOTAL income or (loss). Combine lines 29, 33, 37, 38, and 41. Enter total here and on Form 1040, line 17 . . . . ▶ | 42 | 0
43 Farmers and fishermen: Enter your share of GROSS FARMING AND FISHING INCOME applicable to Parts I, II, and III (see Instructions) . . . | 43 |

☆ U.S.G.P.O.: 1987 - 183-104

Appendix 11
Shareholders' Agreement Provisions

WHEREAS, the stockholders are the sole stockholders of the corporation and the corporation has made an S election; and

WHEREAS, if the corporation lost its S status without the written consent of more than 50% of the outstanding stock prior thereto it would tend to disrupt the affairs of the corporation.

WHEREAS, the corporation and the stockholders realize that in the event of the death of any one of them, or the sale of his, her, or its stock during his, her, or its lifetime, should in any such event the stock of the corporation owned by such stockholder pass into the ownership or control of a person other than the remaining stockholders it would tend to disrupt the harmonious and successful management and control of the corporation; and

WHEREAS, it is the earnest desire of the corporation and the stockholders to avoid the happening of any such unfortunate contingency by assuring to the remaining stockholders a succession to the ownership and control of the corporation through the acquisition of the shares of a stockholder at the time of his or her death or upon prior sale; and

NOW, THEREFORE, in consideration of the mutual promises of the parties hereto and of the mutual benefits to be gained by the performance thereof, the parties hereto hereby AGREE:

1. The outstanding capital stock of the corporation consists of _____ shares of common stock, which are owned by the stockholders as follows:

    (shareholder) . . . . _____ shares common
    (shareholder) . . . . _____ shares common
    (shareholder) . . . . _____ shares nonvoting common
    (shareholder) . . . . _____ shares nonvoting common

The stockholders agree to endorse the certificate or certificates of stock held by them, or hereafter acquired, as follows: "This certificate of stock is subject to a stock purchase agreement dated _____, 19____, between [Name of Corporation] and its stockholders to, inter alia, preserve S corporate status and is transferable only in accordance with such agreement."

For a discussion of this form, see Chapters 9.8 and 10.3.

A. Except as herein provided each shareholder, as a party hereto, shall not sell, give, assign, transfer, encumber, pledge, hypothecate or otherwise dispose of his, hers or its shares of the corporation now or hereafter owned by him, her or it except under and pursuant and in compliance with the terms and conditions of this agreement and the corporation agrees that it will not transfer or recognize any transfer of such shares except in compliance herewith, and any such transfer or attempted transfer not in accordance with the terms and conditions contained in this agreement shall be of no effect, null and void. Further, each shareholder agrees that no person or entity may acquire the ownership of any shares (beneficial or otherwise) of the corporation's stock, if such transfer or acquisition would cause this corporation to lose its S status, unless the shareholder(s) owning more than 50% of the outstanding stock in writing consent otherwise prior to the transfer. A copy of this agreement shall be filed in the offices of the corporation.

B. Except as herein provided, each of the stockholders covenants and agrees with each other and the corporation to keep registered in his, her or its respective name upon the books of the corporation the certificates representing the ownership of his, her or its capital stock in the corporation.

Appendix 12
Form 8082

For a discussion of this form, see Chapter 9.18.

Form **8082**
(Rev. December 1987)

Department of the Treasury
Internal Revenue Service

Notice of Inconsistent Treatment or Amended Return
(Administrative Adjustment Request (AAR))

(For use by partners, S corporation shareholders, REMIC residual holders, and TMPs)
(See separate instructions.)

OMB No. 1545-0790
Expires 9-30-90

Attachment
Sequence No. **84**

Your name(s) as shown on your return

Your identifying number as shown on your return

| **Part I** | **General Information** |

1 Notice of (check boxes that apply):
  a ☐ Inconsistent treatment of (check only one): **(1)** ☐ Partnership item(s) **(2)** ☐ S corporation item(s) **(3)** ☐ REMIC item(s)
  b ☐ Amended return (administrative adjustment request (AAR)) of (check only one):
    (1) ☐ Partnership item(s) **(2)** ☐ S corporation item(s) **(3)** ☐ REMIC item(s)

2 Name, address, and ZIP code of partnership, S corporation, or REMIC

3a Taxpayer identifying number of partnership, S corporation, or REMIC

b Tax shelter registration number (if applicable) of partnership or S corporation

4 Internal Revenue Service Center where partnership, S corporation or REMIC filed its return

5a Partnership, S corporation or REMIC's tax year
  / / to / /

b Your tax year
  / / to / /

| **Part II** | **Inconsistent or Amended (Administrative Adjustment Request (AAR)) Items** |

(a) Description of inconsistent or amended (administrative adjustment request (AAR)) item(s) (see instructions)	(b) Inconsistency is in, or amendment (AAR) is to, (check boxes that apply)		(c) Amount as shown on Schedule K-1, Schedule Q, or similar statement, or your return, whichever applies (see instructions)	(d) Amount you are reporting	(e) Difference between (c) and (d)
	Amount of item	Treatment of item			
6					
7					
8					
9					

| **Part III** | **Explanation(s)** |

6 ....
....

7 ....
....

8 ....
....

9 ....
....

For Paperwork Reduction Act Notice, see separate instructions.

☆ U.S. GPO: 1987—201-993/60158

Form **8082** (Rev. 12-87)

Appendix 13
Notice of Revocation of Subchapter S Election Under Section 1362(a)

CERTIFIED MAIL
RETURN RECEIPT REQUESTED
Internal Revenue Service Center
[Address]

Name:

Address:

Employer Identification
Number:

Service Center:

Voting shares issued and outstanding:

Nonvoting shares issued and outstanding:

The above corporation, [Name of Corporation], hereby revokes its election made under Sec. 1362(a) to be taxed as an S corporation, made by it on Form 2553 filed with the District Director, on _____. It is intended that this revocation shall be effective on _____. Attached are the consents to the revocation by shareholders owning more than one-half of the issued and outstanding shares.

Dated:

[Corporation Name]

By: _____

[Name, Title]

For a discussion of this form, see Chapter 10.2.

Appendix 14
Consent to Election to Have Items Assigned Under Normal Accounting Rules—Section 1362(e)(3)(B)

The undersigned, being all of the shareholders, [Name of Corporation], at any time during the S short year beginning _____, and all shareholders on the first day of the C short year, beginning _____ hereby consent to the aforementioned corporation's election under Section 1362(e)(3)(B) to have the rules in Section 1362(e)(2) not apply.

Dated:

[Corporate Name]

By: _____
[Name, Title]

Name of Shareholder	Shareholder Identification No.	
_____	_____	_____
		Date
_____	_____	_____
		Date

_____

For a discussion of this form, see Chapters 10.7.A and 10.7.A.2.

Appendix 15
Election to Close Books upon Termination of Interest by S Corporation Shareholder— Section 1377(a)(2)

CERTIFIED MAIL
RETURN RECEIPT REQUESTED
Internal Revenue Service Center
[Address]

Name:

Address:

Employer Identification
Number:

Service Center:

The above corporation, [Name of Corporation], hereby elects under Section 1377(a)(2) to have the rules provided in Section 1377(a)(1) applied as if the taxable year consisted of two taxable years.

    Date corporate year ends:

    Name of shareholder who terminated entire interest in corporation:

    Cause of termination:

    Date of termination:

Dated:

Corporate Name

by: _____
[Name, Title]

For a discussion of this form, see Chapter 10.8.D.1.

Appendix 16
Shareholders' Consent—Section 1377(a)(2)*

We the undersigned shareholders of [Name of Corporation, Address, Identification Number] hereby consent to the election to close the books of the corporation pursuant to Section 1377(a)(2).

Shareholder   Identification No.   Date

_____ _____ _____

_____ _____ _____

* To be appended to Appendix 15.
_____

For discussion of this form, see Chapter 10.8.D.1.

Form 1120S

Department of the Treasury
Internal Revenue Service

U.S. Income Tax Return for an S Corporation

For the calendar year 1987 or tax year beginning ...., 1987, ending ...., 19 ....

▶ For Paperwork Reduction Act Notice, see page 1 of the instructions.

OMB No. 1545-0130

1987

A Date of election as an S corporation
12/01/86

Use IRS label. Otherwise, please print or type.

10-4487964   DEC87   D74   3070
ESTEX FABRICATORS, INC
482 WINSTON ST
METRO CITY   OH   43704

C Employer identification number

D Date incorporated
3/01/72

B Business code no. (see Specific Instructions)
3070

E Total assets (see Specific Instructions)

	Dollars	Cents
$	921,714	

F Check applicable boxes: (1) ☐ Initial return (2) ☐ Final return (3) ☐ Change in address (4) ☐ Amended return

G Check this box if this is an S corporation subject to the consolidated audit procedures of sections 6241 through 6245 (see instructions) . . . . ▶ ☐

H Was this corporation in operation at the end of 1987 (see instructions)? . . . . Yes ☒ No ☐

I How many months in 1987 was this corporation in operation (see instructions)? . . . . ▶ 12

Caution: Include **only** trade or business income and expenses on lines 1a through 21. See the instructions for more information.

Income				
1a	Gross receipts or sales 2,010,000 **b** Less returns and allowances 21,000 Balance ▶	1c	1,989,000	
2	Cost of goods sold and/or operations (Schedule A, line 7)	2	1,520,000	
3	Gross profit (subtract line 2 from line 1c)	3	469,000	
4	Net gain (or loss) from Form 4797, line 18 (see instructions)	4		
5	Other income (see instructions—attach schedule)	5	1,000	
6	TOTAL income (loss)—Combine lines 3, 4 and 5 and enter here . . . ▶	6	470,000	

Deductions (See instructions for limitations.)				
7	Compensation of officers	7	70,000	
8a	Salaries and wages 44,000 **b** Less jobs credit 6,000 Balance ▶	8c	38,000	
9	Repairs	9	800	
10	Bad debts (see instructions)	10	1,600	
11	Rents	11	9,200	
12	Taxes	12	15,000	
13	Deductible interest expense not claimed or reported elsewhere on return (see instructions)	13	24,200	
14a	Depreciation from Form 4562 (attach Form 4562) 14a 17,600			
b	Depreciation reported on Schedule A and elsewhere on return 14b 12,400			
c	Subtract line 14b from line 14a	14c	5,200	
15	Depletion (**Do not deduct oil and gas depletion.** See instructions.) . . .	15		
16	Advertising	16	8,700	
17	Pension, profit-sharing, etc. plans	17		
18	Employee benefit programs	18		
19	Other deductions (attach schedule)	19	78,300	
20	TOTAL deductions—Add lines 7 through 19 and enter here . . . ▶	20	251,000	
21	Ordinary income (loss) from trade or business activity(ies)—Subtract line 20 from line 6	21	219,000	

Tax and Payments				
22	Tax:			
a	Excess net passive income tax (attach schedule) 22a			
b	Tax from Schedule D (Form 1120S) 22b			
c	Add lines 22a and 22b	22c		
23	Payments:			
a	Tax deposited with Form 7004 . . . . 23a			
b	Credit for Federal tax on gasoline and special fuels (attach Form 4136) 23b			
c	Add lines 23a and 23b	23c		
24	**TAX DUE** (subtract line 23c from line 22c). See instructions for Paying the Tax . . ▶	24		
25	**OVERPAYMENT** (subtract line 22c from line 23c) . . . . ▶	25		

Please Sign Here

Under penalties of perjury, I declare that I have examined this return, including accompanying schedules and statements, and to the best of my knowledge and belief, it is true, correct, and complete. Declaration of preparer (other than taxpayer) is based on all information of which preparer has any knowledge.

▶ *John H. Anders*   Signature of officer   3/9/88   Date   ▶ President   Title

Paid Preparer's Use Only

Preparer's signature ▶		Date		Check if self-employed ▶ ☐	Preparer's social security number
Firm's name (or yours if self-employed) and address ▶				E.I. No. ▶	
				ZIP code ▶	

Form **1120S** (1987)

Schedule A — Cost of Goods Sold and/or Operations (See instructions for Schedule A.)

1	Inventory at beginning of year	126,000
2	Purchases	1,127,100
3	Cost of labor	402,000
4a	Additional section 263A costs (attach schedule)	60,000
b	Other costs (attach schedule)	103,300
5	Total—Add lines 1 through 4b	1,818,400
6	Inventory at end of year	298,400
7	Cost of goods sold and/or operations—Subtract line 6 from line 5. Enter here and on line 2, page 1	1,520,000

8a Check all methods used for valuing closing inventory:

(i) ☐ Cost

(ii) ☒ Lower of cost or market as described in Regulations section 1.471-4 (see instructions)

(iii) ☐ Writedown of "subnormal" goods as described in Regulations section 1.471-2(c) (see instructions)

(iv) ☐ Other (Specify method used and attach explanation) ▶ ----------------------------------

b Check this box if the LIFO inventory method was adopted this tax year for any goods (if checked, attach Form 970) . . . . . ☐

c If the LIFO inventory method was used for this tax year, enter percentage (or amounts) of closing inventory computed under LIFO . . . . . **8c** |

d Do the rules of section 263A (with respect to property produced or acquired for resale) apply to the corporation? . . . ☐ Yes ☒ No

e Was there any change (other than for section 263A purposes) in determining quantities, cost, or valuations between opening and closing inventory? (If "Yes," attach explanation.) . . . . . ☐ Yes ☒ No

Additional Information Required

		Yes	No
J	Did you at the end of the tax year own, directly or indirectly, 50% or more of the voting stock of a domestic corporation? (For rules of attribution, see section 267(c).)		X
	If "Yes," attach a schedule showing: (1) Name, address, and employer identification number; (3) Highest amount owed by you to such corporation during the year; and (2) Percentage owned; (4) Highest amount owed to you by such corporation during the year. (Note: For purposes of J(3) and J(4), "highest amount owed" includes loans and accounts receivable/payable.)		
K	Refer to the listing of business activity codes at the end of the Instructions for Form 1120S and state your principal: Business activity ▶ ----------------------- ; Product or service ▶ -----------------------		X
L	Were you a member of a controlled group subject to the provisions of section 1561?		
M	Did you claim a deduction for expenses connected with:		
	(1) Entertainment facilities (boat, resort, ranch, etc.)?		X
	(2) Living accommodations (except for employees on business)?		X
	(3) Employees attending conventions or meetings outside the North American area? (See section 274(h).)		X
	(4) Employees' families at conventions or meetings?		X
	If "Yes," were any of these conventions or meetings outside the North American area? (See section 274(h).)		
	(5) Employee or family vacations not reported on Form W-2?		X
N	At any time during the tax year, did you have an interest in or a signature or other authority over a financial account in a foreign country (such as a bank account, securities account, or other financial account)? (See instructions for exceptions and filing requirements for form TD F 90-22.1.)		X
	If "Yes," enter the name of the foreign country ▶ -----------------------		
O	Were you the grantor of, or transferor to, a foreign trust which existed during the current tax year, whether or not you have any beneficial interest in it? If "Yes," you may have to file Forms 3520, 3520-A, or 926		X
P	During this tax year did you maintain any part of your accounting/tax records on a computerized system?		X
Q	Check method of accounting: (1)☐ Cash (2)☒ Accrual (3)☐ Other (specify) ▶ -----------------------		
R	Check this box if the S corporation has filed or is required to file Form 8264, Application for Registration of a Tax Shelter . . . . ▶☐		
S	Check this box if the corporation issued publicly offered debt instruments with original issue discount . . . . ▶☐ If so, the corporation may have to file Form 8281, Information Return for Publicly Offered Original Issue Discount Instruments.		
T	If section 1374 (new built-in gains tax) applies to the corporation, enter the corporation's net unrealized built-in gain as defined in section 1374(d)(1) (see instructions) ▶		

Designation of Tax Matters Person

The following shareholder is hereby designated as the tax matters person (TMP) for the tax year for which this tax return is filed:

Name of designated TMP ▶	John H. Anders	Identifying number of TMP ▶	458 - 00 - 0327
Address of designated TMP ▶	4340 Holmes Parkway Metro City, Ohio 43704		

Schedule K Shareholders' Shares of Income, Credits, Deductions, etc. (See Instructions.)

	(a) Distributive share items		(b) Total amount
Income (Losses) and Deductions			
1	Ordinary income (loss) from trade or business activity(ies) (page 1, line 21)	1	219,000
2a	Gross income from rental real estate activity(ies).	**2a**	
b	Minus expenses (attach schedule)	**2b**	
c	Balance: net income (loss) from rental real estate activity(ies).	2c	
3a	Gross income from other rental activity(ies)	**3a**	
b	Minus expenses (attach schedule)	**3b**	
c	Balance: net income (loss) from other rental activity(ies)	3c	
4	Portfolio income (loss):		
a	Interest income	4a	4,000
b	Dividend income	4b	16,000
c	Royalty income	4c	
d	Net short-term capital gain (loss) (Schedule D (Form 1120S)).	4d	
e	Net long-term capital gain (loss) (Schedule D (Form 1120S))	4e	
f	Other portfolio income (loss) (attach schedule)	4f	
5	Net gain (loss) under section 1231 (other than due to casualty or theft)	5	
6	Other income (loss) (attach schedule)	6	
7	Charitable contributions (attach schedule)	7	24,000
8	Section 179 expense deduction (attach schedule)	8	
9	Expenses related to portfolio income (loss) (attach schedule) (see instructions)	9	
10	Other deductions (attach schedule)	10	
Credits			
11a	Jobs credit (attach Form 5884)	11a	6,000
b	Low-income housing credit (attach Form 8586)	11b	
c	Qualified rehabilitation expenditures related to rental real estate activity(ies) (attach schedule)	11c	
d	Credits related to rental real estate activity(ies) other than on lines 11b and 11c (attach schedule)	11d	
e	Credit(s) related to rental activity(ies) other than on lines 11b, 11c, and 11d (attach schedule)	11e	
12	Other credits (attach schedule)	12	
Tax Preference and Adjustment Items			
13a	Accelerated depreciation of real property placed in service before 1987	13a	
b	Accelerated depreciation of leased personal property placed in service before 1987	13b	
c	Depreciation adjustment on property placed in service after 1986	13c	
d	Depletion (other than oil and gas)	13d	
e	(1) Gross income from oil, gas, or geothermal properties	13e(1)	
	(2) Gross deductions allocable to oil, gas, or geothermal properties	13e(2)	
f	Other items (attach schedule)	13f	
Investment Interest			
14a	Interest expense on investment debts	14a	3,000
b	(1) Investment income included on lines 4a through 4f, Schedule K	14b(1)	20,000
	(2) Investment expenses included on line 9, Schedule K	14b(2)	
Foreign Taxes			
15a	Type of income		
b	Name of foreign country or U.S. possession		
c	Total gross income from sources outside the U.S. (attach schedule)	15c	
d	Total applicable deductions and losses (attach schedule)	15d	
e	Total foreign taxes (check one): ▶ ☐ Paid ☐ Accrued	15e	
f	Reduction in taxes available for credit (attach schedule)	15f	
g	Other (attach schedule)	15g	
Other Items			
16	Total property distributions (including cash) other than dividend distributions reported on line 18, Schedule K	16	65,000
17	Other items and amounts not included in lines 1 through 16, Schedule K, that are required to be reported separately to shareholders (attach schedule).		
18	Total dividend distributions paid from accumulated earnings and profits contained in other retained earnings (line 26 of Schedule L)	18	

Schedule L — Balance Sheets

Assets	Beginning of tax year (a)	(b)	End of tax year (c)	(d)
1 Cash		14,700		64,514
2 Trade notes and accounts receivable	98,400		83,700	
a Less allowance for bad debts		98,400		83,700
3 Inventories		126,000		298,400
4 Federal and state government obligations		100,000		120,000
5 Other current assets (attach schedule)		26,300		26,300
6 Loans to shareholders				
7 Mortgage and real estate loans				
8 Other investments (attach schedule)		100,000		100,000
9 Buildings and other depreciable assets	272,400		299,400	
a Less accumulated depreciation	88,300	184,100	105,900	193,500
10 Depletable assets				
a Less accumulated depletion				
11 Land (net of any amortization)		20,000		20,000
12 Intangible assets (amortizable only)				
a Less accumulated amortization				
13 Other assets (attach schedule)		14,800		19,300
14 Total assets		684,300		925,714
Liabilities and Shareholders' Equity				
15 Accounts payable		28,500		34,834
16 Mortgages, notes, bonds payable in less than 1 year		4,300		4,300
17 Other current liabilities (attach schedule)		6,800		7,400
18 Loans from shareholders				
19 Mortgages, notes, bonds payable in 1 year or more		176,700		265,180
20 Other liabilities (attach schedule)		200,000		200,000
21 Capital stock				
22 Paid-in or capital surplus			141,000	
23 Accumulated adjustments account			5,000	
24 Other adjustments account				
25 Shareholders' undistributed taxable income previously taxed				
26 Other retained earnings (see instructions)	268,000		268,000	
Check this box if the corporation has subchapter C earnings and profits at the close of the tax year ▶ ☐ (see instructions)				
27 Total retained earnings per books—Combine amounts on lines 23 through 26, columns (a) and (c) (see instructions)		268,000		414,000
28 Less cost of treasury stock		( )		( )
29 Total liabilities and shareholders' equity		684,300		925,714

Schedule M — Analysis of Accumulated Adjustments Account, Other Adjustments Account, and Shareholders' Undistributed Taxable Income Previously Taxed (If Schedule L, column (c), amounts for lines 23, 24, or 25 are not the same as corresponding amounts on line 9 of Schedule M, attach a schedule explaining any differences. See instructions.)

	Accumulated adjustments account	Other adjustments account	Shareholders' undistributed taxable income previously taxed
1 Balance at beginning of year	-0-	-0-	
2 Ordinary income from page 1, line 21	214,000		
3 Other additions	20,000	5,000	
4 Total of lines 1, 2, and 3	234,000	5,000	
5 Distributions other than dividend distributions	65,000	-0-	
6 Loss from page 1, line 21	-0-		
7 Other reductions	33,000	-0-	
8 Add lines 5, 6, and 7	98,000	-0-	
9 Balance at end of tax year—Subtract line 8 from line 4	141,000	5,000	

SCHEDULE K-1
(Form 1120S)

Department of the Treasury
Internal Revenue Service

Shareholder's Share of Income, Credits, Deductions, etc.

For calendar year 1987 or tax year

beginning _____ 1987, and ending _____ 19 ____

▶ For Paperwork Reduction Act Notice, see page 1 of Instructions for Form 1120S.

OMB No. 1545-0130

1987

Shareholder's identifying number ▶	Corporation's identifying number ▶
Shareholder's name, address, and ZIP code John H. Anders 4340 Holmes Parkway Metro City, Ohio 43707	Corporation's name, address, and ZIP code Estex Fabricators, Inc. 482 Winston St. Metro City, Ohio 43704

A (1) Shareholder's percentage of stock ownership for tax year (see instructions for Schedule K-1) . . . . ▶ 45 %

(2) Number of shares owned by shareholder at tax year end . . . . ▶ 4500

B Internal Revenue Service Center where corporation filed its return ▶ Cincinnati, OH

C Tax shelter registration number (see Instructions for Schedule K-1) . . . . ▶

D Did the shareholder materially participate in the trade or business activity(ies) of the corporation? (See instructions for Schedule K-1. Leave the check boxes blank if there are no trade or business activities.) . . . . ☒ Yes ☐ No

E Did the shareholder actively participate in the rental real estate activity(ies) of the corporation? (See instructions for Schedule K-1. Leave the check boxes blank if there are no rental real estate activities.) . . . . ☐ Yes ☐ No

F If (1) question D is checked "No" or income or loss is reported on line 2 or 3 and (2) the shareholder acquired corporate stock after 10/22/86, check here ▶ ☐ and enter the shareholder's weighted percentage increase in stock ownership for 1987 (see instructions for Schedule K-1) . . . . ▶ %

G If question D is checked "No" and any activity referred to in question D was started or acquired by the corporation after 10/22/86, check here ▶ ☐ and enter the date of start up or acquisition in the date space on line 1. Also, if an activity for which income or loss is reported on line 2 or 3 was started after 10/22/86, check the box and enter the start up date in the date space on line 2 or 3.

H If the short tax year shown above was a result of a change in tax year required by section 1378, check here . . . . . ▶ ☐

Caution: Refer to Shareholder's Instructions for Schedule K-1 before entering information from Schedule K-1 on your tax return.

		(a) Distributive share items	(b) Amount	(c) Form 1040 filers enter the amount in column (b) on:
Income (Losses) and Deductions	1	Ordinary income (loss) from trade or business activity(ies). Date:_____	48,550	See Shareholder's Instructions for Schedule K-1 (Form 1120S).
	2	Income or loss from rental real estate activity(ies). Date: _____		
	3	Income or loss from rental activity(ies) other than line 2 above. Date: _____		
	4	Portfolio income (loss):		
	a	Interest	1,800	Sch. B, Part I, line 2
	b	Dividends	1,200	Sch. B, Part II, line 4
	c	Royalties		Sch. E, Part I, line 5
	d	Net short-term capital gain (loss)		Sch. D, line 5, col. (f) or (g)
	e	Net long-term capital gain (loss)		Sch. D, line 12, col. (f) or (g)
	f	Other portfolio income (loss)		(Enter on applicable line of your return.)
	5	Net gain (loss) under section 1231 (other than due to casualty or theft)		Form 4797, line 1
	6	Other income (loss) (attach schedule)		(Enter on applicable line of your return.)
	7	Charitable contributions	10,800	See Form 1040 Instructions.
	8	Section 179 expense deduction (attach schedule)		See Shareholder's Instructions for Schedule K-1 (Form 1120S).
	9	Deductions related to portfolio income (loss) (attach schedule)		
	10	Other deductions (attach schedule)		
Credits	11a	Jobs credit	2,700	Form 5884
	b	Low-income housing credit		Form 8586, line 8
	c	Qualified rehabilitation expenditures related to rental real estate activity(ies) (attach schedule)	/////	See Shareholder's Instructions for Schedule K-1 (Form 1120S).
	d	Credits related to rental real estate activity(ies) other than on lines 11b and 11c (attach schedule)	/////	
	e	Credits related to rental activity(ies) other than on lines 11b, c, and d (attach schedule)	/////	
	12	Other credits (attach schedule)		
Tax Preference and Adjustment Items	13a	Accelerated depreciation of real property placed in service before 1987		Form 6251, line 5a
	b	Accelerated depreciation of leased personal property placed in service before 1987	/////	Form 6251, line 5b
	c	Depreciation adjustment on property placed in service after 1986		Form 6251, line 4g
	d	Depletion (other than oil and gas)		Form 6251, line 5h
	e	(1) Gross income from oil, gas, or geothermal properties		See Form 6251 Instructions.
		(2) Gross deductions allocable to oil, gas, or geothermal properties		See Shareholder's Instructions for Schedule K-1 (Form 1120S)
	f	Other items (attach schedule)		

	(a) Distributive share items			(b) Amount	(c) Form 1040 filers enter the amount in column (b) on:
Investment Interest	**14a**	Interest expense on investment debts		1,350	Form 4952, line 1
	b	**(1)** Investment income included on Schedule K-1, lines 4a through 4f .		9,000	See Shareholder's Instructions for Schedule K-1 (Form 1120S).
		(2) Investment expenses included on Schedule K-1, line 9			
Foreign Taxes	**15a**	Type of income ▶			Form 1116, Check boxes
	b	Name of foreign country or U.S. possession ▶			Form 1116, Part I
	c	Total gross income from sources outside the U.S. (attach schedule) . .			Form 1116, Part I
	d	Total applicable deductions and losses (attach schedule)			Form 1116, Part I
	e	Total foreign taxes (check one): ▶ ☐ Paid ☐ Accrued			Form 1116, Part II
	f	Reduction in taxes available for credit (attach schedule)			Form 1116, Part III
	g	Other (attach schedule)			See Form 1116 Instructions.
Other Items	**16**	Property distributions (including cash) other than dividend distributions reported to you on Form 1099-DIV		29,250	See Shareholder's Instructions for Schedule K-1 (Form 1120S).
	17	Amount of loan repayments for "Loans from Shareholders"			

	18	Properties:	**A**	**B**	**C**	
Property Subject to Recapture of Investment Credit	**a**	Description of property (State whether recovery or non-recovery property. If recovery property, state whether regular percentage method or section 48(q) election used.).				Form 4255, top
	b	Date placed in service .				Form 4255, line 2
	c	Cost or other basis . .				Form 4255, line 3
	d	Class of recovery property or original estimated useful life .				Form 4255, line 4
	e	Date item ceased to be investment credit property				Form 4255, line 8

	19	Supplemental information for lines 1 through 18 that is required to be reported separately to each shareholder (attach additional schedules if more space is needed):
Supplemental Schedules		Tax-exempt interest — $ 2,250
		Nondeductible salaries and wages due to the jobs credit — $ 2,700

Appendix 17
Sample Return

Estex Fabricators, Inc., is the corporation for which the sample return is filled out. Estex is engaged in the business of manufacturing and selling various plastic products. It uses an accrual method of accounting and files its returns on the basis of the calendar year. At the beginning of the year, Estex Fabricators, Inc., made a timely and proper choice to be treated as an S corporation.

Page 1

Line 1. Gross sales for the year totaled $2,010,000 (line 1a), determined on the accrual method of accounting. After subtracting returned goods and allowances of $21,000 (line 1b), net sales of $1,989,000 are entered on line 1c.

Line 2. Cost of goods sold is deducted on line 2. This figure, $1,520,000, is the total brought over from Schedule A (line 7) on page 2.

Line 3. Net sales less cost of goods sold result in gross profit of $470,000.

Line 5. Estex revalued its beginning inventory pursuant to Section 263A with the required adjustment being $1,000.

Line 6. Total income on line 6 is $470,000.

Line 7. The salaries of the company president, vice president, and secretary-treasurer total $70,000 and are included on line 7. Compensation paid to corporate officers must be separated from other salaries and wages and must be entered on line 7 rather than on line 8.

Line 8. Other salaries and wages are entered on line 8a. The entry includes only salaries and wages not included in line 7 and not deducted as part of cost of goods sold. For a manufacturing company such as Estex, this amount represents nonmanufacturing salaries and wages, such as office salaries. Salaries and wages on line 8a are reduced by $6,000, the amount of jobs credit (discussed later) passed through to the shareholders on line 8b.

Line 9. Repairs include only payments for items which do not add to the value of the assets repaired or substantially increase their useful lives. Estex incurred $800 of repairs.

Line 10. Estex uses the specific charge-off method for bad debts. Actual accounts written off during the year total $1,600.

314

Line 11. Rental expense for Estex's office facilities was $9,200 for the year.

Line 12. Deductible taxes totaled $15,000.

Line 13. Interest expense accrued during the year amounted to $24,200. This included interest on debts for business operations only. Interest to carry tax-exempt securities is not included. Interest on the debt to carry investments that produce taxable income is $3,000, shown on line 9 of Schedule K and passed through to the shareholders on Schedule K-1.

Lines 14a and 14b. Depreciation of $17,600 is brought forward from Form 4562, Depreciation and Amortization (not illustrated). The amount on line 14a is reduced by the depreciation claimed on Line 4, other costs, of Schedule A ($12,400). The balance, $5,200, deducted on line 14c, is depreciation on the nonmanufacturing assets used in the business. If Estex has a section 179 deduction, it would not be included here. It is passed through to the shareholders on Schedule K-1.

Line 16. Advertising expenses of $8,700 is entered on line 16.

Line 19. Other ordinary and necessary business deductions totaled $78,300. These included miscellaneous office expenses, sales commissions, legal fees, and so on. A schedule itemizing these expenses must be attached to the return, even though it has not been shown in this example.

Line 20. Total deductions are $251,000.

Line 21. Ordinary income (nonseparately computed income) is $219,000.

Lines 22 through 25. Line 22a is for the tax on excess net passive income. The tax is figured on a worksheet in the Form 1120S instructions. Line 22b is for the tax on capital gains, including any minimum tax. The capital gains tax is figured on Schedule D (Form 1120S). If Estex were liable for the repayment of investment credit that it has claimed before it became an S corporation, it would figure the amount on Form 4255 and include it in the total on 22c. Since none of these taxes apply to Estex, no tax is shown.

Estex did not deposit any tax with Form 7004 and does not have a fuel tax credit. Therefore, Estex has nothing to enter on lines 23a and 23b. There is no tax due or overpayment on line 24 or 25.

The corporation return must be signed manually by the corporate office authorized to sign. Use of the corporate seal is optional.

Page 2

Schedule A. Use Schedule A to report the cost of goods sold. Basically, this figure is beginning inventory plus merchandise bought or produced during the year less ending inventory. Because it is a manufacturer, Estex must account for its costs of manufacturing as part of cost of goods sold. Goods on hand at the beginning of the year were valued at $126,000, using the lower of cost or market valuation method. Cost of goods manufactured during the year is added to beginning inventory. This cost is made up of three components, direct materials, direct labor, and overhead which includes Section 263A. The full absorption method of inventory costing is required for all taxpayers engaged in manufacturing or production operations. Goods on hand at the end of the year were valued at $298,400.

Materials cost of $1,127,100 is listed on line 2 of Schedule A; this includes subcontracted parts as well as raw materials.

Salaries and wages of $402,000 are entered on line 3 of Schedule A. This amount includes wages paid to production-line workers and also the portion of supervisory salaries attributable to actual production of goods. Care should be taken not to deduct payments already on lines 10 or 11 of page 1.

Additional costs required to be included because of the revised rules under Section 263A amounted to $60,000 with this figure being reported on line 4a.

Other costs of $103,300 appear on line 4 of Schedule A. The supporting itemization is not illustrated, but these costs consist basically of factory overhead such as electricity, fuel, water, small tools, and depreciation on production-line machinery. Note that this depreciation, $12,400, represents depreciation on assets used directly in the manufacturing operations of the business.

Estex had goods on hand at the end of the year valued at $298,400 reportable on line 6 of Schedule A.

All applicable questions on line 8 of Schedule A should be answered.

Additional Information. All applicable questions in this section should be answered. Also, indicate the business activity, product, or service and check the appropriate boxes.

Page 3

Schedule K and Schedule K-1 are extremely important parts of Form 1120S. Schedule K summarizes the shareholders' share of the corporation's income, deductions, credits, and so on. Schedule K-1 shows each shareholder's separate share.

Schedule K. On line 1 Estex shows the nonseparately computed income of $219,000 from line 21, page 1.

Line 4 is used to report portfolio items. Estex had the following: taxable interest income of $4,000 reportable on line 4a; taxable dividends of $16,000 reportable on line 4b.

Line 5 is for gains or losses on section 1231 property (other than due to casualty or theft); and line 6 is for other types of separately computed income or loss such as net gains or losses from involuntary conversions due to casualty or theft. Estex has no other income, gains or losses to report on these lines in 1987.

Line 7 is for charitable contributions. During 1987 Estex contributed $11,400 to the United Community Fund and $12,600 to the State University Scholarship Fund. The total of $24,000 is entered after 50% and in the total column on line 7. (It is assumed that the reader knows the differences between 20%, 30% and 50% charities.)

Line 9 is for expenses (other than investment interest) related to portfolio income and (loss) items listed on line 4. Estex had no such expenses.

Line 10 is for other separately computed deductions. Estex has no other deductions that separately pass through to the shareholders.

Line 11a is for the jobs credit. Estex has $6,000 of jobs credit in 1987. The credit was figured on Form 5884. Jobs Credit (not illustrated).

Lines 11b through 11e and 12 are for other credits. Estex has no other credits.

Lines 13a through 13f list the items of tax preference that must be taken into account by each individual shareholder. Estex has none of these items.

Lines 14a and 14b list the items used in the computation of interest on investment indebtedness, which must be taken into account by each individual shareholder. Line 14b is used for investment income. Estex had investment interest of $3,000. Line 14b is used for investment income. Estex had taxable interest from investments (line 4a) totalling $4,000. Estex also had dividends from investments (line 4b) totalling $16,000. Therefore, Estex must enter $20,000 on line 14b. Each shareholder's share of these items must be reported on Schedule K-1.

Line 16 is for distributions other than those reported on line 18. Estex distributed $65,000 in 1987.

Line 17 is for other adjustments that would affect shareholder's bases in their S corporation stock. In 1987, Estex earned $5,000 of tax-exempt interest from state bonds, and had $6,000 of nondeductible salaries and wages due to the jobs credit. A separate schedule (not shown here) is attached to the return to show what the $5,000 and $6,000 consist of.

Schedule K-1. A separate Schedule K-1 is completed by the S corporation for each shareholder.

Generally, shareholders must treat items of income, loss, deduction, credit, etc. on their returns consistent with the way the S corporation reported them on its return. A shareholder who shows the items differently than the way the S corporation reported them on Schedule K-1 should complete Form 8082, (Appendix 12) Notice of Inconsistent Treatment or Amended Return (Administrative Adjustment Request (AAR)).

Copy A of Schedule K-1 for each shareholder should be filed with Form 1120S. Give each shareholder Copy B with attached instructions. Retain Copy C for each shareholder.

Estex must prepare a Schedule K-1 for each shareholder. The illustrated Schedule K-1 is for John H. Anders, who owns 9,000 shares (45%) of the corporation's stock, which he acquired on March 3, 1972. Mr. Anders devotes 100% of his time to the business for which he is compensated $40,000.

Lines 1 through 10 are for each shareholder's distributive share of nonseparately stated income or loss and separately stated income or loss and deductions.

Line 1 shows Mr. Anders' share of nonseparately computed income of $98,550. It makes no difference whether or not this income was distributed to Mr. Anders in 1987. Mr. Anders must report $98,550 on Schedule E (Form 1040) when he files his individual income tax return, Form 1040.

Line 4 is for portfolio income and (loss) items. Mr. Anders' share of interest income is $1,800 and his share of dividend income is $7,200.

Line 7 is for Mr. Anders' share of Estex's charitable contributions for 1987. His share is $10,800. Because all of Estex's contributions were given to public charities, they qualify for the 50% limitation.

Lines 11 and 12 are for each shareholder's distributive share of credits.

Line 11a is for the jobs credit. Mr. Anders share of Estex's job credit is $2,700.

Line 12 is for other credits that Estex did not have in 1987.

Line 13a through 13f are for tax preference and adjustment items.

Line 14a shows Mr. Anders' share of Estex's investment interest expense, $1,350 (45% × $3,000). Investment interest expense is that part of Estex's total interest that is for loans made to carry its investment. Line 14b(1) shows Mr. Anders' share of Extex's investment income $9,000 ($20,000 × 45%). This represents Extex's income from ordinary dividends and interest, but does not include interest on municipal bond investments, which is tax-exempt.

Lines 15a through 15g are used for reporting foreign taxes. Shareholders of an S corporation decide individually whether to claim a deduction or a credit for foreign income taxes.

Lines 16 through 17 are for other items that affect a shareholder's basis in the stock of an S corporation.

Line 16 is for distributions paid during the year other than those paid from accumulated earnings and profits and reported on Form 1099. During 1987, Estex distributed $65,000. Mr. Anders' share of the distribution was $29,250.

Lines 18a through 18e are for information concerning each shareholder's share of properties that may be subject to a recapture of investment credit. Since this only applies to investment credit taken by a shareholder, it does not apply to Estex this year.

Line 19 is for other items that would affect a shareholder's basis in S corporation stock such as nontaxable income, nondeductible expenses, etc. In 1987 Estex had $5,000 of tax-exempt interest from state bonds and $6,000 of nondeductible salaries and wages due to the jobs credit.

Mr. Anders' share of the tax-exempt interest and the nondeductible salaries and wages was $2,250 and $2,700 respectively.

Page 4

Schedule L. Comparative balance sheets for the beginning and end of the tax year must be shown on Schedule L. Entries on this page should agree with amounts shown elsewhere on the return. For example, the figures for beginning and ending inventories must be the same as those appearing in the analysis of cost of goods sold.

In addition, the figures on the balance sheet for the beginning of the tax year will normally agree with the balance sheet figures for the end of the last taxable year.

Schedule M. Schedule M shows the accounts affecting shareholders bases in S corporation stock and the taxability of distributions from the corporation.

The first column is the accumulated adjustments account. For an S corporation's first year beginning after 1982, the initial balance in the account is zero. Estex enters zero on line 1. Estex's ordinary income for 1987 (page 1, line 21) is $219,000. Estex enters on line 3 $20,000 (16,000 dividends plus $4,000 interest). Line 4 is $239,00, the total of lines 2 and 3. Estex enters its $65,000 distribution on line 5. Estex has no losses in 1987, so line 6 is zero. On line 7, it enters $33,000. This is made up of $3,000 interest on a loan to carry investments, a $6,000 reduction in salaries and wages due to the jobs credit, and $24,000 of charitable contributions. Line 8 is the total of lines 5, 6, and 7, or $98,000. Line 9 is line 4 less line 8, $141,000.

The second column is the other adjustments account and is for other items, such as tax-exempt income and related expenses. For 1987, the balance at the beginning of the year, line 1, is zero. Estex had $5,000 of tax-free interest income from state bonds. This amount is entered on line 3.

The total of lines 1, 2, and 3, $5,000, is entered on line 4. Because the total distributions, other than dividends, did not exceed the balance in the accumulated adjustments account, none of the distribution is applied to the other adjustments account. Estex enters zero on lines 7 and 8. The balance in the other adjustments account at the end of the year, line 9, is $5,000.

The third column is for undistributed taxable income that was included in shareholders' income for years that began before 1987. Since this is Estex's first year as an S corporation, there are no entries in this column.

Tables

I. Table Setting Forth in General Terms the Method of Computing S Corporation Income and Expenses

The taxable income of an S corporation is figured like the taxable income of an individual, with the following differences.

1. Any items of income (including tax-exempt income), loss, deduction, or credit, the separate treatment of which could affect the tax liability of any shareholder, must be separately stated and passed through to the shareholder.

2. The following items that may be claimed by an individual may not be claimed by an S corporation:
    a. The deduction for personal exemptions
    b. The deduction for certain taxes paid or accrued to foreign countries and U.S. possessions
    c. The deduction for charitable contributions
    d. The net operating loss deduction
    e. The depletion deduction for oil and gas wells
    f. Expenses for the production of income
    g. Medical expenses
    h. Alimony
    i. The deduction for taxes, interest, and business depreciation by a cooperative housing corporation tenant-stockholder
    j. Moving expenses
    k. The deduction for payments to an IRA

3. The S corporation may claim the deduction for corporate organizational costs.

Separately Stated Items. The items of income, loss, expense, and credit that are to be separately stated are those items whose separate treatment on the shareholder's income tax return, as opposed to treating the item as a part of a lump amount, could affect the shareholder's tax liability.

The list of items that are to be separately stated includes, but is not limited to

---

For a discussion of this table, see Chapter 4.1.B.

1. Short-term capital gains and losses
2. Long-term capital gains and losses
3. Gains and losses from sales and exchanges of property used in a trade or business and involuntary conversions
4. Charitable contributions
5. The Section 179 deduction
6. Tax-exempt income
7. Wagering gains and losses
8. Exploration costs for new mineral deposits
9. Interest expense on investments
10. Certain taxes paid or accrued to foreign countries and to U.S. possessions
11. Items used in figuring depletion on S corporation oil and gas properties
12. Soil and water conservation costs the corporation elects to expense
13. Intangible drilling and development costs the corporation elects to expense

Nonseparately Computed Income or Loss. Nonseparately computed income or loss is all items of gross income of the S corporation minus all items of deduction allowed the S corporation, except the items that are separately stated.

Reducing Pass-throughs. If the corporation is subject to the capital gains tax, the minimum tax, or the tax on excess net passive income, it must reduce the amount of the related pass-through items.

If the corporation is subject to the tax on excess net passive income, it must reduce each item of passive investment income by an amount that bears the same ratio to the amount of tax on excess net passive income as the amount of each item of passive investment income bears to the total passive investment income for the tax year.

II. Table of Internal Revenue Code Sections

Section	Text Location
1	1.2.E; 9.3
1(g)	4.1.A
1(j)	4.1.A
6(d)	5.6.B
11	1.2.E.1; 6.2.F
11(b)	4.9.B; 6.4.B
11(c)	5.7.D
30(f)	2.6
38	3.6.H
39	3.6.H
47	9.14
48(q)(6)	7.2.B.4; 7.4(4)
52(a)	2.6
55	1.3.B
55(d)(2)	1.2.E.ii; endnote 10
56	6.2.F
56(f)(1)	1.2.E.2
57(a)(5)(C)(1)	1.2.E.2
57(a)(9)(B)	6.2.F
58(d)	6.2.G
63(a)	6.4.G
67	5.15
72	6.4.C.6
74	6.7.B.2.a; 6.7(i)
67	5.15
79	5.6
101	5.6
101(b)	5.6.A
101–133	4.1.B
105	5.6

Section	Text Location
106	5.6
108(d)(7)	4.10.A
108(d)(7)(A)	4.10.A
108(d)(7)(B)	4.10.A
108(d)(7)(C)	4.10.B
119	5.6
162	5.5
163	5.5; 7.9.A.4.C
163(d)	5.2; 8.3.G.1
163(d)(1)	5.2
163(d)(4)(A)	5.2
163(d)(4)(B)	5.2
163(d)(4)(E)	7.9.M
163(d)(5)(A)	5.2
163(d)(5)(A)(ii)	5.2
163(d)(6)	5.2
163(h)(1)	5.7.B; 5.14
164	5.5
165	7.9.G
165(g)	7.6
166(d)	7.6
168(e)(4)(A)(i)	8.5.C
170	5.3
170(b)(2)	1.3.D; 5.3
170(e)(3)(A)	1.3.D; 5.3
170(e)(4)(D)	1.3.D; 5.3
172	3.6.H; 6.2.F.1; 6.4.E
179	4.1.B; 5.9; 6.4.E; 8.5.C
179(b)(2)	5.9
179(b)(3)	5.9
179(b)(3)(B)	5.9
179(d)(2)(A)	8.5.C
179(d)(8)	5.9
183	5.5; 5.11; 7.5
183(d)	5.11
212	5.5
213	5.6.A
241–250	6.4.E

Section	Text Location
243	1.2.E.2; 6.2.F.1; 9.9.A
247	6.2.F.1
248	5.8
249	6.2.F.1
250	6.2.F.1
267	1.5.C; 5.12
267(a)	5.12.B
267(a)(1)	5.12; 5.12.A; 8.5
267(a)(2)	1.5.A; 5.12.B
267(b)	1.5.A; 5.12.B
267(b)(10)	5.12.A.2
267(b)(11)	5.12.A.2
267(b)(12)	5.12.A.2
267(c)	5.12.A.2
267(c)(1)	5.12.A.2
267(e)	1.5.A; 5.12.B
267(d)	5.12.A.3
267(e)(1)(B)(ii)	5.12.B
267(f)(1)	5.12.A.2
267(f)(2)	5.12
269	1.3.A
280A	5.13
280A(c)(5)	5.13
280A(f)(2)	5.13
301	10.9
301(d)	8.5.B
302	10.9
302(a)	8.3.B.4
303(a)	8.3.B.4
311	4.1.B
312–316	4.9; 6.4.C.5; 6.5.A; 10.4.A
312(a)(3)	8.5.D
318	2.2.B; 5.6.A
318(a)(1)(A)(ii)	4.7.B
318(a)(2)(B)	4.7.B
332	10.10.D
333	10.10; 10.10.C
334(b)(2)	2.5.A.2.a

Section	Text Location
336	6.7.B.2; 10.8
337	2.5.A.2.a; 3.3.B; 6.2.E; 6.4.D; 6.7.B.2; 9.12.A; 9.20.A; 10.8; 10.9; 10.10.A
337(c)(1)(B)	10.10.C
338	2.5.A.2.a; 3.3.B; 6.7.B.2; 10.8.C.4; 10.10; 10.10.B
338(a)	2.5.A.2.a
341	10.8.B
351	7.2.B.1; 7.2.B.5.i; 7.9.K; 9.14
354	4.8.A; 4.1.B; 6.4.D; 8.5.A
355	4.8.A; 6.5.A; 8.5.A
356	4.8.A; 8.5.A
361	6.4.D
368	4.9.A; 10.11.A
368(a)(1)(A)	10.11.A; 10.11.B
368(a)(1)(B)	10.11.C
368(a)(1)(C)	10.11.C
368(a)(1)(D)	10.11.D
368(a)(1)(E)	10.11.E
368(a)(1)(F)	10.11.F
368(a)(1)(A)	10.11.A
368(a)(2)(D) and (E)	10.11.G
381(a)	1.5.A
381(c)(2)	4.9.A
381(c)(4)	1.5.A
401	2.6; 5.7
410	2.6
444	1.4; 3.5.D
453	6.2.C.3; 6.4.D
453(d)	4.1.B
453A	6.2.C.3
465	5.10; 7.2.B.5.d
465(a)	5.10
465(a)(1)(B)	5.10
469	1.2.E; 1.3.A; 5.16.A; 6.4.A; 7.9.A
469(b)	7.9.B
469(a)(1)	7.9.A.1

Section	Text Location
469(c)	7.9.A.4
469(c)(1)	7.9.A.4
469(c)(2)	6.4.B; 7.9.A.4.a
469(c)(3)	7.9.A.2
469(c)(3)(A)	7.9.A.2
469(c)(4)	7.9.A.2
469(d)(1)	7.9.B
469(e)	7.9.A
469(e)(1)	7.9.C
469(e)(1)(A)(i)(II) and (III)	7.9.A.4.b; 7.9(ii)
469(f)(1)	7.9.H
469(g)	7.9.A; 7.9.K
469(g)(1)	7.9.G
469(g)(1)(A)	7.9.G
469(g)(2)	7.9.I
469(g)(3)	7.9.G
469(h)	7.9.A.4.a
469(h)(2)	7.9.A.4.a
469(i)(6)	7.9.D
469(j)(4)	7.9.B
469(j)(6)	7.9.J
469(j)(8)	7.9.D
482	2.6.A; 4.1.B; 6.4.D
483	6.4.C.4
531	8.6.A
535	9.9.A; 10.7.B
541	1.3.C
543	6.4.C.5
543(b)(3)	6.4.C.2.a.; (6.4Ci)
551	6.4.C.5
565	6.4.C.5
585(a)(2)	2.8
593	2.8
617	7.1.D
631(b) and (c)	6.4.C.3
651(a)	2.3.B.2.e
671–677	2.3.B.2.a; (ii)

Section	Text Location
678	2.3.B.2; 2.3.B.2.d; 3.3.J
703(a)(2)(E)	5.5
704	9.10.A.1
704(b)	1.1
704(e)(3)	1.2.D
707(b)(1)	1.5.A; 5.12.B
806(e)	1.4.B
806(e)(2)(C)	1.4.B
901	7.1.D
1001(a)	10.8.A
1012	7.2.D.3.a
1031	6.4.D; 7.9.K
1033	4.3
1066	5.2
1201(a)	6.2.F.2
1231	4.1.A; 4.5; 4.5.B; 4.6.B; 4.8; 7.1; 7.2.2; 7.2.3; 10.8
1231(c)	4.5.B
1239	4.7; 4.8; 8.5.B
1239(b)	4.7.B
1239(b)(1)	4.7.B
1239(d)	4.7.B
1244	7.2.B.5.d; 9.13; 10.8
1245	8.5.B; 9.14; 10.8.C.3
1250	8.5.B; 9.14; 10.8.C.3
1256	6.4.C.6
1256(e)(3)(B)	1.5.A
1271(a)(1)	7.2.E; 9.19
1273	6.4.C.4
1283	6.4.C.4
1361	2.5; 6.7.B.2; 9.11.B; 10.5
1361(b)	2.1; 2.2; 2.2.C; 2.9; 2.3.A
1361(b)(1)	2.3.A; 2.7; 2.9.B
1361(b)(1)(A)	9.11.A.1
1361(b)(1)(B)	2.3.B.1; 2.3.B.2; 2.4.C; 2.4.D; 10.7.A.2
1361(b)(1)(C)	2.4.A
1361(b)(1)(D)	2.9; 10.5; 10.11.E
1361(b)(2)	2.8; 9.9

Section	**Text Location**
1361(b)(2)(A)	2.5; 2.9.A; 10.10.B
1361(c)	2.9.B
1361(c)(1)	2.1.F; 3.3.D
1361(c)(1)(A)(i)	2.3.B.2.b; 2.3(ii)
1361(c)(1)(A)(iv)	2.3.B.2.a; 2.3(i)
1361(c)(2)(A)	2.4.B
1361(c)(2)(A)(i)	2.3.B.2.d
1361(c)(2)(A)(ii)	2.3.B.2.b; 2.3.b.2.d.; 10.10.a.1
1361(c)(2)(A)(iii)	2.3.b.2.c; 10.10.A.1
1361(c)(2)(A)(iv)	2.3.B.2
1361(c)(2)(A)	2.4.B; 6.7.B.2.a; 6.7(i)
1361(c)(2)(A)(iii)	9.11.A.1
1361(c)(2)(B)(iii)	3.3.I
1361(c)(2)(B)(iv)	3.3.G
1361(c)(3)	2.3.E
1361(c)(4)	2.9.A
1361(c)(5)	2.9.B.2; 9.15
1361(c)(5)(A)	2.9.B.2
1361(c)(6)	2.5.A.1; 2.5.A.1.b
1361(d)	2.3.C
1361(d)(1)	2.3.D; 10.1
1361(d)(2)(D)	2.3.D
1362	10.8.D.1
1362(a)	8.6
1362(a)(2)	3.1.A
1362(b)(1)(B)	3.1.A.2
1362(b)(2)(B)(i)	2.5; 3.1.A.3
1362(b)(2)(B)(ii)	3.1.A
1362(b)(4)	3.1.A.2
1362(d)	3.2; 6.4.B; 8.5; 10.6
1362(d)(1)	10.2; 10.3; 10.5
1362(d)(1)(c)	10.1.B.1; 10.1.C
1362(d)(1)(c)(i)	10.1.B.1
1362(d)(1)(c)(ii)	10.1.B.1
1362(d)(1)(B)	10.1.B.2
1362(d)(2)(B)	10.3; 10.11.B
1362(d)(1)(D)	10.1.B.2; 10.1.C; 10.7
1362(d)(2)	9.11.A.1; 10.3; 10.3.A; 10.5; 10.6

Section	Text Location
1362(d)(3)	3.6.E; 4.9.B; 6.4.B; 6.4.C; 6.4.C.1; 6.4.C.2.a; 6.4.C.7; 6.4.D; 6.4.K; 6.5; 8.3.G; 10.4; 10.5; 10.6
1362(d)(3)(A)	10.4
1362(d)(3)(A)(ii)	10.4
1362(d)(3)(A)(iii)	10.4
1362(d)(3)(B)	10.4.A
1362(d)(3)(D)	6.4.H.2
1362(d)(3)(i)	6.4.B; 6.5.B
1362(d)(3)(D)(1)	6.4.C.1; 6.4.C.2
1362(d)(3)(D)(i)	6.4.C.7; 6.5.A
1362(d)(3)(D)(ii)	6.4.C.4
1362(d)(3)(D)(iv)	6.4.C.2; 6.4.C.7
1362(d)(3)(D)(v)	6.4.C.2; 6.4.C.7
1362(e)(1)(A)	10.7
1362(e)(2)	10.7; 10.7.A; 10.7.C; 10.8.A; 10.8.D
1362(e)(3)	7.1.B.2; 10.7.A; 10.7.A.2
1362(e)(3)(D)	10.8.G
1362(e)(5)	10.7.A
1362(e)(6)(C)	10.7.A
1362(e)(6)(B)	10.7.A.1; 10.11.B.1
1362(e)(6)(D)	7.1.B.3; 10.7.A; 10.7.C
1362(f)	3.4; 10.1; 10.3; 10.5; 10.11.B.1
1362(f)(1)	10.1
1362(g)	3.1.A.4; 10.1; 10.5; 10.6; 10.11.B.1; 10.11.D.2
1363	6.2.G
1363(b)	4.1.B; 6.2.F.2
1363(b)(2)	3.6.F; 5.5; 5.6.A
1363(b)(3)	5.8
1363(c)	7.1.D
1363(c)(1)	4.3; 5.9
1363(c)(2)	4.3
1363(d)	4.8; 8.5; 8.5.A; 8.5.C; 9.19
1363(e)	4.8.B; 8.5.A
1363(f)	3.6.I; 6.7.B.2
1363(e)(3)(B)	10.7.A
1366	4.5.B; 4.8; 5.4.B; 9.12.B
1366(a)(1)	4.1.A; 7.1; 7.1.B; 7.1.E; 8.2

Section	Text Location
1366(a)(1)(A)	1.3.D; 5.2; 5.4
1366(a)(1)(B)	8.2
1366(d)	7.2.A; 7.3; 7.4.A
1366(d)(1)	5.3; 7.4.A
1366(d)(2)	7.4.B; 7.7
1366(d)(3)	7.4.B; 7.4.C; 9.19
1366(e)	1.2.D; 9.3
1366(f)(2)	6.2.H
1366(f)(2)(B)	6.2.H
1366(f)(3)	6.4.J
1367	7.2.C; 7.2.D.3; 7.3.A; 8.3.D
1367(a)	8.3.B.5; 8.3(5)
1367(a)(1)	7.2.B.2; 8.3.B
1367(a)(1)(A)	7.2.B.2
1367(a)(1)(B)	7.2.B.2; 8.2
1367(a)(2)	5.16.A; 7.2.B.5.b; 8.2
1367(a)(2)(A)	7.2.B.3
1367(a)(2)(B)	7.2.B.3; 7.2.C
1367(a)(2)(C)	7.2.B.3; 8.2.C
1367(a)(2)(D)	7.2.B.3
1367(a)(2)(E)	7.2.B.3
1367(b)(1)	7.2.B.5
1367(b)(2)	7.3.A
1367(b)(2)(A)	7.2.C; 7.2.D.3.a
1367(b)(2)(B)-(E)	7.2.C; 7.2.D.3.b
1367(b)(3)	7.6
1368	5.4.B; 5.16.A; 5.16.B; 8.2
1368(a)(1)	8.2
1368(a)(1)(A)	10.11.B.2
1368(b)	8.2
1368(b)(1) and (2)	8.2; 8.2.C
1368(c)	8.3.C
1368(c)(1)	8.3.B
1368(c)(3)	8.3.F; 8.3.G
1368(d)	4.8
1368(d)(1)	8.2
1368(e)(1)	8.3.B
1368(e)(1)(A)	8.3.B; 8.3.D
1368(e)(1)(B)	8.3.B.4

Section	Text Location
1368(e)(2)	8.3.B
1368(e)(3)	3.6.E; 4.9.C; 6.4.K; 8.2; 8.3.G; 10.4.A
1368(f)(3)	6.4.J
1371	3.3.D
1371(a)(1)	10.11.A
1371(b)(1)	3.6.H
1371(b)(3)	3.6.H
1371(c)(1)	4.9.A; 8.2
1371(c)(2)	4.9.A; 4.9.D.3; 8.3.A
1371(d)(1)	3.6.C
1371(d)(2)	3.6.C; 6.1; 6.3; 9.17.A
1371(d)(3)	8.3.A; 8.6.A
1371(e)	7.4.C.1; 10.7.A.3
1371(e)(1)	8.6
1371(e)(2)	8.6.A
1372	5.6.A; 6.4.C.2; 6.4.C.4; 6.4.C.7; 10.6
1372(b)	5.6.A.1
1372(a)(1)	5.6.A
1372(a)(2)	5.6.A
1372(b)	5.6.A.1
1374	1.3.B; 3.6.G; 4.8; 4.8.B; 6.1; 6.2.B.1; 6.2.B.2; 6.2.C; 6.2.C.3; 6.2.F.2; 6.2.F.3; 6.7; 6.7.B.2; 8.5.B; 9.12.A.1
1374(2)	6.7.B.2
1374(a)	3.6.G; 6.2.B.2; 6.2.C.2; 6.2.E; 6.2.F; 6.2.F.1; 6.2.F.2; 6.7.B
1374(a)(1)	6.2.B.2
1374(a)(2)	6.2.B.2
1374(b)	6.2.F.1; 6.2.G.1; 6.2.G.2; 6.2.H
1374(b)(1)	6.2.F.1; 6.7.B.2
1374(b)(2)	6.2.F.1; 6.7.F.2
1374(b)(3)(B)	6.7.B.2
1374(c)	6.2.F.1; 7.8
1374(c)(1)	6.2.D.1; 6.7.B
1374(c)(2)	6.2.D.1; 6.7.B.2
1374(e)(2)(A)	6.7.B.2
1374(c)(3)	6.2.D.1; 6.2.F.2
1374(d)	6.4.H

Section	**Text Location**
1374(d)(2)	6.7.B.2
1374(d)(4)	6.4.G
1375	4.6; 4.8; 4.9.B; 5.16.B; 6.1; 6.2.F.3; 6.4.B; 6.4.C; 6.4.C.2; 6.4.C.2.b; 6.4.D; 6.4.E; 6.4.F; 6.4.G; 6.4.H; 6.4.J; 6.5.A; 8.3; 9.17.A; 10.4
1375(a)(1)	6.4.H
1375(a)(1)	6.4.B
1375(a)(2)	6.4.B
1375(b)(1)(A)	6.4.F
1375(b)(1)(B)	6.4.G; 6.4.H
1375(b)(2)	6.4.B; 6.4.E
1375(c)(1)	6.4.H.1
1375(c)(2)	6.2.F.3; 6.4.H.2
1375(d)	6.4.H.2.a; 8.4
1375(f)	8.4
1377(a)(1)	7.1; 10.8.G
1377(a)(2)	10.7.A.2; 10.8.D; 10.8.G
1377(b)(1)	8.6
1377(b)(2)	8.6
1377(b)(1)(A)	8.6
1377(b)(1)(B)	8.6
1377(b)(2)	8.6
1378	1.4.B.3; 6.2.A
1378(b)	1.4.B
1379(c)	8.4
1401	5.16.B
1402	7.9.A.4.a
1504	2.5
1561	2.6.A; 5.7.D; 6.2.F.1; 10.7.B
1563(a)	2.6
2010	9.11.B
2036(C)	9.11.A.c
2056(b)(7)	9.11.A.1
2503(b)	2.3.B.e; 9.11.B
4975	3.6.A
4975(c)(1)(B)	5.7.B
4975(d)	5.7.B
6062	3.5

Section	Text Location
6037	9.17.A; 10.2
6221–6233	9.17; 9.18.A
6229(a)	9.18.A
6241–6245	7.2.B.5.a; 9.18
6242	9.18.A
6501(a)	9.17.A
6501(e)	9.17.A
6661A	2.3.B.1
6661(b)(2)(C)(ii)	1.5.A
7502	3.4
7519	1.4.B; 3.5.D
7872	9.15

III. Table of Tax Reform Act of 1986 Sections

Section	Text Location
633(d)	4.8.B; 6.2.D.1; 6.7.A.2; 10.10.A.1
633(d)(3)	10.10.A.1
633(d)(5)	10.10.A.1
801	1.5.A

IV. Table of Treasury Regulations

Regulation	Text Location
Reg. Section 1.47-4	9.14
Reg. Section 1.47-4(a)	9.14
Reg. Section 1.47-4(a)(1)	10.7.B.1.c
Reg. Section 1.47-4(a)(2)	10.7.B.1.c; 10.8.C.2
Reg. Section 1.47-4(d)	9.14
Prop. Treas. Reg. Section 1.179-1(f)(2)	5.9; endnote 8
Prop. Treas. Reg. Section 1.179-1(h)	5.9; endnote 7
Reg. Section 1.248-1(b)(3)(i)	5.8; endnote 6
Reg. Section 1.267(d)-1(b)	5.12.A.3
Reg. Section 1.267(d)-1(c)(3)	5.12.A.3
Prop. Reg. Section 1.280A-1(e)(1)	5.13
Prop. Reg. Section 1.280A-1(e)(5)	5.13
Temp. Reg. Section 1.469-2T	7.9.A.4.a; N
Temp. Reg. Section 1.469-5T(a)	7.9.A.4.a; D
Temp. Reg. Section 1.469-11T	7.9.C
Reg. Section 1.355-2(c)	10.11.D.1
Reg. Section 1.404(a)-1(b)	5.7.C
Prop. Reg. Section 1.414(b)(1)-(a)	5.7.D
Prop. Reg. Section 1.465-10(d)	5.10
Reg. Section 1.543-1(b)(5)(i)	6.4.C.7
Reg. Section 1.704-1(d)	7.5
Reg. Section 1.1001-2	7.2.E
Temp. Reg. Section 18.1361-1	2.3.D
Temp. Reg. Section 18.1362-1(a)	3.1.A.1; 3.4; 3.5
Temp. Reg. Section 18.1362-2(a)	3.1.A.1; endnote 4
Temp. Reg. Section 18.1362-2(b)(2)	2.2.F; 3.3.B; 3.3.C; 3.3.E; 3.3.F; 3.3.J; endnotes 7, 14
Temp. Reg. 18.1362-3	10.2
Treas. Reg. Section 1.1371-1(b)	2.7
Reg. Section 1.1371-1(c)(1)	2.5; endnote 19
Reg. Section 1.1371-1(c)(2)(ii)	2.5.A.1; endnote 22
Reg. Section 1.1371-1(d)(1)	2.3(d) endnotes 4; 6; 15; 16

Regulation	Text Location
Reg. Section 1.1371-1(d)(2)	3.3.D; endnote 8
Reg. Section 1.1371-1(d)(2)(i)	2.2.F; endnote 8
Proposed Reg. Section 1.1371-1(d)(3)	2.3.B.2
Reg. Section 1.1371-1(g)	2.9.B; endnote 36
Reg. Section 1.1372-1(c)	10.10.A; endnote 14
Reg. Section 1.1372-3(a)	2.2.F; endnote 7
Reg. Section 1.1372-4(b)(3)	10.3
Reg. Section 1.1372-4(b)(5)(vi)	6.4.C.2; 6.4.C.2.a, endnote 17; 6.4.C.2.b
Reg. Section 1.1372-4(b)(5)(vii)	6.4.C.5
Reg. Section 1.1372-4(b)(5)(viii)	6.4.C.4
Reg. Section 1.1372-4(b)(5)(ix)	6.4.C.6
Reg. Section 1.1372-4(b)(5)(x)	6.4.C.7
Reg. Section 1.1372-4(b)(iv)	6.4.D
Reg. Section 1.1372-4(b)(5)(iv)	6.4.D
Reg. Section 1.1372-4(b)(5)(iv)(b)	6.4.D
Reg. Section 1.1372-5(a)	10.6
Reg. Section 1.1372-5(b)	10.6
Reg. Section 1.1375-1(d)	4.6.B
Reg. Section 1.1375-1A(d)(2)	6.4.G
Reg. Section 1.1376-2(a)(2)	7.3.A
Reg. Section 1.1376-2(a)(2)(ii)	7.3.A
Reg. Section 1.1376-2(a)(3)	7.3.A
Reg. Section 1.1378-2(b)(2)	6.2.C.3
Reg. Section 1.1402(a)-1(b)	5.16.B; endnote 12
Reg. Section 1.1563-1(b)(2)(ii)(c)	6.2.F.2; endnote 10
Reg. Section 1.6037(b)	9.17.A
Reg. Section 1.6037-1(c)	9.17.A

V. Table of Cases

Case	Text Location
Allison, William M., Estate of	2.9.B, endnote 37
Arrowsmith v. *Comm.*	4.4.B, endnote 10
Auld, Finley G.	3.3.M, endnote 15
Bank of Winnfield & Trust Co. v. *U.S.*	2.6, endnote 32
Barnes Motor & Parts Co. v. *U.S.*	2.5, endnote 17
Barr, Bernard	7.2.E, endnote 9
Bell, III, William H.	2.6; endnote 32
Bianchi	5.7.C, endnote 5
Braun	9.3, endnote 1
Bresler, David	4.4.B, endnote 12
Brutsche v. *Comm.*	3.1.A.1, endnote 6
Brutsche, Ralph L.	4.1.B, endnote 8
Bunnel, Robert L.	9.17.A, endnote 9
Cain	9.11.A.1.c
Campbell, T. H., & Bros., Inc.	3.1, endnote 1
Carmelo v. *Ofria*	4.6.B.2
Charbonnet v. *U.S.*	9.14, endnote 8
Corn Products Ref Co. v. *Comm.*	4.49.B, endnote 11
Cromer, Gary H.	5.16.C
Crook, William H.	5.2
Davis, Edwin D.	1.2.D; 5.16.C
Dean, Walter K., Estate of	4.6.B
Diecks, C. A., Estate of	10.8.C.3; endnote 10
Dessauer v. *Comm.*	4.1.B, endnote 6
Farm Equip. Co. v. *U.S.*	3.1
Feingold v. *Comm.*	6.4.C.2.a, endnote 19
Forrester, Homer W.	3.3.D, endnote 13
Gamon, W. C.	2.9.B.2, endnote 42
George v. *Buono*	4.6.B.2
Gonzalez v. *Heckler*	9.6
Guzowski, Ray	2.4.C, endnote 15
Harbour Properties, Inc.	7.2.E

Case	Text Location
Harrison, Lucille M.	4.1.B, endnote 9
Hennessey, Robert A.	4.1.B, endnote 5
Henry, T. J., Associates	1.2.A; 10.2.B.2, endnote 3
Hoffman, Albert N.	10.2.B.1; endnote 2
Imler, Joseph W.	10.9.B
Johnston, Stedwell	4.1.B, endnote 7
Kling, Frederick J.	2.4.C; endnote 14
La Mastro	5.7.C
Leonhart, William H.	1.5.B; endnote 16
Llewellyn v. *Comm.*	6.4.C.4, endnote 34
Lober v. *U.S.*	1.2, endnote 3
McClelland Farm Equipment Co. v. *U.S.*	3.1, endnote 1
McIlhinney v. *Comm.*	6.4.C.2.a; endnote 22
Mitchell Offset Plate Serv., Inc.	3.4, endnote 17
Merrit Sr. v. *Comm.*	5.12.A.3; endnote 10
Meyer Papermaster v. *U.S.*	7.8
Modern Home Fire & Casualty Insurance Co.	1.3; endnote 11
Mora, Ray	3.1, endnote 1; 3.4, endnote 18
Nielsen Co., August F.	2.9.B
Novell, Sam	2.9.B; 7.2.E
Ober, Wesley A.	3.1, endnote 3
Old Virginia Brick Co., Inc.	2.3.B.1, endnote 9
Pacific Coast Music Jobbers, Inc.	3.3.N, endnote 16
Payne, Albert H.	5.11
Poulter, Frank E.	10.2.B.1, endnote 2
Qualley, Olive E.	2.5; endnotes 17, 19
Rocco v. *Comm.*	5.16.C
Rowland v. *U.S.*	3.1, endnote 1
Sauvigne, Donald J.	7.5
Selfe v. *U.S.*	7.2.D.1
Selig v. *U.S.*	9.10
Shea, John F., Estate of	4.4.B, endnote 12
St. Paul Fire & Marine Ins. Co. v. *Cox*	9.5.B, endnote 2
Stinnett, Jr., James L.	2.9.B, endnotes 36, 37
Trucks, Inc. v. *U.S.*	1.2.D
Warrensburg Board & Paper Corp.	6.2.B, endnotes 3, 11
Weiss v. *Comm.*	1.5.B, endnote 16
Wiebusch, George W.	7.2.D.3.c
Zenz v. *Quinlivan*	10.8.E

VI. Table of Revenue Rulings

Ruling	Text Location	Ruling	Text Location
59-221	5.16.B	75-144	7.2.D.1
64-162	7.2.E	75-349	6.4.C.2.b, endnote 27
64-232	6.4.C.2.b, endnote 24	76-48	6.4.C.2.a, endnote 20
64-250	10.11.F	76-23	2.3.B.1, endnote 10
65-40	6.4.C.2.b, endnote 8	76-223	2.3.B
65-83	6.4.C.2.b, endnote 25	76-347	10.10.C
66-116	3.3.B	76-363	1.3.A, endnote 11
66-226	2.2.D, endnote 5	77-220	2.2.A.1; 2.4.C
68-227	3.3.B	78-89	10.10.A, endnote 14
68-537	7.2.E	78-275	10.6
69-125	7.2.D.1	78-307	6.4.C.2.a, endnote 18
70-50	7.2.D.1	78-333	10.6
70-271	7.2.E	78-390	2.2.A.1
71-287	3.3.B, endnote 12	79-10	5.7.D
71-407	6.4.C.3, endnote 32	81-47	6.4.C.2.b
71-455	6.4.D, endnote 35	81-187	7.2.G.5.c
71-522	2.9.A.1.c	81-197	6.4.C.2.b, endnote 29
71-549	10.6, endnote 6	84-161	2.9.A.1.a,c
72-230	10.11.D	85-68	5.7.D
73-496	2.5.A.2	85-161	2.9.A.1.c
74-44	5.16.C	86-141	6.7.B.2
74-150	3.4, endnote 19	87-4	10.10.C, endnote 16

VII. Department of Labor Opinions, Revenue Procedures, Announcements, Technical Memoranda

Department of Labor Opinion

Opinion Number	Text Location
84-4(a)	3.6.A, endnote 2

Table of Prohibited Transaction Exemptions

79-10	5.7.D
85-68	5.7.D

Table of Technical Memoranda

8537007	4.6.B.1

Table of Treasury Information Releases

Section	Text Location
1248	2.9.B, endnote 36

Table of Revenue Procedures

Revenue Procedures	Text Location
74-33	1.4.A.1
83-23	1.4.A.1

Table of Announcements

Announcement	Text Location
Ann. 86-128	6.7.B.2

VIII. Table of Private Letter Rulings

Private Letter Ruling	Text Location
7718007	6.4.C.2.a, endnote 23
7727027	6.4.C.2.b.(4)
7812501	2.5.A.2
7907059	6.4.C.2.a, endnote 21
7951131	2.3.B.1
8203017	3.1.A.4
8211103	6.4.C.2.c, endnote 31
8215007	2.5.A.1, endnote 23
8219071	2.5, endnote 20
8247017	2.9.A.1.a, b
8336069	2.3.B.2.e, endnote 12
8351065	10.6
8336014	10.2.a, endnote 1
8336033	10.2.A, endnote 1
8411057	9.8, endnote 5
8417042	4.1.B, endnote 4
8421025	2.5, endnote 21
8434091	2.3.B.2.e, endnote 13
8435153	2.3.B.2.e
8442053	3.1
8451049	2.5
8514018	2.3.B.2.e
8515056	6.2.C.3, endnote 33
8523097	10.5
8529037	10.11.D, endnote 18
8530100	3.1.A.1, endnote 5
8609052	10.10.A
8651019	6.2.C.1; 6.7.B.3

Index

A

Accounting method. *See* Cash versus accrual basis

Accrual versus cash basis. *See* Cash versus accrual basis

Accumulated adjustments account (AAA):
  consent for Section 1368(e)(3) distributions, sample, 246
  definition of, 169
  distributions and, 169–176, 181, 246

Adjusted net book income, 8

Affiliated group, S corporation as member of, 31–32, 35

Agreement, shareholders', 5, 188, 192, 221
  sample, 300–301

Aliens, nonresident, 30

Alternative minimum tax. *See* Minimum tax, alternative

Amortization of organizational expenses, 79

Announcements, table of, 343

Annuities, 111, 191

At-risk limitation, 81, 150

Audits of partnerships and S corporations, 199–200

B

Bankrupts, as shareholders, 30, 50

Banks, 25

Basis, cash versus accrual. *See* Cash versus accrual basis

Basis, in debt:
  calculation of, 137–138, 141–144
  creation of, 144–145
  importance of, 136
  payment/conversion of debt and, 138–139

Basis, in stock, 165, 220–221
  calculation of, 132–135, 140–144
  creation of, 144–145
  importance of, 132
  preparer penalties and, 145
  timing of, 139–141, 217–218

Borrowing. *See* Debt; Loans

Built-in gains, taxation of certain, 120–123

Business or trade expenses, deduction of, 75

C

Cain redemptions, 192

Calendar year versus fiscal year. *See* Fiscal year versus calendar year

Capital gains:
  taxation of, 54, 60, 62–67, 93–104, 165, 179–180, 195, 225–227
  TRA and, 54, 60, 62–67, 94, 180, 195, 225–227

Carrybacks/carryforwards:
  of foreign tax credits, 54
  of investment tax credits, 54, 153
  of losses, 8, 54, 142, 217

Cases, table of, 340–341

Cash versus accrual basis:
  for C corporation converting to S corporation, 18, 52
  general discussion of, 17
  for partnership converting to S corporation, 18

C corporations (Form 1120 corporations):
  assets of, and sale of an S corporation, 193–194
  conversion of, to S corporations, 10–11, 46–47, 52–55, 67, 93–123, 198
  conversion to, from S corporations, 213–217, 219–220, 230
  liquidation of, 54, 98–99, 179
  as members of controlled group, 34–35
  S corporations as shareholders in, 188
  S corporations compared to, 3, 7–9, 86, 216–217
  as shareholders, 31

Charitable contributions, 3, 9, 61, 74

Children. *See* Minors

Closing the books of the S corporation, 131, 217, 221–222, 224
    sample consent for, 307
    sample form for, 306
Community property, 25, 49
Conditional sale of stock, 50
Consent for closing the books of the S corporation, sample, 307
Consent for Section 1368(e)(3) distributions, sample, 246
Consents, Form 2553, 45–50
    sample letter for, 240
Consent to normal accounting rules, sample, 305
Controlled group, S and C corporations as members of, 34–35
Corporations, C. *See* C corporations
Credits, tax. *See* Tax credits
Custodian, under UGMA, 4–5, 24–25, 48–49

D

Dealer transactions, 63–65
Death of a shareholder, 26, 27–29, 80, 131, 154–155, 190–192
Debt:
    basis in, 136, 137–145
    discharge of, 68–69
    distributions and, 166–167
    pros and cons of, 200–201
    as a second class of stock, 38–39
    what constitutes, 136–138
    See also Loans
Deductions:
    at-risk limitation, 81, 150
    charitable contributions as, 3, 9, 61, 74
    disallowance of, 82–83
    foreign taxes as, 61, 75
    fringe benefits as, 76–77
    interest as a, 61, 62, 73–74, 75, 86
    losses as, 8–9, 68, 75, 81–83, 132, 141–157
    miscellaneous itemized, 86
    oil and gas depletion allowance, 61
    organizational expenses, amortization of, 79
    pass-through of, to shareholders, 9, 60–61, 68, 74, 132
    recovery property, expensing of, 79–80

Deductions (*cont'd*)
    residences as, 84–86
    retirement plans as, 77–79
    suspension of expenses and interest and, 84
    taxes as, 75
    trade or business expenses as, 75
    vacation homes as, 84–86
Depreciation, 224
    recapture of, 220
DISCs, 36
Distributions:
    AAA and, 169–176, 181, 246
    posttermination, 181–182, 215–216
    property, 66–67, 179–181
    reasonable compensation and, 86–89
    sample consent for Section 1368(e)(3), 246
    in S corporations with earnings and profits, 168–176
    in S corporations without earnings and profits, 163–167
    in S corporations with previously taxed income, 176–178
    special, 53
    taxation of, 53, 66–67, 163–182, 187
Dividends:
    declaration of, 53
    income from, 8
    to reduce earnings and profits, 68
    taxation of, 8, 68, 110–111
Domestic corporations, as S corporations, 35

E

Earnings and profits:
    definition of, 210
    distributions in S corporations with, 168–176
    distributions in S corporations without, 163–167
    elimination of, 68, 168, 210
    penalties for, 67
    sample filled-in tax returns, for S corporations with, 283–290, 291–299
    sample filled-in tax returns, for S corporations without, 247–253, 254–264, 265–282
    tax consequences of reductions in, 68
    when an S corporation can have, 67
    See also Income

Election of S corporation status:
  Form 2553 and, 45–55, 238–241
  limits on numbers of shareholders, 23–26
  reasons for, 8–9
  reelection of S corporation status, after termination, 47, 212–213, 230–231
  shareholders and, 23–31, 45–50, 240
  stock class and, 36–39
  statutory requirements for, 23
  types of corporations that cannot be S corporations, 35–36
  types of entities and individuals that can be shareholders, 26–30
  who cannot be shareholders, 30–31
Employee stock ownership trusts (ESOPs), 26, 37, 187
Estates:
  as shareholders, 26, 49
  taxation of, 4, 26, 27, 190–192
Estimated taxes, 216
Excess net passive income, 115, 209–210
Expenses:
  amortization of organizational, 79
  deduction of business or trade, 75
  suspension of, 84
  table showing method of computing income and, 323–324
  See also Deductions

F

FIFO versus LIFO inventory valuation, 54–55
Fiscal year versus calendar year:
  business purpose basis for choosing, 11
  distributions and, 166
  general discussion of, 9–10
  mechanics of, 10–17
  OBRA and, 10–11, 12
  required payments and, 12–16, 53
  shareholders and, 12, 14–17
  TRA and, 11
Foreign:
  income, 3, 60
  losses, 3, 60
  taxes, 54, 61, 62, 74–75, 146
Form 1040, sample filled-in, 251, 258, 263, 269, 274, 280, 287, 296
Form 1099-DIV, sample, 295

Form 1116, 75
Form 1120 corporations. *See* C corporations
Form 1120S, 59, 63, 74, 75, 198–199
  line-by-line explanation of a sample, 314–315
  sample filled-in, 308
Form 2553 election of S corporation status:
  burden of proof regarding filing of, 51
  conditional sale of stock and, 50
  consents, 45–50, 240
  existing corporations and, 48
  gifts of stock and, 50
  incompetent individuals and, 50
  new corporations and, 45–47
  sample form, 238–239
  sample transmittal letter for, 241
  shareholders and, 45–52
  UGMA and, 48–49
  who signs, 48–50, 52
Form 4797, 63
Form 8082, sample, 302–303
Fringe benefits, 186
  deduction of, 76–77
  loss of, 53–54

G

Gains. *See* Capital gains; Earnings and profits; Income
Gifts of passive loss property, 155
Gifts of stock:
  to children, 4–7
  Form 2553 and, 50
  to grandchildren, 6
  to other relatives, 186
  to parents, 6, 185
  to spouses, 6
  taxation of, 4–7, 16–17, 185, 192–193
  UGMA, 4–5, 24–25, 48–49
Grantor trusts, as shareholders, 27–28, 50
Gross income, 61–62
Gross receipts, 113–115
  termination of S corporation status and, 209–210

H

Hagendorf, Stanley, 193
Hobby losses, 75, 81–82

I

Income:
  adjusted net book, 8
  annuities as, 111, 191
  capital gains as, 54, 60, 62–67, 93–104,
      165, 179–180, 225–227
  distributions in S corporations with previ-
      ously taxed, 176–178
  dividends as, 8, 110–111
  fiscal year versus calendar year reporting
      of, 9–17
  foreign, 3, 60
  gross, 61–62
  interest as, 3, 8, 110, 151
  net, 8, 14
  overview of taxation of, 3, 59–61
  passive, 3, 9, 53, 60, 101–102, 105–119,
      145–157
  pass-through of, to shareholders, 3, 9, 60,
      103–104, 118
  reasonable compensation, 86–89
  rents as, 107–109
  royalties as, 109–110
  splitting of, 4–6
  table showing method of computing ex-
      penses and, 323–324
  tax-exempt, 3, 8, 60, 61, 200–201
  when to take into account items of, 129–
      132, 224
  See also Earnings and profits
Income taxes. See Taxation
Incompetent individuals, as shareholders, 50
Insurance companies, 35
Interest:
  deduction of, 61, 62, 73–74, 75, 86
  as income, 3, 8, 110, 151
  investment, 61, 62, 73–74
  self-charged, 151–152
  suspension of, 84
  taxation of, 8, 110
  tax-exempt income from, 3, 8, 60, 61, 200–
      201
  TRA and, 86
Internal Revenue Code, table of sections of,
      325–336
Inventory valuation, LIFO versus FIFO, 54–
      55
Investment interest, 61, 62, 73–74
Investment tax credits:
  carrybacks/carryforwards of, 54, 153

Investment tax credits (cont'd)
  recapture of, 52, 68, 104, 133–134, 171,
      194, 195–196, 216, 219–220, 231

J

Joint tenants, as shareholders, 25, 49

K

"Kiddie tax," 185–186

L

Labor Department opinions, table of, 343
LIFO versus FIFO inventory valuation, 54–
      55
Limitations, statute of, 198–199
Liquidation of a C corporation 54, 98–99, 179
Liquidation of an S corporation:
  partial, 226
  Section 332, 229
  Section 333, 228–229
  Section 337, 226–227
  Section 338, 228
  TRA and, 226–229
Loans:
  below-market, 197
  from retirement plans, 52, 77–78, 216
  from S corporations to shareholders, 52,
      77–78, 197
  from shareholders to S corporations, 38–
      39, 197
  See also Debt
Losses:
  carrybacks/carryforwards of, 8, 54, 142, 217
  deduction of, 8–9, 68, 75, 81–83, 132, 141–
      157
  foreign, 3, 60
  hobby, 75, 81–82
  passive, 7, 9, 145–157
  pass-through of, to shareholders, 8–9, 60,
      68, 132
  tax consequences of, 5–6, 7, 8–9, 54, 60,
      68, 75, 81–83, 132, 141–157, 195
  when to take into account items of loss,
      129–132, 224

M

Minimum tax, alternative:
 pre-TRA, 102–103
 TRA and, 7–8, 9
Minors:
 children, gifts of stock to, 4–7
 grandchildren, gifts of stock to, 6
 "kiddie tax," 185–186
 as shareholders, 4–7, 24–25, 36–37, 48–49
 taxation of, 7, 185–186
 trusts for, 28, 30
 UGMA and, 4–5, 24–25, 48–49

N

Net income:
 adjusted, 8
 definition of, 14
 excess, 115, 209–210
 passive, 115, 209–210
Nominees, as shareholders, 24, 48
Nonqualifying trusts, 30
Nonresident aliens, 30

O

Oil and gas depletion allowance, 61
Omnibus Budget Reconciliation Act of 1987
 (OBRA), 10–11, 12, 223
Organizational expenses, amortization of, 79

P

Parents:
 gifts of stock to, 6, 185
 as shareholders, 6, 24, 185
Partnership(s):
 audits of, 199–200
 conversion of, to S corporations, 18
 S corporation as a partner in a, 12, 189–190
 S corporations compared to, 3
 as shareholders, 31
 SSRA and, 199
 TEFRA and, 199–200

Passive income, 3, 60, 101–102
 built-in gains as, 120–123
 definitions of types of, 107–113
 excess net, 115, 209–210
 gross receipts as, 113–115, 209–210
 net, 115, 209–210
 taxation of, 3, 9, 53, 60, 101–102, 105–119, 145–157
 tests to determine taxable, 53, 105–106, 115–119
 TRA and, 9, 106–107, 116–117, 122, 145–157
Passive losses:
 conversion of activities and, 154
 gifts of property and, 155
 taxable dispositions and, 153–154, 156–157
 TRA and, 7, 9, 145–157
Pass-through:
 of deductions, 9, 60–61, 74, 132
 of income, 3, 9, 60, 103–104, 118
 of losses, 8–9, 60, 68, 132
Private letter rulings, table of, 344
Profits and earnings. *See* Earnings and profits
Prohibited transaction exemptions, table of, 343
Property:
 community, 25, 49
 distributions of, 66–67, 179–181
 gifts of passive-loss, 155
 recovery, expensing of, 79–80

Q

Qualified S Corporation Trusts, as shareholders, 27, 28–30, 50
Qualified terminal interest property trusts
 (QTIPs), as shareholders, 28, 190–191

R

Reasonable compensation, 86–89
Recapture of depreciation, 220
Recapture of investment tax credits, 52, 68, 104, 133–134, 171, 194, 216, 219–220, 231
 ways to eliminate the effects of, 195–196
Recovery property, expensing of, 79–80

Redemptions:
  Cain, 192
  reasons for considering, 225
Reelection of S corporation status, after termination, 47, 212–213, 230–231
Rental activities, definition of, 152–153
Rents, taxation of, 107–109
Reorganization of an S corporation, 194
  Section 368(a)(1)(D), 232–233
  Section 368(a)(1)(E) (recapitalizations), 233
  Section 368(a)(1)(F) (type F), 233
  Sections 368(a)(1)(B) and (C), 231
  Sections 368(a)(2)(D) (E) (hybrid mergers), 233–234
  statutory merger and consolidations, 230–231
  tax effects of, 229–234
Residences, deduction of, 84–86
Retirement plans, 186–187
  deduction of, 77–79
  loans from, 52, 77–78, 216
  TEFRA and, 77–78
Revenue:
  procedures, table of, 343
  rulings, table of, 342
Royalties, taxation of, 109–110

S

Salary, reasonable compensation and, 86–89
Sale of stock, 194
  conditional, 50
  OBRA and, 223
  taxation of, 217–224
  TRA and, 221, 223, 224
Sale of the S corporation, 193–194
Schedule A:
  line-by-line explanation of a sample, 315–316
  sample filled-in, 288, 309
Schedule B, sample filled-in, 297
Schedule D, 63
  sample filled-in, 252, 264, 275, 281, 289, 298
Schedule E, sample filled-in, 253, 259, 270, 276, 282, 290, 299
Schedule K, 59, 63, 74
  line-by-line explanation of a sample, 316–317
  sample filled-in, 310

Schedule K-1, 59, 63, 74, 75
  line-by-line explanation of a sample, 317–318
  sample filled-in, 249–250, 256–257, 261–262, 267–268, 272–273, 278–279, 285–286, 293–294, 312–313
Schedule L:
  line-by-line explanation of a sample, 319
  sample filled-in, 248, 255, 260, 266, 271, 277, 284, 292, 311
Schedule M, 59
  line-by-line explanation of a sample, 319
  sample filled-in, 248, 255, 260, 266, 271, 277, 284, 292, 311
S corporation status, election of. *See* Election of S corporation status
Section 678 trusts, as shareholders, 27, 28, 50
Section 1231 transactions, 63
Section 1239 transactions, 65–66
Self-employment tax, 88, 187
Shareholder(s):
  agreement made by, 5, 188, 192, 221, 300–301
  bankrupts as, 30, 50
  basis, in debt, 136–139, 141–145
  basis, in stock, 132–135, 139–145
  community property and, 25, 49
  death of a, 26, 27–29, 80, 131, 154–155, 190–192
  election of S corporation status and, 23–31, 45–50, 240
  estates as, 26, 49
  exchanges of stock between, 16, 65–66, 111–113, 130–131
  fiscal year versus calendar year and, 12, 14–17
  Form 2553 and, 45–52
  guarantee of debt by, 136
  incompetent individuals as, 50
  joint tenants as, 25, 49
  limits on numbers of, 23–26
  loans from S corporations to, 52, 77–78, 197
  loans to S corporations from, 38–39, 197
  minors as, 4–7, 24–25, 36–37, 48–49
  nominees as, 24, 48
  parents as, 6, 24, 185
  pass-through of deductions to, 9, 60–61, 74, 132

Shareholder(s) (*cont'd*)
    pass-through of income to, 3, 9, 60, 103–104, 118
    pass-through of losses to, 8–9, 60, 68, 132
    S corporations as, in C corporations, 188
    spouses as, 6, 24, 25–26, 49
    tenants in common as, 25
    termination of status as a, 131
    trusts as, 27–30, 49–50, 190–191
    types of entities and individuals that can be, 26–30
    when to take into account items of income and loss, 129–132, 224
    who cannot be, 30–31
    See also Stock
Social security, 187
Splitting, income, 4–6
Spouses:
    community property and, 25, 49
    gifts of stock to, 6
    as shareholders, 6, 24, 25–26, 49
SSRA. *See* Subchapter S Revision Act of 1982
State income taxes, 75, 87, 119
    chart showing, 242–245
Statute of limitations, 198–199
Stock, 129–130
    basis in, 132–135, 139–145, 217–218, 220–221
    class of, 36–39
    conditional sale of, 50
    debt as a second class of, 38–39
    gifts of, 4–7, 16–17, 24–25, 185, 186, 192–193
    nonvoting, 5, 36–39
    sale of, 50, 194, 217–224
    shareholder exchanges of, 16, 65–66, 111–113, 130–131
    voting, 5, 36–39
    See also Shareholder(s)
Subchapter C transactions, 68
Subchapter S Revision Act of 1982 (SSRA), 3, 118–119, 163
    at-risk limitation and, 81
    audits of S corporations and, 199
    fringe benefits and, 76
Subsidiaries:
    inactive, 32–33
    transitory, 33
Suspension of expenses and interest, 84

T

Taxation:
    alternative minimum tax, 7–8, 9, 102–103
    of annuities, 111, 191
    of built-in gains, 120–123
    of capital gains, 54, 60, 62–67, 93–104, 165, 179–180, 195, 225–227
    conversion of C corporations to S corporations and, 52–55, 93–123, 198, 219–220
    conversion of S corporations to C corporations and, 213–217, 219–220
    of distributions, 53, 66–67, 163–182, 187
    of dividends, 8, 68, 110–111
    of estates, 4, 26, 27, 190–192
    estimated taxes, 216
    of exchanges of stock, 111–113, 130–131
    foreign, 54, 61, 62, 74–75, 146
    of gifts of stock, 4–7, 16–17, 185, 192–193
    of interest, 8, 110
    "kiddie tax," 185–186
    losses and, 5–6, 7, 8–9, 54, 60, 68, 75, 81–83, 132, 141–157, 195
    of minors, 7, 185–186
    overview of, 3, 59–61
    of passive income, 3, 9, 53, 60, 101–102, 105–119, 145–157
    rates of, 7, 34–35, 60, 67, 185–186
    reasonable compensation and, 86–89
    reductions in earnings and profits, consequences of, 68
    of rents, 107–109
    reorganizations and, 229–234
    of royalties, 109–110
    sale of stock and, 217–224
    self-employment tax, 88, 187
    situations where the S corporation is liable for income tax, 93
    state income taxes, 75, 87, 119, 242–245
    taxes as deductions, 75
    termination of S corporation status and, 205–234
    See also Tax Equity and Fiscal Responsibility Act of 1982; Tax Reform Act of 1986
Tax credits:
    foreign, 54, 62, 75, 146
    investment, 52, 54, 68, 104, 133–134, 153, 171, 194, 195–196, 216, 219–220

Tax Equity and Fiscal Responsibility Act of 1982 (TEFRA):
  audits of partnerships and, 199–200
  retirement plans and, 77–78
Tax-exempt income, 3, 8, 60, 61, 200–201
Tax Guide for Buying and Selling a Business, 193
Tax Reform Act of 1986 (TRA), 216
  alternative minimum tax and, 7–8, 9
  capital gains and, 54, 60, 62–67, 94, 180, 195, 225–227
  expensing of recovery property and, 80
  fiscal year versus calendar year and, 11
  interest and, 86
  "kiddie tax" and, 185–186
  LIFO versus FIFO inventory valuation and, 54–55
  liquidations and, 226–229
  passive income and, 9, 106–107, 116–117, 122, 145–157
  passive losses and, 7, 9, 145–157
  sale of stock and, 221, 223, 224
  sale of the S corporation and, 193
  table of sections of, 337
  tax rates, 7, 60, 185–186
Tax return(s):
  Form 1040, 251, 258, 263, 269, 274, 280, 287, 296
  Form 1116, 75
  Form 1120S, 59, 63, 74, 75, 198–199, 308
  Form 4797, 63
  line-by-line explanation of a sample, 314–319
  sample filled-in, for S corporations with earnings/profits, 283–290, 291–299
  sample filled-in, for S corporations without earnings/profits, 247–253, 254–264, 265–282
  Schedule A, 288, 309
  Schedule B, 297
  Schedule D, 63, 252, 264, 275, 281, 289, 298
  Schedule E, 253, 259, 270, 276, 282, 290, 299
  Schedule K, 59, 63, 74, 310
  Schedule K-1, 59, 63, 74, 75, 249–250, 256–257, 261–262, 267–268, 272–273, 278–279, 285–286, 293–294, 312–313

Tax return(s) (*cont'd*)
  Schedule L, 248, 255, 260, 266, 271, 277, 284, 292, 311
  Schedule M, 59, 248, 255, 260, 266, 271, 277, 284, 292, 311
Technical memoranda, table of, 343
TEFRA. *See* Tax Equity and Fiscal Responsibility Act of 1982
Tenants in common, as shareholders, 25
Termination of S corporation status:
  change of more than 50 percent interest, 131
  closing of the books, 131, 217, 221–222, 224, 306
  failure to remain as an S corporation, 208–209
  gross receipts and, 209–210
  liquidations, 226–229
  methods of achieving, 205
  posttermination distributions and, 181–182, 215–216
  reasons for choosing, 206
  redemptions, 225
  reelection of S corporation status after, 47, 212–213, 230–231
  reorganizations, 194, 229–234
  sample notice of voluntary revocation of S status, 304
  tax effects of, 205–234
  voluntary revocation of S status, 205–208, 304
  waiver of termination, 211–212
Testamentary trusts, as shareholders, 27, 28, 50, 190–191
TRA. *See* Tax Reform Act of 1986
Trade or business expenses, deduction of, 75
Treasury Department:
  information releases, table of, 343
  regulations, table of, 338–339
Trusts, as shareholders:
  grantor, 27–28, 50
  for minors, 28, 30
  nonqualifying, 30
  Qualified S Corporation, 27, 28–30, 50
  qualified terminal interest property, 28, 190–191
  Section 678, 27, 28, 50
  testamentary, 27, 28, 50, 190–191
  voting, 27, 49

U

Uniform Gifts to Minors Act (UGMA):
   custodian under, 4–5, 24–25, 48–
      49
   Form 2553 and, 48–49

V

Vacation homes, deduction of, 84–
   86
Voting trusts, as shareholders, 27,
   49